Alan Feige

Alpha
Teach Yourself

Retirement
Planning

in 24
hours

ALPHA
A Pearson Education Company

Alpha Teach Yourself Retirement Planning in 24 Hours

International Standard Book Number: 0-02-864212-0
Library of Congress Catalog Card Number: 2001093555

Printed in the United States of America

First printing: 2002

04   03   02   4   3   2   1

Note: This publication contains the opinions and ideas of its authors. It is intended to provide helpful and informative material on the subject matter covered. It is sold with the understanding that the authors and publisher are not engaged in rendering professional services in the book. If the reader requires personal assistance or advice, a competent professional should be consulted.

The authors and publisher specifically disclaim any responsibility for any liability, loss or risk, personal or otherwise, which is incurred as a consequence, directly or indirectly, of the use and application of any of the contents of this book.

Trademarks

CERTIFIED FINANCIAL PLANNER™ is a certification mark owned by the Certified Financial Planner Board of Standards, Inc. It will be used in the remainder of this book without the trademark symbol. All other terms mentioned in this book that are known to be or are suspected of being trademarks or service marks have been appropriately capitalized. Alpha Books and Pearson Education cannot attest to the accuracy of this information. Use of a term in this book should not be regarded as affecting the validity of any trademark or service mark.

ACQUISITIONS EDITOR
Mike Sanders

DEVELOPMENT EDITOR
Lynn Northrup

PRODUCTION EDITOR
Billy Fields

COPY EDITOR
Susan Aufheimer

INDEXER
Angie Bess

PRODUCTION
John Etchison
Ayanna Lacey

COVER DESIGNER
Alan Clements

BOOK DESIGNER
Gary Adair

MANAGING EDITOR
Jennifer Chisholm

PRODUCT MANAGER
Phil Kitchel

PUBLISHER
Marie Butler-Knight

From Alan Feigenbaum:

This book is dedicated to my beloved late mother, Janet Feigenbaum, who tragically never reached retirement. She taught me the wise use of money while using it only for the benefit of her family and not herself. And to my beloved father, Richard Feigenbaum, who worked so hard for that money and is unable to enjoy retirement because my mother is not with him.

Finally, this book is dedicated to my loving wife, Janet Rose Levy, who has spent 29 years putting up with me being duller, with no common sense—even though I write about dollars and cents.

From Lita Epstein:

This book is dedicated to my beloved late father, Jerome Kirschbrown, whose financial savvy helped me develop mine.

Overview

Introduction   xv

PART I Your Retirement Needs

HOUR 1 Confronting Retirement Realities   3

HOUR 2 Envisioning Your Retirement   19

HOUR 3 Quantifying Retirement Costs   33

HOUR 4 Quantifying Retirement Assets   47

PART II Your Retirement Gap

HOUR 5 Retirement Finance Basics   59

HOUR 6 Retirement Gap Calculation   73

HOUR 7 Introduction to Retirement Gap Calculation   87

HOUR 8 Retirement Gap Solutions   101

PART III Employment/Government Plans

HOUR 9 Social Security   117

HOUR 10 401(k) and Related Plans   131

HOUR 11 Small Business/Self-Employed Plans   149

HOUR 12 Defined-Benefit and Federal Pension Plans   165

HOUR 13 Traditional/Roth IRAs   181

HOUR 14 Medicare and Private Supplementary Insurance   197

Part IV Assembling the Plan

Hour 15 Integrating Retirement Sources   217

Hour 16 Savings/Spending Priorities   233

Hour 17 Retirement Road Detours   247

Hour 18 Retirement Plan Management   261

Hour 19 Completing the Plan   271

Hour 20 Comprehensive Retirement Gap Calculation Example   283

Part V Road to Retirement

Hour 21 Retirement Gap Scenarios   299

Hour 22 Pre-Retirement Planning   313

Hour 23 Managing Retirement Distributions   329

Hour 24 Retirement Pitfalls, Shortfalls, and Surpluses   343

Appendixes

Appendix A 20-Minute Recap   355

Appendix B Resources   361

Appendix C Answers to Quiz Questions   373

Appendix D Retirement Gap Data and Calculation Worksheets   377

Index   419

Contents

Introduction   ix

PART I Your Retirement Needs

HOUR 1 Confronting Retirement Realities   3

Increasing Life Spans 4

Retirement Stages...5

Demographic Trends...6

    Sandwich Generation 6

    Divorce 7

    Retirement Gender Gap 8

    Disability 9

Benefit Cutbacks...10

    Employer Cutbacks 10

    Government Benefit Cutbacks 11

Economic Trends 12

Shift to Personal Responsibility 13

Hour's Up!..14

HOUR 2 Envisioning Your Retirement   19

Decide When 20

    The Cost of When 21

    When to Say When 22

Decide Where...23

    Location Considerations 24

    Location Choices..25

Decide About Working Part-Time...26

Decide on Leisure and Travel Goals 27

    Decide on Your Overall Living Standard 28

Hour's Up!..29

HOUR 3 Quantifying Retirement Costs   33

Estimate Food and Shelter Costs 34

    Active Adult Retirement Communities (AARC).....................35

    Continuing Care Retirement Communities (CCRC) 36

    Concentrated Retirement Care Living Options.........................37

    Homeowner's Insurance 38

Estimate Healthcare Costs 38
  Estimate Leisure and Travel Costs 39
Estimate Other Recurring Budget Items 40
  Personal Care...40
  Clothing and Local Transportation 41
  Professional Services and Insurance 42
  Taxes and Lump-Sum Expenses 43
Combine Estimates into Total Budget 43
Hour's Up!...44

HOUR 4 Quantifying Retirement Assets   **47**

Your Financial Assets 47
  Inventory Cash-Equivalent Savings 48
  Inventory Market and Insurance Investments 49
  Inventory Personal Retirement Assets 50
  Inventory Employer Retirement Benefits...................50
  Inventory Government (Aided) Retirement Benefits 51
  Inventory Home Equity, Real Estate..........................52
  Inventory Property, Collectibles, Business Value 52
  Inventory Potential Gifts and Inheritance 53
Understand Your Liabilities 53
Your Retirement-Ready Net Worth 54
Compile Your Inventory..55
What You Can Do Now 55
Hour's Up!...56

PART II Your Retirement Gap

HOUR 5 Retirement Finance Basics   **59**

Understand Inflation and Interest Rates 59
Return on Investment 61
  Rate of Return..61
  Historical Rate-of-Return Yardsticks 62
Understand Taxation Basics...63
Understand After-Tax Cash Flow 64
Understand Time Value of Money...................................65
Understand Estimation and Assumption 67
Hour's Up!...70

HOUR 6 Retirement Gap Calculation   **73**

Understanding the Retirement Gap Concept 73
Financial Formulas Used in Calculations 74
    Inflation 75
    Investment Return 76
    Synchronize for Growth with Inflation 78
Retirement Need Gap Calculation 79
Hour's Up! 85

HOUR 7 Introduction to Retirement Gap Calculation   **87**

Setting the Stage 87
Preparing the Worksheets 88
Retirement Need Gap Calculation Procedure 90
Calculating Your Own Retirement Gap 99
Hour's Up! 100

HOUR 8 Retirement Gap Solutions   **101**

Budgeting Basics 102
Investing Basics 104
Utilize Tax Reduction/Deferral Basics 105
Benefit Utilization Basics 107
Understand Dual-Purpose Resources 109
    Your Home 109
    Tax-Deferred Retirement Savings 110
    Invest in Your Earning Potential 111
What Can You Do? 112
Hour's Up! 112

PART III Employment/Government Plans

HOUR 9 Social Security   **117**

Understand Contributions and Eligibility 117
Estimate Standard Benefit 120
Evaluate Early/Delayed Benefit Options 121
    Early Retirement 121
    Delayed Retirement 122
Estimate Supplementary Income Effects 122
Evaluate Taxation of Benefits 124
Anticipate Social Security Trends/Revisions 125
Hour's Up! 128

HOUR 10 401(k) and Related Plans   **131**

Defined-Contribution Salary-Reduction Plans 132
    A Closer Look at 401(k)s 133
    A Closer Look at 403(b)s 136
Employer and Employee Contributions 138
Contribution and Investment (Re)Allocations............................140
    Allocation Alternatives 140
    Allocation Rules 141
Income-Tax Impacts 141
Rules: Vesting, Borrowing, Withdrawals, Portability...................142
    Borrowing from Your 401(k)......................................142
    Plan Trends and Your Rights.......................................143
    Your Rights 144
Hour's Up!...145

HOUR 11 Small Business/Self-Employed Plans   **149**

Understand SEP-IRA, SIMPLE IRA, and Keogh Basics...............150
    SEP-IRAs..151
    SIMPLE IRAs 153
    Keogh Plans...155
Income Tax Impacts 158
Understand Vesting, Withdrawals, and Portability 158
Comparison of Small Business/Self-Employed Plans.....................159
Hour's Up!...160

HOUR 12 Defined-Benefit and Federal Pension Plans   **165**

Traditional Defined-Benefit Pensions 165
Cash-Balance Defined-Benefit Pensions 169
Pension Politics: Controversial Conversions....................................171
Normal and Early Retirement Options 173
Employee Rights and Pension Trends 175
Pension Trends 176
U.S. Federal Employee Pensions 177
    Two Retirement Systems...178
    Thrift Savings Plan 178
Hour's Up!...179

HOUR 13 Traditional/Roth IRAs   **181**

IRA Eligibility and Contribution Basics 181
    Tax-Deductible IRA Eligibility and Contributions 183
    Roth IRA Eligibility and Contributions....................................184

Non-Tax-Deductible IRA Eligibility and Contributions 185
Common Rules 185
IRA Withdrawal Rules 186
Rollovers and Roth Conversions 187
Compare IRA Alternatives 188
Understand Investment Alternatives...............................191
Plan Trends 192
Hour's Up!..193

Hour 14 Medicare and Private Supplementary Insurance 197

The Medicare Problem..198
Understand Medicare Basics 199
Understand the Enrollment Window 200
Understand Medicare Reimbursement...........................201
Understand Private Supplementary Insurance (Medigap) 203
Understand Shopping for Supplementary Insurance......................207
Understand Long-Term-Care Insurance 208
Hour's Up!..210

Part IV Assembling the Plan

Hour 15 Integrating Retirement Sources 217

Build a Long-Term Investment Portfolio........................217
Employer/Government Plan Resources 218
Other Savings Sources at Work 220
Profit-Sharing Plans 220
Employee Stock Ownership Plans (ESOP) 220
Employee Stock Purchase Plans 221
Thrift Plans 221
Employee Stock Options..221
Variable Universal Life Insurance and Variable Annuities 222
Other Investments 224
Collectibles 225
Home Equity and Other Real Estate 225
Capital-Based Business Opportunities 227
Inheritance and Other Windfalls.................................228
Hour's Up!..229

Hour 16 Savings/Spending Priorities 233

Ration Overall Spending vs. Retirement Saving 234
Ration House Down Payment vs. Retirement Saving....................235
Ration Debt Payoff vs. Investing 237

Ration Education vs. Investing 239
    Ration Between Other Choices 241
    Setting Priorities 242
    Insurance vs. Retirement Saving 242
Hour's Up!..244

HOUR 17 Retirement Road Detours   **247**

Expect the Unexpected 247
    Premature Death or Disability 248
    Family Medical Crises 249
    Sudden Benefit Losses 250
    Divorce 251
Expect the Expected..253
    Family-Need Crunches 253
    Early Retirement and Layoffs 256
    Anticipate/Handle Widow(er)hood 256
Minimize the Detour Damage 257
    Insurance 257
    Shielding Assets 259
Hour's Up!..259

HOUR 18 Retirement Plan Management   **261**

Changing Jobs..261
Portability Options 263
Using the Catch-Up Provisions 264
Max Out Your Retirement Savings Options 265
Portfolio Balancing and Investment Reallocation...........265
Early Withdrawal Rules Without Penalty, If You Must.................267
Roth Conversion Strategies 268
Hour's Up!..270

HOUR 19 Completing the Plan   **271**

Determine Planning Parameters...........................271
    Planning Time Frame 271
    Determine Risk Tolerance by Life Stage 273
    Economic and Investment Assumptions 274
Investment Amounts and Allocations....................275
Project Contributions to Plans/Investments 275
    Determine Asset Allocation Strategy....................276
    Bonds 277
    Stocks..278
Adjusting Calculations and Assessing Performance 279
Hour's Up!..281

HOUR 20 Comprehensive Retirement Gap Calculation Example   **283**

Setting the Stage 283
Preparing the Worksheets...286
Retirement Need Gap Calculation Procedure.....................287
Use of Estimations and Assumptions 294
Hour's Up!...294

PART V Road to Retirement

HOUR 21 Retirement Gap Scenarios   **299**

Typical Young Single Situation 299
    Planning Advice 300
    Savings Advice 301
Typical Young Married Situation 302
    Debt and Houses 302
    Kids 303
Typical Mid-Life Couple Situation 304
Typical Divorced Couple Situation 305
Typical Permanent Single Situation 307
Pre-Retirees..308
The Right Financial Advisor 308
    Make Sure They Have Good Qualifications 308
    Find an Advisor with a Compatible Style 308
    Find a Compatible Advisor...309
    Understand How Your Advisor Gets Paid 309
    Have Confidence in the Methods Your Advisor Uses 310
Hour's Up!...311

HOUR 22 Pre-Retirement Planning   **313**

Revisit Retirement Scenario 314
    Determine the Attainability of Your Original Goal.................314
    Determine Whether Your Objectives Have Changed 315
Revise Retirement Scenario 315
    Consider Your Current Life Circumstances and Health 316
    Consider Your Desire/Ability to Continue Working 316
    Envision Retirement Life More Realistically 317
Pre-Retirement Lifestyle and Work Actions 318
    Continuing Work or Starting a Business 318
    Phasing Down or Out of a Business 318
Pre-Retirement Financial Actions 321
    Restructure Investments for Retirement.........................321
    Social Security, Medicare, Long-Term Care....................322

Viatical Settlements 324
Reverse Mortgages...325
Annuities..326
Hour's Up!..327

HOUR 23 Managing Retirement Distributions   **329**

Pensions 330
Lump Sums vs. Annuities 330
Annuity Withdrawal Options..331
Lump-Sum Withdrawal Options...332
Pension Plan Errors 334
All Other Retirement Plans...334
Understand Differing IRS Withdrawal Rules.......................334
Understand Tax Ramifications of Withdrawals 336
Evaluate Retirement Withdrawal Options 338
Social Security Rules for Widows and Widowers 340
Revisiting Your Withdrawal Options Annually.........................341
Hour's Up!..342

HOUR 24 Retirement Pitfalls, Shortfalls, and Surpluses   **343**

Monitor Your Retirement Plan's Performance.........................344
Avoid Ripoff Retirement "Opportunities" 345
Remarriage and Other Complications 349
Retirement Dreams Deferred 349
Retirement Sweet Dreams, for Good..350
Hour's Up!..353

Appendixes

APPENDIX A 20-Minute Recap   **355**

APPENDIX B Resources   **361**

APPENDIX C Answers to Quiz Questions   **373**

APPENDIX D Retirement Gap Data and Calculation Worksheets   **377**

Index   **419**

Introduction

Did you chuckle upon seeing the Charles Schwab Super Bowl commercial in which the unlikely duo of Charles Barkley and Tara Lipinski were occupants of an old-age retirement home? Why not, with that priceless image of bodacious Sir Charles knitting with precocious Ms. Lipinski. It humorously, yet effectively, highlights our highly stereotyped notions of retirement. Our outdated images totally obscure the real challenges that planning retirement presents for the vast majority of people who lack the celebrity cachet and financial wherewithal to do what they please.

For example, in the real world it's no laughing matter that millions of 50-somethings find themselves put out to professional pasture. They don't come close to having the big bucks that might finance a future political run for Barkley or enable Lipinski to own and operate a new professional skating tour. In other words, those stars are not only rich celebrities, but they really have a life ahead. Meanwhile, many involuntary retirees are terrified about having enough to live on, let alone what they're going to do with their remaining lives.

But let's not overlook those who have (or think they have) planned well financially. Most have not put nearly the effort into realistically envisioning themselves in retirement, other than some hackneyed version of the life of the new millennium's Riley. And when the time comes, they might end up shocked at how current labor, economic, and political forces are conspiring against their dreams of carefree senior days.

This book, then, is for all of you for whom retirement planning is definitely no slam dunk, or who just need more help preparing to skate carefree through it when the time comes. In other words, it's for practically everyone in today's workforce, including those who've recently returned after the market let the air out of their inflated tech-stock portfolios.

Furthermore, whether you wear pajamas to work in your study, sneakers with no socks at your dress-down startup, or don thousand-dollar tailored suits to walk the marble floors of your corporate headquarters, we'd like to think this book speaks you language. It starts with a right-brained approach to framing your retirement challenge, and continues with a left-brained approach to some serious (but only algebra-level) number-crunching. In the end, you'll have quantified highly qualitative objectives, and will have drawn yourself a businesslike blueprint for achieving them.

And, to toot our own horns, you'll be doing this with a (potentially patentable) far more accurate and realistic approach than any you've seen before. It thumbs its nose at the inadequate rules of thumb used by virtually every retirement calculator you'll find in computer software or on the Web. And to save you the trouble of thumbing through the book before getting started, here's how it's organized.

What You'll Find in This Book

Part I, "Your Retirement Needs," will give you a clean slate to draw your own conclusions about what the future of retirement is going to look like in general, and for you in particular. By the time you're through, you'll have a good idea of just how much your life in retirement will cost you and what you're starting with now on the road to building a portfolio that will get you there.

Part II, "Your Retirement Gap," will give you the arithmetical and financial basics to do retirement math, and then take you through this book's unique approach to calculating the gap you must fill with savings and investments beyond your current program. When you finish, you'll also have some idea about strategies to start getting there.

Part III, "Employment/Government Plans," will give you the real scoop on today's topsy-turvy pension world, tax-advantaged 401(k) and related plans, and what's really going on with, and into, Social Security and Medicare.

Part IV, "Assembling the Plan," helps you develop a customized retirement strategy based on what you now know about your financial situation and the programs available to you. And it takes the kid gloves off to help you knock out a more realistic, detailed calculation of your retirement gap than the simpler one presented to get you started in Part II.

Part V, "Road to Retirement," helps you put your own situation in perspective by profiling the retirement strategies and challenges of hypothetical people in several different life-stage situations. It then moves from hypothesis to the real-life moves you should make in the years immediately preceding retirement, and on to guidelines for the complex task of managing your funds to last the rest of your life during retirement. Finally, it takes you into the beginning of your retirement, with no-holds-barred advice on getting it off on the right track.

EXTRAS

Last but not least, this book features numerous miscellaneous cross-references, tips, shortcuts, and warning sidebar boxes. Here's how they stack up:

GO TO ▶
This sidebar cross-references you to another point in the book to learn more about a particular topic.

JUST A MINUTE

 Just a Minute sidebars offer advice or teach an easier way to do something.

TIME SAVER

 Time Saver sidebars give you a faster way to do something.

STRICTLY DEFINED

Strictly Defined boxes offer definitions of words you may not know.

PROCEED WITH CAUTION

 Proceed with Caution boxes are warnings. They warn you about potential problems and help you steer clear of trouble.

 These are quick references to direct you toward further reading and examples in other sources.

About the Authors

Alan Feigenbaum, CERTIFIED FINANCIAL PLANNER, devotes himself full-time to writing about personal finance for a variety of print and Web-based publications. His credits include regular columns or frequent features for *Bloomberg Wealth Manager, CBS MarketWatch, Worth Interactive, Raleigh News & Observer, Financial Web (Stock Detective), Raging Bull,* and *Chapel Hill News.* He's also been published in *The New York Times* and *LA Times Syndicate,* is a columnist for *Strong Mutual Funds,* and has written for subscription newsletters and other Web sites.

Alan has covered virtually every aspect of personal money management, with particular focus on comprehensive financial planning, retirement, college funding, employee benefits, budgeting and debt management, and home ownership. His passionate advocacy of financial-services consumerism is a common thread throughout his writing. Nevertheless, he flavors his serious financial writing with a sense of humor, which he also brings to his avocation of writing political satire and op-ed—his most recent published piece appearing in the *Boston Globe*.

Alan resides in Chapel Hill, North Carolina, where he, his wife, and three daughters all root for the Tar Heels. Alan also roots for Jesse Helms to retire and hopes that he'll take the hint when Alan sends him this book.

Lita Epstein is an Emory University MBA who resides in Atlanta with her husband. She combines her business, finance, and writing skills producing and teaching online investing courses at Bloomberg.com and SmartPlanet. com on topics including Investing for Retirement, Introduction to the Stock Market and Investing, Mutual Funds 101, and Picking the Best Tech Stocks. Lita was also the editorial content director for the financial-services Web site, MostChoice.com; wrote *Tip World's* daily Mutual Fund Tip; and was the editorial guide for the About.com Investing for Women site.

Previously, Lita was a daily newspaper reporter for the *Jersey Journal*, a magazine editor for *Popular Photography*, a press secretary for a U.S. Congressman, and an associate director for fund-raising at the (President Jimmy) Carter Center.

Acknowledgments

Alan offers a huge thank you to Heather Linton, CERTIFIED FINANCIAL PLANNER and CPA. She reviewed and helped improve the retirement-gap calculation methodology, and has been an excellent expert source throughout his personal-finance writing career.

PART I
Your Retirement Needs

Hour 1 Confronting Retirement Realities

Hour 2 Envisioning Your Retirement

Hour 3 Quantifying Retirement Costs

Hour 4 Quantifying Retirement Assets

Hour 1

Confronting Retirement Realities

Chapter Summary

LESSON PLAN:

In this Hour you will learn about …

- What lifestyle to expect when you retire.
- What living longer means financially.
- What retirement has in store for Baby Boomers.
- Your financial responsibility for your retirement.
- Demographic trends affecting your retirement.

Do you have 20-20 vision? If not, put on your glasses (or bifocals, for you Baby Boomers) so that you can see clearly to the year 2020. By then more than 100 million Americans will be at least the traditional 65 retirement age, but millions of them won't retire. For some it will be due to the good news that people are staying healthier longer, they like to work, and their lifetimes of experience are still valued by employers. For too many, though, it will be due to the bad news that they simply can't afford to stop working and live the retirement life they'd dreamed.

"Tsk, tsk," say hundreds of articles about these unfortunate folks. "They never learned to live within their means and are simply getting what they deserve." You probably know such people, and might even take some silent satisfaction in knowing that they're the Joneses with whom keeping up was an option you wisely chose to reject. But, I dare say you might even be among those smitten Smiths who couldn't resist the temptation of Jones-type materialism.

FYI About two thirds of Baby Boomers carry some credit card debt, and the average amount they've saved is less than $40,000. Furthermore, women have saved an average of $10,000 less than men, yet the typical woman's savings will have to last about five years longer than men's.

On the other hand, you might be one of the countless Jones and Smith families who must delay retirement through no fault of your own. How could you have known that employers en masse would suddenly revamp their great pension plans and terminate their retiree medical coverage? How could you have anticipated a 25 percent chance of divorce by your mid-30s—and end up paying for two apartment rents and the lawyers' Model 401 sports cars, instead of funding 401(k)s? Could you ever have guessed that FDR's New Deal Social Security would become the Congressional "let's make a deal" social insecurity of potential delayed or reduced benefits? And, if you're younger and Social Security doesn't get cut, how could you have known that you'd have to give up an ever-increasing percentage of your pay to ensure Social Security for all those imminent retirees?

However, regardless of your age or how well you've prepared, you can still do something to create a brighter 2020, or later. Let's start by taking a clear look at the details of societal, demographic, and economic changes that you must factor into developing or improving your retirement plan.

INCREASING LIFE SPANS

When Social Security began in 1935 (and started paying benefits in 1940), it did begin rescuing millions from a destitute old age or disability. Yet its more significant real value then was embodied in the popular Orphan Annie comic strip—the survivor benefits for children under 18. At a time before antibiotics and vaccinations, during which there were two world wars in 30 years, the average life expectancy was 63, so it verged on miraculous to live long during retirement.

Today, the children (currently Baby Boomers) of those often-orphaned children have the opposite problem. They are the leading edge of the baby boom (the 78 million Americans born between 1946 and 1964) whose average life expectancy is 77 and rising, and many will consider themselves economically lucky *not* to live until age 95. This trend has retirement-planning professionals scurrying to revise their traditional assumption that anyone who had sufficient savings and income to last them 20 years beyond retirement was literally and figuratively golden. Instead, the new approach is to look at each individual's circumstances to determine a unique life expectancy and add a cushion for error—based on current health, family health history, and lifestyle.

PROCEED WITH CAUTION

You should periodically recalculate your life expectancy, because the older you get, the better your chance of getting still older yet. Ninety-eight-year-old Strom Thurmond has a realistic chance of living until his Senate term ends in January 2003.

RETIREMENT STAGES

The "threat" of living too long is not the whole story, however. Because so many people now live retirements as long as their childhoods, researchers have recognized that there are distinct stages to retirement—each with different activity and economic-need levels.

During the *active* phase, many retirees still work part-time, either for pay or as volunteers, while engaging in more high-energy recreation and entertainment that 60-hour workweeks didn't allow. Others truly do retire and spend time traveling, shopping, and playing golf, and generally indulging themselves as part of an initial retirement-living lifestyle that undermines the traditional assumption that it costs far less to live in retirement.

For all but the hyperactive, however, retired people eventually do slow down. Picture the front-porch, rocking-chair, stereotypical *passive* retirement—although it's often now replaced by life in a senior housing development, or in individual homes located near active senior centers. Unless retirees choose a pricey senior enclave, this is the least expensive phase of retirement. Even though most seniors no longer work part-time during this phase, that income loss is more than offset by the disappearance of certain expenses such as a second car, and the shrinking of others—such as business and social wardrobes. Unfortunately, this period of taking it easy, and cheap living while in good health, is often regrettably short.

That's because people now live much longer in the third and final retirement phase, a state of declining health and dependence. Forty percent of today's Boomers will eventually require round-the-clock medical and personal-care assistance that's beyond what families, friends, or hired caretakers can provide. While some will end up in wonderful facilities offering tender (almost) loving care, the majority will spend significant time in long-term "we care only if you pay us enough" facilities, or "worsing" homes.

The sarcasm is intentional, given the corporatization of these facilities, and the increasing problems they have in getting competent, caring staff while maintaining rigid cost controls. Even those blessed with somewhat better health and larger, more supportive families still end up living with prolonged, high-cost medical care—including substantial drug bills, mostly paid out of pocket. And when their families become overwhelmed, the under-supply and over-demand for private-duty nurses results in huge costs.

Yes, this view of retirement life probably resembles a stern lecture meant to increase your anxiety and motivate you to act, but it's not intended to demoralize or discourage you. Instead think of it as kindly "forewarned is forearmed" advice from your (grand)parents. Oddly enough, for them, these retirement phases were or are the exception rather than the rule. But for you, be assured they'll be the rule rather than the exception.

Demographic Trends

If you've now accepted the likelihood of a long, expensive-at-times retirement, you're ready to deal with "that won't happen to me" denial about adverse preretirement life phases, starting with the consequences of your own parents' retirement.

Sandwich Generation

You probably have little clue about your parents' financial condition, so now there are two reasons to discuss it with them. First, with this book and other resources, you might be able to help them in better managing their money in retirement. Second, you might discover that they will, indeed, need your financial help later, or you'll be pleasantly surprised that they intend to ease yours.

If you're lucky, your folks are *millionaire-next-door* types who've quietly amassed a considerable nest egg through old-fashioned hard work and thrift, and will never need your help. If you're even more fortunate, they recognized the long-term growth of the American economy and combined a sound savings plan with prudent investment, resulting in a nest egg so large that you'll inherit a tidy sum, even if the estate tax still exists by then. But the younger your parents are now, the more likely they've been caught up in our consumer culture, and they might very well need your financial help during their later years.

> **Millionaire-next-door** types are the frugal, super-saving, and conservative-investing seniors of today. They've quietly amassed a sizeable cash stash, but nobody would know it based on the modest way they've continued living since becoming wealthy. They're described in more detail in the book *The Millionaire Next Door* by Thomas Stanley and William Danko (see Appendix B, "Resources").

That's fair, considering all they've done for you, but what about your kids, if you have any? If you haven't saved enough for their college education, you might be paying back loans at the same time your parents need the help. And maybe you're also the only financially successful sibling among several children and you're also helping out your sister with her son who has serious medical/developmental problems in addition to helping your parents and kids. In other words, you're sandwiched between the needs of your older, younger, and perhaps even peer generations. You might even be a divorced woman faced with all this, in which case you're spread too thin in a "worst-case scenario" sandwich.

 The average American woman spends about 20 years raising children and another 20 helping elderly parents, not necessarily at the same time; about 40 percent of women do both simultaneously. This sandwich burden falls squarely on women, who provide three quarters of all family caring for elderly parents, which is much greater than 30 years ago when few women worked. Today, half of women caring for parents are also holding full-time jobs.

DIVORCE

Even without the sandwich, divorce alone deals a deadly blow to many retirement plans. Although two people can't quite live as cheaply together as one person alone, divorce brings the cruel realization that one household lives far more cheaply than two. At a time when putting away money for long-term growth is crucial to accumulating an ample retirement nest egg, it's usually all divorced people can do to just stay out of debt. Given the 50 percent divorce rate, you're just as likely to end up as a half—not as a member of the lucky half.

Although the odds of divorce are 50-50, the burdens it places on people when it does occur aren't equal. While men suffer a larger average loss of standard of living initially, women get the worst of it in the long run. Not only does their alimony or child support eventually run out, but they generally get only half the value of their husband's pension at the time of divorce—losing out on the heavy later-career growth years of traditional pensions. Most important, they no longer have the support base at a time when many married women are poised to move beyond the earning-power limitations of concentrated motherhood.

RETIREMENT GENDER GAP

Divorced, never married, or still married, until mid-life, mothers have generally had career disruptions, are in lower-paying jobs, are out of work longer after involuntarily losing a job, and have continued responsibility for kids that limits their ability to get further training and education needed to catch up. Although those who remain married face these obstacles to a lesser degree, these factors are the important reasons why women overall save and invest far less for retirement. Then add the financial phobia often attributable to mid-life women's upbringing, and the unexplainable *pay inequity* suffered by even childless, never-married women. The conclusion is undeniable: Women compete on a tilted retirement-preparation playing field.

STRICTLY DEFINED

Pay inequity refers to the differences in pay between men and women with the same qualifications doing the same job. The gap falls short of Census Bureau's report of women's 73 cents for each male dollar—experts estimate it at 10 to 20 percent depending on profession. Lower pay also translates to women receiving lower pensions and accumulating smaller 401(k)s due to lower allowed contributions and matching.

No, this isn't a boo-hoo sob story meant to increase intergender tension, but a bit of demographic detective work that Joe Friday might say is, "just the facts, ma'am—and man." And as a further irony, a cruel quirk of nature that seems to benefit women actually makes things worse: They live longer. Without good financial planning, widows whose husbands didn't have adequate life insurance join divorced and always-single women in having to make their smaller nest eggs last for an average five years longer than men do.

In fairness, though, let's wrap up these demographic detours to a prosperous retirement with this disproportionate male disadvantage. Although women exceed 50 percent of the work force, men remain bearers of the primary breadwinning burden in intact families—sometimes two families. Nature's double standard has led to many mid-life men who'd normally be thinking of empty-nest retirement instead starting a second nest with a younger woman after leaving first wives. Forget the original plan to start taking retirement distributions at age 65 for backpacking trips to the Grand Canyon. Instead, they're still working full-time at age 68, paying for second-round children's scout camping trips while also trying to rebuild divorce-split retirement accounts.

DISABILITY

Those ex-husbands' retirement-funding stress probably doesn't garner much sympathy from first wives, but husbands who stay around deserve some understanding.

Men are the large majority of the one third of workers who are out of work for nonmaternity reasons at least a year with major disabilities before age 55. That period of missed work, in which savings are severely depleted to cover living expenses and excess medical bills, can set retirement planning behind for several years. Combined with family obligations, it causes men even more stress to catch up when they report back to work.

Of course, disability doesn't have to damage retirement if the employee carries long-term disability insurance. It was once automatic or an optional add-on in many employer benefit plans. But it's fallen victim to markedly rising claims costs that have led to companies either dropping it or making it an option that employees can "buy" in a *cafeteria benefits plan*. It's cheaper as a group policy than it is as an individual policy, which is the only option for most individuals whose employers don't offer it. But either way, it's pricey, siphoning off significant amounts that could go into retirement savings. Thus, most people who don't get it free from employers roll the dice and skip it.

STRICTLY DEFINED

A company's **cafeteria benefits plan** allocates an amount of money for employees to use as they wish to buy from an employer's menu of benefits. Thus, the employee might choose bare-bones or no medical coverage if the spouse has a good policy, and use the money saved to buy long-term-care insurance. Most employers allow additional payroll deductions if the employee's choices cost more than the company allocation.

BENEFIT CUTBACKS

Employee benefit deficiencies that harm retirement savings go beyond just a lack of disability insurance. A substantially lower percentage of today's employees have full benefits—as companies have increasingly relied on part-time, temporary, and contract labor.

EMPLOYER CUTBACKS

Employees also suffer benefit deficiencies when they skip from company to company, or contract firm to contract firm, having accumulated little or no vested pension benefit. Meanwhile, loyal long-term employees who've been fortunate to dodge downsizing bullets are increasingly seeing their devotion rewarded by a new form of pension that chops them off at the knees: cash-balance pension plans. To attract younger workers who place little value on a possible pension benefit 30 years hence, companies have changed their plans to make monthly deposits into a pension account that becomes port-able after vesting. But to pay for front-loading more dollars to younger employees, they've also converted mid-career employee pensions into cash accounts reflecting the current value of their eventual pensions. The result is that most long-term employees who stay with the company end up with anywhere from a 25 to 75 percent lower annual pension payment upon retirement than they would have under the previous pension system.

PROCEED WITH CAUTION

 Several major court actions and decisions are slowing the frantic pace of conversion to cash-balance plans. For example, courts have ruled that the Bank of Boston and Georgia-Pacific Company undervalued employee conversion amounts.

Unfair, sure, but perfectly legal. Pension law protects only what employees have already earned, so pensions can always be changed regarding future employer contributions, and even terminated. In fact, long before the cash-balance pension came along, employers were getting stingier with or termi-nating defined-benefit pension plans that provide a retirement income based on a known formula involving salary, years of service, and age at retirement. That provided a huge impetus for the once-obscure 401(k) and other *defined-contribution plans* to take center stage as the prime source of future retirement assets for most current U.S. workers.

STRICTLY DEFINED

> **Defined contribution plans**—such as 401(k) and 403(b) plans—are qualified (IRS approved) employee savings and investment plans. They're offered primarily by companies and state or local governments to either replace or supplement traditional defined benefit pension plans. Employees defer tax on an allowed percentage of their pay by contributing it to their plan accounts, which grow tax-deferred—usually until retirement. Companies offering 401(k)s often add partial-matching, tax-deferred amounts to employee accounts.

If all this makes you queasy, and you're nearing or in retirement, then recover quickly. It's perfectly legal for employers to start charging retirees for healthcare coverage, or terminate it altogether—with no chance of litigation except a loss in the court of public opinion. That's an increasingly palatable option for employers willing to sacrifice rewarding their loyal ex-employees in order to pay for rising healthcare costs to keep their current employees. So have a healthy dose of skepticism about the likelihood that you'll eventually or continue to get free or any retiree health coverage.

GOVERNMENT BENEFIT CUTBACKS

No problem, you might say, because there's always Medicare—perhaps more aptly renamed Med-Don't-Care. If you rely on it, you will care when you find out that, on top of the 20 percent co-payment, doctors often make you pay part of the difference between their charges and what Medicare authorizes. True, you can find medical service that will fully accept Medicare, but unless you recognize your provider as one of the hardcore minority of heroic altruists still wearing stethoscopes, remember the adage about whether it's wise to accept the lowest bid for building a bridge. As for prescription-drug benefits, be sure to bring your calculator to the pharmacist so you can check the arithmetic on the three-figure bills you'll be paying most visits.

 Facts about "senior" drugs (based on insurance claims):

- One third of seniors have no insurance coverage for drugs.

- Since 1994, prices of the 50 most commonly used "senior" drugs have increased double the inflation rate.

- Half of those 50 drugs each cost more than $500 per year.

- Many seniors have high cholesterol, hypertension, acid reflux, and diabetes. Their annual cost for the four drugs most commonly prescribed for those conditions is approximately $3,500.

In fact, your annual Social Security benefits might just about pay your annual out-of-pocket medical expenses—if Social Security survives. It probably will, in some form, if the 75-million-strong Baby Boomer lobby can successfully navigate future versions of the butterfly ballot. However, it's best to treat Social Security as play money—which Congress will surely play around with for decades to come.

ECONOMIC TRENDS

Okay, then, so you can't count on your employers or the government to provide for your retirement. At least the robust American economy continues to hum along. Surely, well-educated, industrious folks with budgetary discipline can save enough for retirement from generous salaries, right?

Well, in part it depends on what you mean by humming, industrious, discipline, and generous. Despite obituaries by TV talking heads, in 2001 we're reminded that the Old Economy isn't dead—so expect to hear periodic cracks of static in our humming economy. The business cycle we learned in Economics 101 is back—with its boom, overheat, cool, and resume-growth phases. Regardless of your religious beliefs, it's wise to heed the Biblical lesson of storing away extra during the seven fat years.

That will take more discipline than evidenced during the last 10 boom years. Many Americans came to believe that they might be able to ride their existing stock portfolios to early retirement—while letting the good times roll with unbridled spending. Instead, stories abound of portfolios sliced in half, or down two thirds. Former paper multimillionaires are now looking at having to work beyond even normal retirement. Or, they'll have to be more industrious than ever in putting in the 60-hour weeks to either advance to higher-paid positions or accumulate overtime wages.

But can they expect to continue receiving generous salary increases, or even rely on continued salary?

The business media's daily trumpeting of new market highs has been replaced with daily reports of major layoffs or worker concessions to avoid them. Under intense pressure to act in the best interest of shareholders, executives are quick to the payroll-chopping knife, feeling they can't afford to think of the longer term picture and keep employees just because they're good. Furthermore, after a decade of low inflation, the goods and services companies need to produce their own products are showing signs of increasing in cost—which would raise the cost of goods sold, further pressure profits, and make it more urgent to reduce labor costs.

Those same inflationary pressures will also affect household budgets. With the world population expected to double in the next 50 years, energy and clean water will become much scarcer resources—which could send their prices sky-rocketing. Of course, new technologies could deliver more low-pollution energy and endless clean water, but they'll come at heavy initial costs that will be passed on as taxes or higher prices. And as developing countries become more prosperous, they'll start bidding more for scarce resources. Finally, inflation might occur just because we're unable to keep up outstanding productivity gains—especially with so many workers being aging Baby Boomers.

Of course, the need for aging workers might prove to be a saving grace. If inflation and occasional economic slumps cut into workers' ability to save, at least there's a good chance of gainful employment well beyond normal retirement age—at least for the next 20 to 30 years. Nevertheless, your retirement planning must factor in looming economic uncertainties that were largely hidden by our recent prosperity sunshine.

JUST A MINUTE

The percentage of employers providing health insurance for those who retire before Medicare eligibility is declining. Partly as a consequence, the uninsured rate among early retirees has almost doubled, from 7 to 13 percent.

SHIFT TO PERSONAL RESPONSIBILITY

Where does all this leave your retirement planning? Start with the recognition that "all for one and one for all" is a noble ideal that has given way to today's reality of "everybody for themselves." The vast majority of today's (and tomorrow's) employers will provide only the benefits that they deem necessary to compete at any given time or those required by law. In fact, many financial planners and benefits experts speculate that the next big change will be eliminating employer-provided healthcare altogether, perhaps paying employees something extra to compensate, and leaving it up to them to get their own coverage.

Similarly, regardless of party affiliation, our politics are continually shifting toward the notion of government being a facilitator or enabler of individual, industry, and community initiatives to meet social welfare needs. So expect more tax incentives for individuals to fund their own retirements, and companies and institutions to dismantle their retirement programs and instead supplement their employees' efforts. As we move toward 2020, your retirement focus must clearly be on "eye"—not we.

The bad news is that this chapter's glances into the future exposed some financial images that are vividly stark and dark. The good news is that your eyes are now adjusted to the dark, and you'll be able to use the rest of the book to find your way to brighter retirement possibilities.

HOUR'S UP!

It's time for a check on retirement realities—which might have brought you to tears. That's why this quiz is designed with the hope that you'll laugh until you cry.

1. One reason saving for retirement is more difficult than ever is because …

   a. People can now easily get a seemingly limitless number of credit cards, which they can use to gamble, buy pornographic materials, and shop till they drop on the Internet.

   b. People can buy the Miata 401k and the Infiniti 403b with no money down.

   c. The landmark Smith vs. Jones case established that your retirement savings can be dissolved in a bankruptcy settlement if you went into debt trying to upgrade your life style.

2. The fact that men and women have different life spans is a problem because …

   a. Men who are widowers are hopeless about shopping for the best deals on Viagra and other prescription drugs.

   b. Widows who don't have men around to nag anymore nag each other, raising everyone's blood pressure and the amount they must spend on prescription drugs.

   c. Women have smaller pensions and Social Security, and must make them last longer.

3. It's most important to understand which of the following three-phase schemes …

    a. Childhood, adulthood, and retirement. Retirement is usually called second childhood because it's when women finally have enough time to give men toilet (seat-lowering) training.

    b. Active, passive, and decline. The three phases of retirement, each associated with different spending levels for different reasons.

    c. Dumb, dumber, and dumbest. Dumb when you don't save for retirement. Dumber when you don't save for retirement even though your employer makes matching contributions to your 401(k). Dumbest when you don't save for retirement even after reading this book.

4. Long-term care is …

    a. An AARP initiative aimed at convincing people they must think decades ahead and care about providing themselves and family members a comfortable retirement.

    b. A Justice Department initiative to give 10-year-minimum prison terms to administrators who allow elderly residents of nursing homes to be abused.

    c. Something that will hopefully be a long way off, if ever, but will provide you round-the-clock assisted living and intensive medical care as needed.

5. The millionaire-next-door is an important societal reality because …

    a. She's likely to keep her house up, thus raising property values and giving you more equity to use in retirement when you eventually sell your house.

    b. Someone whose acquaintance will improve your retirement life because he's mastered an exercise program to overcome arthritis and tightly pinch pennies.

    c. A nuisance because it means your monthly budget will be taxed by an expensive alarm system that you'll need because of a greater chance of neighborhood burglary.

6. Sandwiches play an important role in retirement because …

    a. Wives have had it with a lifetime of cooking for everybody.

    b. Your retirement savings are affected by various generations of family squeezing you between their demands for bread.

    c. If you don't eat enough of them by brown-bagging while working, you'll definitely be eating them your entire retirement.

7. The 50 percent divorce rate …

    a. Is partly attributable to so many professional women working overtime on Fridays to wait for the repairman, who was "just here to fix the fax, ma'am."

    b. Has increased the burden on the Social Security trust fund, because women are then entitled to the same amount from Uncle Sam that their ex-husbands get.

    c. Is a great boon to the aggregate retirement savings of landlords and lawyers.

8. Employer retirement benefits aren't what they were because …

    a. You can't sell a gold watch for what you once could.

    b. Today's employee retires with higher hypertension and a lower-type (if any) pension.

    c. Employers have cut way back in order to continue their commitments to full employment, regardless of the economy.

9. It's the *which* economy, stupid?

    a. The old, because then you could have a national depression, and yet nobody had to cut into retirement savings to buy Prozac.

    b. The new, because you could have all booms and no busts, thus diverting the immense fortune spent at Victoria's Secret toward retirement savings.

    c. The economy, period, because there will continue to be cycles of booms and busts, and we know that recycling will eventually prove invaluable to our prosperity.

10. Long-term disability …

   a. Puts a strain on your family when you're out of work, and a strain on your retirement when you're no longer working.

   b. Can be costly, but it's offset by the time you save by being able to park in handicapped spaces, thus allowing more overtime work to save for retirement.

   c. Refers to the seemingly endless inability of long-term-care providers to upgrade their facilities.

QUIZ

HOUR 2

Envisioning Your Retirement

CHAPTER SUMMARY

LESSON PLAN:

In this Hour you will learn about …

- The best timing for retirement.
- Good retirement locations and situations.
- Allocating retirement money and time between travel, leisure, and part-time work.
- The financial implications of your desired retirement lifestyle.

Remember your first day of Drivers Education back in high school and how they attempted to scare the living whatever out of you with gruesome films full of car wrecks? But the next day they started with the good stuff—leading to actually getting behind the wheel of the car.

Think of this book's Hour 1 and Hour 2 in the same way. Hour 1, "Confronting Retirement Realities," was meant to jolt you to attention about the possible grim realities of an unprepared-for retirement. But Hour 2 is meant to wipe away all vestiges of that dark mood. It's time for some soothing meditation, with a warm feeling throughout your body as you envision the kind of retirement life you'd like. For a mantra while doing this, keep repeating to yourself, "anything is possible," because the object of this exercise is to figure out what you really want, without imposing advance restrictions on the possibility that you'll be able to make your dreams come true.

Perhaps you're now squirming a bit, thinking that you bought this book for some solid, how-to advice on planning your retirement, and not to engage in futile wishing for something that can't possibly come true. Of course you did, but for many people, the mechanics of financial preparedness are far less daunting than the scary prospect of "just what the heck am I going to do with all that free time?" That's why you must wait a bit to start the heavy lifting, and allow yourself the freedom to imagine, to make a movie in your mind of what your retirement could be like.

JUST A MINUTE

David Demko, a gerontologist and editor in chief of Age Venture News Service, proposes a formula for determining the age that you *feel*—an important determinant of your retirement quality of life. His "neo-years" (www.demko.com/neoyear.htm) are the average of these four ages: chronological (actual) anatomical (health and physical condition), social (activity and engagement level), and emotional (coping and adaptation skills).

If this notion throws you for a loop, you might want to bookmark this page and take a break for some fact-finding. Start by talking to friends who are either in or near retirement, or who have parents and friends who are. Where are they living? What are they doing? What type of retirement life did they originally visualize? What adjustments did they make to new circumstances? What would they do differently if they had it to do over again?

These narratives of actual experience and impressions should come first, sort of like seeing a real fashion model in the flesh before trying to make yourself over into the touched-up, colorized images in ads, commercials, and videos. Then, fitted with your realism filter, plunge into the books, videos, and magazine articles that offer idyllic images of places to travel and live, and all the fabulous people and amenities you'll find there.

Assuming your mind is now filled with possibilities, let's proceed with the dreaming.

DECIDE WHEN

It's not surprising that in a society where early retirement has acquired considerable sex appeal, most people first think of *when* in planning their retirements. Yet, except for the rich, asking when is only a recent phenomenon resulting from the increased longevity and prosperity of the adult generation that emerged from World War II. Ironically, the children of the younger part of that generation—the Baby Boomers—show signs that they abhor the prospect of one thing that retirement represents: being or feeling old—or even being perceived that way. So experts are unsure what to expect about when they'll retire and whether it will look anything like our current view of the golden years.

A 1999 American Association of Retired Persons (AARP) survey of Baby-Boomer retirement attitudes (http://research.aarp.org/econ/boomer_seg_toc.html) found that 80 percent expect to work at least part-time during retirement. Researchers classified 30 percent of Boomers as "self-reliants"—characterized by their expectation of maintaining health throughout most of retirement and not requiring family help in their old age.

THE COST OF WHEN

Although the de-emphasis on retirement age is born of Boomer vanity, it could be a good thing. *When* overly emphasizes the financial aspects of your retirement decision—as reflected in articles gracing the pages and screens of virtually every financial magazine and Web site—and even many general publications such as *Reader's Digest*. Not to be outdone, within the last year, publishers have released at least five significant books with "early retirement" in the title.

Do you want more specifics on the financial timing of early retirement? Start with abundant media articles and financial-institution literature on 401(k) to IRA lump-sum rollovers, and early withdrawals from 401(k) plans and IRA accounts. Then check out Social Security Administration's publication, "When To Retire," for the financial consequences of earliest possible age 62 retirement vs. the normal 65 or 67, depending on your birth year. Finally, this uncertain economy has led virtually all sizeable companies to encourage early retirement of older workers. You might have access to computer software or an internal Web site that enables you to calculate the pension you'd receive by retiring on a chosen date—including a possible incentive sweetener that performs the calculation as though the date you choose is up to five years later.

FYI By age 62, only about 40 percent of men and 25 percent of women still work full-time. Those percentages are dropping further as concerns about a slowing economy prompt more early retirement offers, and first-wave Baby Boomers reach normal corporate early retirement age (55) in 2001. However, within 10 years, employers are expected to start offering reverse late retirement to bolster an inadequate supply of incoming "baby-bust" workers.

Researchers bring other financial perspectives to the question of when—some even practical. For example, an Urban Institute study focuses on the health-insurance gap that early retirees must bridge. It looks at what they do or don't do about getting coverage between the lapse of employer coverage and the onset of Medicare eligibility—which, unlike Social Security, can't take place until age 65.

Other studies, like those done by a professor at the University of South Wales, are a little more esoteric. To the professor, retirement timing boils down to a fascinating mathematical problem with two elegant solutions. The first uses nine variables related to your retirement decision and is based on an "isoelastic form of the utility function and a non-negative rate of time preference." If by some chance you took only two years of high school calculus instead of four, there's good news; the second function uses only four variables and is "based on a log form of the utility function and a zero rate of time preference."

If your preference is something you can actually use, choose from a variety of retirement calculators. Typically, they require that you input your age, salary, desired retirement age, and some economic assumption. In return, you find out how much you have to save annually to meet your goal. If you use some offered by banks and other financial institutions and you'll be comforted to know you can retire sometime before you die—but only if you stop spending money and invest every last dollar with that particular company.

GO TO ▶
Help is on the way in developing the judgment you need to intelligently use retirement calculators. Refer to Hour 5, "Retirement Finance Basics," for a discussion of inflation, interest rates, investment rates of return, and other measures that most retirement calculators require you to estimate.

Other calculators are so simple that they let you get away with broad outrageous assumptions about what your expenses, salary, and investment returns will be—allowing you to conclude that you can retire pretty much whenever you'd like. Good calculators do exist, but they require careful judgement about assumptions and estimates; sometimes slight variations involving them can cause calculated results to vary significantly. Furthermore, no matter how good calculators are, they beg nonfinancial questions that you should answer before using them.

WHEN TO SAY WHEN

Make *when* the last thing you consider, after first figuring out what you want to do with the rest of your life. Instead of asking whether you can retire early, or when you can retire normally, ask yourself when you can fit retirement among all your goals regarding work, family, play, and societal contributions.

Some financial planners facilitate this thinking by having their clients drop retirement from their vocabulary. Instead, planners talk about when their clients will achieve financial independence—defined by no longer needing actively generated income. To make this more real, they have clients imagine they've just won a sweepstakes or lottery, or inherited a fortune, and ask them what they'd then do for the rest of their lives. They then ask again, for a few different ages. Then they guide clients into understanding that this is the same type of problem they'd face if at retirement if they received a large lump-sum pension or profit-sharing plan payoff.

By separating the concept of retirement from financial independence, the question of when can be seen as often depending on where you want to be after the current phase of your life. For example, suppose you want to live out your life overseas as an expatriate, or in some out-of-the-way domestic locale. Even if you've retired financially, you might not want to make the move until after you or your spouse has completed involvement in local politics or social action, or in providing your children hands-on help with your grandchildren. These are things that can't be done if you're not a local resident, or are too far away or remote to regularly be there or easily visit.

JUST A MINUTE

About two million retired Americans live abroad—mostly in Argentina, Belize, Canada, Costa Rica, Ecuador, Greece, Ireland, Italy, Mexico, Panama, Portugal, and Spain. Many retired early by taking advantage of some combination of lower taxes, favorable exchange rates, and lower cost of living. Others returned to homelands or are fulfilling Shangri-la dreams.

After doing this kind of thinking, you might decide that early retirement is not all that attractive an option—even if you can afford it. After all, many children of wealthy families fail to ever discover a reason for being and suffer through privileged, but empty lives.

Of course, you're a grown, accomplished person already, and probably not burdened by enormous wealth. Nevertheless, if you set your sights on early retirement, make sure you're convinced that you won't fall prey to a life of uncomfortable, excess leisure that will leave you feeling unfulfilled.

DECIDE WHERE

Regardless of when you retire, however, you're less likely to endure suffocating boredom if you pick a geographical location and housing community that fosters your interests. For a growing segment of retirees that translates to placing more emphasis on proximity of family and friends, and less on the stereotypical desire to live in the sunbelt for year-round warmth and cheaper housing.

 FYI The 2000 Census shows that among the 10 percent of retirees who move out of state, a smaller portion are choosing Florida and Arizona. Perhaps remembering the music of their youth, today's retirees prefer four seasons—increasingly landing in a new sunbelt that includes Oregon, North Carolina, Georgia, (lower-altitude parts of) Colorado, and several other moderate-climate destinations.

LOCATION CONSIDERATIONS

Recognizing the no-longer homogenous retiree population, developers nationwide have responded with a miniboom of senior-oriented housing communities with recreational, health, and assisted-living amenities. Now you're likely to find housing designed with retirees in mind in any state or significant-sized city you choose. Be aware, though, that two seemingly similar places—such as the senior-laden college towns of Iowa City, Iowa and Chapel Hill, North Carolina—might be worlds apart culturally and politically.

JUST A MINUTE

 If college towns appeal to you, you're almost certain to find one that suits your cultural and political tastes. To meet a strong demand among seniors to (re)live the college life, between 50 and 100 major senior housing communities have already been built nationwide in or near college towns. Perks for seniors include free tuition and free or highly discounted on-campus admission to lectures, concerts, and other entertainment and cultural activities.

Also watch for whether demographic harmony exists in places where retirees are concentrated. Some communities with similar percentages of seniors and growing families boast support of tax rates that provide ample services to all. In others, though, open war prevails between the camps. For example, many communities have thousands of longtime-resident, middle-class seniors who don't want to pay inordinately high taxes for schools, and thousands more relatively affluent families who are willing to pay whatever tax rates it takes to provide their oodles of small children with ample educational space and facilities.

So make sure you consider both sociological and meteorological climate factors in your view of a retirement paradise. Do you prefer rural, urban, new-urban, or suburban? Do you want an executive, professional, academic, artsy, or ordinary-folks feel? Are you more comfortable with small-town stability or go-with-the-flow growth? Do you crave unlimited theatrical, musical, performance, and athletic-event options, or will you be content with a quieter existence offering plenty of opportunities for hiking, bird-watching, and other nature ventures?

If you have difficulty answering these questions, think about what you love, like, dislike, and hate about where you live and have lived. Also, what qualities were missing in those places? By parsing all this information, you'll have a much better idea of the kind of place you're looking for, and the kind you want to avoid like the plague. But remember, while past likes and dislikes are useful, you're going to be 55 or 65, not 25 or 35, in the place you choose—so allow for that in weighting your preferences.

PROCEED WITH CAUTION

In choosing where to retire, consider retirement role changes that occur because your social life no longer revolves around work associates or parenting. Furthermore, midlife hormonal changes sometimes make men more social, nurturing, and laid-back, and women more goal oriented. For more on these and other nonfinancial retirement issues, check out *Retire & Thrive* by Robert Otterbourg (see Appendix B, "Resources").

LOCATION CHOICES

Of course, you considered these same types of factors in deciding on each place you've lived. But then you were under the duress of a different set of priorities—mainly where the jobs were. In retirement, though, if you do proper planning, employment opportunities will play second fiddle to quality-of-life opportunities. So start off on the right note by savoring the experience. This is your chance to relive the excitement of having chosen a college or finding your first post-graduate job—without the unpleasant pressures, time expended, and travel costs associated with those decisions.

Start by thinking about your preferences in your spare moments and keeping a running list of the attributes you consider most desirable in a retirement locale—and perhaps a few definite "don't wants." Then, spend a few hours of computer or library time making lists of cities and retirement communities meeting your criteria.

TIME SAVER

Not sure where you'd like to retire? The following books can help you narrow down the choices (see Appendix B for details):

- *50 Fabulous Places to Retire in America* by Ken Stern

- *America's Best Places to Retire* by Robert L. Fox

- *Where to Retire: America's Best and Most Affordable Places* by John Howells

- *Retirement Places Rated* by David Savageau

- *The World's Top Retirement Havens* by Margaret J. Goldstein

- *America's 100 Best Places to Retire: The Only Guide You Need to Today's Top Retirement Towns* by Robert L. Fox

Expect some of your choices to stay on your mind. Those are the places you should start incorporating into your vacation plans. Get to know the area. Among the happiest retirees who picked up stakes upon retirement are those who'd visited their new locations repeatedly over a period of years before moving there.

DECIDE ABOUT WORKING PART-TIME

Retirement has become a less decisive act as the percentage of workers who "earn retirement" from particular companies, government, or other organizations decreases. Retirement is becoming distinguished by the subtle shift from basing one's lifestyle and life circumstances on work. Instead, most retirees base their choice of whether, how much, and where to work, on their higher-priority location and lifestyle preferences.

That's somewhat reflected in the approximate 20 percent of today's retirees who operate a business or work either full-time or part-time, even though they don't need the money. However, another 25 percent are still working because they do need the money.

It's the Boomers, however, who'll seal the deal about retirement work. Forty percent plan to work for pay even though they don't need the money, and another 40 percent because they do. Furthermore, many who need the money now plan to keep working even after they don't. And most of the 20 percent who don't plan to work for pay do plan substantial volunteer work. Regardless of need, the almost-unanimous intent of Boomers to do some kind of retirement work is driven by what they say are the psychological and social rewards of meeting challenges, being valued, and feeling needed and connected.

PROCEED WITH CAUTION

 These figures are based on a combination of surveys done within the last few years— and on behavior and attitudes that preceded the dramatic 2000-2001 tech-stock collapse. With many of the portfolios that Boomers and retirees thought were (nearly) sufficient for retirement now down 25 to 75 percent, it's likely that a much higher percentage of both groups will now be working during retirement due to need.

DECIDE ON LEISURE AND TRAVEL GOALS

Retirement can be a virtual utopia if you love to travel and have at least a modest fun cash stash. Freed from a schedule, you can pack at a moment's notice to take advantage of tremendous savings available from last-minute bookings on undersold cruises and tours. You can buy that unlimited-travel train fare and leave without knowing when you're coming back or where you'll be stopping. Or you can book air travel that departs and returns mid-week to get the best deals. Closer to home, you can play golf or attend week-day matinees at hours when fees and admission prices are much lower and there are fewer people. However, unless you've been at least a little sponta-neous before, you might not adjust to such a freewheeling lifestyle.

Similarly, your retirement dreams probably include many activities that you've always been meaning to get to, but never do. That's fine if you're one of those super-efficient people who always gets all the "A" items done first on your to-do list, and gets to others only when possible. More likely, though, you share the frustration of most folks who never seem to get to some things they consider important—perhaps regular exercise, spending more time with the kids, or doing volunteer work. So beware, because the act of retiring doesn't trigger a magic spell that enables you to suddenly change your personality or behavior style, or do things you've never done before.

Therefore, while still ignoring cost, do make your dreams realistic with hon-est self-examination of who you really are, and how adaptable you'll be to a regimen of pursuits that are now foreign to you. On the other hand, avoid being the kid in the empty candy store thinking that you'll finally be able to devote unlimited time to things you now love, because those things might lose their joyful kick when they become routine and repetitive. As many retirees have come to realize, "there's only so much golf you can play."

FYI In his book *Virtues of Aging* (see Appendix B), former President Jimmy Carter talks about retirement being the best time of his life. He cites the freedom to do more of something you didn't have enough time for, or taking up totally new things. For example, in addition to becoming an author (13 books and counting), his 60s firsts include skiing, climbing mountains, and becoming a college professor.

In other words, don't plan a retirement either based on new things you'll never do at all, or favorite things you'll never do as much as you think you will. Avoid that mistake by brainstorming exhaustively about all the things you've ever done, and make notes next to each one about why you liked it or didn't like it—and under what circumstances you might like it either less or more as a retirement pursuit. Perhaps that rock collection you once kept will become an archaeological dig during retirement. Maybe those times you cooked for an international potluck dinner will turn into an interest in gourmet cooking.

Keep in mind that you're just doing a rough sketch of your ideal retirement life. Broaden your horizons now by trying new things and then repeat this exercise at least annually. You should find that your sketch will start to take on definition, and eventually become a detailed, multicolored canvas of your bright retirement dreams.

DECIDE ON YOUR OVERALL LIVING STANDARD

The 1990 book *Your Money or Your Life* (see Appendix B) wasn't about retirement, but about artificial expectations. Authors Joe Dominguez and Vicki Robin asked readers to first answer the question "how much stuff is enough?" That led to their theme: Once you know you have enough to get you that much stuff, you're able to stop the unending material quest and be at peace with yourself and what you have; and chances are that you'll discover you'll be content with less than you thought. They then proceeded to show readers what they believed was a way to ensure continued financial security. It required an act of faith—that once you know what will satisfy you, it's possible to combine an amount of money and investment philosophy that constitutes a sustaining threshold at which you can live that satisfied life.

It's time for you to show the same faith—that this book will enable you to home in on your sustaining retirement threshold, and show you how to get there. So far, you've pondered what kind of retirement you want, qualitatively. You don't have to decide on the specifics now—in fact, you probably can't—but what we've covered this hour should give you a sense of the standard-of-living level that will make you comfortable in retirement. In Hour 3, "Quantifying Retirement Costs," we'll break down that standard-of-living level into a specific forecast of your retirement expenses by detailed category.

FYI *Your Money or Your Life* proved to be a seminal work in defining a condition of American society that came to be known as "affluenza." Quickly following were many how-to books on frugal living. When the stock market started soaring, all that seemed to be quickly forgotten, but it's worth revisiting in regards to your retirement, now that we've been reintroduced to sober economic realities.

HOUR'S UP!

Look at the clock and calendar on the wall and focus on your date of retirement. You're getting very sleepy. When you hear fingers snap, wake up and take advantage of your hypnotic state to answer these questions about your retirement hopes and dreams.

1. Which of these best describes the value of dreaming about retirement?

   a. It's therapeutic, because at least if you're not able to live all your dreams during retirement, you'll get the pleasure of dreaming about them.

   b. In your career, you've got to dream big if you hope to do big things. So in retirement planning, you've got to dream first so that you can focus on what you really want.

   c. Dreaming just leads to disappointment and resentment; chances are that if you're a dreamer about retirement, you're a dreamer on the job who never gets anything done.

2. Most people view part-time work during retirement in the following way:

   a. The pay is only a small part; the real value is the great discounts on the living staples that most retail firms give senior workers, and they don't have to pay a dime of tax.

   b. It's a necessary evil if you enter retirement with less than a million-dollar nest egg.

   c. After a life of being defined by the work they do, many retirees still want the psychological satisfaction it provides, even if they don't need the money.

QUIZ

3. The most important development in helping people visualize their retirement is …

   a. The fact that good retirement housing and communities can be found almost anywhere in the country, so that geography is now far less of a limitation in deciding where to retire.

   b. The recent discovery that just as hypnosis can tap repressed childhood memories, so can it help get at the deep dreams and desires that people have about their retirements.

   c. Webcams set up in most major retirement communities, allowing people to get a real picture of what retirement life is like.

4. Which of these is the best time to retire?

   a. The date that hell freezes over, which is when Congress will change the law to provide complete retiree medical coverage under Medicare.

   b. When you are ready financially, psychologically, and emotionally.

   c. When you are no longer invisible to teenage boys and girls, but they wish you were.

5. The greatest thing about retirement calculators is …

   a. They're available for a 50 percent discount from national office superstores if you show proof that you're at least 55 years old.

   b. Although they're guaranteed to be only 95 percent accurate, that's close enough because you can always work part-time for a little while during retirement if you come up slightly short.

   c. They turn the mindset of save, save, save, and save some more into one of this is where I am now, this is where I need to be, and this is what I have to do to get there.

6. Which combination of factors is the best reason to retire overseas?

   a. Reduced-fee privileges at the World Bank and ground-floor opportunities to participate in IPO-like economic redevelopment ventures following civil unrest.

   b. Appeals to a sense of adventure and usually offers overall economic advantage.

   c. The cost of living is always lower and taxes are practically nonexistent because those governments are far more efficient than the U.S.

7. The most important reason college towns appeal to many as a place to retire is ...

    a. Because of the multifaceted lifestyle they offer retirees.

    b. You can buy a house and take in a student as a tenant for a delightfully obscene high rent.

    c. It's been proven that a glass of wine every night for dinner can reduce risk of heart attack, and wine and spirits are much cheaper in such towns.

8. Fewer retirees are seeking the traditional sunbelt locales for the following reason:

    a. With many more being Baby Boomers, they prefer places like New Jersey, where the Four Seasons are played in virtually every karaoke club.

    b. They're worried about whether they'll be allowed to register to vote in Florida.

    c. With retirement becoming more an extension of the rest of your life, warmth and proximity to myriad other retirees are becoming less important.

9. The most important reason you should be wary of retiring early is ...

    a. For every year that you retire before you're allowed to take Social Security, one year is chopped off a surviving spouse's eventual Social Security benefit.

    b. Medicare is not available until normal Social Security retirement age, thus creating a health insurance gap that you must individually fill.

    c. If you still have children in college and refuse to cover the full costs of the college of their choice, they can sue you to make you resume work.

QUIZ

10. The most accurate thing you can say about your retirement standard of living is …

    a. First you have to determine what you want to do in retirement, and then whether it's realistic to accumulate the funds necessary to do it.

    b. It's usually about the same standard of living you had when you were in your 30s.

    c. It's dictated by your good fortune, or lack thereof, in what you are able to earn from jobs and investments during your working years.

HOUR 3

Quantifying Retirement Costs

CHAPTER SUMMARY

LESSON PLAN:

In this Hour you will learn about …

- Problems with retirement cost rules-of-thumb estimation based on current expenses.
- Various possible costs.
- Most important costs to estimate as accurately as possible.
- Realistically estimating both big-item costs and all other expenses.

To determine how much it will cost you to live in retirement, let's consider what it costs dogs. Generally, they eat less in their golden (retriever) years, with fewer fancy treats. And they also play less, so they don't need as many new toys and other gadgets. However, they develop hip dysplasia and other physical problems, so vet expenses increase. Thus, as a rule of thumb, let's say that a dog's retirement budget is about 95 percent of its current budget.

Of course, that 95 percent is just a rule of thumb, but dogs shouldn't be opposed to using it because they don't have opposable thumbs. However, as humans with opposable thumbs, we should oppose using the standard rule of thumb for how much annual retirement income (in today's dollars) we'll need to cover expenses. Many experts say that you should use 80 percent of your current annual income if you're a family with children at home.

Okay, our opposable thumbs don't really have anything to do with retirement expenses—unless we twiddle them for the last 30 years of life, thus drastically reducing our expenditures. Yet the logic that many retirement "experts" use in arriving at our 80 percent rule of thumb is about as silly and oversimplified as the 95 percent dog example. That's why we should take a different lesson from dogs: Be as painstaking in preparing an estimated retirement budget as they are in burying bones. Unless you list every possible expense and estimate its yearly cost in today's dollars, you're simply barking up the wrong retirement-planning tree. Here's how to fetch those expenses.

TIME SAVER

If your time is severely limited, continue reading, but skip determining the individual expense details for now and use that 80 percent rule of thumb. Adjust it to 100 percent if you're accustomed to living well, and to 70 percent if you consider yourself thrifty. Come back to this chapter later when you're ready to make more exact estimates.

ESTIMATE FOOD AND SHELTER COSTS

Regardless of your retirement lifestyle, you need the basics—a roof over your head and daily nutrition. They sound easy to estimate, but there are many factors to consider. If you simply stay in place, or perhaps move to a smaller home, you might still be paying off a mortgage or be taking on an entirely new one. Either way, your property taxes should decrease if your home is smaller or you move to a more senior-populated area with low or no school taxes.

Regardless of your property taxes, though, the effort involved in home ownership becomes increasingly more taxing with age. You're unlikely to continue clearing your own gutters, fixing roof shingles, or doing your own inside or outside painting—and that's just a small sample. Furthermore, consider the fact that both you and your house will become creakier with age. That means you'll need more routine maintenance help and require more repairs—including building in costly senior-friendly accommodations. Thus, plan to pay for both more routine maintenance help and more repairs. In short, consider the overall costs of home ownership in planning your retirement budget.

If that's not enough food for thought about increased retirement costs, here's something else that's hard to swallow. Although your groceries will be considerably less than they are now if you still have kids at home, you'll likely dine out more often as part of a more active outside entertainment and recreation schedule. However, if you're now buying takeout food frequently because of a hectic lifestyle, those costs could drop drastically—particularly because you're less likely to eat such foods when you join the ranks of typically more health-conscious seniors.

PROCEED WITH CAUTION

Your food costs might not go down if you regard dietary supplements as part of your food budget rather than your medical budget. If you're currently a "health nut," you know how expensive these can be. And you'll likely use even more of these items to meet greater needs and less-efficient digestion when you're older.

All bets are off, though, if you choose some type of retirement community. You might be paying a hefty fee for shared community recreation and other amenities. You might have the opportunity to purchase meals at a community facility at times you don't want to cook in your smaller kitchen. Or you could even be on a meal plan that adds to a monthly rental or installment-payment cost—much like room and board if you lived in a college dorm.

To illustrate these differences, let's examine the features of the major types of retirement communities and living facilities.

Active Adult Retirement Communities (AARC)

AARCs are clusters of attached or small detached homes, designed for pre-retirees and active, healthy retirees. They generally include golf courses, swimming pools, fitness courses and rooms, and other activity centers. But they sell the "youth image" by excluding medical and living-assistance facilities and staff. However, some have reserved extra land on which assisted-living facilities might be built as the residents age.

Although some AARCs have rentals, the ones with significant amenities usually require home purchase—typically ranging from $100,000 to $300,000—and an annual maintenance fee that is usually larger than the average condominium or homeowners association fee. Some also provide meals, housekeeping, and laundry services—either bundled into the fee or paid for by those who use them.

FYI Sun City, Arizona (near Phoenix) is the best-known AARC. It's an entire city completely populated by 45,000 "rockin' retirees"—requiring at least one person over 55 in each household and nobody under 19. Home prices range from $50,000 to over $200,000, with small annual recreation and golf-privilege fees, and property taxes under 1 percent.

If the AARC lifestyle appeals to you, be sure to thoroughly research it, so that you'll have a realistic idea of the upfront and continuing costs. Prices can vary widely for virtually identical facilities—usually due to desirability with respect to the following factors:

- Cost of living, and level of property and state income taxes
- Location outside of but near a bigger city—preferably with a major air hub and plentiful, quality lodging
- Mild climate, excellent medical facilities, and low crime rate
- Ample public transportation and opportunities for adult education and retiree-oriented social/cultural activities

CONTINUING CARE RETIREMENT COMMUNITIES (CCRC)

A CCRC serves people retiring at the normal age, ready to leave a house they stayed in after retirement, or ready to phase out of the higher-energy AARC. CCRCs are designed to allow residents to "age in place" by providing independent, supervised, and assisted-living units on one campus. For example, residents might start in a small detached or attached home, taking their meals in the centralized dining room, and fully participating in the recreation and transportation included in the package.

Later, they might move into an apartment where cleaning and other personal services are included. Eventually, they'll be in dormitory-type assisted-living unit or nursing home, where intensive physical-aid or medical services are routinely provided.

CCRCs currently house only about 1,000,000 people. But they're in the early stages of explosive growth leading to total national capacity exceeding 10,000,000 as Baby Boomers start retiring in significant numbers. That growth is an answer to uncertainty, because CCRCs are a sort of insurance policy that guarantees care as people age.

That insurance comes at the substantial cost of entry fees ranging from tens of thousands to hundreds of thousands, and monthly maintenance fees of hundreds to thousands. For many residents, that translates to paying the entry fee from the equity left after selling a home. The maintenance fee is often covered with monthly Social Security and pension proceeds—with continuing residence assured even if those amounts decrease (such as exhausting an IRA).

The financial arrangements involved in a CCRC contract can be as complex as investment in sophisticated life insurance or annuities—and they're not regulated by an SEC-like organization. For example, some make all or part of the entrance fee refundable if you decide to move—but that's not as great a deal as it sounds. Meanwhile, the owners are investing your money to make themselves money.

PROCEED WITH CAUTION

 Although CCRCs provide medical care and facilities, the level varies widely and isn't necessarily comprehensive. You might still be responsible for hospital costs, specialist-physician fees, and prescription drugs. Because so many CCRCs are so new, beware of a repeat of what befell some of the first ones: excessive promises that might never be fulfilled due to over-ambitious expansion leading to bankruptcy.

So buyer beware: Think about all the effort and research you put into buying your first home, and double or triple it. Meanwhile, though, if you're years from retirement now, it's realistic to assume you'll be living in a CCRC at some point, and to include the cost in your retirement-need calculation.

Concentrated Retirement Care Living Options

While CCRCs provide the whole package for aging in place after retirees start slowing down, the majority of retirees still choose the option of aging in place in their own homes—assisted by paid companions, home health aides, and adult day care. If they require a higher level of assistance or their health deteriorates, they then move into the same type of stand-alone assisted living, group home, or long-term-care facilities that are sometimes part of a CCRC.

Costs vary widely. Assisted living is often government subsidized on a sliding scale as low as a few hundred dollars per month, keyed to income. At the other end, private facilities can be several thousand dollars monthly. Long-term-care facilities are even more expensive and far less frequently subsidized.

Fortunately, most home support, assisted living, or long-term care can be covered with Medicaid or Medicare if you're very poor in retirement—although the facilities leave much to be desired. You will want to look seriously at the other option—long-term-care insurance. Although it's expensive, it's one important way to protect yourself from a dismal old age and ensure your assets will last as long as you live.

GO TO ▶
Refer to Hours 17, "Retirement Road Detours," and 22, "Pre-Retirement Planning," for explanations of how long-term care insurance can help offset killer medical and living expenses during retirement.

HOMEOWNER'S INSURANCE

Regardless of what style housing you choose, make sure to budget for some form of homeowner's insurance, although it's possible it would be included in the fees for a community. However, don't assume it's included without checking, because whenever you occupy a specific property, whether owning or renting, you are responsible for insuring it and your own property that you keep there.

ESTIMATE HEALTHCARE COSTS

Future healthcare costs are extremely hard to predict as it is, but more so for retirees due to their potential overlap with the food and shelter costs just discussed. Just as with health maintenance organizations (HMOs), CCRCs that purport to offer complete medical care might have a different definition of what that means from what you have—and you could end up with substantial uncovered costs.

GO TO ▷
Hour 17 also includes a discussion on the overall role of retirement health coverage in preventing asset erosion from exorbitant medical expenses.

Even if you don't go the CCRC route, long-term-care policies substantially differ in the medical care they provide. Furthermore, although tremendous emphasis has been placed on "saving Social Security," Medicare is in far greater trouble ultimately. The certain reforms to come will mean either more out-of-pocket expense due to less coverage, or much higher premiums for the supplemental government and private coverages.

Finally, there is employer-provided retiree health coverage. Millions of retirees are now discovering that just because that coverage was included in their original retirement package, companies have the right to ask retirees to share in paying the premiums or to simply drop the coverage. The only exception is when a company has made a specific guarantee or promise to employees that the coverage will continue.

So how do you deal with all this uncertainty in projecting retirement healthcare costs? To start, although it's not fully in your control, the chances are good that your future costs will be correlated to both your inherited (genetic) medical predispositions and the type of lifestyle you have now and will have in the years to come. Therefore, in using the following definite or average costs in your estimates, rate yourself from 1 to 5 to apply the appropriate cost factor. A 1 means the entire cast of television's *ER* is on alert for you daily, and a 5 means your health insurer always sends you valentines.

Then, apply that rating in using the following table as a guide in compiling a retirement healthcare estimate:

Item	Cost (C)	1	2	3	4	5
Medicare	Free	NA	NA	NA	NA	NA
Medicare B	____	NA	NA	C	NA	NA
Medigap	____	NA	NA	C	NA	NA
Average Drugs	____	$2 \times C$	$1.5 \times C$	C	$.75 \times C$	$.5 \times C$
Average Uncovered	____	$2 \times C$	$1.5 \times A$	C	$.75 \times C$	$.5 \times C$

GO TO ▷
Hour 14, "Medicare and Private Supplementary Insurance," explains the features of the basic Medicare, the optional Medicare B that gives you extra coverage in exchange for a monthly premium you pay the government, and private-insurer Medigap policies that partially cover some things not covered by either type of Medicare.

ESTIMATE LEISURE AND TRAVEL COSTS

They might be saddled with high, uncovered medical bills, and be hostages to their frugal nature. Nevertheless, today's retirees definitely spend more on travel and leisure pursuits than they did during their working years. Therefore, it's a no-brainer that future retirees will continue that trend—especially the free-spending Boomers. For example, don't you now regard your computers somewhat like cars—buying a new model every few years? Although computers might eventually be master controllers for your house, you should still regard them as recreational expenses, for now.

In fact, you might even buy a computer fully dedicated to a new hobby such as genealogy. But even if new hobbies don't need dedicated computers, they will require funding, so don't forget to include them. In particular, don't fail to include a "hobby" that many retirees take up for health reasons—particularly if they're widow(er)s, pet ownership, which studies have shown helps overcome depression and extends life.

Finally, if you're getting anywhere close to retirement, you've probably heard the joke about the retirement hobby (or ritual) of checking the obituaries daily to make sure you're not in them. Although that costs only a newspaper subscription, make sure you include the increasing cost of sudden funeral or consolation trips for the illnesses or deaths of close friends as you get older.

FYI Many Boomers don't see themselves as aging, but as "middle-aging"—until at least age 75. For more on the "new retiree," check out *Refirement, A Boomer's Guide to Life After 50* by James V. Gambone and *Time of Your Life: Why Almost Everything Gets Better After 50* by Jane Glenn Haas and Leah Komaiko. Details on both books are in Appendix B, "Resources."

A new school of thought suggests that overall leisure and travel costs might not be so steep. If future retirees will already be so accustomed to playing hard, perhaps they won't be bursting from the retirement starting gate to board the next cruise ship. Of course, believing themselves immortal, they won't even own rocking chairs, and will be more active than ever. However, they'll center this activity close to home and be less self-centered than their reputation—reverting to their 1960s rebellious roots in trying to change society through volunteer activism.

So you decide, if all those mileage clubs have made travel same-ole, same-ole for you, to project your travel expenses as only moderately higher than currently, and your other leisure expenses 25 to 50 percent higher. But if you have your sights set on an around-the-world or even out-of-this-world (yes, it's more likely the younger you are) trip, then think double or triple.

 You probably won't have to spend the $20 million reportedly charged the first commercial space passenger, Dennis Tito, when he hooked up with the Russian Soyuz in April 2001. In fact, the firm that arranged the flight, Space Adventures, says it has several customers on the waiting list for $100,000 suborbital flights.

ESTIMATE OTHER RECURRING BUDGET ITEMS

Thinking in both multiples and fractions is wise when it comes to mundane aspects of your retirement budget. For example, the "medicine cabinet" now mostly filled with cosmetic items might actually become filled with mostly medicine! This information might help you determine the medicine cabinet's side effects on your budget.

PERSONAL CARE

Start with how good you want to look and feel—which could greatly affect how you feel about how your budget looks. For example, it's possible that former career women might be a little less fastidious about makeup, hair care, and related items in the more casual retirement atmosphere. But that reduction will probably be more than compensated by the overall much higher costs of personal-care items for both men and women that enhance day-to-day life as we age.

In fact, advertisers are finally catching on to the aging Baby Boomers, and will follow them to their graves pushing every conceivable vanity and health-enhancing, over-the-counter products. And who knows how many more Viagra, Niagra, and similar romantic-rehabilitation products not covered by medical insurance will appear on the horizon. And when bed-bouncing gives way to partial bed confinement, dignity-maintenance products such as Depends will fill the gap. Thus, it's probably wise to double or triple what you now spend on personal care, depending on how important appearances are to you.

CLOTHING AND LOCAL TRANSPORTATION

Of course, even those with off-the-scale vanity will probably spend less on clothing during retirement, so cut your budget there by 25 to 50 percent. That probably means you'll also spend less caring for your clothing—particularly if you're no longer wearing your weekday finest to work. Don't go overboard, though, because you're likely to be doing a lot of volunteer work and attending senior programming that sometimes require semiformal attire.

JUST A MINUTE

There's no way you can really estimate this, but it's good to know you can take some tax deductions related to your volunteer work. You can't count donation of your time, but you can sometimes deduct the cost of lodging, meals, and transportation for overnight travel exclusively related to volunteer work. You can also deduct driving-mileage charges to and from volunteer sites, and the cost of hosting parties related to the volunteer efforts.

If you plan on doing volunteer work, you'd be making a mistake to assume your local transportation costs will go way down. Instead of one daily trip to work for both you and your spouse, and perhaps one together for shopping or other activities, you'll be making several shorter trips—perhaps separately, as related to different spousal interests, and maybe part-time jobs.

The question is, will the Department of Motor Vehicles allow you to make all those trips as you get older? Recent startling statistics on the soaring fatal-accident rates among senior drivers suggest that your insurance costs could become almost prohibitive. While that might lead to less or no advanced-senior driving, it won't get you out of the local-transportation woods. Instead, it means that you could become reliant on far-more-expensive local transportation—such as taxis and vans. Or, despite the dot-com failure of Webvan, you'll use "proxy driving"—such as paying for grocery shopping and delivery.

PROFESSIONAL SERVICES AND INSURANCE

Aging could also make you prone to other deadly consequences, such as financially fatal errors regarding taxes, estate planning, vulnerability to scams, and failure to keep up payments for crucial needs such as insurance. Thus, even if you're now the type who uses software to do all your own finances and to prepare wills, you'd be wise to assume you'll need help with those matters during retirement.

PROCEED WITH CAUTION

In early 2001, the IRS commissioner admitted that the agency is currently ill-equipped to effectively act on an estimated one-quarter trillion dollars of annual tax avoidance and cheating. This is largely due to antiquated computer systems (another lesson in the cost of not maintaining yourself when younger) that are currently being revamped and should be fully ready to call you on the carpet for future audits.

For one thing, if you have substantial assets, you'll probably want a good financial planner to help you figure out how to do your retirement distributions to minimize taxes and ensure your money lasts. Your financial planner can also help you determine if you still should keep up your life insurance, long-term disability, and long-term care insurance, and advise you on how much umbrella coverage you should have to protect you from major lawsuits.

You also want to use a CPA for tax filing in years your affairs are complex, because it could be a nightmare to be audited when you're older.

Furthermore, while it might now be wise to do a new will every 5 to 10 years, as you get older, you might want to revise it every year or two as your financial situation changes. Also, the older you get, the more specific you'll want to be in drawing up powers of attorney and other capacity-related documents.

Then there's the matter of planning gifts to family members and organizations to do good and right with your money, and make your mark. Don't be fooled, despite the fact the estate tax is now being phased out by 2010 (only to be resumed in 2011), some significant form of tax will always affect the property comprising your estate. All this adds up to much higher legal bills in retirement to sort it all out.

TAXES AND LUMP-SUM EXPENSES

The fact you'll need all that financial help suggests how hard it can be to estimate your retirement budget for taxes. As a result, although taxes can be substantial, they won't be included in your retirement budget (although they will in your current budget). Instead, retirement taxation will be worked into the need-gap calculations in Hour 6, "Retirement Gap Calculation."

That leaves the big-ticket items you plan between now and retirement, or after retirement. For example, perhaps you're going to use seed money for a business, buy that RV or a sailboat, or build that greenhouse you'd always hoped to have but didn't have the time to tend. You might not think so now, but chances are that you're going to want something big to celebrate and symbolize some important rites of passage—when you finally have an empty nest, and when you retire. So, while you're to be commended if you don't have any big expenditures in mind, that's not realistic. Do some serious sleep or day dreaming to think of some big-cost items or activities you're likely to have. That way you can underestimate the lump sums you might need during retirement.

COMBINE ESTIMATES INTO TOTAL BUDGET

Speaking of estimating, the time has come to use the information in this chapter to take a shot at assembling your retirement expense budget (see Appendix D, "Retirement Gap Data and Calculation Worksheets"). Actually, you'll be filling in four budgets: one being your current annual budget and the other three representing annual budgets for the three phases of retirement—although there's no need right now to decide how long each of those phases will last. Nor should you now try to anticipate how inflation will change the price of goods and services by the time you retire; the amounts you enter for all four budgets should be based on today's dollars.

Finally, note that although these budgets contain a business seed money category, they don't include any expenses for a side or main business or service that you own or provide. That's because we'll assume that those expenses are incorporated in the net gain or net loss from the business reflected in your income.

Obviously, the closer you are to retirement, the more realistic you can be in making your estimates. But no matter what your current age, if you really give some thought to the numbers, you'll end up with a far better basis to plan your retirement than you would with a rule of thumb. As to the accuracy of your current budget, if you anticipate it soon changing significantly—because you're about to buy a home, for example—then use your anticipated new budget instead.

FYI The itemized budget in Appendix D, and some of the earlier ideas about estimating expenses, are partly courtesy of financial planner, Errold Moody, who has a similar budget with very detailed explanations on his free, information-packed Web site (www.erroldmoody.com).

In Hour 6, you'll use that information, along with the retirement-ready assets form you'll complete after Hour 4, "Quantifying Retirement Assets," to calculate your retirement gap. That will show you where you stand in your progress toward the goal of being financially able to retire. You'll then be able to make the best use of the information in the rest of the book to help you start closing the gap and become increasingly prepared for your retirement.

HOUR'S UP!

Remember all those times somebody told you, "that's going to cost you"? Well, they were talking about retirement, and now it's time to find out if you know how much.

Answer True or False to the following statements:

1. Senior Citizen's Early Bird restaurant discounts mean you'll be paying far less overall for food as a retiree.

2. If you've paid off your mortgage, continuing to live in your house is by far the cheapest housing alternative.

3. Long-term-care policies are expensive, but can cover exorbitant costs that you might incur from Alzheimer's—which might otherwise ruin your family financially.

4. The best thing about retirement communities that are oriented to youthful retirees as young as 55 is that they guarantee aging in place for the duration of your life.

5. If you pass the income-ceiling test, assisted-living communities are ideal because the subsidy keeps your costs below government-established maximums.

6. For many people, the fact that Medicare normally doesn't start until age 65 might be the most important factor in deciding not to retire early.

7. It's easy to underestimate how long you'll be healthy and active in retirement, desiring and able to spend unexpectedly large sums on travel and leisure.

8. Fortunately, seniors these days are so informal that clothing is usually a miniscule portion of their budgets.

9. You should plan to pay much higher rates for auto insurance as you get into later retirement, if you're still able to drive.

10. One of the unfortunate and ironic things about being a senior is that you can no longer count on your digestive system to process economical and nutritious beans, but you can count on paying more for financial bean-counting professionals.

HOUR 4

Quantifying Retirement Assets

CHAPTER SUMMARY

LESSON PLAN:

In this Hour you will learn about ...

- The value of your liquid, capital-gain, home-equity, and insurance cash-value assets.
- The value of your employer-provided, government-provided, and tax-deferred assets.
- The potential value of future gifts and inheritances.
- The liabilities that cancel out some of your assets.

We Americans pride ourselves on spending first and then figuring out how to pay the bills. So, patriotically, we first looked at retirement expenditures in Hour 3, "Quantifying Retirement Costs." Now let's examine the retirement assets that will pay for them.

That's easier said than done, however, because assets don't come with labels on them that signify either "use now" or "save for retirement." It's true that IRAs and 401(k)s are designed to be used for retirement purposes. But there's nothing to stop someone from using them (usually foolishly) at any time—the little that's left after taxes and penalties for premature withdrawals, anyway.

Therefore, we'll start with the assumption that all your assets are earmarked for retirement. Later, we'll figure out which and what parts of those assets will actually be available for retirement—taking into account normal preretirement spending, taxation, liabilities, and the cost of protecting those assets through insurance and other means. So get out your stickers and indelible-ink markers, it's time to do inventory.

YOUR FINANCIAL ASSETS

Admittedly, taking inventory of your assets is deadly boring if you have considerable net worth, or depressing if you have mostly no worth. In either case, though, it's deadly in a good way—it's the same exercise you'll use in preparing an estate plan. Knowing that, aren't you just dying to start?

PROCEED WITH CAUTION

In valuing your assets, we're being conservative by determining what you'd actually net for them (before taxes) if you were to sell them immediately. In some cases, that undervalues them because you're not selling them now, but it's the best way to avoid over-optimistic projections that understate the gap between your assets and retirement needs.

INVENTORY CASH-EQUIVALENT SAVINGS

These are assets that are not subject to market fluctuation—other than possible interest-rate changes that affect how much they earn at any given time. However, we're concerned only with what they're worth right now.

Most cash items are pretty obvious, starting with how much is in your checking, savings, and money-market accounts. Then add up the current value, and don't assess any penalties that would occur if you were to cash them in now (which, of course, you won't).

Next are any government bonds—including U.S. savings bonds and Treasury bonds, bills, or notes. You can find the current values of your savings bonds at the "Treasury Direct" Web site (www.publicdebt.treas.gov/sav/savcalc.htm). For other bonds, it's important to realize that although they have face values, their market values fluctuate with interest rates. Therefore to get an accurate current valuation, you must look them up in a newspaper such as *Investor's Business Daily* or the *Wall Street Journal*. Also, you can find the value of Treasury, corporate, municipal, and other bonds, at www.investinginbonds.com.

Another important cash item is the cash value of any permanent life insurance you own—in other words, what the insurance company would pay you if you surrendered the policy. Don't confuse this with the death benefit, because the cash value is usually much smaller unless you've had the policy in force for more than 15 years. You should be able to find this value from annual statements sent by the insurance company.

Of course, if you have term insurance, it won't have any cash value, because then you're paying strictly for protection. In fact, term insurance is usually the kind you should have, as we'll discuss in Hour 17, "Retirement Road Detours."

Finally, have you made informal loans to friends, kids, or other family members? Add in the total of all loans that you're confident will be paid back. Also add any major insurance claim payments and similar items.

Inventory Market and Insurance Investments

Now for taking stock of stock—and related investments held outside any IRA, 401(k), or other tax-deferred retirement plans. Stock prices are easy to find in virtually any newspaper. Be sure to record the brokerage commissions you'd pay to sell. In doing an inventory of your stock holdings, don't forget to include any shares you might hold in an *employee stock purchase plan*.

STRICTLY DEFINED

An **employee stock purchase plan** is an excellent way of using what's called dollar-cost averaging to invest in the growth of your company. It usually involves designating a dollar amount or percentage of your salary to go toward buying shares each month. To encourage this, companies frequently give a 10 or 15 percent discount on these shares.

Chances are, though, that you hold most of your equities in mutual funds. Your quarterly or monthly statements provide values, but daily fluctuations can significantly change them. Thus, an accurate valuation requires looking up each fund's individual net asset value (NAV) and multiplying it by the number of units of that fund you hold. Then you must subtract whatever load or sales commission you'd have to pay to sell that fund—which might be based on how long you've owned it, and could possibly be as high as 4 percent.

You might also hold annuities, which are contracts for which you make one-time or monthly payments now in exchange for future monthly payments from an insurance company. The idea is that you're guaranteed those future payments for your lifetime.

PROCEED WITH CAUTION

Variable annuities are aggressively marketed products that are usually inappropriate for investors who don't have very high incomes. Financial salespeople love them because they sometimes generate several thousand dollars in commission for a single large sale. For most people, the only kind of annuity that's ever appropriate is what's called an immediate fixed annuity that you buy upon retirement to generate a predictable income stream.

Thus, there are two ways to value an annuity for retirement purposes. If it's mature—already paid for—then you can think of it in terms of the payments it will later generate, but if it's not paid for then you should think of it in terms of an investment that is worth a certain amount if you cash it in.

That amount is called the surrender value, the actual current value of the annuity minus the cost of surrendering it—often high due to premature surrender penalties. Although it's unlikely you'd liquidate your annuity while subject to such large penalties, for now we'll use the surrender value that you should be able to find on your insurance-company statement. If the annuity is mature, you'll still find a surrender value. However, you should also be able to find what payments you should expect and when they start—although they're subject to change if you have a variable annuity (covered in Hour 15, "Integrating Retirement Sources").

Now for the major nuisance, estimating your "basis"—the amount you paid (including commission) for your stocks, mutual funds, and annuities. One break, though: We'll assume that you'll sell any of these only after they become long-term gain, so there's no need to indicate when you bought them.

 FYI You might be wondering why we're not considering taxes if we are considering the cost of buying and selling the asset—especially assets in an IRA or 401(k) that could be taxed heavily. The answer is that we'll consider taxes later, because taxation often depends on how and when the asset is liquidated.

INVENTORY PERSONAL RETIREMENT ASSETS

Now it's time to look at the same types of investments (such as mutual funds and stocks) held inside an IRA. These should be easier to value, because most institutions offering IRAs report the total account values in monthly or quarterly mailed reports, and in daily online updates. You should come up with separate totals for the three types of IRAs: Roth, traditional, and non-deductible.

INVENTORY EMPLOYER RETIREMENT BENEFITS

Similarly, it should be easy to determine an aggregate value for your 401(k), 403(b), or 457 employment-related plan. And if you're self-employed or work for a small company, you might have a Simplified Employee Pension (SEP), Savings Incentive Match Plan for Employees (SIMPLE), or Keogh tax-deferred retirement savings plan. In all cases, be sure to separately note the part of the account value that is vested, and the part that isn't.

Finally, perhaps you're fortunate enough to work for a company that still provides a pension—either a traditional one tied to years of service and recent salary history, or a cash-balance pension. In either case, you need to determine your pension's value if you were to leave your job today. In some cases, you must find out that value in two forms: first, a monthly payment; second, a lump-sum value.

INVENTORY GOVERNMENT (AIDED) RETIREMENT BENEFITS

Nobody can guarantee that Social Security will be there for you if you're just entering the work force, but it will undoubtedly be around awhile, given the Baby-Boomer lobby. The closer you are to retirement, the more you can rely on the benefit.

Unlike pensions, Social Security is strictly available in annuity form (monthly payments). For the purposes of this initial exercise, assume you'll retire at the normal retirement age, and use information from the Social Security Administration (SSA) to calculate your expected benefit in one of these ways:

- Use the calculators on the Social Security Web site (www.ssa.gov/ OACT/ANYPIA/).

- Request an Earnings and Benefits Estimate Statement (EBES) online to be emailed or mailed to you (https://s00dace.ssa.gov/pro/batch-pebes/bp-7004home.shtml).

- Request the Earnings and Benefits Estimate Statement by filing Form SSA-7004. You can obtain it online (www.ssa.gov/online/ssa-7004.html), or by calling Social Security at 1-800-772-1213.

JUST A MINUTE

To do the estimate online, you need the information from the Earnings and Benefits Estimate Statement (EBES), although estimating your past annual earnings is sufficient for this exercise. However, it's a good idea to request the EBES anyway, because you should check it at least every three years to correct any mistakes (even though the government never makes them).

INVENTORY HOME EQUITY, REAL ESTATE

In the hope that you're finally feeling at home doing this asset inventory, it's time to include the value of your home, and any other real estate. No, you don't have to hire an appraiser, but use what you know about recent sales to estimate your home's market value. Include the actual value, because we'll list the mortgage and any home equity loans elsewhere.

PROCEED WITH CAUTION

Of course, it is possible to avoid taxation on the gain of a second or vacation home by making it your primary residence after selling your original primary residence. It's even possible to convert rental property along somewhat the same lines, although it's far more complicated. Note that we do not subtract the cost of selling the homes because that can vary widely—and is sometimes zero in a "by owner" sale.

Then list the value of any vacation home, second home, or investment real estate that you own. Then provide information on the basis (purchase price, plus improvements, minus depreciation taken) on each. We're listing these separately because unlike the profit on your personal residence (unless you're so wealthy you probably shouldn't be reading this book), selling these will incur capital gains taxes.

INVENTORY PROPERTY, COLLECTIBLES, BUSINESS VALUE

Unlike the home inventory you'd conduct for insurance purposes, the goal here is *not* to put a value on everything you own. Stick to items that might fetch several thousand dollars each—such as pianos, fine furniture, decorating accessories, boats, and nonheirloom jewelry. Don't include cars unless they are luxury cars that might prove wise to sell and "buy down" in order to generate more investment capital. Because these items are generally depreciated noninvestment items, we'll assume that no capital gains or losses would be involved in their sale.

Then move on to collectibles such as antiques, art, and coins—this time including basis information because these are capital-gain items. Again, no formal appraisal is necessary—just a rough idea of their worth.

Now put your mind to your own business, if you have one. Estimate how much it's worth. Then determine its basis, how much you paid for it or spent building it—in other words, your capital costs (but not operating expenses).

Also make a note that we must later reconcile the value of this business with the source of income it provides. In other words, you can't have your cake and eat it too—the business will either generate income or be an asset for sale, but not both at the same time.

JUST A MINUTE

If your business has any substantial value, you should already have an idea of what it is because of the need to have a life-insurance (based) succession plan. Such plans enable a business to stay intact while they allow someone inheriting your share of a business to cash out, or estate taxes to be paid. For one reference on valuing a small business, check out *The Small Business Valuation Book* by Lawrence W. Tuller (see Appendix B, "Resources").

INVENTORY POTENTIAL GIFTS AND INHERITANCE

We're ready to move from solid ground to the shifting sands of supposition—what you might expect in the way of gifts and inheritances. Although you might be dubious, remember that this is retirement *planning*. The potential for major money from this source is so considerable for the children and grandchildren of today's seniors that it can't be ignored.

 Some studies have claimed that as much as $15 trillion will be inherited in the first half of the twenty-first century by about 100 million Americans—or an average of $150 thousand per person. However, a widely cited analysis by respected economists makes many good arguments to debunk this theory of unprecedented wealth transfer—claiming that much of the inheritance will never materialize. The lesson: Don't be complacent by expecting an inherited windfall.

Of course, be conservatively realistic, preferably by discussing this point-blank with your parents. Many financial planners recommend such talks between parents and children based on the need for planning, not a request for money.

UNDERSTAND YOUR LIABILITIES

Moving from the plus to the minus column, it's time to find the final piece of your net asset puzzle by identifying your financial liabilities. Here's the place to list mortgages, home equity borrowing, credit-card debt, college and automobile loans, and other major bills—but not routine outstanding bills for utilities and other recurring or daily-life expenses.

Instead, we'll consider those routine bills later in examining your budget to determine how much in savings you can generate towards retirement. Similarly, unless you've already contracted for them, we won't include major expenses you expect to incur. That's because your retirement planning is so crucial that you should consider all your work-life goals negotiable until you examine them in light of your preparation for retirement.

In addition to the actual debts, make sure you gather information about their applicable interest rates and terms. That information will be important in later decisions about how quickly to liquidate debt vs. hanging onto it to keep more capital free for retirement investing.

PROCEED WITH CAUTION

Before establishing a retirement plan, you must put an end to high-interest debt burdens that suck the life out of any attempt to save for retirement. Even with generous 401(k) matching and its tax deferral, investing in a 401(k) must come after paying off 18 percent credit-card debt. For free or low-cost debt-management guidance, contact your local nonprofit Consumer Credit Counseling Service.

Your Retirement-Ready Net Worth

At this point, we've effectively gathered the information necessary to determine what we might call your retirement-ready net worth. That would be the difference between your assets and liabilities—without including routine personal property such as normal cars, furniture, and recreational equipment.

Theoretically, all of these assets could be put to use toward retirement, while you use current earnings to live on until then. In practice, however, a substantial portion of those assets will be consumed before retirement for big needs that can't fit into your normal budget.

For example, if a few years out of college, you're probably planning to apply most of your assets toward purchasing a home, paying for a wedding, buying a better car, starting a family, doing some travel before settling down, or for many other possible purposes. Or, if you have teenage children, you might be planning to buy an additional car, pay for their college educations and weddings, or remodel your home. Meanwhile, through systematic savings, you'll attempt to replenish—and then some—the assets you consume now toward (re)building your retirement nest egg.

If you're planning to get married, consider a modest wedding instead of doing your part to continue inflating the now-average $20,000 spent on American weddings. It's no wonder that many couples actually suggest money as a wedding gift (which is tacky, by the way). They recognize just what a dent the wedding cost puts into their plans to buy a house and start a family, thus also delaying their retirement saving.

Later, it will be necessary to separate these assets to determine what portion of your retirement-ready net worth is left to start your retirement nest egg. For now, though, you're just compiling the information that will go into making that calculation.

To complete this preparation, make a serious wish list of the nonretirement items we've just discussed that might consume some of your assets. Note how much each costs, and when you anticipate needing the money for them.

Compile Your Inventory

Now you're ready to pull all this information together to fill out the form you'll find in Appendix D, "Retirement Gap Data and Calculation Worksheets," which corresponds to the sections in this Hour. In Hour 6, "Retirement Gap Calculation," you'll combine it with the completed form from Appendix D, which you filled in after Hour 3 in order to calculate your retirement gap.

What You Can Do Now

Compile a list of what we've defined as not being a part of retirement-ready assets: home furnishings, furniture, clothing, and other belongings. These are items that won't be included in eventually selling your home, and for which you'll never recover nearly what you paid for them.

Next to this list, make two columns. The first is about how much you paid for the item—including interest charges if you bought it on installment or credit. The second column is about how much you can realistically expect to get back if you were to sell it now.

Then, total the two columns and subtract the second from the first. This is an estimate of how much you've poured into disposable assets that don't contribute to your net worth. Of course, we won't include any value for these items in calculating your retirement-ready assets, but if you're a stickler, it does give you an estimate of the actual worth of assets that have depreciated away.

Hour's Up!

Once you total them up, you'll know if you need a swift kick in your assets in order to be poised for a successful retirement. But before you start, we have a few questions to ask about assets.

Answer True or False to the following statements:

1. It's much better to have totally solid assets such as precious metals, rather than liquid assets, which evaporate easily from inflation's effects.

2. In retirement, you'll generally pay less tax on capital gains than on long-term gains associated with withdrawals from 401(k) accounts.

3. Home equity is a real problem in retirement, because here you finally thought you could stop playing keep up with the Joneses, yet you're still trying to maintain equity with your neighbors.

4. The great thing about cash-value life insurance is that it guarantees that you can quit the policy at any time and get back the cash value (every dollar you ever paid) in premiums.

5. 401(k)s are such good investments that you should always fund them fully before paying off any credit-card debt.

6. You shouldn't hesitate to contact your Congressional representative to get an annual update of your projected Social Security benefits. That's part of his or her job.

7. Taking careful advantage of the benefits offered by your employer can substantially help you build up assets.

8. It's important to prepare for retirement, but if you're a Baby Boomer you'll likely be fine regardless, because of the enormous inheritances due your generation.

9. Liabilities shouldn't be considered in tallying up your retirement-ready assets, because you can assume you'll be paying them off with future work income.

10. Regarding retirement, the problem with weddings is that after paying for them, there's nothing much left to have and to hold.

PART II

Your Retirement Gap

HOUR 5   Retirement Finance Basics

HOUR 6   Retirement Gap Calculation

HOUR 7   Introduction to Retirement Gap
Calculation

HOUR 8   Retirement Gap Solutions

HOUR 5

Retirement Finance Basics

CHAPTER SUMMARY

LESSON PLAN:
In this Hour you will learn about ...

- The relationship between inflation and interest rates.
- Calculating rate of return.
- Taxation and how it impacts your retirement savings.
- Calculating after-tax cash flows.
- How time impacts the value of money.
- How to estimate your needs based on various assumptions you make, so you can avoid facing a huge retirement gap.

"Will I have enough for retirement?" That is a question asked by almost everyone. In order to feel confident in your ability to answer yes to that question you must learn some basic retirement finance. When you hear the term finance, it may bring back horrible memories of finance and economic classes required in college that you were relieved you passed and hoped you would never have to revisit again.

It should be easier this time around because we'll be reviewing these techniques with your money and future in mind, rather than looking at the financials of some make-believe company. After reviewing basics here, you'll assess your retirement needs in future Hours that will take you step by step through the calculations.

UNDERSTAND INFLATION AND INTEREST RATES

Our first stop in learning to calculate whether we'll have enough for retirement will be to review the impact inflation and interest rates has on our savings and spending power. We all witness rising prices almost daily and are well aware of the impact they have on our purchasing power. For example in the 1970s, people could find gas for as little as 28 cents per gallon. This year, it might hit $3 a gallon in some areas.

Alan Greenspan and the Federal Reserve (the Fed) attempt to manage the rate of inflation by managing the interest rate charged to member banks. Any change to this rate ultimately affects the amount of interest you can earn on CDs or other savings instruments—or on what you pay to borrow for a mortgage on a new home or as interest on credit cards.

The Fed considers numerous economic factors when deciding what monetary policy to set, but the two key indicators are Consumer Price Index (CPI) and Producer Price Index (PPI). The CPI measures price changes in consumer goods and services, such as gasoline, food, clothing and cars. The PPI measures price changes faced by sellers and manufacturers.

By tweaking interest rates, the Fed seeks to stabilize prices, moderate growth, and maintain maximum employment. When you hear the Fed announce a rate increase, it's intended to fight inflation by tightening the flow of money and reducing spending by increasing the cost of debt and making financing more expensive. Conversely, when the Fed cuts interest rates it is hoping to encourage economic growth by making money less costly to borrow. Of course, some people think the role of the Fed is overstated, and that Alan Greenspan should spend more time fighting inflation of his ego.

How does inflation impact your retirement savings? It all depends upon the type of assets your hold. The key is to earn enough on your investments so you can beat inflation and have enough at retirement. While an insured savings account may be the safest investment for preservation of capital, the key risk you take keeping your entire portfolio in that type of investment is that your money may not grow enough to exceed the rate of inflation and provide the retirement nest egg you need. We'll now take a look at how rate of return impacts your portfolio's potential success.

RETURN ON INVESTMENT

Return is a measurement of the ratio of profit or loss from an investment to the amount invested. It takes into account the cost of investing (Cost), which can include commissions and income taxes. Most market investments involve two types of profit: increase in capital value (CV), and payment of interest or dividends (Pay). Thus, return can be defined mathematically:

$$Return = ([CCV - OCV] + Pay - Cost]) \div (OCV)$$

Or more simply, Return is $^{Gain}/_{OCV}$ (or Gain $\div$ OCV), where Gain results from calculating the numerator: CCV – OCV + Pay – Cost.

RATE OF RETURN

Rate of return takes this one step further, measuring how fast the return is achieved—usually stating it in terms of annual compounded return. Let's illustrate all this with an example:

Let's say that two years ago, you bought a share of stock for $100. You just sold it for $130 and also received two annual dividend checks of $3 each since buying it—thus achieving a gain of 30 + 6 = $36. However, you paid $10 to sell it and paid another $5 in total taxes (never mind explaining the tax rates!), leaving you with a net two-year gain of $21, or a return of $^{21}/_{100}$ (or 21 $\div$ 100) = 21%.

If we were using something called simple (interest) return, the annual gain would be 21 percent divided by 2, or 10.5 percent annually. Fortunately for your retirement planning, however, we usually reinvest any gains we make, so instead we must look at compounded growth to get a true measure of return.

Thus, let's make this simpler by assuming we started with $100, which grows 10 percent to $110 after one year (already taking into account costs). In the second year, the $110 grows 10 percent to $121 (after costs). Consequently, because we can see that the two years of 10 percent growth compound to a total of 21 percent growth, 10 percent is the actual Rate of (annual) Return.

Just to make this perfectly clear (even if you're not a Nixon Republican), we started with $100 and ended with $121, and that can be achieved by a constant gain of 10 percent a year, like so: 100(1.10)(1.10) = 121.

 FYI Here are the average annual return rates since 1926 from some of the key types of investments:

- U.S. Treasury bills, which roughly equal what you could get in a savings account, averaged 3.8 percent annually.

- Long-term government bonds averaged 5.3 percent annually.

- Large-company stocks, while risky for short-term investing, have averaged 11.2 percent annually.

HISTORICAL RATE-OF-RETURN YARDSTICKS

Using 10 percent return as an example is no accident. Due to the '90s boom, many newer investors who came to believe they could achieve high-teen rates consistently have since discovered the hard way that those rates weren't sustainable. Now chastened, they have prudent financial advisors telling them there's only one reliable way to start recovering their recent losses: Aim for that more realistic overall 10 percent rate, sustainable when investing in about 80 percent quality stocks, the rest in "safer"—but lower-return—investments. Understanding these numbers is crucial to developing a two-pronged retirement savings strategy to nurture your nest egg. First, continually add savings to investments. Second, grow those investments at a rate that comfortably exceeds inflation (historically averaging a little more than the current 3.5 percent annually).

JUST A MINUTE

 To put this 10 percent example into perspective, until the stock market started a major decline toward the end of Year 2000, many investors held portfolios that had increased about 150 percent over the previous five years. The movement was far from even year by year (in fact, many portfolios were down during 1997), but it worked out to a rate of about 20 percent annually.

It's not only inflation, though, that reduces your real rate of return. Taxes are like axes chopping away big chunks of your gains. We'll now take a look at how and how much.

UNDERSTAND TAXATION BASICS

There is no way to avoid paying taxes, but when it comes to retirement investing you can certainly put it off for a very long time. You can even put some of your money in a retirement account for which you will never owe taxes, the Roth IRA. First we'll take a look at what type of taxes your investments will incur.

Interest and dividends are taxed at whatever your tax rate is for current income unless you shelter that income in some form of tax-deferred retirement savings. Capital gains, which you can earn on stock, bonds, or mutual funds, varies by the amount of time you hold your investment and in what type of account the investment is being held. Short-term capital gains, which you earn from the sale of an asset that was held for less than a year, are taxed at your current highest income tax rate, unless the investment is held in a tax-deferred retirement savings. Long-term capital gains, which are earned on investments held over a year, are taxed at a rate of 10 percent for people in the 15 percent tax bracket and 20 percent for all other tax brackets.

FYI In 1997, a new tax law was passed that lowered these long-term rates even more if investments are held for at least five years and purchased after January 1, 2001. These new longer long-term rates are 8 percent for those in the 15 percent tax bracket and 18 percent for all others.

Obviously, the longer you can hold on to your money so it can earn you more money the better off you are. Retirement savings programs such as tax-deferred or tax-free IRAs, 401(k)s and other employer sponsored plans, and self-employed retirement plans allow you to avoid the tax man until retirement.

Right now just know that there are many options available to delay paying the taxes. The following chart shows you how much faster your money can grow if you use the various tax-deferred alternatives.

GO TO ▶
You'll get the full scoop on these tax-deferral savings/ investing plans in Part III, "Employment/ Government Plans," which covers all retirement- relevant employer and government plans.

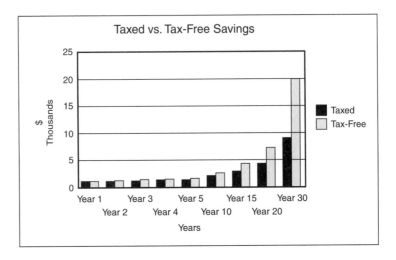

UNDERSTAND AFTER-TAX CASH FLOW

Unfortunately, unless it's from a Roth IRA, you'll owe taxes on monies drawn from IRA and employer accounts during retirement. Unfortunately, it might not be at the tax rates you originally thought. In figuring your after-tax cash flow look at estimates for several tax rates to review both best-case and worst-case scenarios for how much money you can expect to have after paying taxes.

GO TO ▶
Hour 23, "Managing Retirement Distributions," addresses the complex issues involved in liquidating investments during retirement. The challenge is to meet your current income needs while making the money last as long as possible.

Unfortunately, even though you have a great tax avoidance benefit while your money grows in a tax-deferred plan, your distributions from that plan will usually be treated as ordinary income, regardless of sources of income in the plan. You can't take advantage of the special capital gains tax benefits offered investments held outside a qualified retirement plan.

If all your investments for retirement are held in a tax-deferred account, your after-tax cash flow is relatively easy to calculate (ET = Estimated Taxes):

$$ET = \text{Annual Income Estimated} \times \text{Tax Rate Estimated}$$

Once you know your estimated taxes, you can calculate your after-tax cash flow by subtracting:

$$\text{After-Tax Cash Flow} = \text{Annual Income Estimated} - ET$$

These computations become much more complex when you are considering investments held outside a qualified retirement plan. If the investment was held for a year or less, you can calculate the amount of money to be taxed at your current income tax rate by subtracting:

Capital Gain or Loss = Asset Sale Price – Asset Cost

If this Capital Gain is derived from an asset held longer than a year, you would then be able to use the lower capital gains rate of 20 percent if your current tax rate is 28 percent or above; or 10 percent if your current tax rate is 15 percent. Now we'll look at time's effect on the value of money.

PROCEED WITH CAUTION

If you do win the lottery, get a large inheritance, or receive some other type of windfall, a bigger problem is simply not blowing it. Unfortunately, lottery winners have a history of doing just that—often ending up worse off than before. It's well worth the price to obtain competent financial advice if you should be so lucky.

UNDERSTAND TIME VALUE OF MONEY

The classic time value of money question is which option should you choose if you win the million-dollar lottery:

- Take one million dollars in cash.
- Take $5,000 a month for 25 years, which totals $1.5 million.

Would you know which one to pick? In making this type of choice you must understand whether it is better to take all the cash up front and invest it yourself, after you pay the taxes that would be due on the lump sum. Or, would you be better off taking the lower monthly amount and have a guaranteed income for which you would not have to worry about finding the best investment alternatives.

TIME SAVER

The Hewlett Packard HP12C is probably the most commonly used college business/finance course calculator. It's programmable, so more expensive, but is available by discount for about $50. The Texas Instrument BA II is also popular, and has a few more capabilities and better Web support than the HP10B, which has fewer options than its more expensive cousin the HP12C. Both the BA II and HP10B sell for about $25 to $30 (discounted).

When you are looking at whether to take money now or in the future there are a number of ways to consider the problem. We will not be exploring the individual calculations because they can get rather complex and thankfully today you can buy a basic financial calculator for under $50 with a time value of money feature on it that will do this for you.

In using one of these calculators there are a number of key figures you will need. When working with these calculators you can solve for any of the missing variables which include …

- **Number (N).** The amount of time for which you are comparing an investment option. For the million-dollar lottery scenario, it is 25 years with a payout possible on a monthly basis or a total of 300 (12 × 25) segments or payments.

- **Interest (I).** This reflects the rate of return you can expect to earn on the investment. As we mentioned earlier, savings accounts can be expect to earn an average of 3.8 percent, bonds 5.3 percent and stocks 11.2 percent. It is up to you to decide which variable would make sense based on what you think you may do with the money.

- **Present Value (PV).** That would represent the cash you have on hand. In the million-dollar lottery scenario it is either $1 million (adjusted for tax bite) or $0 depending upon which option you are considering.

- **Payment (PMT).** The payment would be the amount you expect to receive on a monthly basis. In the million-dollar lottery scenarios there would be no payment for the lump sum and a payment of $5,000 for the second option.

- **Future Value (FV).** The future value represents what the choice you have made will be worth in 25 years given these variables. In some situations you can put in a future value and solve for a present value or payment. You would most likely use this option to figure out what you need to invest now in order to meet some future goal.

To show you how this calculation would work, here is a chart that gives you the answers for these million-dollar winner scenarios. Taxes are not included in the calculations to simplify the chart for this illustration, since everyone's tax consequences can vary based on individual circumstances.

Which option would you choose? It is not always an easy question to answer because you have to balance it with what you know about yourself and how disciplined you can be about your money. Someone who will not be tempted to just go out and spend it frivolously on current wants and desires may be more willing to take the lump sum. Another person who prefers the security that a regular monthly income would provide might decide that it is worth taking a bit less to know he or she will have the income over 25 years. As you can see from the previous chart, $1 million taken as a lump sum and invested wisely will be worth a lot more in 25 years than the annual payments totaling $1.5 million, even if they were invested as received.

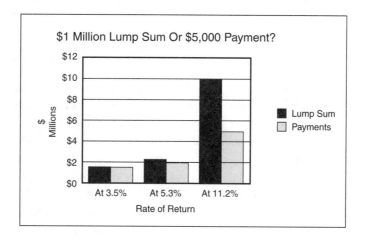

For most people these calculations don't involve something as exciting as winning the lottery, but are more involved with the choices of how much money one needs to save now so there will be enough money at the time one retires. Another common use is to figure out how to stretch the amount of money you currently have to make sure it doesn't run out during your lifetime. To begin looking at these issues, we first have to understand the basics of estimation and assumption.

UNDERSTAND ESTIMATION AND ASSUMPTION

Throughout this Hour we made certain estimations, such as estimating the rate of return on an investment, and assumptions, such as which tax rate bracket you might be in at the time you reach retirement. You can never really guarantee anything based on estimates and assumption, but you also can't do any future planning without at least starting with an assumption. Since the future is never certain, you can only estimate based on past performance and future guesses that this historical information will reflect as closely as possible what might happen in the future.

There are three key assumptions that anyone planning for retirement must make:

GO TO ▶
Hour 6, "Retirement Gap Calculation," explains the approach used in this book, which relies on actual calculations of your retirement needs, rather than depending on a rule of thumb.

1. You must estimate the annual income you think you will need at the time of retirement. Until recently, most financial planners assumed you'd need less than you did before retirement. Their assumption was that your actual cost of living will drop because you will not have the daily costs related to working and you will most likely have paid off your mortgage or moved into a smaller home. However, many now assume you'll need just as much as you did in the years immediately before retirement.

2. You must estimate the growth rate you expect on your investments after considering the impact of taxes and inflation. These growth rates may be higher if you are younger and take more risk and could drop as you get older and shift your portfolio toward more conservative investments.

3. The third assumption makes you try to answer the most difficult question—how long will you live. Of course, that is a big guess but without making some estimate of how long you think you will need the money, it is impossible to figure out how much money you will need.

The good news is that none of the estimates and assumptions is cut in stone and all should be revisited throughout your life to see if your initial assumptions are correct. If there is a correction needed, as long as you review your retirement planning yearly, you should have plenty of time to make up for any shortfall. You also do not want to overestimate what you need for retirement and force yourself to live too frugally through much of your life. Remember, you can't take it with you, so you should plan to enjoy a reasonable amount of the money while you are young and able to do things you might not be physically able to do when you reach retirement.

FYI In his book *The Prosperous Retirement* (see Appendix B, "Resources"), Fred Waddell says that expenses for the active phase of retirement may be similar to the expenses incurred during the working years. People then move to a passive phase, when they must slow down their pace because of physical complications, but incur increased medical expenses.

The next big assumption is what rate of return you can expect for your investments, so you can estimate how much money you need to save to meet your goals. It's not as simple as saying you'll put everything into stocks and choose the largest return possible. Most people should diversify their investments by mixing their assets to reduce the risks they take. Ibbotson Associates, who developed the most commonly used rate of return figures cited earlier in the Hour, also reviewed common asset allocation mixes to project what a diversified portfolio may expect to earn. In their study "Stocks, Bonds, Bills, and Inflation" (1998), Ibbotson looked at numerous portfolios and their earnings between 1950 and 1997. Returns for two of the most common mixes were …

- Earnings of 12.2 percent annually before taxes on a portfolio comprised of 80 percent stock, 10 percent bonds, and 10 percent cash.

- Earnings of only 9.2 percent annually on a portfolio with 40 percent stock, 50 percent bonds, and 10 percent cash.

You can see from this study that making estimates can get very complex because you have to consider not only what type of investments you want to include in your retirement portfolio, but you also must consider what proportion of your funds you want to allocate to each type of investment. These proportions will change as you get closer to retirement. The more time you have before retirement the greater risk you can take investing in stocks, which could result in higher returns.

JUST A MINUTE

MSN MoneyCentral (http://moneycentral.msn.com/investor/calcs/n_expect/main.asp) has a sophisticated life expectancy calculator that takes into account lifestyle and family-history factors. Of course, it would be really useful if there was a quality-of-life expectancy factor to get an idea of how long each of the phases of retirement would last, but at least this is a far better planning tool than just relying on an insurance table keyed to only gender and age.

The final assumption is the hardest to even think about—how long you will live. Retirees are living longer today than ever before. A couple that retires at age 65 can expect that at least one partner will live another 25 years to age 90. Some clues you may have to estimate your personal life span include family history and personal health habits, such as diet, exercise, and smoking. If your family has a history of long-lived ancestors who have taken good care of themselves, you probably want to plan for a life span that at least matches that history.

Hour's Up!

It's time to find out whether you have learned the basics of retirement finance. Here are a few key points for you to check your success at learning the basics:

1. When interest rates are raised by the Federal Reserve the following will likely happen:

    a. The cost of borrowing money for a mortgage will rise.

    b. The interest you pay on your credit cards will rise.

    c. The amount of spending will decrease, which will reduce the pressure on the possibility that the rate of inflation will rise.

    d. All of the above are likely to occur.

2. What average annual inflation rate should you use when calculating the impact of inflation on your long-term planning?

    a. 3.5 percent which reflects the average since 1988.

    b. 4.5 percent which reflects the average since 1960.

    c. Either. It's just a matter of luck if you pick the right one.

    d. Both. Your long-range retirement goals should consider both rates so you can develop a best-case and worst-case scenario.

3. If you are looking to earn the greatest amount on your money and are not concerned about risk of loss, which alternative should you choose for your retirement investments?

    a. Buying bonds

    b. Buying stocks

    c. Depositing the money in a savings account

    d. Keeping close tabs on the money by putting it under your mattress

4. What is the average annual rate of return you can expect if you put your money safely away in a U.S. Treasury Bill?

    a. 11.2 percent

    b. 5.3 percent

    c. 3.8 percent

    d. 2.5 percent

5. What is the impact on a bond when interest rates change?

    a. If interest rates go up the bond price will drop because investors will prefer the bonds that have a higher yield.

    b. If interest rates go up the bond price will go up in sympathy.

    c. If interest rates go down the bond price will rise because investors will prefer the older bonds that pay higher interest.

    d. Both (a) and (c) are correct.

6. Which are factors in computing your capital gains on the sale of a stock or bond?

    a. The amount of money you paid for the stock or bond.

    b. The amount of money at which you sold the stock or bond.

    c. The amount of time you held the asset.

    d. All of the above are factors when you figure the amount of capital gains you will need to report to the Internal Revenue Service.

7. What tax rates offer you the opportunity to keep more money in your pocket and give less back to the government?

    a. The tax on current interest earnings because you pay them yearly and get them out of the way

    b. The tax on short-term capital gains, so you are not stuck with a tax bill by holding the investment too long

    c. The tax on longer long-term capital gains, which are paid on investments bought after January 1, 2001, and sold after holding them for at least five years

    d. The tax on long-term capital gains, which are paid on investments you held for over a year

8. When calculating the time value of money, what are the most important factors?

    a. Time frame that you have to meet your goals

    b. The amount of interest or rate of return you can earn on the money that you plan to invest

    c. The amount of money you plan to invest

    d. All are key factors in trying to calculate the time value of money.

QUIZ

9. When trying to plan for retirement you must make assumptions in order to figure out how much money to save. What are these assumptions?

    a. You must estimate the annual income you think you will need at the time of retirement.

    b. You must estimate the growth rate you expect on your investments after considering the impact of taxes and inflation.

    c. You must try to answer the most difficult question—how long will you live.

    d. All of the above.

10. A diversified portfolio will include a mix of what type of investments?

    a. Stocks and bonds only

    b. Stocks and cash only

    c. Stocks, bonds, and cash

    d. Bonds and cash only

Hour 6

Retirement Gap Calculation

Chapter Summary

LESSON PLAN:

In this Hour you will learn about ...

- Your retirement gap (a key concept in this book).
- Basic time-value-of-money procedures for retirement financial analysis.
- Applying these procedures to learn a method you'll use in Hour 7, "Introduction to Retirement Gap Calculation."

If you make intelligent use of your current assets, and continue saving at your current rate, will you be able to afford retirement early, or even at normal age? If not, how much will you fall short?

During this hour, you'll learn about a method for answering that question far more accurately than you can with many of the snapshot retirement-analysis calculators based on oversimplified rules of thumb about retirement needs. By necessity, therefore, the method isn't simple—requiring you to apply the basic time-value-of-money techniques of present value and future value. However, once you get the hang of it, you'll find it's a straightforward yet powerful way to quickly develop a clearer picture of your finances. Before you know it, you'll have the pleasure of tracking your retirement progress and applying what's coming in later lessons toward realizing your goals.

Understanding the Retirement Gap Concept

During retirement, will you be able to fully enjoy the fruits of what you have and are earning now? To find out, you must compare apples to apples—and imagine for a moment that it's the green ones that are good and the red ones that are bad. Specifically, will the current assets, continued savings, and investment growth represented by your good green apples outweigh the current liabilities, additional interest charges, and future expenses represented by your rotten red apples? To make this comparison accurate, you must place all these apples side by side at the same future point in time.

That common point in time is the year you would normally retire, not when you plan to retire. That's because if you retire early, you don't yet get Social Security or pension payments—and you might have to pay tax penalties to freely dip into your 401(k) and IRA. Furthermore, you don't have employer medical coverage and you're too young to get Medicare. So retiring early is more like being unemployed and living on something better than government unemployment benefits.

If you do retire early, we're going to deal with those years with a separate interim budget. On the other hand, if you retire late, we'll treat it as though you retired at normal age, because unlike early retirement, it's not fundamentally different. Your retirement benefits might be enhanced by your extra years of work, and you might have more savings income and fewer insurance expenses than the typical retiree.

Therefore, the analysis starts by lining up all your assets and liabilities in your normal retirement year. You'll find the future value, at that time of your current retirement-ready assets and continued savings and investments. You must also find the then-present value of the earnings and expenses you'll have during your retirement.

Once your apples are all in that retirement-year barrel, you can find out if you have a preponderance of good green—in which case your retirement will be more fun than a barrel of apples. Or you might discover an excess of rotten red, which means that you'll need to go bobbing for more good green apples, or try not to grow so many rotten red ones.

Performing this analysis requires being fruitful and multiplying—as well as adding, subtracting, dividing, and using exponents. In other words, we must raise the dreaded specter of some elementary math. How do you like them apples?

FINANCIAL FORMULAS USED IN CALCULATIONS

If it weren't for the economic realities introduced in Hour 5, "Retirement Finance Basics," the calculation to determine your retirement gap would involve only arithmetic, not true mathematics. But it's complicated by the fact that we need more money in the future because it loses value due to inflation, and we invest for growth to overcome that inflation. Let's look at how this is represented mathematically.

FYI Have you ever wondered just how much impact inflation has had throughout history, let alone in recent times? An online resource called Current Value of Old Money (www.ex.ac.uk/~RDavies/arian/current/howmuch.html) contains some fascinating facts and figures, and some neat calculators to compare money throughout history.

INFLATION

If inflation is 5 percent annually, it means that one year from now, something that costs one dollar today will cost that same dollar plus 5 percent of that dollar—in other words:

$$1 + (.05)(1) \text{ or } (1.05)(1) = 1.05$$

Note: Parenthetic expressions that appear next to each other are assumed to be multiplied together. In other words, (1.2)(5) means 1.2 times 5.

What about two years from now? Now we take next year's $1.05 and grow it by another 5 percent:

$$1.05 + (.05)(1.05) \text{ or } 1.05(1.05) = 1.1025 \ (\$1.10 + \tfrac{1}{4} \text{ cent})$$

But we didn't have to do this in two steps. Instead, we could have found how much it would take in dollars two years from now, assuming inflation, to buy what one dollar does today by doing this:

$$1 \times (1.05)^2$$

In other words, knowing inflation is 5 percent, we know the inflation factor is 1.05, and we raise that factor to the power representing the number of years of inflation. So let's look at a more realistic example. Suppose you're now 55 and planning to retire at 65. You currently spend $4,500 a month, and see no reason why your spending budget will be different 10 years from now when you retire. However, there *is* a reason that it will be—a current inflation rate of about 3.5 percent. Let's assume that inflation rate remains constant (things continue costing 3.5 percent more each year than the year before) and calculate how much you'll need to spend 10 years from now to cover the monthly expenses you're now covering with $4,500.

Of course, inflation doesn't remain constant, it tends to run in cycles that somewhat correspond to economic cycles. It tends to be higher when the economy overheats and there's more demand for goods than there's supply, and quite low during periods of economic weakness—although we had "stagflation" in the late '70s: economic stagnation and high inflation. Despite the cycles, however, we're assuming the highs and lows even out over long periods of time, and in later-hour calculations, we'll assume a long-run rate of 3 percent.

The key elements are an inflation factor of 1.035, 10 years, and $4,500, thus:

$$4,500 \times (1.035)^{10} = \$6,438 \text{ (to the nearest dollar)}$$

Another way to look at this is to consider an amount of money we have now, and determine what it will be worth in the future. Suppose we have $100 and inflation is running at 5 percent annually. How much in buying power will our $100 be worth a year from now? We know that at 5 percent inflation it will take $105 a year from now to be equivalent to $100 today. That means that if our $100 doesn't grow between now and next year, a year from now we'll have only 100/105ths of the amount we need. Thus our $100 will be worth only $100 \times (^{100}/_{105}) = \$95.24$ in this year's dollars next year.

From this we can develop a general rule. Given an inflation rate of I, buying power decreases by a factor of $1/(1 + I)$ after one year, $1/(1 + I)^2$ after two years, and $1/(1 + I)^N$ after N years. Thus, returning to our example of $100, in 10 years, that $100 will have a buying power of only $100 \times (^1/_1 + .05^{10}) = \$61.39$.

INVESTMENT RETURN

Now let's return to the $4,500 monthly expenses in today's dollars that we've determined is equivalent in buying power to $6,348 in 10 years from now. That means we know we'll need about $75,000 for the whole first year of retirement. Assume we have about $40,000 saved that we're going to invest for the next 10 years, but we're unable to save any additional money. Will our $40,000 grow enough to cover the $75,000 we'll need?

We're not including taxes in this analysis, which of course is not realistic. We will consider taxes in the actual procedures in which growth of money formulas will be used.

Well, it depends on how much it will grow. Let's assume we can earn 9 percent annually on that money. A year from now, that means we'll have this much:

$1.09 \times 40,000 = 43,600$

A year after that: $1.09 \times 43,600 = 47,524$

Or in one step: $40,000 \times (1.09)^2 = \$47,524$

Thus, in 10 years, $40,000 \times (1.09)^{10} = \$94,695$ (more than the $75,000 needed).

Just to be clear, inflation does not grow money. We did the inflation calculation on the $4,500 to find out how much money was need in the future to purchase what $4,500 does now. In contrast, the investment growth calculation on the $40,000, although done the same way, is actually showing the growth of the money.

Now let's return to our challenge of having enough for that first year of retirement. We know we need $75,000 that first year, and want to know how much we need to invest now to grow to exactly $75,000. That way, we can use some of that $40,000 now to cover sudden current unexpected expenses. With CA standing for Current Amount, the problem would look like this:

$CA \times (1.09)^{10} = \$75,000$

Then, perish the thought, you can use algebra, and divide both sides of the equation by $(1.09)^{10}$!

$CA = \$75,000 \div (1.09)^{10} = \$31,681$

In other words, if $31,681 grows at 9 percent a year compounded for 10 years, it will accumulate to $75,000. That means we can set aside more than $8,000 of that $40,000 for current use.

TIME SAVER

If you're now muttering things that can't be printed on these pages, relax. You're not going to have to take a refresher course in algebra, and you needn't do all these calculations manually. Instead, you'll be able to arrive at an identical or approximately equal result by applying the formulas we develop on a handheld or online financial calculator, or a program such as Microsoft Money or Quicken.

SYNCHRONIZE FOR GROWTH WITH INFLATION

With this basic understanding of growth and inflation, let's look at how we'll combine them. The cornerstone of our approach will be to synchronize all monies accumulated and all monies needed to one point in time—your normal retirement age. Here's how:

1. **Future Value of Asset and Investment Cash Flow.** You'll project all current retirement-ready assets and ongoing retirement investments forward, using investment rate-of-return and real-estate appreciation growth factors, to a total pot of money you'll have at retirement age.

2. **Inflation-Adjusted Annual Retirement Expenses.** You'll use the inflation factor to project your anticipated retirement expenses forward to your retirement years.

3. **Inflation-Adjusted Annual Retirement Income.** You'll determine the tax-adjusted combined annual amount—as of your normal retirement year—of pension, Social Security, and other annuity-like payments you'll receive during retirement.

4. **Synchronized Retirement-Year Income vs. Expense Gap.** You'll take the difference between (2) and (3) to determine your annual gap. You'll then use an assumed growth rate to "discount" those amounts back to your normal retirement year, factoring in an inflation-amount assumption. That will be the total amount you'll need to have accumulated by your retirement year in order to spin off enough cash from planned investment and depletion to meet your inflation-adjusted specific needs throughout retirement.

This calculation uses what's called an inflation-adjusted present value (PV) of all your annual gap amounts, combining the rate of return with the inflation factor. Let's look at a simple case of how it works, in which we've calculated your annual gap at age 75 to be $20,000, and want to know how much you'll need at age 65 to fill the inflation-adjusted value of $20,000 you'll need at age 75.

JUST A MINUTE

Until recently, the notion of investing for growth during retirement was disparaged as too risky. But now that substantial numbers of people are going to be retired for almost as long as they worked, it's recognized that most people simply can't live off the income from safe investments for 30 years. However, you will want your portfolio to be increasingly conservative the older you get.

To find how much you'll need to invest when you're 65 years old to meet that need, we'll use this formula that combines 4 percent inflation and 8 percent growth:

Age 65 Need = $(20,000 \times (1.04)^{10}) \times (1/(1.08)^{10})$

In other words, we're inflating the $20,000 forward 10 years at a rate of 4 percent a year to represent how much you'd need to have, taking into account inflation. Then we discount that amount backwards 10 years at the 8 percent annual rate of return. That gives us the age-65 amount to invest at 8 percent to reach that inflated age-75 amount.

The result is $13,712, and to show this is right, do the following two calculations:

$20,000 \times (1.04)^{10} = \$29,603$

$13,712 \times (1.08)^{10} = \$29,603$

In other words, we're looking at the future inflated amount, $29,603, that is equivalent to $20,000 at retirement, and then looking at how the $13,712 we calculated we'd need at retirement will grow at 8 percent to reach that future amount of $29,603.

RETIREMENT NEED GAP CALCULATION

With the fundamentals about time value of money covered, the future is now (or there's no time like the present) to look at the steps in which they'll be used to calculate your retirement need gap. In the remainder of this Hour, we'll review these steps in conceptual terms. Then, in Hour 7, we'll take an actual detailed (but simple) example and work through the steps to calculate the retirement need gap using these steps.

Later, in Hour 20, "Comprehensive Retirement Gap Calculation Example," we'll expand on the Hour 7 example for an even more realistic look at the kind of calculation that your own circumstances might require. Once you've gone through that more complicated example, you should be ready to tackle your own retirement gap. Meanwhile, in Hours 8 through 19, you'll be learning what to do to close a retirement gap, no matter how large it is.

Now that you know where this is all leading, let's find out what the retirement gap calculation is all about.

1. **Compile and total current and retirement budgets.** Use the table in Appendix D, "Retirement Gap Data and Calculation Worksheets," in conjunction with the information in Hour 3, "Quantifying Retirement Costs." You'll be developing either four or five complete budgets: Current Budget (Phase 0, pre-retirement, active phase), the one with which you'll begin early retirement, if applicable; (Phase 1, normal active phase), the one with which you'll begin normal-age (65) retirement; (Phase 2, passive phase), the one for the period of retirement during which you gear down; and (Phase 3, declining phase), the one during which, unfortunately, your activity and health might go way down.

   You must decide the ages when Phases 0 (if applicable), 2, and 3 will begin—based on your own assessment of health and life expectancy. Assume Phase 1 begins at 65, the normal time (currently) for starting Medicare and Social Security. Once you've completed your budgets, sum up an annual total of expenses (not one-time lump sum expenditures, to be handled separately) for each. This way you'll know how much you expect to spend in the years representing the three (or four) critical junctures of retirement.

   Remember, the figures you use in your budgets should be based on current dollars. We'll later use inflation assumptions to project these dollars to the appropriate future retirement years.

2. **Determine inflation-adjusted retirement budgets.** Use the total budget amounts from Step 1 for the years that begin Phases 0 (if applicable), 1, 2, and 3. Then apply the inflation factor for the appropriate

number of years to each, thus projecting each amount the appropriate number of years into the future.

3. **Determine inflation-adjusted retirement income.** You'll calculate your income for the years that start retirement Phases 1, 2, and 3. These amounts will include Social Security, defined-benefit pension payments, and other already established annuities.

   You'll start with the calculation for the year you reach 65, the beginning of Phase 1, but won't apply inflation factors to project forward to that year. That's because inflation is already factored into that year's calculations of expected pension, Social Security, and annuities. (Be sure to choose the option that calculates your Social Security benefit in future inflated dollars rather than today's dollars.)

JUST A MINUTE

Inflation is definitely factored into the Social Security Administration's benefit estimates, and is almost always factored into private-pension estimates calculated by your company. However, the majority of private pension payments are not further inflation adjusted once they're initially determined. An estimated maximum of 30 percent of private pension recipients get annual cost of living adjustments (COLA), averaging only 2 percent. Uncle Sam retirees do get realistic COLA adjustments, however.

   Inflation is in play—for the years starting Phases 2 and 3—regarding Social Security, which uses an annual cost of living adjustment (COLA) factor. However, you won't apply inflation to annual pension payments or annuity amounts if you know those amounts won't be adjusted for inflation—and usually they're not.

4. **Determine individual retirement-year need gaps.** This is simply the difference between the Steps 2 and 3 totals for the starting years of Phases 1, 2, and 3.

5. **Determine inflation-adjusted present values of the total gaps for each of the three retirement phases.** In this step, a formula is used that applies inflation factors to the first-year gap in each retirement phase in order to determine each year's gap during that phase.

   In other words, if your Phase 2 starts when you turn 75, then the formula will apply inflation to your (Phase 1 starting) age-65 retirement gap and determine your gaps at age 66, 67, and so on until age 74. The formula then does the same for all the Phase 2 years and Phase 3 years.

You won't actually see these individual year values, but the gaps for each year of retirement are separately calculated.

The formula then applies the rate of return (ROR), or growth rate, to each year's gap amount and discounts it back to the first year of its phase. For example, it applies the ROR to discount your age-74 gap back nine years to age 65, your age-73 gap back eight years, age-72 gap back seven years, and so on. The result is that you'll have all those annual gaps stated in age-65 dollars. You'll then add them together to get your total Phase 1 gap. The formula will then do the same thing for Phase 2 and Phase 3 to determine total gaps as of those years.

Finally, this step separately discounts the total Phase 2 and 3 gaps back to age 65. Now that the total gap amounts for all 3 phases are stated in age-65 dollars, you add those three amounts together to get one number that represents the total retirement gap as of age 65.

That number is the present value of the total gap between Social Security income and living expenses throughout retirement. However, if you will be receiving a pension or other form of annuity, you will also do Preliminary Step 5 (which you'll find after Step 10). That extra step uses a very similar procedure to this regular Step 5 in order to determine the present value of all your pension and annuity income throughout retirement. You then add that number to your Social Security gap to get your total income-vs.-expense gap during retirement.

PROCEED WITH CAUTION

It's a huge assumption to plan steadily saved amounts every month that will go up with predictable salary increases. Neither your salary nor expenses will be predictable. But it's the best we can do now to develop an actionable plan with a mathematical basis. With that unpredictability, however, you're always better off maximizing savings whenever possible—particularly when you're younger, with more time for the money to grow.

6. **Calculate how much you can annually save and invest.** Use the information in Hour 3 and your associated (completed) Appendix D table to determine how much you can currently save per year. Include what's in your budget already in contributions to employer plans and other savings vehicles, plus the difference between your gross income and your total outlays (including taxes and those savings). Also add employer's matching amounts.

7. **Project the amount that your invested ongoing savings will grow to by the time you retire.** This calculation factors in how inflation boosts both your salary and expenses every year. It applies a rate-of-return (growth) factor to grow your increasing annual savings, starting now, to an age-65 lump sum. It then takes basis (amount originally invested) and differing tax rates (tax-free Roth, tax-deferred, and long-term capital gains) into account to determine your after-tax lump sum.

   These tax calculations might seem unrealistic because you won't cash in all assets upon retirement—and if you did, your tax rate would balloon higher. However, this assumption greatly simplifies the calculation—maintaining reasonable accuracy by simulating regular liquidation of these assets throughout retirement.

TIME SAVER

 If you're really serious about retiring early, you'll use the Alternative Step 7, which is lengthier and more complex. But first assume retiring at normal retirement age and do the far simpler calculation to see if you'll be solid retiring then. If so, and you're patient and number-savvy, do the more complex Alternative Step 7. But also consider professional financial-planning help for a more exact, detailed analysis.

   If you're retiring early, do this step twice, because you'll be dealing with two different budgets: current working-years budget and Phase 0 budget. First, find the value, as of your early retirement year, of your ongoing invested savings between now and that year. Project that lump sum forward to normal retirement (age 65), and determine the after-tax amount. Second, you'll project the ongoing invested savings from your early retirement year until age 65. You'll then find the after-tax amount and sum the two after-tax amounts.

   Finally, identify your current mortgage, car loan, or other amortized debts that you pay off on a regular monthly schedule. You must look ahead to when those debts will be paid off, which will create extra funds for you to invest toward retirement. You'll then use the same methodology to project those individual streams of additional funds forward at the investment rate of return to age 65, and then determine their after-tax values.

8. **Project your age-65 retirement-ready asset value.** Use Hour 4, "Quantifying Retirement Assets," and Appendix D to calculate your current and anticipated (inheritances, gifts, and so on) retirement-ready assets. If your current cash exceeds your current debts, you'll

apply a safe-investment rate of return to your excess cash assets to determine their value at age 65. However, if your current debt exceeds your cash assets, you'll apply an investment rate of return to your excess debts to determine your future liability at age 65.

Finally, you'll apply an investment rate of return to your market investments to project their value to age 65, completing the calculation by subtracting taxes. You'll separately apply a real-estate (inflation) appreciation rate to your home to determine its value at age 65, assuming no taxation. Finally, you'll have to do your own analysis to determine the retirement-age after-tax value of assets such as investment real estate and collectibles, since there's no good way to apply a general rule to them.

9. **Calculate your total age-65 retirement gap/surplus.** Add the results of Steps 7 and 8 (which should be positive) to yield your total after-tax assets as of age 65. Then add the (likely) negative amount of your Step 5 retirement-expense gap—the additional amount you'll need to carry you through retirement by covering all the expenses you project.

   The result is likely a negative number representing your total retirement gap. It's the amount to "make up" between now and retirement with more earning and saving, less spending, and better investment returns. If your "gap" is positive, however, it suggests a surplus that will more than fully fund your retirement.

   Of course, this result is only an estimate, the result of several simplifying taxation and other assumptions. There's no sense getting overly complex when we're only capable of reasonable estimates. Nor should we throw up our hands and not try just because we can't predict tax rates and timing, or be sure about other variables.

10. **Determine additional annual savings needed to close the Step 9 gap; adjust budgets to free those savings.** Because of taxes, this step can't be done by simply using financial functions on your calculator. Instead, it's based on the formulas behind those financial functions, expressed as worksheet steps (instead of a hideous-looking equation). The result is how much you must add to your current ongoing investments annually in order to close your gap by the time you retire. To achieve those extra savings you can you could take a second look at your retirement goals and adjust your retirement budget downward if feasible and appropriate. You'd then repeat Steps 4, 5, and 9 to determine your adjusted gap. Or, you can play with other assumptions (such

as growth rate and inflation) to repeat all the steps in this analysis and see how the final result is affected.

JUST A MINUTE

This analysis assumes approximately same-age spouses—unlikely! If you're less than 10 years apart, adjust by assuming you'll both retire halfway between your normal retirement years—and that's when you'll both get Social Security and pension. For larger age differences, do separate analyses, making reasonable assumptions about division of your assets. Better yet, consult a financial planner; retirement and estate planning are very tricky when spouses are very different ages.

Hour's Up!

There's a method to the madness of calculating a retirement gap. So if trying to follow the method hasn't driven you mad, answer these questions to see if you really understood it.

Answer True or False to the following statements:

1. The method outlined requires developing three different retirement budgets for the three stages, and then averaging all the amounts.

2. Inflation is insignificant enough that we don't complicate the calculations by including it.

3. More people would appreciate their Social Security cost of living adjustment (COLA) if the government sent a video featuring Britney Spears to explain it.

4. Before taking into account your current retirement-ready assets and ongoing savings, you'll likely have large gaps between your retirement expenses and the income you'll be receiving in retirement from pensions and Social Security.

5. Time value of money is best illustrated by the fact that $10 invested today in money-market funds will probably grow fast enough to buy a watch from Wal-Mart next year, and will probably grow enough to buy a Rolex (at today's prices) by next millennium.

6. Unfortunately, except if you get promoted or look for a higher paying job, you have little influence over the amount you've available to invest annually.

7. It's best to assume that the inflation rate and rate of return are approximately equal.

QUIZ

8. The rate of return we're assuming for real estate shows why it's always a much better investment than stocks as long as you have enough to invest.

9. Although this procedure is detailed, the good thing is that you'll need to do it only once, and your retirement planning will be set for life.

10. The final step will work best if you apply both the law of successive approximations and the law of successful approximations.

Hour 7

Introduction to Retirement Gap Calculation

CHAPTER SUMMARY

LESSON PLAN:
In this Hour you will learn about ...

- A case study based on the method described in Hour 6, "Retirement Gap Calculation."
- Calculations for finding the retirement gap.
- Applying the case to your own retirement gap calculation.
- Gauging the effects of estimation and assumption.

You've made it through the hard part—learning the concepts of retirement gap calculation. They probably haven't quite sunk in yet and it will help to practice using a realistic made-up example. Once you've worked through it, you'll be more confident about applying this method to your own retirement planning.

SETTING THE STAGE

First let's set the stage for this drama. We're going to look in on a couple, with two teenagers, who are planning for retirement. Mark and Mary Moneystrapped are both 40 years old and expect to live until age 90. They plan to start their retirement at age 65. They believe they'll reach Phase 2 of their retirement planning at age 75 and Phase 3 at age 85.

The Moneystrappeds have a joint gross income of $100,000. Their annual expenses total $98,000, including taxes and deposits in their 401(k)—leaving a $2,000 surplus for net annual additional savings. Their 401(k) savings are $6,000 annually, including $1,000 from employer match.

We're going to calculate the Moneystrappeds' retirement gap assuming the inflation rate is 3 percent and their rate of return on investments until age 65 is 9 percent. From age 65 to 75, we'll assume they'll move investments into more conservative choices and earn an average of 8 percent. From age 75 to 85, they'll again shift to a more

GO TO ▶

The Moneystrappeds could have bought an additional $1,000,000 in umbrella liability insurance for about $150 more per year. Hour 17, "Retirement Road Detours," covers umbrella liability and other types of insurance and forms of asset protection.

conservative investment allocation that earns 7 percent. Finally, after age 85 all investments are virtually safe, earning 6 percent.

Currently their retirement resources are $30,000 in their 401(k)s, $14,000 in their Roth IRAs, and $9,000 in cash or other liquid assets. Their taxable stock portfolio currently has a market value of $12,000 with a cost basis of $5,000. Their home is valued at $330,000, and has a $200,000 mortgage balance due in 25 years, at retirement. Their annual Social Security income at age 65 is estimated to be $25,000.

Fortunately, the grandparents have set up a trust fund to cover college for their two children. Unfortunately, Moneystrappeds have just been assessed a huge judgment in a lawsuit involving a car accident. Although their umbrella liability insurance covered $1,000,000 of it, they still owe an additional $125,000. To cover that, they've tapped a home equity line of credit.

They anticipate needing annual after-tax income, in today's dollars, of $90,000 at the beginning of Phase 1 (age 65), $50,000 at the beginning of Phase 2 (age 75), and $75,000 starting Phase 3 (age 85). Inflation will increase these amounts yearly during each phase.

PREPARING THE WORKSHEETS

Our first step will be to set up this information in worksheets used to compile retirement gap calculations.

In Appendix D, "Retirement Gap Data and Calculation Worksheets," you'll find a budget worksheet to set your own budget for Phases 1, 2, and 3. It includes an extensive list of items to consider for your budget. Following is an example of how we can use the information we have to develop Mark and Mary's budget within the stated assumptions. In this example we're going to simplify line items considerably. However, when completing your personal budget worksheet, use the one in Appendix D. The additional line-by-line detail will help you estimate each of these major line items.

Expense Item	Now	Phase 1	Phase 2	Phase 3	Lump Sum	Lump Sum Year
Home ownership	$5,000	$3,500	$3,500	$3,500		
Utilities	$4,000	$5,000	$6,000	$7,000		
Insurance	$6,000	$8,500	$8,500	$9,500		
Food/personal care	$7,000	$8,000	$8,000	$20,000		

Expense Item	Now	Phase 1	Phase 2	Phase 3	Lump Sum	Lump Sum Year
Entertainment/ travel	$8,000	$18,000	$3,000	$2,000		
Transportation	$7,000	$9,000	$3,000	$3,000		
Clothing	$8,000	$8,000	$4,000	$3,000		
Religion/charity	$5,000	$5,000				
Savings/ investments	$5,000	$0	$0	$0		
FICA/taxes	$35,000	$12,000	$2,000	$2,000		
Health/child care	$6,000	$10,000	$10,000	$23,000		
Professional fees/dues	$2,000	$3,000	$2,000	$2,000		
Additional savings	$2,000					
Total	**$100,000**	**$90,000**	**$50,000**	**$75,000**		

JUST A MINUTE

Note that the Moneystrappeds' projected expenses in the first phase of retirement are 90 percent of their preretirement income. That's a higher amount than the 70 percent to 80 percent that many "quickie" retirement-needs calculators assume. Instead of assuming, we're looking at what those expenses are really expected to be.

In the preceding budget example, we assume the home loans are paid off, but there are still property taxes and maintenance costs. Insurance escalates to cover long-term care insurance costs. We assume Phase 1 will include extensive travel plans, while that will not be part of Phases 2 and 3. For Phases 3, we assume that personal care and healthcare needs will rise because assistance may be needed for daily needs.

Remember, this is a simplified look at retirement needs, just to give you an opportunity to learn how to work with the calculations. When you start planning retirement, other issues will need to be considered. Are you thinking about moving to a retirement community or continuing-care community? If so, you will need to plan for a lump sum to buy into the community as well as to cover annual fees. The lump sum could be covered primarily by the sale of your principal residence, and annual fees could be at least partially offset by no longer having property taxes and home mainte-nance costs.

The next worksheet you will need to develop is the Retirement Ready Assets worksheet that you'll find in Appendix D. This will include investments, luxury cars, valuables, personal property, real estate, and other miscellaneous assets. Here is a sample developed from Mark and Mary's assets from the previous section:

Asset Category	Asset Name	Value	Cost to Sell	Basis
Investment	401(k)s	$30,000	-	-
Investment	Roth IRAs	$9,000	-	-
Investment	Stock	$12,000	$720	$5,000
Real Estate	Home	$330,000	$10,000	$275,000

Now we'll move on to practice the calculations using the numbers in these worksheets, as well as the additional assumptions stated previously in the "Setting the Stage" section.

RETIREMENT NEED GAP CALCULATION PROCEDURE

If you felt a little overwhelmed with the information presented in Hour 6, don't despair. In this section we'll look at each of these steps, carry out the calculations, and explain the fine points.

This procedure contains some simplifying assumptions, such as the way taxes are calculated, that will make the result different from a more detailed, exact procedure. But these simplifications are biased toward overstating your retirement gap. Thus you won't get overconfident and you'll still have a far better idea where you stand than with the rule-of-thumb methods.

When you do the calculations for your own situation, you'll use a blank version of the Retirement Gap Calculation Worksheet that you'll find in Appendix D.

Step 1: Determine the ages for each phase and determine your expected annual budget amount in current dollars. Remember, the three different budgets represent the three retirement stages, so the result of this step should be separate totals for Phases 1, 2, and 3:

Ages for Phase 1 are __65–74__; annual budget ____$90,000____

Ages for Phase 2 are __75–84__; annual budget ____$50,000____

Ages for Phase 3 are __85+__; annual budget ____$75,000____

PROCEED WITH CAUTION

 If you plan to retire before normal retirement age, you'll need to do a second budget for the year you plan to retire because that budget will definitely be different from the one you'll be using up until that time. The more extensive example in Hour 20, "Comprehensive Retirement Gap Calculation Example," includes an early retirement scenario.

Step 2: Determine the inflation-adjusted budget amounts for each year in retirement by using the results of Step 1 and applying the inflation factor to project to the future. To simplify, we have rounded to the nearest $1,000. Do this only for the years that start Phase 1, Phase 2, and Phase 3:

For Phase 1:

$$\$90,000 \underline{\hspace{1cm}} \times (1.03 \underline{\hspace{1cm}})^{25} = \$188,000$$

| Budget Amount | Inflation Factor | Years to Phase 1 | P1 Inflation-Adjusted Budget Amount |

For Phase 2:

$$\$50,000 \underline{\hspace{1cm}} \times (1.03 \underline{\hspace{1cm}})^{35} = \$141,000$$

| Budget Amount | Inflation Factor | Years to Phase 2 | P2 Inflation-Adjusted Budget Amount |

For Phase 3:

$$\$75,000 \underline{\hspace{1cm}} \times (1.03 \underline{\hspace{1cm}})^{45} = \$284,000$$

| Budget Amount | Inflation Factor | Years to Phase 3 | P3 Inflation-Adjusted Budget Amount |

Step 3: Determine inflation-adjusted income during each year of retirement from Social Security, pensions, and other already established annuities. In Mark and Mary's situation, we are including only Social Security.

For Phase 1:

$$\$25,000 \underline{\hspace{1cm}} \times (1.03 \underline{\hspace{1cm}})^{25} = \$52,000$$

| Social Security Income Amount | Inflation Factor | Years to Phase 1 | Phase 1 (P1) Inflation-Adjusted Soc Sec Income |

For Phase 2:

$25,000 _____ × (1.03 _____)^{35} = $70,000

| Social Security Income Amount | Inflation Factor | Years to Phase 2 | Phase 2 (P2) Inflation-Adjusted Soc Sec Income |

For Phase 3:

$25,000 _____ × (1.03 _____)^{45} = $95,000

| Social Security Income Amount | Inflation Factor | Years to Phase 3 | Phase 3 (P3) Inflation-Adjusted Soc Sec Income |

Step 4: Find the need gap. Use the numbers in Step 2 to show the amount needed and subtract them from Step 3 to get first-year amounts for each phase. Remember, we aren't including any of the investment assets in this step. It only includes Social Security, so don't panic:

For Phase 1:

$188,000 – $52,000 = $136,000

| Inflation-Adjusted Budget | Inflation-Adjusted Income | Phase 1 (P1) Gap |

For Phase 2:

$141,000 – $70,000 = $71,000

| Inflation-Adjusted Budget | Inflation-Adjusted Income | Phase 2 (P2) Gap |

For Phase 3:

$284,000 – $95,000 = $189,000

| Inflation-Adjusted Budget | Inflation-Adjusted Income | Phase 3 (P3) Gap |

Step 5: This step calculates the total gap between retirement income and retirement expenses as of the beginning of retirement. It does this by combining the expected effects of inflation and rate of return on the gap amounts from Step 4 to get your total gaps at the beginning of each of the phases of retirement.

First find the inflation-adjusted interest rate. This is different for each phase, with a suggested inflation rate of 3 percent (or inflation factor of 1.03), and the following suggested growth rates/factors: Phase 3 = 6 percent or 1.06; Phase 2 = 7 percent or 1.07; Phase 1 = 8 percent or 1.08. Do not feel bound to these choices; feel free to use what you think makes sense.

(1.08 _____ ÷ 1.03 _____) – 1 = .0485_____(4.85%)

P1 Growth Factor   Inflation Factor   P1 Inflation
                                                Adjusted-
                                                Interest Rate

(1.07 _____ ÷ 1.03 _____) – 1 = .0388_____(3.88%)

P2 Growth Factor   Inflation Factor   P2 Inflation
                                                Adjusted-
                                                Interest Rate

(1.06 _____ ÷ 1.03 _____) – 1 = .0291_____(2.91%)

P3 Growth Factor   Inflation Factor   P3 Inflation
                                                Adjusted-
                                                Interest Rate

For Phase 1:

Using your financial calculator (remember to set it in begin mode and one payment per year), enter …

> N (number) = Number of years in the Phase = 10
> I (interest) = P1 Inflation-Adjusted Interest Rate = 4.85%
> PMT (payment) = Phase 1 Gap from Step 4 = $136,000
> FV (future value) = N/A
> Solve for PV (present value) = $1,109,154

Phase 1 (P1) Gap at
Start of Phase 1 (P1)

For Phase 2:

Using your financial calculator (remember to set it in begin mode and one payment per year), enter …

> N (number) = Number of years in the Phase = 10
> I (interest) = P2 Inflation-Adjusted Interest Rate = 3.88
> PMT (payment) = Phase 2 Gap from Step 4 = $71,000
> FV (future value) = N/A
> Solve for PV (present value) = $602,000

Phase 2 (P2) Gap at
Start of Phase 2 (P2)

Then discount back to the beginning of retirement (Phase 1) using the Phase 1 growth rate (suggested 8% or .08) by entering ...

FV = PV just found (P2 gap at start of P2) = $602,000

PMT = N/A
N = Number of years back from Phase 2 to Phase 1 = 10
I = Growth rate for Phase 1 (not inflation adjusted) = 8%
Solve for PV (present value) = $279,000

Phase 2 (P2) Gap at
Start of Phase 1 (P1)

For Phase 3:

Using your financial calculator (remember to set it in begin mode and one payment per year), enter ...

N (number) = Number of years in the Phase
I (interest) = P3 Inflation-Adjusted Interest Rate = 2.91%
PMT (payment) = Phase 3 Gap from Step 4 = $189,000
FV (future value) = N/A
Solve for PV (present value) = $893,000

Phase 3 (P3) Gap at
Start of Phase 3 (P3)

Then discount back to the beginning of Phase 2 using the Phase 2 growth rate (suggested 7% or .07) by entering ...

FV = PV just found (P3 gap at start of P3) = $893,000
PMT = N/A
N = Number of years back from Phase 3 to Phase 2
I = Growth rate for Phase 2 (not inflation adjusted)
Solve for PV (present value) = $454,000

Phase 3 (P3) Gap at
Start of Phase 2 (P2)

Then discount back to the beginning of retirement (Phase 1) using the Phase 1 growth rate (suggested 8% or .08) by entering ...

FV = PV just found (P3 gap at start of P2) = $454,000
PMT = N/A

N = Number of years back from Phase 2 to Phase 1
I = Growth rate for Phase 1 (not inflation adjusted)
Solve for PV (present value) = $210,000

Phase 3 (P3) Gap at
Start of Phase 1 (P1)

Add the just-calculated gaps (as of the beginning of Phase 1) for Phases 1, 2, and 3 to find the total Social-Security gap at the beginning of retirement …

$1,109,154 _____ + $279,000 _____ + $210,000 _____ = $1,598,000

| P1 Gap at | P2 Gap at | P3 Gap at | Total Social |
| Beginning of P1 | Beginning of P1 | Beginning of P1 | Security Gap |

Step 6: Calculate the amount available to save and invest annually. Remember, by saving money in tax-deferred accounts such as the 401(k), Mary and Mark were able to reduce taxes and have more money to save, which helped to create part of the $2,000 annual savings shown here. Mary and Mark's total savings are:

Your retirement contribution at work	$5,000
Employer contribution	$1,000
If married and your spouse works, his or her retirement contribution at work	$0
Spouse's employer contribution	$0
Your IRA contributions	$0
Spouse's IRA contributions	$0
Other investments and savings	$2,000

PROCEED WITH CAUTION

In this example, we're assuming only one of the two spouses has a 401(k) available, so the additional savings will go into taxable investing. Otherwise it would be better to contribute to the 401(k). Also note that the total going into the 401(k) is $5,000 from one of the spouses, and a $1,000 employer match.

Step 7: Project the amount that your invested ongoing savings will grow to by the time you retire. Don't include money already saved. That is used in Step 8.

First, combine the rate of return with the inflation rate to determine the enhanced growth rate (taking salary inflation into account) by which your annual savings are estimate to grow as they build toward retirement:

$$(1 + \underline{\quad .09 \quad}) \times (1 + \underline{\quad .03}) - 1 = .0123\ (12.3\%)$$

Growth	Inflation	Enhanced Growth
Rate	Rate	Rate

Next, calculate the Future Value of your annual payments using:

Payment = __$6,000__ (total 401(k) savings)
N = Number of years until retirement __25__
I = Adjusted Growth Rate = 12.3%
PV = 0
Solve for FV __$940,000__

Payment = $2,000__ (total additional savings)
N = Number of years until retirement __25__
I = Adjusted Growth Rate = 12.3%
PV = 0
Solve for FV __$314,000__

Next, calculate your after-tax lump sum on tax-deferred retirement accounts, using the ordinary income rate of 25 percent that is now slated to be in effect at age 65 as the result of the just-enacted tax legislation. Include only those retirement accounts for which you will be taxed. For example, a Roth IRA is not taxed. Investments held outside a retirement account will be taxed at the capital gains rate:

.75	×	$940,000	=	$705,000
1 – Tax Rate		Tax-Deferred Lump Sum		After-Tax Lump Sum

For savings invested outside a retirement tax shelter, calculate your after-tax lump sum for those accounts. Remember in this scenario the $2,000 per year for 25 years, or $50,000, is the cost basis and is subtracted from the gain. When you're calculating capital gains tax, always remember to subtract the cost basis of the investment:

$314,000	–	[.2	×	($314,000	–	$50,000)]	=	$261,000
Taxable				Capital Gains	Taxable Investment			After-Tax
Lump Sum				Tax Rate	Lump Sum Basis			Lump Sum

Add all your after-tax savings:

$705,000	+ $261,000	+ 0	+ 0	= $966,000
Tax-Deferred	Taxable	Nontaxable	Nondeductible	Total
After-Tax	After-Tax	Roth	IRA	After-Tax
Lump Sum	Lump Sum	Lump Sum	Lump Sum	Lump Sum

Step 8: We'll now calculate Mary and Mark's current and anticipated retirement-ready assets and then apply the 9 percent investment rate of return to those assets to determine their value at age 65, completing the calculation by subtracting taxes. We'll separately apply a real-estate (inflation) appreciation rate to their home to determine its value at age 65.

To start, set your calculator in the end mode and for one payment per year. For each calculation, enter …

N (Number) = Number of years until retirement ___25___
I (Interest) = Interest Rate ___9%___
PV (Present Value) = _____
Solve for FV (Future Value) _____

First, we'll consider the cash on hand and debt. Mary and Mark have $9,000 but needed to take a $125,000 emergency loan because they needed to pay the judgment against them. They actually will be paying it off, but on no particular schedule, so we're representing payoff by projecting what the debt would grow to by age 65 and what your means to pay it off would grow to by the same time.

Cash on Hand: $9,000 – $125,000 = –$116,000
Future Value ___–$1,000,000___

Roth IRA: $14,000
Future Value ___$121,000___ (nontaxable)

401(k): $30,000
Future Value ___$259,000___
After-Tax Value ___.725 × ($259,000) = $188,000___

Taxable Investments: $12,000 (with $5,000 basis)
Future Value ___$103,000___
After-Tax Value $103,000 – [.2 × ($103,000 – $5,000)] = $83,000

Home Value: $330,000
Future Value (@ 3% Inflation Growth Rate): ___$692,000___

Cost basis on the home was $300,000 so gain is $392,000 and the first $500,000 of gain is tax free on your personal residence. So we don't have to worry about taxes on this amount.

Total Retirement Ready Assets

Add all the Step 8 intermediate results:

−1,000,000 + $121,000 + $188,000 + $83,000 + $692,000 = $84,000

Step 9: Calculate Mary and Mark's total age-65 retirement gap. Add the results of Steps 7 and 8 to yield your total after-tax assets as of age 65. Then subtract that amount from your Step 5 retirement expense gap—the additional amount you'll need to carry you through retirement by covering all the expenses you project:

−$1,598,000	+	$966,000	+	$84,000	=	$552,000
Retirement Income minus Expenses (Step 5)		After-Tax Savings (Step 7)		Pre-Retirement Assets/Expenses (Step 8)		Retirement Gap

Step 10: Determine additional annual savings needed to close the Step 9 total retirement gap. There's no direct way to do this with financial-calculator functions, so instead, this calculation is based on adapting the formulas behind those calculator functions. Thus, you'll use only normal calculator arithmetic.

Determine additional annual savings needed to close the Step 9 gap of $552,000.

(i) 5 × Total Retirement Gap (Step 9) = $2,760,000

5 × $552,000 = $2,760,000

(Call this result the Full Numerator)

(ii) 1 + Growth Rate = (suggest 1 + .09 = 1.09) = 1.09

(Call this result the Growth Factor)

(iii) [(Growth Factor)$^{\text{Years to Retirement}}$] − 1 = 2.64

$(1.09)^{25} − 1 = 8.62$

Raising Growth Factor of 1.09 to the power of the number of years (25) from now to retirement. Then subtract 1 from that result.

(iv) Multiply results of Steps (ii) and (iii) = 7.62

$(1.09) \times 7.62 = 8.31$

(v) Multiply Step (iv) result (of 8.31) by 4 = 33.24

(Call this the Partial Denominator)

(vi) (Partial Denominator) ÷ Growth Rate = 369.3

Use .09 Growth Rate from Step (ii)

(vii) (Years to Retirement) + (Step (vi) Result) = 143.4

$25 + 369.3 = 394.3$

(Call this result the Full Denominator)

(viii) Full Numerator ÷ Full Denominator = $7,000

Step (i) result (2,510,000) divided by Step (vii) result (394.3)

You can now confirm that this is the correct amount as follows:

Determine the Future Value of 25 years of $7,000 payments at a 9 percent growth rate, which is about $646,000.

Determine the Basis: $25 \times \$7,000 = \$175,000$

Taxes = $.2 \times (646,000 - 175,000) = \$94,000$ (approximate)

$646,000 - \$94,000 = \$552,000$ (your retirement gap)

CALCULATING YOUR OWN RETIREMENT GAP

You made it. Now you can tackle your own numbers. If you haven't done it yet, first complete the blank Expenses, Planned Expenditures, and Liabilities Worksheet and the Retirement-Ready Assets Worksheet in Appendix D. Before starting, you may want to make a few copies to work with and leave the originals in the book blank, so you can use them again in the future as your priorities, estimates, and assumptions change.

To make your work easier, use the Retirement Gap Calculation Worksheet in Appendix D, which has the steps laid out for you. All you need to do is

GO TO ▶
In Hour 16, "Savings/Spending Priorities," we'll start looking at that balancing act. Then in Hour 20 I'll show you how to handle some of the more complex calculations, such as early retirement and planning for your child's education or wedding. At that point, you'll be ready to tackle your own calculation.

fill in the blanks as we did in the sample (skipping the parts that don't apply to this example).

If you don't feel ready to do your own calculation yet, that's okay. It's safe to assume that you'll have a significant retirement gap, and Hours 8 through 19 will teach you how to attack it. Then, Hour 20 will build on this example with more complexity that makes it more realistic for most people—such as large lump-sum expenses that will eat away at your ability to save. Once you've completed Hour 20, you should feel confident in doing your own calculation, regardless of how different it might be from what you see here.

Hour's Up!

You're probably delighted to see those words. You know now the basics of calculating your retirement gap. Let's see how much you've learned.

Answer True or False to the following statements:

1. When beginning the calculations for your retirement gap you must first decide on when you will retire and how many phases you will need to plan for in retirement.

2. Once you figure out your budget, the first calculation you must complete is to adjust that budget for inflation.

3. You do not have to worry about adjusting your income for inflation.

4. Insurance costs will rise during retirement because you'll continue to pay for supplemental health insurance plus long-term care.

5. An inflation-adjusted interest rate is needed to calculate the retirement gap.

6. When calculating after-tax lump sums on accounts held in taxable investments, do not forget to subtract out your cost basis.

7. When calculating after-tax lump sums on tax-deferred investments, cost basis is not a factor.

8. When calculating the future value of a home, you should use the inflation rate and not the interest rate used for other investments.

9. When calculating after-tax lump sums on a home, you must subtract long-term capital gains taxes from the entire gain on the home.

10. The retirement gap is based on many estimates and assumptions, so it is important to revisit these calculations regularly through your life as life events change your ability to save and your future needs.

Hour 8

Retirement Gap Solutions

Chapter Summary

LESSON PLAN:

In this Hour you will learn about …

- Budgeting to free up money for investment.
- "Increasing" your salary by making better use of benefits.
- Investing for growth.
- Investing for tax advantage.
- How assets you have now will also be available for retirement.

No more wishful thinking. By getting this far, your eyes are now wide open to the gap between what you have set aside for retirement and how much you'll actually need. Of course, it's only a rough estimate—but it's an estimate customized to your situation, not based on an outdated, overused rule of thumb.

So, now what? Despair is not the answer, even if your gap seems impossibly large. And don't overdo the celebration if the numbers show you're in great shape. Instead, think of the size of your gap as representing the score of a basketball game, and your age as being how much of the game has been played.

As the coach, you must develop a strategy so that you'll win in the end. Oh, and one nice rule change—you're allowed to declare an overtime, even if you're behind when the game is over. In other words, think in terms of when you're going to close the gap, not if.

For example, if you have more than a few years left until retirement, and your gap is small, you're winning. Depending on the size of your lead, you'll play conservatively to milk it. Conversely, if you have relatively few years left and are way behind, you need to play aggressively, without getting out of control. You're aiming to close the gap as much as possible by your desired retirement age, and minimize the overtime period it will take before you're ready to retire.

BUDGETING BASICS

Instead of providing you with a boring laundry list of money-saving tips that you'll likely never use, let's aim for motivation with a little philosophy. No matter how much money you accumulate for retirement, it's not going to be enough if you spend it all before you're ready to bid the world adieu. That's why budgeting is the essential ingredient in successfully implementing a retirement plan. True, you might get lucky and get great returns on investments, or have a hugely successful business—but both of those ventures still rely on a trite, but true adage: It takes money to make money.

That money is going to come from spending less than what you earn. Unfortunately, too many Americans try it the other way, endeavoring to earn more than they spend. In doing so, they argue that in order to achieve career success that will bring those high salaries, they must avail themselves of conveniences that save time. Consequently, they buy takeout or ready-preparation foods almost daily, pay other people to clean their houses and cut their lawns, and rely heavily on professional clothes laundering—but we won't talk about the ones that rely on money laundering.

FYI If you're at a loss on how to budget and are willing to invest a small amount to start saving a lot quickly, consider *The Pocket Idiot's Guide to Living on a Budget* by Peter J. Sander and Jennifer Basye Sander (see Appendix B, "Resources"). The first chapter will open your eyes to how much money you are likely frittering away without even realizing it.

Furthermore, they feel the need to indulge themselves in the little downtime they have. Enter the big-screen TVs, elaborate sound systems, leased luxury cars, and the premium-priced mini-vacations or spa weekends. With that mindset, why shouldn't they also get weekly manicures, exquisite monthly hairstyling, and regular visits to or from a personal trainer?

Unfortunately, the unpredictability, or basic unfairness, of life too often gets in the way: The fast-track career derails from the still-runaway lifestyle train. Preventing this tragedy doesn't preclude career-climbing ambition, but does require matching lifestyle to current, not potential, success.

In doing so, you acquire the most important skill needed to achieve budget success, how to invest sweat equity. When doing the math on what the value of your time is, consider what you're actually paying to have services performed for you. For that $20 takeout meal, you must earn almost $30 if you're in the 36 percent federal tax bracket—after adding in FICA and state tax. Now consider how much extra you spend for time-saving conveniences and decide whether you can ever earn enough to regain what you're wasting.

JUST A MINUTE

You can actually figure out what your time is worth. It involves figuring out your true hourly wage—taking into account overtime on a salaried job. Then subtract taxes and all the expenses related to doing that work. MSN MoneyCentral (http://moneycentral.msn.com) puts it together in a neat time value calculator.

So instead of spending money to save time, spend time to save money. Here are a few major money savers that rely on this philosophy:

- Shop especially carefully for big-ticket items. There's no excuse not to—what with all the consumer information available now in well-researched magazines, and the instant comparison pricing you can do on the Internet.

- Park your vanity in the back so that you can park an owned, reliable, fuel-efficient automobile in the front—which you'll drive till it drops. Why? First, compare the many cars getting 36 miles per gallon in the city to the SUVs getting 12 miles per gallon. That means you save two thirds on what you're currently paying for gas if you trade in the SUV. Second, serial car leasing, even in the unlikely event you've negotiated a fair deal, is usually the most expensive form of "ownership." Most importantly, though, consumer studies scream with data demonstrating savings of tens of thousands of dollars over your lifetime by buying economical quality new cars and driving them into the ground. That makes it well worth the extra time you'll spend with more frequent mechanics' visits as cars age.

- Double your savings by making your own meals more often and investing in a healthier lifestyle. You can definitely reduce your estimates for future medical care if you take care of yourself all throughout your life. In fact, long-term disability from heart attacks and strokes helps contribute to the startling statistic that one in four workers is forced to retire early for health reasons.

- Stop shielding your kids from financial realities. Obedience to a budget fails in too many cases because the tail (children) wags the dog (parents). Let your kids know that a little deprivation now will save them from either supporting you later, or at least having to feel guilty if they don't. You might find they'll welcome the opportunity to use their natural creativity to promote savings.

TIME SAVER

For a jumpstart in teaching your children financial responsibility, consider reading *Piggy Bank to Credit Card* by Linda Barbanel, a social worker who helps you understand the emotional guilt associated with indulging children. For a more business-oriented perspective, try *Money Doesn't Grow on Trees* by Neale S. Godfrey and Carolina Edwards. (See Appendix B for details.)

INVESTING BASICS

Developing an ingrained savings habit is the first and hardest step, but it's not enough. Even if you're already a great saver who has accumulated the necessary retirement nest egg, you'll reopen the gap if you sit pat. Due to inflation, it's necessary to invest in enough growth to maintain your spending power.

But just keeping pace is usually insufficient, because most people can't meet their retirement needs fully by just saving. Instead, it's necessary to take moderate risk by investing in growth that will exceed inflation. The trick is, however, to be reasonable in the amount of growth you need to meet your goals. The fundamental rule, "the more risk, the more return," is often misinterpreted to mean that you *will* achieve that return if you take the risk.

The risk of loss from a specific investment is only one of several types of investment-related risk. There is also the risk of inflation, the overall market risk associated with ups and downs in the economy, the risk associated with the uncertainties of interest rates, and the risk associated with foreign-exchange rates for companies doing some of their business overseas. All these risks can affect the performance of an investment.

Instead, the rule, in effect, means that you'll almost never achieve a high level of return if you don't take a high level of risk. What's left unsaid is that the higher the risk, the less likely that you will achieve that return. Thus, if you're trying to achieve a 20 percent return over the long haul, you'll be dealing with investments that have only a few percent chance of paying off that big, and even when they do, it might happen for only a few extended periods over many years. The bottom line: You'll achieve that long-run return only if you're very lucky. More likely, you'll eventually lose all your money by making investments that can potentially achieve that return.

By relying on moderate risk, however, especially with proper diversification, you will achieve desired returns and sometimes more—often enough over the long term to offset a "law of averages" virtual certainty that for some extended periods your return will be lower or even negative.

So, instead of the hair-raising experience of dabbling in risky investments, take a lesson from the tortoise who raised the hare's eyebrows: Slow, boring, and steady wins the investing race to meet your retirement goals. That's why many financial planners advise long-term investors to use *index mutual funds*. By doing so, you're making a bet on the long-range growth of the economy, and you'll perform about as well as the economy does—while also minimizing fees that sap your returns.

STRICTLY DEFINED

> An **index mutual fund** consists of a portfolio of stocks that closely mirror stock market indexes such as the S&P 500, Russell 2000, and Wilshire 5000. An S&P 500 index fund, for example, will invest in the securities comprising the actual S&P 500 in a similar proportion to the way the S&P 500 average is calculated. An index fund's return, therefore, should be very close to the return on the market index it mimics.

UTILIZE TAX REDUCTION/DEFERRAL BASICS

While it's true that nothing is certain but death and taxes, you can take advantage of uncertainty concerning both the time of death and the amount of taxes. For example, another advantage of investing in index funds is that they make only modest annual capital-gains distributions—unlike actively managed funds that distribute substantial taxable gains annually. That allows taxation on most gain to be deferred for years or decades.

That deferral is the reason why 401(k)s and the original IRA accounts are so popular. It allows you to avoid immediate taxation on the amount you invest originally, and then allows that investment to grow, unfettered by taxes, until retirement. At that time, you might be at a lower tax rate when you start withdrawing some of the money, so you're able to keep more of it. And even if you're not initially at a lower tax rate in retirement, you probably will be at some later point, so you still end up losing less of your investment gains to taxes.

The Roth IRA, though, is even better. You pay taxes immediately on the original amount you invest, but then all investment earnings you generate over the years are yours to keep in retirement—with no tax ever due on them. It's a deal too good to not take advantage of every year. In fact, you should encourage your children to get jobs as soon as possible when they're teens so that they can put their first $2,000 (going up to $3,000 next year and gradually to $5,000 by 2008) in earnings annually into Roth IRAs, and have 50 or more years of tax-free earnings. Starting in 2006, you'll be able to add to those tax-free earnings if your employer offers the Roth 401(k)s just authorized in the newly passed 2001 tax bill. They'll enable you to set aside part of your salary after-tax, perhaps with employer matching, in an account that works just like a Roth IRA.

Even without tax deferral or avoidance, though, that long period of investment earnings is motivation enough to look for ways to save on taxes. If you immediately invest every tax dollar you save, you'll generate quite a nest egg with that money alone.

JUST A MINUTE

Match withholding to actual tax owed by estimating a given year's tax liability at the beginning of that year. For example, use Quicken's online Tax Estimator (www. quicken.com/taxes/estimator/). Then get your company's payroll department to help you file a new W-4 form with the number of allowances that will withhold approximately what you'll owe—rather than using the rule-of-thumb guidelines the instructions provide.

The power of immediate investing is also the reason why you should never get a tax refund. Instead, you should plan your withholding so that you take home the maximum pay and owe nothing at tax-filing time. For example, if you're now getting a $1,200 refund, you'll be ahead in the long run if you get a zero refund next year and invest that extra $100 each month.

That's why it pays to pay attention to every reasonable opportunity to save on taxes, and to learn to file your own taxes when you're young. You save the fee you would have paid for the service, and you become more aware of how taxes work. Nobody you hire will ever be as motivated as you are to minimize your taxes, and to get your return right so you don't end up paying interest or penalties. Here are just a few examples of tax-saving tips:

- If your total itemized deductions are not much more than the standard deduction, bunch your deductions so that you take the standard deduction every other year and are able to claim large itemized deductions in the alternate years. This will allow you more total deductions over each two-year period, thus saving more in taxes.

You can do this, for example, by making double charitable donations in alternate years, and skipping them in alternate years. You can also time the payment of certain deductible taxes so that you pay only in alternate years. Similarly, if you know you're moving into a higher tax bracket due to a salary increase, defer deductions into the year you move into the higher bracket.

- If you're paying back student loans, don't fail to claim a deduction for the interest you pay on them. It's deductible even if you don't itemize. Also, if you're making a fairly low salary while going to school part-time, look into whether you qualify for the Earned Income Credit, which can sometimes almost wipe out any taxes you might otherwise owe.

- Consider gifting appreciated stock you've held at least a year to your (at least) 14-year-old children, and have them sell it and use it for discretionary expenses—those things for which you are not actually obligated to provide for them. By doing that, you shift the capital gain from your own (probably) 20 percent bracket to their likely 10 percent bracket.

BENEFIT UTILIZATION BASICS

You can also save taxes while enjoying a $500 meal at a gala charitable benefit, but here's a better idea: Use your company benefits for your own personal charity—your retirement savings. Start with that old standby, the 401(k) plan, into which most employers provide full or partial matching of a certain percentage of your contributions. Similarly, employers frequently offer employee stock savings plans that allow you to purchase company shares on a monthly basis at a 10 or 15 percent discount.

But wise use of benefits also helps you save for retirement indirectly by saving you money. For example, if you're young and healthy, perhaps you should consider the highest deductible medical insurance your company offers. Sure, that means you might not be covered for any of your medical expenses during a year, but the premiums you save will either put more money in your paycheck or give you more money with which to buy other company benefits in a cafeteria benefits plan. For example, it might enable you to buy better dental insurance so that you can do more preventive care. Doing so could avoid thousands of future dollars spent on costly root canal, dental crowns, and similar procedures that take a huge bite out of senior budgets.

Remember, the purpose of insurance is not to recover all expenses, but to protect you from incurring expenses you can't afford to pay. And if your company offers a benefit called flexible reimbursement medical accounts, you can use Uncle Sam to help pay some of those uncovered bills. You do this by setting aside a certain amount of your salary to pay for the bills—an amount that is then subtracted from your salary for tax purposes. Thus, if you're in the 28 percent tax bracket, you wind up saving 28 cents of every dollar in taxes, effectively getting a 28 percent discount on those uncovered bills. (Adjust this accordingly as the 28 percent bracket gradually goes down to 25 percent by 2006 under the just-enacted 2001 tax bill.)

PROCEED WITH CAUTION

While a $5,000 flexible reimbursement account can save you more than $1,500 in income taxes if you're in the highest brackets (and about $750 in the lowest), you can also lose money. Namely, you must decide your allocation in advance, and if you don't wind up having that much in expenses on which to collect reimbursement, you lose the excess allocation forever.

Now that you have a healthy respect for the tax-saving power of flexible health reimbursement accounts, you're ready for another pleasant possibility—also saving taxes on your child-care expenses. In exactly the same fashion, you can set aside pre-tax dollars to pay those expenses—even including summer day camps that are authorized as child-care providers. If you're not in the lowest 10 percent or 15 percent brackets, doing that will save more on taxes than claiming the dependent-care credit. If you discover your employer doesn't have either this flexible dependent-care plan or flexible health reimbursement plan, ask why not. It's a tremendous benefit that costs very little to administer.

It also costs very little of your time to fully investigate your company's benefit plan to make sure you are taking full advantage of it. For example, what about tuition reimbursement. In today's world a college graduate might expect to pursue an average of three careers during his or her career. Thus, continuing education is a virtual must—not an option—and it can increasingly be obtained online through legitimate Web-based courses offered by major universities. Getting your company to subsidize your career development is a great investment toward increased employability and higher earnings that will help you achieve the retirement you seek.

Similarly, many companies offer fitness benefits that will pay part of the cost of belonging to a health club or taking exercise classes. As mentioned previously, investing in your health now can make all the difference in living a retirement that isn't ruined by excessive medical expenses.

FYI Although they're adversely affected by the current economic slowdown, so-called work/life programs are on the rise as an employee benefit. These include services such as helping employees locate quality care for their children and parents, wellness programs, and subscriptions to online homework services for kids. Although it's generally in a company's interest to promote such programs when they offer them, many fall short on publicity, so ask around.

Finally, spouses should make the best use of their benefits by putting their heads together. By picking and choosing the best features of each one's benefit package, and taking full advantage of employer savings subsidies, they can save hundreds or thousands of dollars combined in taxes, and bills that would otherwise be out-of-pocket.

UNDERSTAND DUAL-PURPOSE RESOURCES

Just as you should analyze employee benefits that can be used by both spouses, you should analyze assets that can provide benefits both before and after retirement. Think of your treatment of these assets as though you had two sets of books, legally.

YOUR HOME

Although you must spend money to keep up your home, historically it appreciates at a rate that exceeds inflation enough that even those expenses get reflected in its value. Thus, at retirement you have an asset that can be used in one of the following ways:

- Sell it and use the proceeds to pay for a different type of housing that more suits your retirement lifestyle. In some cases, that allows you to pocket considerable cash that can be used for other purposes.

- Sell it and use part of the proceeds to generate income that will let you rent, and another part for other purposes.

- Put a reverse mortgage on your home, generating income that comes from the bank gradually taking ownership of your home.

Reverse mortgages, discussed further in Hour 22, "Pre-Retirement Planning," are still a relatively new product that has been used by some unscrupulous institutions to exploit cash-poor elderly. However, if shopped for carefully, it can be a win-win situation for both seniors and the financial institution.

TAX-DEFERRED RETIREMENT SAVINGS

Winning is easy if you develop good savings habits to sock away the maximum toward retirement in IRA and 401(k) plans as early in life as possible. That's because tax laws allow these assets to be used in many ways before retirement without penalty.

For example, you can withdraw money from an IRA to pay college expenses for any immediate family member, and you owe only the ordinary tax, not the 10 percent penalty. Even better, though, is how colleges treat the assets in your IRA and 401(k). They're not included in your assets when colleges consider your child's ability to pay in the financial need calculation that helps determine financial aid. Thus, it could be a far better deal to keep your assets in the accounts to generate maximum financial aid, and borrow as needed to make college payments.

JUST A MINUTE

Although it won't directly help your retirement, your finances can indirectly benefit from your children investing any earnings they have into Roth IRAs. That's because the college financial need process weights children's assets much more heavily, so it pays to have little or no money in nonretirement accounts in the child's name. Meanwhile, your child gets a fabulous start on retirement savings or toward a first house.

Unfortunately, you can't use 401(k) withdrawals to pay for your own college education, but you can borrow against your 401(k)—usually up to half the balance, depending on your employer's rules. In fact, you can borrow for any reason, so this is also a potential source for business seed money if you can't find it from a bank.

Borrowing against your 401(k) is a double-edged sword, however. The good news is that you pay yourself back the interest, along with the principal. The bad news is that borrowing against your 401(k) creates double taxation. You pay tax on the money you use to pay back the loan, and then you pay tax on it again when you withdraw it during retirement. In general, use 401(k) loans as a last resort.

INVEST IN YOUR EARNING POTENTIAL

Wall Street offers no sure things, but investing in Nearby U or Online U in order to invest in yourself is a guaranteed winner—especially if you diversify. In other words, take courses to increase skills that will help you get promoted in your current position, as well as other courses that might help you get a new job or start a side business. Finally, take courses in personal finance and real estate that can help you manage your money more effectively, invest more successfully, and possibly become a landlord.

As an important side benefit, making a habit of educating yourself will likely reduce frivolous expenditures in your budget. After all, the more time you devote to education, the less time you have for aimless shopping or expensive outings. And just making the commitment to spend the money will make you more budget conscious and likely lead to better control of your expenses.

Better yet, you might not have to pay for those courses if you're able to get tuition assistance from your company for career-related courses. But even if that's not available, you can take courses at a discount by claiming miscellaneous tax deductions if they're specifically geared to advancement in your job. (However, the miscellaneous deduction is available only to the extent that your total miscellaneous deductions exceed 2 percent of your Adjusted Gross Income.) Or, if the courses help you start a business in that same year, you can probably deduct their cost as a business expense. And even if you can't deduct them for those reasons, you can claim either the Hope Credit or Lifetime Learning Credit—direct tax rebates for all or part of the tuition you pay.

Be aware, though, that you cannot claim the Hope or Lifetime Learning Credit for the same expenses that you claim as miscellaneous deductions, although you might be able to combine credits for part of the tuition and deductions for another part. Finally, both of these credits phase out the higher your income. See IRS Publications 508 (Educational Expenses) and 970 (Tax Benefits for Higher Education).

PROCEED WITH CAUTION

The just-enacted 2001 tax bill also contains provisions that allow deductions of up to $3,000 annually for qualified education expenses. If you use this deduction, you cannot claim the Hope or Lifetime Learning Credit. However, possible allowed use of this deduction in tandem with the miscellaneous education expense deduction remains to be clarified.

What Can You Do?

It's one thing to talk about closing your retirement gap, and another to do something about it. These exercises should get you more ready to be a doer:

1. Assume you have to cut your current budget by 10 percent and invest what you save in order to meet your retirement goals. Figure out what your budget is now and then come up with a way to do it.

2. Find out whether your employer's benefits include tuition assistance and flexible reimbursement accounts for medical expenses and dependent care.

3. Find out these details of your employer's 401(k) plan: the percentage of your contributions that are matched, and how the loan program works.

Hour's Up!

If selling clothes to teeny-boppers and college preppies appeals to you, you can get a job as the late-shift manager at a national chain store, and learn all about closing The Gap. Or, you can take this quiz and test your gap-closing capabilities.

Answer True or False to each of the following statements:

1. Unless you increase your earnings substantially, it won't help much to close the gap because it all gets taken away in taxes.

2. Despite facing an enormous gap, it is still possible to retire when you had originally hoped.

3. Making good use of employee benefits can free up cash to be used in closing the gap.

QUIZ

4. Fortunately, even if you're stuck in a dead-end job with little chance for pay increase, you can always increase your investment risk and achieve the profits you need, as long as you're willing to wait long enough.

5. Tax-deferred savings are over hyped because they give you the illusion that you're reaching your goals but you're no better off when the taxes are collected during retirement.

6. Roth IRAs are especially good because the government matches half of what you invest in them.

7. Believe it or not, the government actually offers pretty good tax incentives for pursuing more education to increase job skills.

8. Shakespeare said that neither a predatory lender nor a 401(k) borrower should one be; and even if he didn't, he should have.

9. If you don't take steps to close your retirement gap now, then in retirement you might end up earning minimum wage to "clothes" The Gap.

10. Flexible reimbursement accounts are a spine-tingling opportunity to take pre-tax payroll deductions that you can then use to pay for yoga and similar fitness courses.

PART III

Employment/ Government Plans

Hour 9   Social Security

Hour 10   401(k) and Related Plans

Hour 11   Small Business/Self-Employed Plans

Hour 12   Defined-Benefit and Federal Pension Plans

Hour 13   Traditional/Roth IRAs

Hour 14   Medicare and Private Supplementary Insurance

HOUR 9

Social Security

CHAPTER SUMMARY

LESSON PLAN:

In this Hour you will learn about ...

- Contributions you are now making to Social Security.
- Options of early retirement and delayed retirement.
- Supplementing your Social Security with other income and how it affects your benefits.
- Calculating after-tax cash flows.
- Benefits taxation and ideas for minimizing those taxes.
- How current trends in Social Security and plans may change your future benefits.

Y ou have seen many stories talking about the Social Security Trust Fund running out of money in the 2030s. You are probably asking yourself can I count on Social Security being there through my retirement. Answers to these questions are still developing and you should keep your eye on any plans that discuss making changes to Social Security benefits.

The fact of the matter is that 16 percent of people depend on Social Security as their only source of income after the age of 65 according to a 1994 Bureau of Census population survey. More than 65 percent of people over 65 get at least 50 percent of their income from Social Security.

In all likelihood, there will be some form of the Social Security safety net available at the time you retire. But the fact you're reading this book means that for your retirement needs, that amount will be gravy at best. To live in retirement as you'd like, your money "meat" will have to come from your own invested savings.

UNDERSTAND CONTRIBUTIONS AND ELIGIBILITY

Our first stop will be to explore the contributions you and your employer make toward your future Social Security benefits. Then we'll look at eligibility issues.

FYI According to a 1994 Bureau of Census population survey, the average family with persons 65 and older get 46 percent of their income from Social Security. Other retirement systems provide another 18.4 percent. Investments, including income produced from interest, dividends, and rents, add another 18 percent. Earnings from working are another 14 percent. All other income totals 3.3 percent.

How do you contribute to Social Security? For most people your contribution can be found on your pay stub next to abbreviation FICA, which stands for the Federal Insurance Contributions Act. These tax provisions of the Social Security Act of 1935 were made part of Internal Revenue Code in 1939.

As an employee you contribute 6.2 percent of your income, which is matched equally by your employer. This was based on the first $76,200 of income in 2000, and will be based on the first $80,400 income in 2001. If you are self-employed, you must pay 12.4 percent into the Self-Employment Contributions Act (SECA). In other words, you're paying double, also covering the employer's share.

SECA is paid at the time you make your quarterly estimated tax payments and calculated annually when you file your taxes. People who are self-employed compute the 12.4 percent SECA tax using 92.35 percent of net earnings. One half of the tax becomes deductible for income tax purposes, so you actually pay a little less than double normal employee's Social Security.

The taxes collected from workers' earnings toward Social Security totaled $493 billion in 2000, which represented 87 percent of the total income collected. The rest of the funds needed to meet payouts came from Trust Fund interest earnings, which totaled $65 billion or 11 percent and from taxation of Social Security benefits, which totaled $12 billion or 2 percent.

There are some people who are not obligated to pay into the Social Security System:

- State and local government workers who participate in alternative retirement systems
- Election workers who earn less than $1,000 a year
- Career Federal employees hired before 1984 who did not choose Social Security coverage
- College students who work at their academic institutions

- Ministers who choose not to be covered
- Household workers who earn less than $1,100 annually
- Self-employed workers who have net earnings below $400

Enough about paying into Social Security, you say, what about collecting? For starters, be aware that collecting Social Security is becoming like buying airline tickets. Just as everybody seems to have paid different ticket prices, soon it will seem like everybody has different ages at which they're eligible to collect.

For now, however, there are two important ages. The current normal retirement age for most people is 65. However, you're eligible to start receiving Social Security benefits as early as age 62, with a big catch: You'll have to accept a permanent reduction in your benefit amount.

However, although the early-retirement age will remain at 62, change is afoot for normal retirement. The actual age of retirement now changes according to calendar year in which you were born. That's because of a 1983 law to "save Social Security" that gradually increases the age at which you become eligible for full benefits. People born in 1938 are the first to feel the impact of this change, but as you can see from the following table, it only delays their eligibility by two months.

Use this table to determine when you become eligible for Social Security. Go to the year of your birth and find your retirement age in the column "Full Retirement Age." We'll be using this table again when we look at the impact of early retirement.

GO TO ▶

For more information on figuring out how your benefits are impacted by early retirement, go to the section "Evaluate Early/Delayed Benefit Options" a little later in this chapter.

Social Security Full Retirement and Reductions* by Age (from the Social Security Administration)

Year of Birth**	Full Retirement Age	Age 62 Reduction Months	Monthly % Reduction	Total % Reduction
1937 or earlier	65	36	.555	20.00
1938	65 and 2 months	38	.548	20.83
1939	65 and 4 months	40	.541	21.67
1940	65 and 6 months	42	.535	22.50

continues

Social Security Full Retirement and Reductions* by Age (from the Social Security Administration) (continued)

Year of Birth**	Full Retirement Age	Age 62 Reduction Months	Monthly % Reduction	Total % Reduction
1941	65 and 8 months	44	.530	23.33
1942	65 and 10 months	46	.525	24.17
1943–1954	66	48	.520	25.00
1955	66 and 2 months	50	.516	25.84
1956	66 and 4 months	52	.512	26.66
1957	66 and 6 months	54	.509	27.50
1958	66 and 8 months	56	.505	28.33
1959	66 and 10 months	58	.502	29.17
1960 and later	67	60	.500	30.00

*Percentage monthly and total reductions are approximate due to rounding. The actual reductions are .555 or 5/9 of 1 percent per month for the first 36 months and .416 or 5/12 of 1 percent for subsequent months.

**Persons born on January 1 of any year should refer to the previous year.

ESTIMATE STANDARD BENEFIT

Now that you know what your eligibility age is for full Social Security benefits, let's take a look at how those benefits are calculated. The process looks complicated, but there are ways around doing this yourself. Call Social Security (1-800-772-1213) or visit its Web site (www.ssa.gov/planners/calculators.htm) and use their online calculators.

The Social Security benefit is based on your average earnings over your working lifetime, using three steps keyed to your earnings base. For people born after 1928 and retiring in 1991 or later, that base number is your 35 highest years of earnings. Fewer years are used for people born in 1928 or earlier. Here are the steps:

1. Earnings are adjusted in base years for wage inflation.

2. An average monthly earnings figure is determined over the number of years in Step 1. If you don't have 35 different years of earnings, some years with $0 will be used to do this calculation.

3. The average adjusted monthly earnings is calculated using this formula:

   90 percent of the first $531 of average monthly earnings;

   32 percent of the amount between $531 and $3202; and

   15 percent of everything over $3202.

This formula usually results in benefits that reflect about 42 percent of what was earned while working for people who were middle-income wage earners. It is weighted toward low-income earners because they have less opportunity to save during their working years. If you were a high-income earner, you will probably find that your Social Security benefit will fall below 42 percent of earnings.

FYI Unlike most private pension plans, calculation of your Social Security is not based on your last five years or your highest three years. Instead, it looks at your entire earnings history. Basically, the more in total you earned over your lifetime, the higher the benefit, although most well-paid people hit the max benefit.

Let's look at how Social Security benefits are impacted by decisions to retire early or delay retirement.

EVALUATE EARLY/DELAYED BENEFIT OPTIONS

Social Security was obviously not designed by Charles Darwin: The early-retirement birds catch the skimpy worms, and the late birds catch the fat ones. Let's look at the separate benefit-calculation treatments of retiring before your normal retirement age, and after.

EARLY RETIREMENT

As mentioned earlier, anyone eligible may start receiving benefits as early as age 62. The key thing to remember if you make the decision to retire early is that your benefit will be permanently reduced and this decision cannot be reversed once made. The reduction is intended to ensure that you won't get more total benefits from the system than a normal retiree if you both live to your life-expectancy age. The good news (if that's what you want to call it) is that you'll end up with more than a person retiring at normal age if both of you die early, say at age 70. However, if you should outlive that age significantly, and die at, say, 90, the person retiring at the normal age will end up collecting more benefits overall.

To estimate how much your benefits will be reduced by retiring early, go back to the earlier table, "Social Security Full Retirement and Reductions by Age." Use the column "Age 62 Reduction Months" to find the number of months by which the benefit will be reduced. Then use "Monthly % Reduction" to calculate an approximate reduction percentage based on the number of months you'd retire early. For age 62, you can find the "Total % Reduction" based on the year you were born.

PROCEED WITH CAUTION

 A decision to start receiving Social Security benefits early will result in a permanent reduction of your benefits. Everyone's situation is different. What is best for you needs to be balanced with other resources you have available at retirement. Before you make this decision be certain you have carefully considered all options. There is no going back once you've taken the step to apply for benefits.

DELAYED RETIREMENT

We looked at what it costs you in monthly benefit amounts if you retire early. We'll now take a look at what you gain by delaying your retirement past your full retirement age. People born before 1938 get an increase in benefits between 3 and 4 percent for each year they delay retirement between age 65 and 70.

This percentage begins to rise for people born in 1938 and beyond. Those born in 1938 will get a 6.5 percent increase for each year up to age 70 they delay full retirement. After that it increases one half of 1 percent for persons born between 1938 and 1943. In 1943, the credit for delaying receiving benefits reaches its maximum at 8 percent per year of delay. There is no reason to delay applying for benefits beyond age 70 because there will be no increase to your benefit amount if you delay any longer.

ESTIMATE SUPPLEMENTARY INCOME EFFECTS

Many people supplement their Social Security benefits with work because their fixed incomes are not enough to maintain the lifestyle they seek. A decision to work after you begin receiving your Social Security benefits can result in a temporary reduction in benefits if you make too much money.

Ironically, and fortunately, though, going back to work can sometimes permanently increase your benefits. In fact, it's possible to increase them permanently from earning too much in a year in which you had them reduced temporarily! That happens if you earn more in any year than in one of the years used to compute your original benefit.

To explain all this, let's first clarify what earned income is for Social Security purposes. Income that could result in a benefit reduction is solely income you earn through gainful employment. It does not include passive income sources such as interest, dividends, or rental income. Nor does it include distributions from IRAs, pensions, and retirement plans.

FYI Until a bill was passed in 2000, retirees ages 65 to 69 lost $1 in benefits for every $3 earned over $17,000. Today, retirees age 66 and older can earn as much as they want with no forfeiture of Social Security benefits. The old law was an outdated relic of earlier high-unemployment times. It caused many much-needed older workers, especially when unemployment was low, to feel they were unduly penalized, and they refused to work.

There are limitations on how much you can earn before risking a reduction in benefits. Between the ages of 62 and 64, the limitation in 2001 was $10,680 per year. Earnings above that amount resulted in a loss of $1 in benefits for every $2 of excess. Retirees 65 years old can earn up to $25,000 with no risk of forfeiture. Above $25,000 they lose $1 for every $3 of excess. There is no forfeiture of benefits for earnings after the age of 66.

As we noted earlier, working after you begin collecting benefits can help to increase the benefits you will receive. For example, if a woman had no earnings for 10 years while raising children, 10 of the 35 years used to calculate her benefit would be $0. By going back to work after she starts collecting Social Security, the $0 dollar years will be replaced with the higher earning years during post-retirement work. Even if she only earns $10,000 a year for five years, that is a lot better than the $0 years she is replacing. This will increase her average earnings base and the benefit for which she will then be entitled to receive. The Social Security Administration has an automatic process for reviewing the earnings of beneficiaries to see if the new earnings years are higher than those previously used in the calculation. If the answer is yes, the benefit amount is adjusted upward.

EVALUATE TAXATION OF BENEFITS

We all wish we would be done with the tax collector at retirement, but unfortunately that is not the case. Your Social Security benefits are taxable once you exceed the base amount. Your base amount depends on your filing status:

- $25,000 if you are single, head of household, or qualifying widow(er)
- $25,000 if you are married filing separately and lived apart from your spouse for all of 2000
- $32,000 if you are married filing jointly
- $0 if you are married filing separately and lived with your spouse at any time during 2000

JUST A MINUTE

For the full scoop on how Social Security Benefits are taxed, order Publication 915, "Social Security and Equivalent Railroad Retirement Benefits," from the Internal Revenue Service. For tax withholding, order Publication 505, "Tax Withholding and Estimated Tax." You can read or download either online at www.irs.gov/forms_pubs/index.html.

Will your Social Security benefit be taxable at retirement? To find out, add one half of your benefit amount plus all other earned income, including tax-exempt income. The dreaded answer is yes if this total exceeds the base amount for your filing status. The "good news" is that 15 percent of your benefit cannot be taxed no matter how high your income.

You do have the option to allow federal income tax to be withheld from your Social Security benefits. If you decide to do this, you must complete a Form W-4V. When you complete this form you indicate how much you want to be withheld from you total benefit payment. Your options are 7 percent, 15 percent, 28 percent, or 31 percent. If at any time in retirement you want to change your percentage, just complete a new Form W-4V and resubmit it to the Social Security Administration.

You can opt not to have any taxes withheld from your Social Security benefits. If you decide to do this, you may have to request that additional withholding be taken from other income sources or pay estimated tax during the year.

The taxable part of your benefits usually cannot be more than 50 percent. As with all tax laws there are exceptions. Up to 85 percent of your benefits can be taxable if the total of one half of your benefits and all your other income is more than $34,000 ($44,000 if you are married filing jointly). If you are married filing separately and lived with your spouse at any time in the previous year, taxation above 50 percent may also be possible.

 There is a move in Congress to repeal the 85% taxation rule added to the 1993 tax law. The House of Representatives passed the "Social Security Benefits Tax Relief Act" on July 27, 2000 and will most likely try again in the current Congress.

ANTICIPATE SOCIAL SECURITY TRENDS/REVISIONS

We just discussed one possible revision to the tax law that could help some people keep more of their Social Security benefits. There are many other trends and potential revisions that could impact your future benefits. You certainly have heard that Social Security may run out of money before you retire and there are many alternatives being considered to remedy this. Most involve further delay of normal retirement age and possibly even early-retirement age.

There is no question you should be alert to changes being proposed to the Social Security System and the benefits you may someday receive. There is little doubt that changes will be considered in the Congress that opened its doors for business in January 2001. President George W. Bush has made it clear that he will seek to revise the current method for Social Security contributions to include some form of privatization. We'll discuss the alternatives being considered after first debunking some key myths about the current system.

One legend commonly cited as fact is that the solvency problem that everyone is talking about was created because Social Security Trust Funds were raided for use in other government activities. The reality is that every dollar that is collected for Social Security goes to pay benefits or is invested in Treasury Bonds.

Social Security is a pay-as-you-go program. Most money collected for Social Security is paid out in benefits in the same year the money is collected. Only about 22 percent is invested for future benefits.

FYI According to the Social Security Administration, the number of people aged 65 or older receiving benefits totaled 31.1 million in 1994 and climbed to 32.1 million in 1999, a 3.2 percent increase. Beneficiaries 85 or older increased at a greater rate—14 percent during this five-year period.

The problem facing Social Security is not caused by errors in Trust Fund accounting or misuse of funds. Instead, "it's the demographics, stupid"—as President Clinton's political advisors might have said (but not to you readers, of course!). There are now 8 million Baby Boomers. They will begin to retire around 2010. By 2030, twice as many Americans than there are today will be eligible for Social Security.

This problem is compounded by declining numbers of workers—the "baby bust" that followed the widespread use of "the pill" by women of the Baby-Boom generation. It's a bitter pill to swallow for younger workers who will probably have to pay higher FICA payroll taxes. That's because the Social Security Administration estimates that by 2032 there will be only two workers for every beneficiary. Currently there is a 3.3 to 1 ratio.

What are the key dates of concern when it comes to the Social Security Trust Fund? There are four important dates that were cited in the 2001 Trustees Report:

- The year 2016 is the first year projected benefits paid will exceed collected Social Security taxes.
- The year 2026 is the first year that disability insurance trust funds will be exhausted.
- The year 2025 is the first year the projected benefits paid will exceed the taxes collected plus the interest earned on the Trust Fund.
- The year 2038 is when the Social Security Trust Fund's assets are projected to be completely exhausted.

PROCEED WITH CAUTION

Who is most at risk if Social Security goes bust? A 1998 White House study found that elderly unmarried women—including widows—get 51 percent of their total income from Social Security. Unmarried elderly men get 39 percent, while elderly married couples get 36 percent of their income from Social Security.

All of these dates are, of course, dependent on the fact that there are no changes between now and 2038. Most people do expect that there will be legislative action prior to that time in attempting to fix the problem. In reality there will probably be numerous attempts made to accomplish a fix between now and then.

What are the key changes being considered to fix this potential problem? Right now there are none actually on the table. In May of 2001, President Bush appointed a commission to draft plans to overhaul Social Security. He appears to have selected members who mostly support allowing workers to invest some of their contributions in stocks and other private accounts. However, opponents of partial privatization believe that the recommendations of this "unbalanced commission" will not be adopted due to the economic and political realities of the recent stock slide and the mid-term election. Thus, any reforms will probably have to wait until after the mid-term election, and if history holds, that will change Congress significantly.

FYI The National Council of Women's Organizations (NCWO), which represents over 6 million women, strongly opposes privatization. NCWO Chair Martha Burk said, "Privatization might work for some woman making $100,000 a year, but it's absolutely bad news for the vast majority of women."

If a Democratic majority emerges, privatization will probably be dead for two reasons they cite. One is the perceived loss of some of the safety net of guaranteed benefits. The other more significant concern is that similar to 401(k) experience, administrative fees will seep, then flood, into the process, reducing actual returns on the private accounts. The Social Security Network believes that the administrative costs alone could end up lowering benefits. In a study completed by the network they found that administrative costs for Social Security currently amount to less than 1 percent of benefits. Private insurers average 12 percent to 14 percent for administrative costs of retirement programs that they administer.

Millions of small accounts would have to be administered if privatization were approved. The costs would increase even more if each investor were allowed to manage his or her own account. In addition to management fees, there would likely be costs for marketing incurred by private groups as they compete with each other to win the lucrative new private accounts.

Economist Peter Diamond studied the effect of administrative costs in countries that have adopted the use of individual accounts, which include Britain, Chile, Argentina, and Mexico. He found that actual benefits could be reduced by 20 to 30 percent after looking at how these experiments are working.

So, what's the forecast for reform? Despite its current high visibility, it could be several years before what's now in place will change. Whatever your views, make your voice heard politically. But most important, follow the story and any actual changes made to assess their impact on your retirement. Once a plan actually passes Congress, be certain you adjust your long-term plans to match any changes proposed.

HOUR'S UP!

It's time to find out whether you have learned the basics of Social Security, how you contribute to the program, and what benefits you can expect to receive:

1. If you work in a job where FICA (Federal Insurance Contributions Act) taxes are taken out of your paycheck, what percentage actually goes to the Social Security Administration?

   a. You contribute 6.2 percent of your gross income and that is the total that goes to Social Security.

   b. Your employer contributes 6.2 percent of your gross income and that is the total that goes to Social Security.

   c. You and your employer contribute a total of 12.4 percent of your gross income.

   d. Zero goes to Social Security because you opted not to participate.

2. If you are self-employed in 2001, you must pay 12.4 percent of what percentage of your income to Social Security under the provisions of SECA (Self-Employment Contributions Act)?

   a. 100 percent of my gross receipts under $80,400

   b. 92.35 percent of my gross receipts under $80,400

   c. 92.35 percent of my net earnings under $80,400

   d. 100 percent of my net earnings under $80,400

3. When calculating your Social Security contribution for the year 2001, how much of your income should be included in that calculation?

   a. Only the first $80,400 of income is subject to taxes in 2001.

   b. All income is subject to Social Security taxes in 2001.

   c. Only the first $76,200 of income is subject to taxes in 2001.

   d. None; I don't intend to pay it.

4. There are some people who are not obligated to pay into the Social Security System. You may be one of the lucky few. Possible exceptions include …

    a. State and local government workers who participate in alternative retirement systems.

    b. Career Federal employees hired before 1984 who did not choose Social Security coverage.

    c. College students who work at their academic institutions.

    d. All of the above are groups that do not have to pay into Social Security.

5. You are thinking of retiring early. What could happen to your benefits if you begin to collect them at age 62?

    a. The benefits would be permanently reduced, but will likely be paid for a longer period of time.

    b. It is generally believed that ultimately you will collect the same total benefits no matter what age you choose to retire.

    c. Everyone's individual situation is different and it is critical that a careful assessment is made of all retirement alternatives before deciding to begin collecting benefits.

    d. All of the above are correct.

6. Which of the following are steps in calculating your standard Social Security benefits?

    a. If born after 1928, you must calculate an earnings base including 35 years of income.

    b. If you do not have a total of 35 years of income, it is possible for $0 to be added to the calculation for the nonearning years.

    c. The top five earnings years are averaged to arrive at an earnings base.

    d. Both (a) and (b) are part of the steps in calculating benefits.

7. If you decide to delay collecting your Social Security benefits until age 70, what is likely to happen to your monthly amount?

   a. A percentage varying from 3 percent to 8 percent will be added to the monthly benefit amount depending upon your birth year for each year you delay.

   b. There will be a loss in benefits because you did not apply to collect them on time.

   c. There is no change to the benefit to be collected. You reach the maximum benefit amount possible at age 65.

   d. You must be crazy to continue working until age 70 and therefore you don't need any benefits.

8. If you decide to go back to work after you start collecting Social Security, what happens to your benefits?

   a. The benefits stop until you stop working again.

   b. The benefits are reduced after you earn above the income limitation allowed between the ages of 62 and 65.

   c. There is no effect on benefits after the age of 70.

   d. Both (b) and (c) are correct.

9. What percentage of your Social Security benefits are likely to be taxed?

   a. 85 percent.

   b. 50 percent.

   c. 100 percent.

   d. Social Security benefits are not likely to be taxed unless you make a mistake.

10. What are the key reasons that the Social Security Trust Fund is facing a crisis?

   a. People are living longer and collecting benefits longer.

   b. The Baby Boomers will soon enter their retirement years and there will be more retirees than there are workers.

   c. The Social Security Trust Fund has been used to pay for other government programs.

   d. Only (a) and (b) are correct.

QUIZ

Hour 10

401(k) and Related Plans

LESSON PLAN:

In this Hour you will learn about …

- Basic plan features and future trends.
- Whether and how contributions are matched.
- The importance of investment allocation.
- Immediate tax breaks and eventual taxation.
- Vesting, portability, and withdrawals.
- Your rights and responsibilities.

4̸01(k) and 403(b) probably sound more like stadium seating sections than IRS retirement savings plan tax codes. But that's okay, because 401(k) and 403(b) plans are probably the most important things you can cheer about in today's difficult environment for affording retirement. Like sports teams that "reward" loyal fans by moving to new cities to make more money, today's employers are increasingly taking traditional pension plans away from their loyal employees. Thus, for a majority of workers in large for-profit companies and nonprofit organizations, 401(k) and 403(b) plans are now the only retirement game in town.

It's a game many are losing, however, because they don't participate at all or enough, or participate when they shouldn't—and even when they should, they often mismanage their plan assets. Like parents who teach their kids to swim by throwing them in the pool, companies have simply thrown their employees' fortunes into the rough savings seas. But unlike the rescue-ready parents at the water's edge, there are no lifeguards on duty to protect your portfolio from being dragged below in the jaws of a vicious market.

Consequently, you must become a savings and investing survivor who can sense the sharks and smell the rats who can take huge bites out of your of your financial future. That way you can live to be an old-age survivor who will never be financially forced to just sit around watching inane television shows. In this Hour you'll learn essential employer retirement plan investing and saving survival skills.

DEFINED-CONTRIBUTION SALARY-REDUCTION PLANS

Employer-offered tax-advantaged retirement savings plans enable you to make investments directly from salary, reducing your reported taxable income. The percentage or dollar amount that you designate is deposited tax deferred in an investment account in your name and it (hopefully) will grow tax-free until retirement. As a bonus incentive for you to contribute to 401(k)s, most employers will match a portion of your contributions.

The 401(k) is offered mostly by for-profit companies and the 403(b) is offered by nonprofit organizations, including schools, universities, hospitals, foundations, and charitable enterprises. In fact, if you work for a nonprofit you may not even realize you are part of a 403(b) because they're sometimes referred to as Tax Sheltered Annuities (TSAs) or savings plans. Section 457 plans offered to state employees are similar to 403(b)s.

FYI More than $1 trillion is invested in 401(k) plans by about 35,000,000 employees, almost 80 percent of those eligible. 403(b) and 457 participant numbers and percentages, and total dollars invested are far lower.

The 401(k), 403(b) and Section 457 all fit into the category of Defined Contribution Plans—defining the contributions to be made by employer and employee. In contrast, rapidly disappearing traditional defined-benefit pension plans require employers to set aside money for employees in amounts determined by their salary history, years of service, and age at the time of retirement. Thus, defined-contribution plans are a radical change—putting the onus on employees to nurture growth of their accounts so that they become a major source of the funds they'll live on in retirement.

These plans give you more control over how the money is invested, but you take more risk. If your contributions are inadequate or your investment choices aren't sound—either too risky, too conservative, or not sufficiently diversified—you might come up short at retirement.

Furthermore, investment options are not the only thing that can put at risk your success in meeting your retirement goals. Both 401(k)s and 403(b)s have risks inherent in how the plans are administered overall, the quality and breadth of the investment choices offered, and the guidance provided for your best use of them.

A Closer Look at 401(k)s

The 401(k) provides an excellent opportunity for millions of employees nationwide to have their retirement savings, while eating them too—as tax savings. However, some employees can lose their savings appetite after sniffing out rotten features in their plans. For example, in *Robbing You Blind* (see Appendix B, "Resources"), former Wall-Streeter Mark Dempsey reveals many ways middle-class investors are parted from their money through unjustified high fees in 401(k) plans and virtually every type of investment product. In addition, *Kiplinger's, Money,* and *Smart Money* are among the many prominent financial publications that have highlighted the 401(k) fee problem.

Start with the far-from-free lunch featuring two courses of your hard-earned contributions. First, employees' contributions are consumed by 12b-1 (marketing fees) and other internal mutual-fund fees. Then, for dessert, more than 25 percent of employers are gobbling more employee assets in compensatory administrative fees that they've been assessed by plan providers. These fees are a gaping ulcer leaking an estimated annual average 2 percent to 3 percent of employee plan value. But you don't feel the pain, because you're not writing a check, and unless you know where to look, you don't even see a bill. However, you'll have major heartburn and heartache if you discover how much this is costing you upon reaching retirement.

For example, assume you're age 40, with $100,000 in your 401(k), on which you can expect to earn an average 10 percent annualized over the next 25 years. Further, assume the average hidden fees are 1.25 percent annually, and that—although unrealistic—you don't invest any more in it. Your account will grow to about $791,000. However, raise those fees to 2.25 percent annually, and your account grows only to about $613,000. That "insignificant" 1 percent difference costs almost a quarter of your nest egg.

FYI The U.S. Department of Labor Pension and Welfare Benefits Administration (DOL PWBA) has published a number of excellent advisories concerning employer-sponsored retirement plans. You can order them by regular mail, or read them on the Web at www.dol.gov/dol/pwba/public/pension.htm.

Complaints about these fees prompted the Department of Labor (DOL) to study them and issue a scathing report in 1998. It confirmed the widespread existence of excessive fees, and emphasized the failure of employers to live up to their fiduciary responsibilities to limit employee cost under the

Employee Retirement Income Security Act (*ERISA*) rules governing qualified plans (tax-advantage benefit plans that meet IRS and other Federal requirements).

STRICTLY DEFINED

> **ERISA** refers to the numerous retirement and other qualified employee benefit regulations that the U.S. Department of Labor Pension and Welfare Benefits Administration (DOL PWBA) enforces as a consequence of the Employee Retirement Income Security Act of 1974.

In addition, the DOL has found that employers are falling short concerning other 401(k)-administration ERISA rules. These include failure to provide either adequate education or an ample and varied selection of investment choices. To encourage employees to push for improvements, as well as report serious employer violations, the DOL published a *Protect Your Pension* pamphlet. Here are some questions from that pamphlet to give you food for thought about 401(k) fees and investment options that may be eating away at your 401(k):

1. What investment options are offered under your company's 401(k) plan?
2. Do you have all available documentation about the investment choices under your plan and the fees charged to your plan?
3. What types of investment education are available under your plan?
4. What arrangement is used to provide services under your plan (are any or all of the services or investment alternatives provided by a single provider)?
5. Do you and other participants use most or all the optional services offered under your 401(k) plan, such as participant loan programs and insurance coverages?
6. If administrative services are paid separately from investment management fees, are they paid for by the plan, your employer, or are they shared?
7. Are the investment options tracking an established market index or is there a higher level of investment management services being provided?
8. Do any of the investment options under your plan include sales charges (such as loads or commissions)?

9. Do any of the investment options under your plan include any fees related to specific investments, such as 12b-1 fees, insurance charges, or surrender fees, and what do they cover?

10. Does your plan offer any special funds or special classes of stock (generally sold to larger group investors)?

If plan fees and features weren't and aren't enough for you and the DOL to worry about, there are difficulties and temptations related to the huge pot of funds employers funnel from you to your account. In smaller companies, particularly, employers frequently delay depositing your contributions and their matches into the plan—through either ineptitude or malfeasance.

That delay, either way, is a no-no, because ERISA requires companies to deposit employee contributions into their 401(k)s as soon as possible, but no later than the 15th business day of the month following the month in which the contributions were withheld. If the DOL PWBA finds that a company violates this regulation, it can ask the company to make an immediate contribution and also request additional deposits to replace the money lost to participants in earnings on that money. How can you recognize if your company may be abusing your 401(k) funds? The DOL PWBA cites 10 warning signs:

1. Your 401(k) statement is consistently late or comes at irregular intervals.

2. Your account balance doesn't appear to be accurate.

3. Your 401(k) statement shows your paycheck contributions weren't made.

4. Your account balance drops sharply for reasons unexplained by market fluctuation.

5. Your employer is having severe financial troubles.

6. Your employer failed to transmit your contribution on a timely basis.

7. Investments listed on your statement are not what you authorized.

8. Former employees are having trouble getting their benefits paid on time or in the correct amounts.

9. You see unusual transactions, such as a loan to the employer, a corporate officer, or one of the plan trustees.

10. You find there are frequent and unexplained changes in investment managers or consultants.

FYI The DOL PWBA launched an enforcement program to protect 401(k) plans in 1995. In just five years it found over 1,900 situations with violations, recovering about $75 million in lost funds. Recently, DOL PWBA began investigating 401(k) funds that might have been misappropriated by dot-coms in last-ditch efforts to stay afloat.

If you see any of these warning signs, you should discuss them with your employer. If you are not comfortable with doing so or if you're not satisfied with the response you get, you should contact the nearest field office of the U.S. Department of Labor Pension and Welfare Benefits Administration.

Excessive fees, limited choices, and questionable accounting practices are certainly serious 401(k) problems, but don't let them automatically scare you off. If your employer provides a decent contribution match, and at least some good investment choices, you'll still come out ahead by contributing at least what gets matched. All bets are off, though, if you think you might actually lose your 401(k) money due to illegal employer actions.

A Closer Look at 403(b)s

If you're in a 403(b), you might feel relieved that you don't have these problems. Unfortunately, 403(b)s present different problems you must be aware of and manage. These problems revolve around the limitations and inappropriateness of investment choices, and the information available about making them. While 401(k) providers can offer most types of securities, 403(b) participants are often restricted to high-fee choices that are also unsuitable as long-term retirement-savings vehicles. And unlike 401(k) participants, for whom employers must provide education about their plans in an (ostensibly) unbiased fashion, employee 403(b) education usually amounts to a sales presentation. To minimize plan administration costs, many nonprofit employers allow "fox in charge of the chicken coop" insurance company representatives to provide that education. And to cement their continued status as provider, insurance companies sign a "hold harmless" agreement that protects the employer from any costs or penalties deriving from accounting errors or IRS assessments.

The 403(b) is offered in two forms. The first, a 403(b)(1) plan, offers only tax-deferred annuity contracts, usually through insurance companies. These are often absurd on their face, because the 403(b) already defers taxes, so why would you want to pick an investment with tax deferral already built into it.

Normally, you'd expect such investments would offer lower returns, and standard annuity contracts that have fixed rates of return certainly qualify in that regard.

FYI "401 Krusader" Tim Younkin's site (www.timyounkin.com/) has a wealth of information about your 401(k)and 403(b) plan features, laws, rules, regulations, your rights—and key trends affecting all of that.

You can "play the market" with variable annuities, whose returns are generally keyed to underlying stock portfolios. However, the return you achieve is often much lower than if you owned that portfolio directly. That's due to exorbitant fees often built into the contract to pay fat annuity-salesperson commissions.

In fairness, financial institutions have responded to a broadside of criticism concerning their profits on selling annuities by designing lower-fee products. This is partly attributable to the Internet, which allows them to lower marketing costs. Unfortunately, though, many employers, such as school systems, look for whatever 403(b) provider will cost them the least—which are not those likely to cost *you* the least.

If you're thinking that all these shortcomings make these 403(b)leak plans, then here's a 403(b)right spot. An increasing number of nonprofit employers are offering 403(b)(7) plans that allow you to establish custodial accounts with a financial institution offering mutual funds. Usually, both the administrative and built-in fees are substantially lower than those associated with tax-deferred annuities. However, the 6 percent excise tax assessed on excess contributions is a serious drawback. It puts the onus on you to make sure that both you and the provider are in compliance with contribution limits.

Unfortunately, the 403(b) follows the story script of the failed-parachute diver who fortunately missed the pitchfork, but unfortunately also missed the haystack. Corporations have a hard enough time getting the kind of strong 401(k) participation from middle-income employees that's needed to give the full benefit to higher-income employees. Even when matching is generous and vested immediately, many budget-squeezed employees in the lowest (15 percent) tax bracket look at the meager potential tax savings, and just say no to contributing.

So why would you have any more desire to make 403(b) contributions if you're the typical modestly paid nonprofit employee—especially if your employer doesn't match even a dime. In fact, 403(b) employers rarely match, either because they can't afford it, or want to avoid additional regulations imposed on "matchers." Thus, you'd be right to think thrice (!) about 403(b) investing if your employer adds no sweetener, the investments are limited and inappropriate, and you're gagged with fees. You might be better off using a buy-and-hold strategy of investing long term in index mutual funds. Assuming they rise substantially over the long haul, you'll defer most taxation until sale during retirement, or even before, paying lower capital-gains rates instead of possibly higher ordinary-income rates.

However, don't dismiss 403(b) plans out of hand, either. Even without matching, they could be a winner if they allow low-fee mutual fund investing—especially if you're in the same or lower retirement tax bracket. For example, assume you invest $10,000, unmatched, in a 403(b)-7 with fees equal to the alternative of investing $10,000 directly in the same mutual fund. You then invest the tax savings outside the 403(b). Assume the fees are zero in both cases, your ordinary income tax bracket applied to the 403(b) results is 28 percent now and in retirement, and the capital gains rate remains at 20 percent. You'll net $102,280 after tax from the 25-year 403(b) scenario versus $86,678 from the straight mutual fund.

PROCEED WITH CAUTION

 Problems with 403(b) plans are getting more press, particularly the experiences of millions of teachers across the country. Insurance salespeople invited in by districts get friendly with teachers and convince them they need to invest as a forced form of savings and to save on taxes, but never disclose the obscene annuity fees they'll unknowingly pay.

EMPLOYER AND EMPLOYEE CONTRIBUTIONS

Assuming you've analyzed your plan and decided it's worthy of your participation, the next step is deciding how much to contribute. Preferably, that should be as much as you can possibly afford, although the government sets absolute maximums. For a 401(k) you can contribute up to 15 percent of your salary with a maximum of $10,500 in 2000. For a 403(b) the $10,500 cap is the same, but you can contribute up to 20 percent of your salary. These maximums will increase to $11,000 in 2002 under the provisions of the new tax bill passed in May 2001, and will increase $1,000 per year after that until the new max of $15,000 in 2006, which will be indexed to inflation after that. People over 50 can make even higher catch-up contributions (discussed in Hour 18, "Retirement Plan Management").

The new tax law also provides a new option in 2006—Roth-like 401(k) or 403(b) accounts. The employee contributions would go into the Roth account and employer contributions would still go into a traditional tax-deferred account. There are not many details available yet about how these plans will be set up.

GO TO ▶
Will a Roth 401(k)/403(b) make sense for you? The discussions about the Roth IRA versus a tradition IRA in Hour 13, "Traditional/Roth IRAs," will help you decide.

If you're highly paid, however, you might not be able to contribute the 401(k) maximum if your company fails to encourage enough participation among more modestly compensated employees (all those making less than $85,000 annually). You're limited to contributing 2 percent more of your salary than the percentage they contribute of theirs. Thus, if you make $150,000 annually and their average contribution rate is 4 percent, you're limited to 6 percent, or $9,000. Because companies don't know what contributions will be until a year ends, that sometimes means you'll be refunded some of your contributions at the end of a year if you exceed that internal cap.

Those maximums don't include the employer match—which most 401(k) employers provide in some form, precisely because they want to boost participation to better reward their highly valued employees. Employers match an average 50 percent of everything you contribute up to a certain percentage—although some match less and many match more. Along with your contributions, which always belong to you, the matching contributions become totally yours (usually) 3 to 5 years after you start participating in the plan—when you're fully vested.

Unfortunately, after years of improvement in the matching that employers provide, recent evidence shows that they are cutting back as the economy softens. Apparently, a cooler labor market makes it less imperative to compete as vigorously with higher matching, and cutting back helps profits or reduces losses. If this trend continues, it will be particularly alarming in a climate where traditional pensions are disappearing—putting even more of an onus on employees to invest as much as possible both in and outside employer-provided retirement plans.

CONTRIBUTION AND INVESTMENT (RE)ALLOCATIONS

Those matching contributions, along with your direct ones, must be allocated into investment choices. Although employers now offer an average nine investment choices, increasing and broadening them continues to be an important emphasis of those seeking improvements.

ALLOCATION ALTERNATIVES

In a for-profit company, investment choices usually include company stock, a few mutual funds, a few bond funds, and a cash investment. Although ERISA requires that the employees' interests be paramount, sometimes these choices put employers' interests over employees', such as maintaining an existing provider relationship.

PROCEED WITH CAUTION

 Be certain that you understand your options and do not allow your 401(k) portfolio to become too heavily laden with company stock. Your current income is dependent on the company. You increase your risks dramatically by filling your retirement portfolio with stock in the same company. It is important to diversify your holdings.

Frequently, the employer match is in the stock of the company. That reduces your diversification and also increases your overall financial dependence on company performance. Thus, financial advisors generally recommend that you don't ever select contributions to company stock, and that you shift matched contributions from company stock if and when you're allowed.

As mentioned earlier 403(b)s have more limited investment options. They usually include annuities or mutual funds. The largest manager of 403(b) assets is Teachers Insurance and Annuity Association-College Retirement Equities Fund (TIAA-CREF), which manages funds for many colleges, universities, and nonprofit educational institutions.

Regardless of plan, your choices also include the opportunity to reallocate (transfer) all or part of any investment you've chosen into a different investment. You might want to do that if the plan has added better new choices or if you realize your choice is getting worse—perhaps due to increasing fees. Also, if a particular choice is doing extremely well, you might want to "take profits" and shift some into other choices in order to maintain a balanced portfolio. Almost every plan allows such shifts, but usually limits the number of times you can make them during a 12-month period.

Allocation Rules

You know that you contribute to these plans through salary reduction, but how do you designate the way these funds should be invested? At the time you signed up for the plans, you were given a choice of investment options. You filled out forms that assigned a percentage allocation for how the money should be invested among the options offered by your employer.

Do you remember the instructions concerning contributions and allocations that you gave your employer? You should confirm them by checking periodic reports from the retirement plan administrator. They should show not only how your portfolio is performing, but how new deposits in the fund are being allocating. You should also get a statement of how all plan investment alternatives are performing. Compare the ones you selected with others available.

Income-Tax Impacts

The income tax benefits while you are working make 401(k) and other defined-contribution plans some of the best deals going for employees. Your money is deposited tax deferred. For example, if you make a $1,000 contribution and are in a 28 percent tax bracket (which will drop to 25 percent by 2006), it actually costs you out of pocket $720. Your employer match is added with no current tax obligation on your part and grows tax-free until retirement.

As you can see, your money grows much faster when taxes do not eat away at your earnings. Unfortunately, it's not a free ride. Withdrawn funds are taxed at your current income rate. However, most people expect to be in the same or at a lower tax bracket at retirement, so this, too, should be a benefit.

There are additional tax risks if you make early withdrawals. Other than for a medical crisis or a few other hardship exceptions, any withdrawals before the age of 59½ will incur a 10 percent penalty, plus you will have to pay taxes at your current tax rate. This can eat up about 30 percent to 40 percent of the withdrawal.

Even if you don't make an early withdrawal, you can suffer a financial setback by mishandling an employment termination. By failing to use "direct transfer" when electing to transfer your balance into an IRA or another employer's 401(k), 20 percent of your balance will be allocated to tax withholding. If you then move your money into a qualified plan within 60 days, you'll recover withholdings when you file your tax return, but you'll have lost all earnings you might have meanwhile garnered.

GO TO ▶
In Hour 18 we'll look at the options for and consequences of handling your 401(k) account balance upon job termination.

Finally, if you have a period of unemployment before you reach age 59½, it can be very tempting to tap your 401(k) to help fill a budget gap. However, you should do this as a last resort—both because you are spending your retirement money prematurely, and you'll suffer tax penalties in most cases. Despite this, an astounding 60 to 70 percent of people leaving jobs squander all or part of their 401(k) balances, instead of maintaining them in continued tax-deferred status.

RULES: VESTING, BORROWING, WITHDRAWALS, PORTABILITY

While the employer benefit match is great, it does come with strings. Most employers impose a vesting period that requires you stay with the company for a certain number of years before the money is 100 percent yours. The most common vesting period is five years at the rate of 20 percent per year. During that time a certain amount vests each year, and those partially vested amounts are yours, regardless of when you leave the company. For example, if your money invests at the rate of 20 percent per year and you leave after three years, you'll walk away with your own contributions, plus 60 percent of the company match, plus earnings. Your employer gets back 40 percent of its matching. The new tax bill does speed up the vesting process by one year. Under the old law a company could wait three years before beginning to vest its contributions to the 401(k). The new law allows only a two-year waiting period. An employee must be fully vested after six years on the job.

BORROWING FROM YOUR 401(K)

Unfortunately, many employees think nothing matches the opportunity to borrow against their 401(k)s and pay themselves back the interest. About 80 percent of plans allow such borrowing and about 20 percent of employees enrolled in 401(k) plans take advantage of it—more than half of the borrowers use it to help buy a home. Although this seems like a worthwhile reason, here are the facts you should consider before possibly dealing a body blow to your retirement savings and investing strategy:

- You can usually borrow 50 percent of the balance, and must usually pay it back within five years. If you don't, the rest is paid back from what's left in the account and you'll suffer steep taxation and penalties. Furthermore, leaving your job usually triggers a demand for immediate, full repayment, with the same negative consequences on your account if you can't.

- Although you're paying yourself back the interest, the cost is double taxation, because you're paying back already-taxed dollars, and you'll pay tax again on those amounts when you ultimately take 401(k) distributions.

- While you have the loan out, you're losing the opportunity for that money to grow tax-deferred within the plan. Furthermore, if you suspend contributions because of your current needs, you might have to wait a year after paying back the loan to resume contributions.

And sealing the bad deal, many borrowers must pay loan fees.

PROCEED WITH CAUTION

 Be wary of a new product that might be offered by commercial lenders, allowing you to borrow against your employer matching—purportedly avoiding some direct 401(k) borrowing problems. It's another way to place your own roadblocks on your path to a successful retirement.

PLAN TRENDS AND YOUR RIGHTS

As you can see, although defined-contribution tax-deferred plans sound simple, it helps to understand their many nuances. Don't stop here, though, because they're a work in progress, constantly being tweaked.

For example, a recent ruling allows employers to automatically enroll newly hired employees into 401(k) plans, unless they specifically opt out. Obviously, this can help boost participation, but it could work against the employee because all automatic-signee contributions are normally put into lower-return, safer investments.

Fortunately, such stealth maneuvers, although legal, are countered by the growing trend to make employee real-time account information accessible through secured-server online access. That way, employees don't have to wait for quarterly or annual statements. They can check their accounts whenever they wish to monitor their performance and make sure contributions and allocations are being handled properly.

Yet another important trend is immediate enrollment, not making employees wait a year. Coupled with that is faster vesting—many employers "sealing their match" after three years, or even immediately. These moves clearly indicate employer desire to boost participation, and that's why they're also stepping up education campaigns. Recent studies confirm that informed employees enroll in greater numbers and contribute higher percentages.

JUST A MINUTE

Take advantage of every opportunity to learn more about these plans, even if you're already fully participating. For one thing, it might mobilize you into the growing corps of advocates for 401(k) improvements. Surprisingly, you might find your employer willing to listen to ideas that will make employees happier, even if they add cost.

YOUR RIGHTS

Knowing how important these plans are to your future, let's take a quick look at what your rights are under current law. There are a number of items your employer must provide:

1. Within 90 days of your eligibility for participating in the plan, your employer must provide you with a Summary Plan Description.

2. Annually, your employer must provide you with a Summary Annual Report free of charge that gives you information about the plan's financial status and a summary of the yearly report filed with the Federal government.

3. You can submit a written request for an Individual Benefit Statement that includes a description of the benefits earned to date and how much of your benefits are vested.

4. You do have the right to ask for a full plan document, which is filled with legal documentation, but your employer can charge a fee for it.

5. You can also ask for the Pension Trust Document, which identifies the trustees of the plan who are financially responsible for the investment alternatives chosen. As it does with the full plan document, the employer can charge a fee for it.

HOUR'S UP!

It's time to find out whether you have learned the basics of employer-sponsored retirement programs such as 401(k)s and 403(b)s:

1. There are many terms thrown around to describe employer-sponsored retirement plans. Which of the following does not accurately describe these plans?

    a. 401(k), 403(b), and Section 457 are parts of the IRS tax code.

    b. 401(k), 403(b), and Section 457 are examples of salary reduction plans.

    c. 401(k), 403(b), and Section 457 are examples of defined benefit plans.

    d. 401(k), 403(b), and Section 457 are examples of defined contribution plans.

2. If you participate in a 401(k) or 403(b), the amount that can be contributed is capped by the Federal government. What is the amount of that cap?

    a. $10,500 per year

    b. $2,000 per year

    c. $15,000 per year

    d. $30,000 per year

3. Who has control over how the contribution is allocated among the approved investment alternatives?

    a. The company takes control, so it can be certain you will have enough to live on when you reach retirement.

    b. The plan administrator takes control so he or she can be certain you will have enough to live on when you reach retirement.

    c. The mutual fund or broker that holds the funds decides how the funds are invested so you will have enough when you reach retirement.

    d. The employee is the only person responsible for choosing how the funds are invested among the investment alternatives.

4. Which of the following statements is not true about the employer matching contribution?

   a. The employer matching funds can take a number of years to be fully vested.

   b. The employer is required by law to match all funds.

   c. The employer matches an employee's contribution up to a stated percentage and dollar amount.

   d. All of the above are true statements regarding the employer matching provisions.

5. In many companies, the amount of money the employer contributes to the plan does not automatically belong to the employee. Which of the following statements are true about employer-sponsored plans?

   a. All the money reverts to the company if you leave before retirement.

   b. The employee does not lose the money that he or she contributed, or its earnings, if the employee leaves the company before retirement.

   c. Employer matching funds are vested at a stated percentage over a stated number of years.

   d. Only (b) and (c).

6. Employer-sponsored retirement plans offer you many tax benefits. Which is true?

   a. All the money deposited is tax-deferred and continues to grow tax-deferred until the retirement.

   b. Only the employer's contribution is tax-deferred.

   c. None of the money is tax-deferred.

   d. Only the employee's contribution is tax-deferred.

7. You want to withdraw the money in your employer-sponsored retirement plan before the age of 59½. Which is true?

   a. The money is taxed at your current income tax rate without any additional costs.

   b. The money is taxed at your current income tax rate plus there is a 10 percent penalty for early withdrawal.

c. You can continue to defer your tax bite provided you roll the money over into another qualified retirement plan.

d. Both (b) and (c) are correct.

8. You are allowed to borrow from your 401(k) plan if your employer permits it. Which is a true statement about using this option, if available?

   a. If you lose your job, you will be required to repay it immediately or you could end up paying penalties for early withdrawal.

   b. The money on loan does not continue to grow.

   c. It's your money, you should be able to use it whenever you want to for whatever purpose.

   d. Only 20 percent of employers allow employees to borrow from their 401(k) plans because it is too dangerous.

9. Which documents about your employer-sponsored retirement plan are you entitled to receive?

   a. The Summary Plan Description must be provided for free within 90 days of your eligibility to participate in the plan.

   b. The Summary Annual Report must be provided to you annually at no extra cost.

   c. The Pension Trust Document and full plan description must be provided if you request it, but a fee may be charged.

   d. All of the above are correct.

10. What is the law that regulates retirement plans in all for-profit companies and some nonprofit companies?

   a. The Employee Retirement Income Security Act

   b. The Pension and Welfare Benefits Act

   c. The Individual Retirement Act

   d. The Employee Benefits Act

HOUR 11

Small Business/
Self-Employed Plans

You might work in a small business, but that doesn't mean your need for retirement savings is small potatoes. Although small businesses generally find costs too prohibitive to have 401(k) plans, cost-effective tax-deferred alternatives are available, both to them and self-employed individuals.

If individuals or small business employers don't use them, they're doing an unacceptable disservice to millions of Americans. Small businesses make up more than 99 percent of all employers and employ 52 percent of private-sector workers—almost 67 million people. Self-employed workers are another 7.2 percent of the private-sector workforce not employed by large corporations. All these workers belong to an underprivileged club that doesn't include resources to financially prepare for retirement among its membership privileges.

This creates even bigger challenges for you to meet your retirement needs. The Employee Benefits Research Institute (EBRI) reports that only 46 percent of businesses with 100 or fewer employees offer retirement plans. Even when these plans are offered, EBRI found that only one fifth of people working for small employers actually participate in a plan. In contrast, about 80 percent of large firms offer retirement plans (covered in Hour 10, "401(k) and Related Plans"), with about 78 percent employee participation.

CHAPTER SUMMARY

LESSON PLAN:

In this Hour you will learn about ...

- Basics of SEP-IRAs, SIMPLE IRAs, and Keoghs.
- Contribution options and employer matching.
- Planning your contribution allocation and assessing your investment allocation.
- Income-tax impacts of participation.
- Vesting, withdrawals, and portability.

FYI In the 2001 Small Employer Retirement Survey conducted by The Employee Benefit Research Institute (EBRI), it was discovered that small businesses perceive little interest or demand from employees to offer a plan. Wages and other benefits like medical and dental plans are considered a priority over retirement plans. The second key reason for not offering a plan cited by small business owners is that revenue is too uncertain to commit to sponsoring a retirement plan.

If you do work for a small company or are self-employed, it is critical that you become aware of the types of plans available and advocate for one of them at your office if it doesn't exist. Unfortunately, you'll have a hard sell because the plans available can seem very confusing, a lot of hassle, or too expensive.

What are the key motivators for getting employers to start a plan? According to 2001 EBRI survey, this is what small business owners want:

1. An increase in the business's profits (44 percent of nonsponsors)
2. Low administrative costs that required no employer contributions (35 percent)
3. Business tax credits for starting a plan (23 percent)
4. A plan that could be tailored to the unique needs of their business (23 percent)
5. Reduced administrative requirements (18 percent)
6. Available easy-to-understand information (19 percent)
7. Allowing key executives to accumulate more in a retirement plan (16 percent)
8. Demand from employees (15 percent)

These are some good points to help you develop your strategy for encouraging these plans at work. Let's cut through the confusing clutter and pave you a smooth road to understanding your employer's plan, getting your employer to start one, or setting one up for yourself.

UNDERSTAND SEP-IRA, SIMPLE IRA, AND KEOGH BASICS

The most commonly used retirement plan is the Simplified Employee Pension (SEP) IRA. However, the 1996 introduction of the Savings Incentive Match Plan (SIMPLE) IRA has been met with enthusiastic response by "larger" small businesses seeking to provide employees a retirement benefit at a more modest cost. The Keogh, the original small-business plan, is particularly valuable to successful sole-proprietor businesses.

The Internal Revenue Service puts out an excellent publication titled "Retirement Plans for Small Business," Publication 560. You can order it by phone at 1-800-829-1040 or find it on the IRS Web site at www.irs.ustreas.gov/basic/forms_pubs/pubs/p560toc.htm.

Each of these plans has its own set of rules for how much can be contributed and by whom. The rules also vary on which employees are eligible and who may be excluded. Let's examine the specifics of each of these plans.

SEP-IRAs

SEP-IRAs are the most flexible and therefore the most popular with small companies, especially those with one to 10 employees. Employers do not have to contribute the same amount each year and can even skip a year if business is bad. They can then make up for skipping contributions by putting in the maximum in good years.

Contributions per employee can be 15 percent of income, but no more than $25,500. If you are self-employed using a SEP-IRA, your contribution is 13.04 percent up to the maximum of $25,500.

Equality is the rule for the SEP. The employer must contribute the exact same percentage of earnings to the plan for every eligible employee. Newly minted SEPs do not have any provisions for employees to contribute. That possibility ended with passage of the 1996 Small Business Job Protection Act. If you're looking for a plan that can include employee contributions, you should skip to the next section on SIMPLE IRAs.

PROCEED WITH CAUTION

 For people who are self-employed, SEP contributions are based on net income, not gross income. A self-employed person must first figure net earnings on Schedule C by subtracting business expenses and 50 percent of the self-employment tax. The computation is further complicated by having to subtract your SEP contribution to arrive at your eligible net income figure, effectively reducing your permitted contribution from 15 percent to 13.0435 percent.

In 1999, $70 billion of the $76 billion of employer-sponsored IRAs in mutual funds were in SEP-IRAs, according to the Investment Company Institute. SEP-IRAs can be set up with banks, insurance companies, or other qualified financial institutions. Since there are no annual reports required by the Federal government about SEP plans, there is no central repository collecting information about total assets held in SEPs.

Employer contributions made to the plan for the benefit of participating employees are tax deductible. SEPs are set up in individual retirement accounts (IRAs) under each employee's name. Unlike the 401(k), employees are immediately 100 percent vested in the plan. Contributions are excluded from income rather than deducted from it.

If you work for a company that established its SEP-IRA before 1996, you may be permitted to defer taxes contributing a portion of your earnings as a salary reduction. If so, you can contribute up to $10,500 in 2001, provided you haven't already contributed that to another retirement plan in which you participate. Under the tax bill that was passed in May 2001, you will be able to increase your contribution to $11,000 in 2002. It will then go up $1,000 per year until 2006. After that time, increases will be indexed to inflation. If you are over 50, there are additional catch-up contributions allowed, which are covered in greater depth in Hour 18, "Retirement Plan Management."

JUST A MINUTE

The salary reduction provision of the SEP-IRA was prohibited for any SEP-IRAs after the introduction of the SIMPLE IRA in 1996. If, as an employee, you are able to make contributions into your SEP-IRA at work, then it is actually a Salary Reduction SEP (SARSEP-IRA), which will gradually become extinct.

Who is an eligible employee? A SEP-IRA must be set up for each qualifying employee and may be required for leased employees. A qualifying employee is one who is at least 21 years old, worked at least three out of five of the immediately preceding tax years, and earned at least $400 in the current tax year. The employer may establish less restrictive participation requirements for its employees, as long as this is consistent across the board. More restrictive ones cannot be established.

Leased employees are people who are hired by a leasing organization but perform services for another. To be eligible to participate in the SEP, you must meet these three conditions: 1) provide services under an agreement between the recipient and the leasing organization; 2) perform these services for the recipient or related persons substantially full-time for at least one year; and 3) perform services under the primary direction and control of the recipient.

An employer can exclude employees covered by a union agreement, if their retirement benefits were bargained for in good faith by their union and their employer. Nonresident aliens can also be excluded if they have no U.S. source of earned income from their employer.

PROCEED WITH CAUTION

There are a number of restrictions unique to a SEP-IRA. You cannot do a SEP rollover into a new employer's retirement plan. Employers cannot prohibit withdrawals, and may not specify, as a condition of accepting contributions to a SEP-IRA, that an employee must keep any part of the contributions in a SEP.

Timing is another critical issue especially for the self-employed. Frequently, the self-employed do not know what their earnings will be until the end of the year. This makes it difficult to fund a SEP until tax returns have been compiled. There are penalties if too much is invested and one must withdraw the funds.

This timing complication also has a silver lining. Employers can delay their SEP contribution until their taxes are actually filed. So if cash is tight at the end of a calendar year, but a big contract payment is due before the time taxes are filed, then employers can take advantage of this provision and delay adding to their SEP up to August 15 of the next year, the last day for tax filing extensions.

SIMPLE IRAs

We'll now take a look at the new kid on the block: the SIMPLE IRA or Savings Incentive Match Plan for Employees. This alternative for small business was established as part of the Small Business Job Protection Act of 1996 for businesses of 100 or fewer employees. The SIMPLE IRA took a while to catch on, but its growth tripled between 1998 and 1999.

The SIMPLE IRA is a tax-deferred salary reduction plan that permits employees to make elective annual contributions that reduce taxable income of up to $6,500. It is essentially a simplified 401(k) plan developed to encourage its use by small businesses. Employers must either match the employee's contribution dollar for dollar up to 3 percent of the employee's compensation or provide a 2 percent contribution for all eligible employees up to a maximum of $3,400.

Beginning in 2002, the employee contribution allowed will begin to increase under the new tax law passed in May 2001. In 2002, the maximum contribution increases to $7,000. After that it will increase $1,000 per year until

2005, when it maxes out at $10,000. After 2005, the maximum contribution will be indexed to inflation. There are also catch-up provisions for employees over 50. These will be covered in greater detail in Hour 18.

SIMPLE IRAs are set up as separate IRAs in each employee's name. That means you are 100 percent vested in the plan from the time it is first established, unlike many 401(k) plans where there is a waiting period before you are fully vested in the plan and entitled to 100 percent of the employer's contribution if you leave the company. That makes it easily portable if you change jobs.

PROCEED WITH CAUTION

You can move your funds by a rollover or trustee-to-trustee transfer to another IRA without incurring tax, provided the account has been opened for at least two years or you will incur a 25 percent tax penalty to move the funds. Since you are fully vested and the SIMPLE IRA account is opened in your name, it's best to wait the full two-year period even if you switch jobs.

The downside is that SIMPLE IRAs have stricter rules on tax-free transfers and early withdrawals than most of the other retirement plans. The account must be opened for at least two years before you can move the money or take it out. If you must withdraw or transfer the funds before the two years are up, you will owe a 25 percent penalty rather than the 10 percent penalty that is common with other retirement plan options. Aside from this stiff two-year rule, the remaining rules about distribution and tax obligation are similar to the traditional IRA.

You must be allowed to participate in the plan if you earn at least $5,000 during any two years prior to the current year, and expect to earn at least that much during the calendar year for which the contributions are made. For SIMPLE plan purposes, the term "employee" includes the self-employed individual with earned income.

You can be excluded from participating in the plan if your retirement benefits are covered by a collective bargaining agreement (union contract), you are a nonresident alien and received no earned income from sources in the United States, or if you became an eligible employee as part of an acquisition or similar transaction during the year.

You will be asked to sign a salary reduction agreement during a 60-day period prior to the beginning of any year. Participation is voluntary. At that time, you can elect to contribute a percentage of your compensation or a specific dollar amount (if the employer makes this option available). You may cancel your election at any time during the year.

 FYI You are in control when deciding how much to contribute to a SIMPLE IRA. The only restriction the employer can make on the contribution amount is that you remain in compliance with the contributions limit set by Federal law, currently $6,500. Your employer cannot limit your contribution percentage for any other reason.

KEOGH PLANS

The Keogh Plan, established in 1962, is primarily for businesses that operate as sole proprietorships or partnerships. You're eligible for a Keogh if you own your own business and file Schedule C, have a Subchapter S corporation, are self-employed, are a partner in a business that files a Schedule K, or do freelance work. If you're part of a limited liability company (LLC) you also can use a Keogh, but must actually perform personal services for the business—not merely be a passive investor. Other corporate structures cannot use Keoghs.

Keoghs offer similarities to the structures available in large corporate pension plans. They're also the most complex of all small business retirement plans, offer the maximum tax-sheltered amounts among retirement plans, and allow business owners flexibility in establishing criteria for employee participation qualification.

Keogh Plans can be set up as defined-contribution—or defined-benefit—plans, just like traditional pension plans. While this Hour focuses on defined-contribution plans, we are including the defined-benefit option since Keoghs offer both possibilities. Also, like a traditional pension plan, you can borrow against funds accumulated in your plan, which is not an option with SIMPLE IRA or SEP-IRA plans.

PROCEED WITH CAUTION

 Be aware that if your business closes you can't continue to contribute to a Keogh, although you can disband it and roll the money over into an IRA. You're out the substantial fees you might have paid professionals to help you set up the Keogh, and there could be penalties depending on the type of Keogh you set up.

What's the catch? It's complexity. There are three different sets of Keogh regulations: one for the self-employed, one for small business owners, and one for employees of a company that has a plan.

You must name a plan administrator, even if that person is you. You must file an IRS-approved plan and annual plan reports. You can get a standardized plan from a bank or financial institution, but to gain your greatest flexibility, it is probably wise to have one designed for your specific situation with the help of a lawyer or CPA who is a Keogh specialist to draw up the required documents that define the plan.

You can establish a Keogh plan even if you are a full-time employee with a defined-benefit pension plan at work, provided you earn additional income in one of the ways that meet Keogh qualifications. The money deposited in the Keogh must also come from sources that meet these qualifications.

Keogh Plans can be established as a profit-sharing defined-contribution plan, a money-purchase defined-contribution plan, a paired plan, or a defined-benefit plan. You can customize the plan to best meet your individual situation.

The defined-benefit Keogh allows you to contribute up to $135,000 annually. However, most business owners are happy if they earn enough to be allowed the maximum contribution of $35,000 to defined-contribution Keoghs (beginning in 2002 under the new tax law, this will increase to $40,000). Profit-sharing or money-purchase plans have additional restrictions on how much can be contributed.

PROCEED WITH CAUTION

You have numerous ways to define your plan, but be careful. There are penalties if you are not able to make the contribution defined in your original documents that can be as high as 100 percent of the amount that should have been contributed.

Profit-sharing defined-contribution plans are the least complicated and most popular. Each year you decide whether to participate and what your contribution will be. A profit-sharing Keogh allows for a maximum of 15 percent (before adjustments) or $35,000 ($40,000 beginning in 2002), whichever is less.

Money-purchase defined-contribution plans allow the maximum shelter, 25 percent of up to $200,000 (beginning in 2002 under the new tax law; for 2001, it is $170,000) in compensation, but they're also the most rigid. You must specify the percentage of earnings (minimum 3 percent) at the time you set up the plan and deposit that percentage even in bad years. If you don't contribute one year, you'll will owe a penalty up to 100 percent of the amount you should have contributed, but it won't count as a contribution.

Paired plans are the most flexible and combine key provisions of profit-sharing and money-purchase defined-contribution plans. They do lock you into annual contributions, even if you haven't made much money in the business. However, you can set a lower required contribution percentage, such as 10 percent, but still contribute up to 25 percent profit sharing in good years.

Defined-benefit plans are established to guarantee a specific annual payout at 65, which cannot not exceed up to 100 percent of the average of your highest three earnings years or a maximum of $135,000. You can fund the plan to produce the specific payout you choose and may even be able to contribute up to 100 percent of your annual earnings to meet that goal. Determining the actual contribution is complex and you should engage an *actuary* to help design the plan and then review it annually to determine the amount you must deposit to meet your projected payout. The actuary's report must be submitted yearly with you tax return.

STRICTLY DEFINED

An **actuary** analyzes the financial consequences of risk. He or she uses mathematics, statistics, and financial theory to study uncertain future events, such as how much you will need in your Keogh plan to meet the annual benefit you desire in retirement.

A defined-benefit Keogh is a perfect vehicle for catching up late in your career if you have the resources. People approaching retirement can use this option because they can contribute as much as 100 percent of their income to meet desired benefits as established by an actuary. For example, the Keogh is a great tool for helping fill your retirement gap by making contributions from professional consulting on the side.

The biggest Keogh disadvantage is the paperwork. The IRS requires at least one type of report annually, and the extensive Form 5500-C every three years. During the middle two years you can file a simple Form 5500EZ if you are self-employed. If plan assets are less than $100,000, the Form 5500EZ is not required. If you have employees, you must file a Form 5500-R. Many retirement specialists recommend that even if you gather the records yourself, it is probably a good idea to have an accountant or Keogh expert complete the forms.

INCOME TAX IMPACTS

GO TO ▶
To review the tax impacts of 401(k)s, go to the section on Income Tax-Impacts in Hour 10.

The income tax impacts for employees vary according to the type of plan offered. If you are in a SEP-IRA or Keogh that is completely funded by your employer, than there are no immediate tax impacts. You contribute nothing to the plan and therefore have no tax deduction, and the contributions are tax deferred so they cause no immediate tax liability. If your Keogh is set up for employee contributions or you make contributions into your SIMPLE IRA, then your contributions will reduce your taxable income the same way as a 401(k). At the time you start withdrawing the funds from any of these plans, they will be taxed at your current income tax rate.

For a business owner, all contributions made into one of these retirement plans are tax deductible. The business can deduct contributions made toward its owners as well as its employees.

UNDERSTAND VESTING, WITHDRAWALS, AND PORTABILITY

In all the small business retirement plans discussed in this Hour, there is no concern about vesting. All plans are established in the employee's name and are 100 percent vested immediately. This also makes all but the Keogh very portable. For the Keogh the rules vary depending upon the type of program chosen. If you are covered by a Keogh, check with your plan administrator regarding questions of withdrawals and portability.

If you decide to withdraw SEP-IRA funds early, tax penalties and interest are subject to traditional IRA rules: 10 percent plus all funds withdrawn will be taxed as current income. Penalties for the SIMPLE IRA and Keogh are stiffer, as indicated earlier.

If you leave the job before retirement, the most common way to get the funds is to roll them over into an individual IRA. That way you can avoid all taxes. Under the new tax law you will have additional options beginning in 2002. You will be able to roll over any qualified retirement plan, such as a SEP-IRA, SIMPLE IRA, 401(k) or 403(b), into any other qualified plan, provided the employer permits the rollover.

At the time of retirement you have two key options: lump sum or annuity. If you choose the lump sum you can take it as a cash payment or as an IRA rollover. For tax purposes, the IRA rollover will probably be your best choice to avoid a substantial tax bill that year.

The rules for SEP IRA and SIMPLE IRA distributions generally follow those of traditional IRAs. You must begin withdrawing those funds at age 70½, planning the withdrawals based on your lifetime, the joint lifetime of you and your spouse, the joint lifetime of you and your beneficiary, or any period you set that is shorter than the ones mentioned. By naming a beneficiary much younger than yourself, you can spread out your IRA payments over a much longer time.

We've explored the major provisions of small business and self-employed retirement plans. Now we'll take a quick look at how these plans compare and then review the effect of the just-enacted tax bill that makes them even more beneficial and complex.

GO TO ▶

Planning for withdrawals from these plans during retirement involves complex juggling of tax-minimization considerations, income needs and avoiding outliving your funds, and compliance with IRS withdrawal requirements. This planning is covered in Hour 18.

COMPARISON OF SMALL BUSINESS/SELF-EMPLOYED PLANS

Now that you've reviewed the options and all their somewhat confusing details, which plan is right for you? There is no a simple answer; it depends on your individual set of circumstances. This table highlights some key considerations and is followed by some general guidelines that might help you determine which plan is best for your business or self-employed income.

Comparison of SEP-IRAs, SIMPLE IRAS, and Keogh Plans

Limits	15% of income up to $25,500 (13.04% for self-employed).	$6,500 by the employee. Employer match dollar for dollar up to 3% of compensation or 2% for all employees up to $3,400.	25% of compensation paid to employee up to $35,000 (defined-benefit plan can be as high as $135,000 in special situations; see Keogh section).
Pre-tax employee contributions?	No	Yes	Yes
Contributions required?	No	Yes	Yes

continues

Comparison of SEP-IRAs, SIMPLE IRAS, and Keogh Plans (continued)

Annual filing required?	No	No	Yes
Employee eligibility requirements?	Yes	Yes	Yes
Vesting schedule?	No	No	No
Employee loans permitted?	No	No	Yes

If you're self-employed and don't want all the hassles of setting up the legal stuff related to a Keogh or dealing with the annual reports, your best choice is the SEP-IRA. It's simple to set up, does not require annual contributions, and gives you the most flexibility in how and when you make your contributions.

If you're the owner of a small company of 100 or fewer employees and want to offer a plan that allows employees to contribute, then your best choice is the SIMPLE IRA. It has a lot less paperwork requirements and gives you a 401(k)-like benefit that can be a good incentive when recruiting and retaining staff.

If you're a sole proprietor, member of a partnership, or a freelancer, you may want to consider the Keogh. It's especially good for folks who are getting starting later in life, have an income source that meets the requirements of a Keogh, and can afford to put a large chunk of that income in the fund.

HOUR'S UP!

It's time to find out if you've learned the basics of small business and self-employed retirement plans:

1. We've discussed several types of plans available. Which plan is the closest to the 401(k) offered by larger employers?

   a. Simplified Employee Pension or SEP-IRA

   b. Savings Incentive Match Plan or SIMPLE IRA

   c. Keogh Plans

   d. None of the above

QUIZ

2. Of the three types of retirement plans mentioned above, which plan cannot be used by corporations?

    a. Simplified Employee Pension or SEP-IRA

    b. Savings Incentive Match Plan or SIMPLE IRA

    c. Keogh Plans

    d. None of the above

3. Of the three types of retirement plans mentioned above, which plan is the simplest for the company to administer, but does not provide a mechanism for the employee to contribute?

    a. Simplified Employee Pension or SEP-IRA

    b. Savings Incentive Match Plan or SIMPLE IRA

    c. Keogh Plans

    d. None of the above

4. The flexibility of the SEP-IRA is the primary reason they are so popular among small businesses and self-employed workers. Which of the following is true?

    a. The employer must put the exact same percentage of earnings in the plan for every eligible employee.

    b. The plan percentage does not have to be the same each year and a company can skip a year completely if necessary.

    c. The company can put away the maximum allowed in good years to make up for bad years.

    d. (a), (b), and (c) are correct.

5. SIMPLE IRAs are the closest to the 401(k)s offered by large employers. Which of the following statements are true about SIMPLE IRAs?

    a. The SIMPLE IRA is a tax-deferred salary reduction plan that permits employees to make elective annual contributions of up to $6,500, which will increase beginning in 2002 under the new tax bill.

    b. Employers must either match the employee's contribution dollar for dollar up to 3 percent of the employee's compensation or provide a 2 percent contribution for all eligible employees up to a maximum of $3,400.

    c. The SIMPLE IRA was created to encourage more small business to offer retirement plans.

    d. All are correct.

6. There are a number of different ways to structure a Keogh. Which one of these is not an acceptable Keogh structure?

    a. Profit-sharing defined-contribution plan

    b. Money-purchase defined-contribution plan

    c. Non-paired plan

    d. Defined-benefit plan

7. One of the plans could have penalties if your business dissolves and you want to continue making contributions by rolling the funds into a traditional IRA. Which plan is that?

    a. SEP-IRA.

    b. SIMPLE-IRA.

    c. Keogh.

    d. There are never problems with rolling over any of these plans.

8. One advantage offered by the SEP-IRA at tax time is that a business which is having cash flow problems can delay its annual contribution. How long can they delay?

    a. Instead of making the contribution by December 31 of the tax year involved they can delay it until April 15 of the next year.

    b. Instead of making the contribution by December 31 of the tax year involved they can delay it until June 15 of the next year.

    c. Instead of making the contribution by December 31 of the tax year involved, they can delay it until August 15 of the next year.

    d. All the above are correct. The delay in making annual contributions can be made at any time before the time the company actually files its tax forms with the IRS.

9. The rules for the distribution of SEP and SIMPLE IRAs generally follow those of traditional IRAs. Which of the following are true?

    a. You must begin withdrawing those funds at 70½.

    b. You can plan the withdrawals based on your lifetime, the joint lifetime of you and your spouse, the joint lifetime of you and your beneficiary, or any period that is shorter than the ones mentioned. You can set the length of the shorter period.

    c. By naming a beneficiary much younger than yourself, you can spread out your IRA payments over a much longer time.

    d. All of the above are true.

10. The new tax bill passed in May 2001 instituted which of the following changes?

   a. The total that can be contributed including employer and employee funds will increase from $35,000 to $40,000 per year.

   b. The total that an employee can contribute in all of his or her plans will increase from $10,500 to $15,000 and then indexed for inflation after 2006.

   c. There is no benefit to employees of small businesses.

   d. Both (a) and (b) are correct.

Hour 12

Defined-Benefit and Federal Pension Plans

Chapter Summary

LESSON PLAN:

In this Hour you will learn about ...

- How and why traditional pensions are changing and disappearing.
- How new cash-balance plans can put your retirement out of balance.
- Your rights under federal law regarding pensions.
- Future trends in defined-benefit pensions.
- Federal vs. private pensions.

If you're a fan of twentieth-century British drama, you've probably heard dialogue like this—albeit better (with apologies to readers from across the pond):

"Say old man, have you heard from Cecil?"

"Didn't you hear, Reggie, his firm pensioned him off. He rang me up a fortnight ago from Surrey, where he and the Mrs. found themselves a charming little cottage."

Until recently, such scenarios played out regularly in merry old England. But here in the colonies, it's never been easy to live on even a full company pension—and it's rare for retirees to get full pensions these days.

Nevertheless, old-fashioned pensions are still part of about one fourth of company benefit plans. And a combination of defined-contribution plans, such as 401(k)s, newer cash-balance pensions, and supplementary savings plans, have been replacing many traditional plans. So it's crucial that you know what you have now, what might happen to it, what your rights are concerning it, and what many activists are doing to keep the futures they thought they'd been promised from being ripped away.

TRADITIONAL DEFINED-BENEFIT PENSIONS

Defined benefit. It sounds rigid and precise. But in looking at different companies, imagine descendants of Lewis Carroll's Alice filling every HR administrator position and saying: "A benefit means just what I say it means, neither more nor less." Yet, despite how different the definitions are from company to company, they're usually based on a generic formula something like this:

Benefit = RAABP × TYS × BMF × ERF

RAABP (recent average annual base pay): This is often based on the last five years, although sometimes on as much as 10 years. Some companies include bonuses and incentive pay, and others don't.

TYS (total years of service): It seems straightforward, but some companies take away years for breaks in service, such as extended parental leave. Also, some companies cap TYS (for example, at 30 years), even though they allow you to work longer and count post-cap years in determining your RAABP. They might also calculate your base year average salary as of completion of that lower total years of service.

BMF (benefit multiplier factor): This usually ranges between .01 and .02—generally set in conjunction with maximum TYS so that the (multiplication) product is the largest percentage of RAABP your pension payment can be. For example, a BMF of .015 and a 30-year maximum TYS limit gives you a maximum 45 percent of your base-period average salary.

ERF (early retirement fraction): This factor is similar to the factor used in Social Security calculations to reduce your payment when you start receiving your pension before normal retirement age. For example, many companies allow you to retire at age 55, so they use this factor to reduce the payment so that on average you won't receive more in your lifetime than someone with the same years of service and pay who retires at age 65.

FYI It used to be common for companies to integrate your expected Social Security payment into a more complicated formula to ensure you didn't wind up with more than what you were making before retirement.

The overall philosophy behind this formula is that your pension should be a substantial fraction of what you were making before retiring, but not enough to replace it. And that percentage is highest when rewarding your loyalty for longevity—which, admittedly sounds strange, given loyalty is often rewarded with pink slips today.

Even if you're not mathematically sophisticated, it's easy to see that your benefit calculation is heavily influenced by your later years in the company, when you're adding that extra service and possibly increasing your base-pay average substantially.

For example, assume the BMF is .0125, and that the averaging period is five years. Let's look at two colleagues who joined the company together after receiving their MBAs at age 25, are both climbing the corporate ladder, and are making the same amount as each other after 30 years. However, Pam is the only child of parents who are now ill. So she retires at age 55, moves across the country to where her parents live so she can take care of them, and takes a consulting position for the same salary. Pam's friend Liz, though, continues with the company getting promoted two more times and retiring 10 years later. Here are each one's pensions:

30-Year Pam: $80,000 × 30 × .0125 × .8 = $24,000

40-Year Liz: $120,000 × 40 × .0125 = $60,000

By not retiring early and staying 10 more years, boosting her most recent five-year average by $40,000 per year, Liz's pension is two-and-one-half times Pam's. Now, let's make the far-fetched assumption that Pam continued matching Liz's salary, and also gets vested in a partial pension with her new employer. Then throw in the 10 years that Pam will collect that early pension. Even so, all that leaves Pam far short of Liz financially in the long run.

JUST A MINUTE

Just like with Social Security, private-employer early retirees continue receiving the reduced benefit throughout retirement to compensate for the additional years they receive it. However, not all employers provide immediate pension payments to early retirees, instead always starting payments at age 65. That eliminates the early retirement fraction from their pension calculations.

Because traditional pensions are so "late-loaded" in this respect, it's hard for mid-career employees to voluntarily walk away from a company that still offers them. Unfortunately, employers realized this, too, in the last 10 years, and aggressively sought to reduce future financial commitments to veteran employees.

The most obvious was firing them before they were old enough to argue they'd been age-discrimination victims. In the old days, such firing actually totally absolved employers of any pension commitment to their employees. But ERISA (Employment Retirement Income Security Act) and other laws passed since then have required that employees gain early vesting in their pensions.

Thus, if you leave your company after 10 years, voluntarily or otherwise, at age 65 you'll receive a partial pension based on the same or similar formula to the one used for full retirement. However, as we've seen, you'll receive far less than $^{10}/_{30}$ of what you'd be entitled to if you were leaving after 30 years. It's probably only because of the very low unemployment we had in the '90s that companies didn't aggressively wield the dismissal axe to chop off those future fat pensions before they grew too much. So it's no coincidence that employers have recently seemed to be on a semi-automatic firing spree triggered by the first signs of economic weakness.

FYI This "current value" rule protecting the part of the pension you've already earned was one important additive fueling the '80s corporate-takeover frenzy. Raiders targeted companies with "overfunded" pensions required by actuarially determined standards for meeting future pension obligations. But in buying companies and terminating their pension plans, raiders vaporized those future obligations, blasting open a cornucopia of cash.

Even before the current purge, however, employers were moving with aggressive stinginess in modifying their pension programs. You might wonder how they could change the rules in the middle of the game. But ERISA requires only that employees can be given the handfuls of chips they've earned anytime they want, even if they've seemingly been promised a boatload in the future. In other words, in modifying pension programs, employers must only avoid taking away any of the pension's current value—the amount an employee actually already earned as of the day the modification goes into effect.

In addition, employers seeking to maintain morale sometimes just tinkered with their programs, while aggressively continuing to offer the kind of early-retirement incentives that were largely born in the '80s downsizing revolution. Usually, this involves offering employees an artificial increase in age and service years to make them eligible for retirement and boost their pension payments. In return, employees who accepted had to agree to leave within months (usually) and waive their right to sue the company for coerced termination.

Finally, employers threw in generous severance and the same medical benefits at age 65 that other retirees would receive—allowing them to immediately absorb those added costs during good times in order to reduce future costs. This came courtesy of tying pension payments to a much lower salary base, reducing them further by the early-retirement factor, and keeping salary-inflation bloat out of those future pension payments.

Despite signing waivers, older workers might still have grounds to sue employers who don't follow proper procedures under the Older Workers Benefit Protection Act (OWBPA). This follow-up legislation to the original Age Discrimination in Employment Act (ADEA) is intended to protect older workers from discrimination related to severance and other employee benefits.

Contrary to popular wisdom about how people are retiring early to fulfill dreams, it's largely due to this dual carrot-or-stick incentive early retirement or dismissal strategy. Later in this Hour, we'll look at the retirement-planning damage done by forcing out employees in their forties and fifties. First, though, let's examine cash-balance plans—the stealth weapon employers now deploy to bomb the secure-retirement concept back into the Stone Age.

CASH-BALANCE DEFINED-BENEFIT PENSIONS

Let's drop the pretenses—this will not be a balanced treatment of balanced-in-employer-favor cash-balance plans. However, before confronting the controversy, let's first examine the very simple concept underlying these plans. To do that, forget your current pension for now, and assume you're leaving your job to join a brand-new company using a cash-balance plan from the get-go.

Because cash-balance plans (CBP) are based on "accounts," many employees mistakenly liken them to 401(k) plans. However, a CBP is a defined-benefit plan; you don't have control over your account. The employer invests the aggregate funds credited to all employee accounts to ensure they sufficiently cover employees' accrued balances. This is markedly different from investing your own 401(k) balance.

For starters, let's acknowledge that the earlier formula used in traditional defined-benefit plans might as well be a deep corporate secret. Unless they're near retirement, few employees with such plans know how much they're entitled to should they leave the company. In contrast, cash-balance plans take an in-your-face approach of letting you know at all times how much pension you've accumulated. The formula, virtually shouted on the mountaintop, looks something like this:

$$NCB = (SAL \times PCT \times SERVFACT) + (OCB \times I) + OCB$$

NCB (new cash balance): This is the latest lump-sum value of your account, updated (usually) every month.

OCB (old cash balance): This is the amount your account was worth the last time the balance was computed.

SAL (salary base): This is some measure of your current salary, either actual or averaged over a recent period. It is stated as monthly in the formula.

PCT (percent factor): The monthly addition to your account is computed from this percentage of SAL.

SERVFACT (service factor): This starts out as 1 your first year, but is increased to reward longevity.

I (interest rate): Your OCB grows at this rate each month—usually variable, tied to Treasury bill rates. It is stated as monthly ($\frac{1}{12}$ of annual) in the formula.

Taking an example, let's assume I = 6 percent annually (.005 or .5%) monthly, PCT = .06 (6%), and you're starting salary is $36,000 ($3,000 monthly).

$$NCB = (3,000)(.06)(1) + (0)(.005) = \$180$$

Now, let's assume that one year later, interest rates have spiked and I is now 9 percent annually (.075 percent monthly), your end-of-year account balance was $2500, and you've just received a combination raise/promotion to $42,000 ($3,500 monthly).

$$NCB = (3,500)(.06)(1) + (2,500)(.0075) + 2,500 = \$2,897.50$$

Finally, 10 years later, let's assume the same basic formula, but your service factor is raised to 1.25 on your 10-year anniversary. You're a fast tracker now making $90,000 a year ($7,500 monthly), you've accumulated $60,000 in your account, and the yearly interest rate is now 7.5 percent:

$$NCB = (7,500)(.06)(1.25) + (60,000)(.00625) + 60,000 = \$60,937.50$$

In 10 years and one month you've earned 60,937.50 in pension. That far exceeds the amount you'd have accumulated in any traditional defined-benefit pension plan. Thus, rather than being back-loaded, the cash-balance plan is much more evenly loaded, although still somewhat weighted towards longevity because of the rising salary base and service factor.

So, what's wrong with cash-balance plans? Actually, they're better for young employees who are likely to job hop. After five years, they'd be vested and able to take away a much larger balance to roll into an IRA than they would if they'd been in a traditional pension.

FYI Many critics say that cash-balance plans are over-hyped as "portable pensions," because the vesting requirements often mean that early-career employees who work at companies less than five years walk away with nothing.

"Gee, swell," you're probably saying—if you're a mid-career employee who has recently been told you were being switched to a cash-balance plan and discovered that the pension you anticipated is now just a dream. So let's take a closer look at your nightmare.

PENSION POLITICS: CONTROVERSIAL CONVERSIONS

In the last 10 years, millions of mid-life Americans have discovered that they've been playing Charlie Brown to their employers' Lucy. Just as they prepared to kick their heels in anticipation of a golden pension, it was yanked away, leaving them to land in a pile of peanuts.

FYI Following IBM's conversion to a cash-balance plan, IBM employee cash-balance activists maintain a Web site (www.cashpensions.com) with an incredible wealth of information concerning cash-balance plan issues and developments around the country. It includes a listing of about 400 companies that have converted to cash-balance plans (about one fifth of large employers have).

No, they aren't being robbed—legally, anyway. It's just that they're being left holding the bag—a bag full of the amount of money their pensions are now worth. Instead of watching that amount shoot up like a giant weed from now until retirement in their traditional pension, they'll now watch it grow like grass in hot, dry August in a new cash-balance plan.

True, some companies are including a little gardening magic in the conversion. They're adding a layer of sod over the grass in the form of a conversion bonus, and liberally applying seed and fertilizer with a higher service-factor multiple to help it grow faster. In fact, some are even keeping the old pension football in place for employees who were just a few inches (years) away from achieving their original pension goals.

To a growing cadre of unwilling convertees, however, such employer "benevolence" is way short and wide of doing the right thing. They cite studies showing their ultimate cash-balance pensions will be from 25 percent to two thirds less than what they would have finally grown to in the traditional plan. Their anger has been heard in a big way in corporate boardrooms such as IBM's, where a 2000 shareholder resolution calling for rescinding the cash-balance conversion garnered about 28 percent support, a highly embarrassing result for a management-opposed resolution.

Although that vote had no effect, intense lobbying by IBM employees did. The hue and cry that immediately followed the 1999 conversion announcement led management to expand the right to keep the old plan. Instead of the original narrow segment of employees within five years of retirement, IBM said that any employee at least age 40 with at least 10 years experience could keep the old plan.

Meanwhile, the IBM clamor attracted sharp government focus on cash-balance plans. Consequently, the IRS announced a moratorium on granting "IRS letters of determination" that would allow companies to proceed with conversions. Soon after, the Department of Labor and Pension Benefits Guarantee Corporation began investigating cash-balance plans. Then the General Accounting Office issued a report saying that companies should give employees more notice a change is coming, and doing a better job of informing them of the personal-financial implications of the conversion.

Then the courts and Congress stepped in. The Supreme Court upheld a ruling in favor of a lawsuit plaintiff who claimed the employer failed to use appropriate interest-rate assumptions. The so-called "whipsaw" ruling now requires employers to use the more employee-favorable conversion-calculation method. Meanwhile, Congress considered banning *wearaway*— a post-conversion account-growth adjustment that was keeping older-worker account balances dead in the water after conversion.

STRICTLY DEFINED

Wearaway refers to the practice of "wearing away" the higher employer termination obligation under the preconversion pension by not adding to the cash-balance account until its lower conversion balance catches up. For example, if the old account is worth $75,000 and the converted amount would be $73,000, the employer doesn't add to the $75,000 until the new account is actually worth $75,000. Confusing and seemingly unfair? You bet!

Unfortunately, all this scrutiny, litigation, and legislation will probably only delay the inevitable resumption of cash-balance plan adoption—especially with the new administration's more hands-off business policies. The good news is that future conversions are likely to be introduced more carefully—with better employee education and more employees having a choice between the old and new plans. The bad news is that your employer might not be among the good (news) guys. In that case, you'd be well advised to watch your back by educating fellow employees, and run both traditional plan and cash-balance retirement scenarios for yourself.

Congress stepped into the fray with the new tax bill passed in May 2001. Now clearer notice to employees of the significant reduction in future benefits would be required within in a reasonable time before the conversion takes place. The only way to avoid the notice requirement is to allow employees the option of choosing the new or old plan. Penalties for failure to notify properly can be as high as $500,000 and based on $100 per day per omitted person. ERISA was amended to include the notification requirements and any cut in early retirement benefits must also be included in these notifications. Full regulations must be in place within 90 days of enactment.

NORMAL AND EARLY RETIREMENT OPTIONS

Whether traditional or cash balance, the bottom line on your defined-benefit retirement plan is the how much, how, and when of receiving its benefits. Not many years ago, virtually all benefits were paid no earlier than the normal retirement age of 65, even if retirement occurred earlier. However, today many plans will start benefits as early as 55, for either normal or solicited early retirement. What's now rare is to delay benefits until 65 if retiring earlier, although most plans stipulate that employers allow that delay upon request of a normal-case early-retiring employee. Employees that request this delay usually intend to continue working or use other resources to fund their early retirement.

Thus, there are a couple of possibilities regarding payout:

- **Leave the company before normal or solicited (early) retirement.** If the lump-sum value of a traditional pension doesn't exceed $3,500, it's given to the employee as a lump sum. If it does, the employee receives monthly payments (or their lump-sum discounted value) at age 65, based on the termination-time partial-vesting formula. However, most cash-balance pension plans stipulate that employees can take any size account balance with them at the time of termination regardless of age.

- **Retire before normal retirement age.** The employee immediately starts receiving permanently reduced (from formula) monthly payments to factor in the longer payment period. However, the reduced amount might be temporarily increased until Social Security kicks in.

  The employee also has the option of receiving a lump sum equal to the actuarially determined present value (until expected death) of these payments. Finally, if retirement was enticed, the monthly payments might start immediately, but be calculated as though the employee was older with more years of service. Usually, such retirement offers are only available in this form, rather than as lump sums, but an additional bonus lump-sum treated as salary might be included with the offer.

- **Retire at or after normal retirement age.** The employee has a choice of receiving either monthly payments based on the normal formula or an equivalent discounted lump sum. Just as with Social Security, the advantage of retiring late is that you might end up with a bigger pension. Some companies allow those extra work years to translate into extra service years and higher average base salary to be used in the ultimate pension calculation.

While the opportunity to retire early can a godsend, it has numerous disadvantages—especially if you're not doing it to grab a sweetener because of fear of an imminent job loss. First and foremost, your monthly payout could easily double or triple if you retire at 60 or 65, instead of 55. Almost as important, when you take payments early, they're based on a less-inflated wage base. Pensions aren't normally adjusted for inflation, so the monthly payment that sounds good now will seem measly 20 years later when you still might have 20 more years to live. Finally, if you're less than age 59½ and take your payments as an equivalent lump sum that you don't roll over into an IRA, you'll pay a 10 percent penalty on top of an unduly high tax rate.

FYI The average age at retirement is now 62 and falling—with more than 30 percent of workers retiring before age 60. This trend is apparently influenced almost as much by employer incentives and layoffs as by individual choice, with 43 percent of retirements occurring earlier than planned.

Against these significant disadvantages, early retirement has at least one minor pleasant surprise: If you choose the monthly-payout option, you won't incur a tax penalty, regardless of age. You'll simply owe tax (but not FICA) as though it was a paycheck. But don't be so grateful to start getting the payments or grabbing the lump sum that you don't check out its accuracy. Because employers frequently make errors in computing pensions, a number of successful consulting businesses have emerged to help employees find such errors—in exchange for a sizeable percentage of restored payout.

Here are several major sources of miscalculation:

- The person doing the calculation failed first grade when the three R's were covered: Readin' (plan rules), 'Ritin' (computer program inputting), and 'Rithmetic (basic math errors).

- Interest rates are wrong or applied incorrectly.

- Mistakes are made in computing salary base or years of service due to poor company records or improper application of rules about bonuses, breaks in service, and so on.

- The wrong balance was carried forward when the plan was updated, or after a merger putting you in the new company's plan.

- The calculation is based on out-of-date information concerning you, or even on a different employee's file!

You don't have to be considering early retirement to worry about these errors, which occur frequently in all types of retirement calculations. In fact, the *Pension Benefit Guaranty Corporation (PBGC)* estimated recently that 8 percent of 1995 retiree pension calculations were erroneous.

STRICTLY DEFINED

The **Pension Benefit Guaranty Corporation (PBGC)** was created as part of the 1974 ERISA legislation. The PBGC acts as an insurance carrier for 43 million Americans enrolled in 38,000 private pension plans, paying what is owed them if their company pension plans fail. That's the rhetoric, anyway. Unfortunately, the PBGC has been a mixed success, plagued by its own underfunding.

EMPLOYEE RIGHTS AND PENSION TRENDS

Perhaps you're now suffering pension paranoia—certainty that your employer is going to get you, either accidentally or intentionally. If so, good, because you're more likely to exercise your considerable rights—under ERISA. One is the right not to remain silent, and instead periodically ask your employer for a projection of your potential future pension benefit. (Technically, you're allowed to request this in writing once every 12 months.) It's a good idea to do that periodically so that if something seems out of kilter, you can start investigating and rectify matters while errors are fresh and you have direct access to benefits staff.

To make sense of the benefits statement, though, you'll also need the summary plan document (SPD), which your employer is required to provide within 90 days of when you become covered by the plan and at certain later intervals when the plan is changed. Although you're less likely to need them, you're also entitled to pay moderate fees to obtain copies of other plan documents filed with ERISA, such as the Form 5500 Annual Report that contains detailed financial information about the entire plan.

Your pension rights also include crucial rights related to an offer of early retirement. For example, you must be given 45 days to consider an offer, and you have seven days to change your mind once you've accepted or rejected it. Early retirement or not, if you're at least in your 40s and appear to be in line for a sizeable pension, it's best to get an early start on understanding all your pension rights. To get the full scoop, obtain "What You Should Know About Your Pension Rights" from the Department of Labor, or access it online at www.dol.gov/dol/pwba/public/pubs/youknow/knowtoc.htm.

Pension Trends

Equally important, you should know about what's likely to happen in general as pensions evolve (or regress) in coming years. Despite the IRS moratorium, cash-balance pension conversions continue. That's because many companies had already received IRS determination letters before the IRS action, and it's just taken time to roll out their new plans. Whether you wind up in a cash-balance plan or not, the chances that your current traditional plan will still exist 20 years from now are pretty small. So in doing your planning, take the benefits it might provide with many grains of salt.

Meanwhile, count on a continuing flow of sugar in the sweeteners companies offer to encourage early retirement. They simply don't want to pay full benefits to a continued heavy retirement wave of Baby Boomers until 2030. Also, expect additional 401(k) sweeteners if your company does convert to a cash-balance plan. Companies do want to rid themselves of fat pension obligations to older workers. But they also anticipate the coming baby bust making it difficult to fully staff anticipated growth while losing so many older workers.

And that's where cash-balance plans might be just the answer, for employees, to a new retirement dynamic beyond their immediate value, to companies, in reducing currently huge future traditional-pension obligations. Many experts predict that ERISA might eventually be modified to recognize something being called "phased retirement." Where many companies now are hiring back normal-age retirees with special skills as contract workers to meet niche needs, companies would rather be able to keep such workers in the first place. The problem is that keeping them would cause their traditional pensions to mushroom out of control as their salaries continued increasing.

FYI A recent study by top benefits-consulting firm, William M. Mercer, confirmed that very few employers have formal programs for phased retirement. However, about 60 percent have a formal policy for rehiring retirees. An amazing 16 percent of companies said they want to encourage continued employment of all their older workers, and about 30 percent want to keep older workers with special skills or roles.

The solution is to keep workers as full-time employees with part-time hours, and a part-time salary to match. But that approach can run afoul of certain current ERISA provisions. However, if a formal, ERISA-sanctioned approach to doing this were approved, it could fit hand in glove with cash-balance pensions, simply continuing to build up worker accounts according to their reduced earnings for part-time hours. So if you're now 40 to 50, and think you want to work beyond normal retirement age for both fulfillment and economic reasons, keep building your skills. You might get your wish by being in the first wave of official phased retirees.

U.S. Federal Employee Pensions

Finally, if you work for Uncle Sam, you might be wondering why you're in the last wave of employees discussed in this Hour. Face it, you're used to a lack of respect, but it's not that, it's just that your plans work so differently from what we've discussed so far. For example, you can retire much younger and receive benefits well before age 55. And, instead of the 401(k) or related DC (defined-contribution) plans covered in Hours 10, "401(k) and Related Plans," and 11, "Small Business/Self-Employed Plans," you have the

(Washington) D.C. Thrift Plan—which has just been given a matching-contribution transfusion to cure its financial anemia. Here's a very brief overview, including references to detailed information provided by the U.S. government.

Two Retirement Systems

Federal employees fall under one of two retirement programs: the old Civil Service Retirement System (CSRS) or the new Federal Employees Retirement System (FERS). FERS was created in the mid '80s due to a new law that put newly hired federal employees into the Social Security program, and thus into FERS. In addition, current employees were given the right to switch to FERS under a complicated conversion process. The result is everything you'd expect of the federal bureaucracy, a two-tiered system that makes the IRS tax code look like a first-grade primer.

Both FERS and CSRS include a defined-benefit pension plan, making federal retirees the only class of employees confident of continued coverage under such pensions for years to come. Each plan also provides a 401(k)-like Thrift Savings Plan, and FERS participants also get Social Security. Thus, the CSRS pension formulas that apply to holdover employees who remain covered under that plan are more generous. Beyond this basic explanation, these plans are far too complicated to adequately explain here. However, Uncle Sam recently created a terrific resource that enables any federal employee to see where they stand in terms of all these plan possibilities— the federal retirement calculator located at www.seniors.gov/fedcalc.html.

JUST A MINUTE

For a better understanding of federal retirement plans than Uncle Sam provides, consider the 2002 *CRS Retirement Planning Guide* and the 2002 *FERS Retirement Planning Guide*. These and other financial-planning publications for federal employees are published by FEDweek (www.fedweek.com/NewPublications/newbookcart.htm).

Thrift Savings Plan

As of early 2001, the defined-contribution Thrift Savings Plan is new and improved, much more like a typical private-sector 401(k) plan. It now has matching contributions, expanded contribution limits, and immediate participation eligibility. Despite adding two new investment options, small-cap and international, it's still stingy in that regard. These details, however, are different, depending on whether you're in the Civil Service Retirement System (CSRS) or the Federal Employees Retirement System (FERS). For complete details, check out the Summary of the Thrift Savings Plan for Federal Employees at www.tsp.gov/cgi-bin/byteserver.cgi/forms/tspbk08.pdf.

Hour's Up!

It's time to see if you understand all the complexities of pension programs and the trends affecting them.

Answer True or False to the following statements:

1. Once you've worked at least 20 years for a company, you're guaranteed half the maximum pension that you could ultimately earn.

2. The consulting firm, William Webster, designed the first defined-benefit plan.

3. Defined-benefit plans were never intended to meet a retiree's complete financial needs.

4. The so-called cash-balance plan was a major step in making employees less dependent on their companies' financial performance, by balancing 50 percent stock payments with 50 percent cash in each pension payment.

5. If you're made an early-retirement offer, it's wise to wonder if this is so good for me, then why is it so good for the company or vice versa.

6. The higher your salary, the more money gets added to your cash-balance account each year.

7. Consumer advocates are extremely worried that the big shift in pension policy will lead to a proliferation of cash-balance checking services charging high fees for loans against your future pension.

8. It's legal to be receiving government pension payments while working for another company from which you might receive a future pension.

9. Many low-fee nonprofit organizations have sprung up that help you find possible huge errors in your pension calculation. They charge for their services on a sliding scale according to ability to pay.

10. The Department of Labor provides helpful information about pensions that you can request by mail or find on a Web site.

HOUR 13

Traditional/Roth IRAs

LESSON PLAN:

In this Hour you will learn about ...

- The basics of self-established IRAs: (traditional) tax-deductible, Roth, non-tax-deductible, and spousal.
- How they differ from employer-established IRAs.
- Determining which is best for you.
- Contribution and withdrawal rules.
- Recent IRA developments and trends.

How much is enough—to retire, that is? As we saw in Hour 12, "Defined-Benefit and Federal Pension Plans," the amount in your employer pension might not be enough. And employer-sponsored defined-contribution accounts from Hours 10, "401(k) and Related Plans" and 11, "Small Business/Self-Employed Plans," will likely do just that—merely contribute. They're unlikely to fully provide your total retirement needs.

Besides, either your current or future employer might not offer either of these retirement components. Thus, you must also act individually, by taking advantage of the opportunity to invest the maximum allowed every year in individual retirement arrangement (IRA) accounts.

IRA ELIGIBILITY AND CONTRIBUTION BASICS

An IRA offers everyone with earned income, or everyone married to someone with earned income, a tax-advantaged way to invest for retirement. That could even include a three-year-old child actor who is allowed to contribute the current maximum of $2,000 annually as long as he or she earns at least that much. Not to be overly dramatic, but just imagine how much that actor's contribution will be worth at age 70!

The tax law passed in May 2001 increases the maximum contributions allowed beginning in 2002. If you are over 50, the maximums are even higher. The following table shows how the maximums will change.

	Over 50	All Others
2002 to 2004	$3,500	$3,000
2005	$4,500	$4,000
2006 to 2007	$5,000	$4,000
2008	$6,000	$5,000

That's the key with IRA accounts: Contribute the maximum as early and as often as possible. To keep things simple, only the current $2,000 maximum is mentioned throughout this Hour, but remember, it's going to be much higher beginning in 2002.

First you must figure out which type(s) of IRA you can invest in, which are best to invest in for your situation, and how you should invest. Doing so requires understanding both eligibility and withdrawal rules, which vary for each type, and allowable investments. This Hour will guide you through all that, directly compare the plans, and provide pointers on determining your best choices.

Let's take a look at the eligibility and contribution rules for each type of IRA—traditional, Roth, and nondeductible. They are government plans, so expect them to be confusing, but we'll simplify them as best possible.

FYI The bible for IRAs is IRS Publication 590. You can call to order it from the IRS at 1-800-829-1040 or download a copy at http://ftp.fedworld.gov/pub/irs-pdf/p590.pdf.

The main requirement for opening an IRA is earned income that matches at least the amount you plan to contribute. Earned income comprises wages, salaries, tips, bonuses, professional fees, and other amounts from providing services. In calculating whether you have enough income to qualify, you cannot use earnings or profits from property, such as rental income, pension or annuity income, deferred compensation payments, or income from a partnership in which you did not provide services.

The first IRA, introduced in 1974, is the tax-deductible version that is now called the traditional IRA. It works just like a 401(k) in that what you contribute reduces your taxable income dollar for dollar. (Unfortunately, the government provides no matching contributions!) In the mid '80s, Congress took the deductibility feature away for most working people who also had an employer-sponsored plan and created the nondeductible IRA. However, as it became apparent that the tax advantage wasn't enticing many middle-class taxpayers, the Roth IRA emerged as a way to accumulate totally tax-free earnings over the years without a current tax deduction.

But if you're unfortunate enough to make too much money (insert violin music) for a traditional or Roth IRA, your Uncle Sam hasn't totally disowned you. You can contribute to a nondeductible IRA, which provides neither tax deduction nor tax-free earnings, but at least allows tax deferral of earnings on your investments until retirement. That's still a big advantage if you're in the above-30 percent tax brackets, because you might pay (the new lower) 25 or 15 percent rates when tapping those earnings during retirement.

With this preliminary snapshot of the IRA landscape, let's now take a hike into the rugged back country of the general and specific contribution rules.

TAX-DEDUCTIBLE IRA ELIGIBILITY AND CONTRIBUTIONS

The tax-deductible (traditional) IRA is primarily for people who have no employer-sponsored retirement plan. There are a number of exceptions that allow working people who have an employer-sponsored plan to open a tax-deductible IRA as well. These exceptions include:

1. A single person with adjusted gross income (AGI) below $43,000 can establish a tax-deductible IRA even when participating in an employer retirement plan—although subject to a deduction *phaseout* when AGI is between $33,000 and $43,000. For example, with a $36,000 AGI in 2001, the contribution (and deduction) is limited to $1,400 (based on the IRS phaseout worksheet in your 1040 tax booklet.)

STRICTLY DEFINED

Phaseouts apply to many tax deductions and credits. The basic principle is that starting at an adjusted gross income (AGI) that we'll call the phaseout-floor AGI (PF AGI), the benefit starts phasing out. It's lost completely at the phaseout ceiling AGI (PC AGI). If your AGI falls between PC AGI and PF AGI, this formula determines your (retained) percentage benefit:

$$100 \times ([PC - Your\ AGI] \div [PC - PF])$$

2. A married couple with joint AGI under $63,000—filing a joint return and both participating in employer-sponsored plans—is eligible to establish a tax-deductible IRA. The phaseout starts at $53,000, so if

their AGI is $57,000, they can contribute $1,200 each (or $2,400 total).

3. If a married couple files a joint return and only one spouse participates in an employer-sponsored plan, the rules change. The person who does not participate in a plan at work is eligible to establish a $2,000 tax-deductible IRA as long as the joint AGI is below $150,000, and proportionately less in the phaseout range, $150,000 to $160,000.

If you're not eligible based on these rules, don't despair. You still may be eligible for a Roth IRA—and will always be eligible for a nondeductible IRA.

JUST A MINUTE

Two special cases apply if you're married, filing separately. If you're not legally separated, forget contributions if either spouse is covered by an employer plan; the AGI limit is ridiculously low. If legally separated (for at least one year) either spouse meeting the eligibility requirements applying to single filers can open an account.

Roth IRA Eligibility and Contributions

The Roth IRA is seen as the best deal in town by many financial planners. You don't have a tax deduction up front, but all your money grows tax-free and you'll never have to pay taxes on it as long as you don't withdraw it before age of $59^1/_2$ (allowing for a few exceptions). Another huge benefit is that, unlike traditional IRAs and 401(k)s, there are no rules about when you must take out the money once you reach $59^1/_2$. You are not obligated to start taking it at any age. Your heirs will be happier, too: They have to pay taxes only on the earnings, not on your contribution amounts.

You can have a Roth IRA and actively participate in your employer-sponsored retirement plan. There are maximum earnings limits, but they are higher than the ones for a tax-deductible IRA. Also like the tax-deductible IRA, your allowed contribution phases out near the maximum:

1. If you are single with an AGI up to $95,000, you can contribute the full $2,000 if you haven't contributed to any other type of IRA. The phaseout range is $95,000 to $110,000.

2. If you're married filing jointly with combined AGI up to $150,000, then you can contribute the full $2,000 each, or a total of $4,000. The phaseout range is $150,000 to $160,000.

3. If you're married filing separately, it's a joke. All contributions based on earnings from $0 to $10,000 are subject to phaseout rules.

Now we'll take a look at the nondeductible traditional IRA, still a great way to build retirement funds tax-deferred if you don't qualify for the Roth.

Non-Tax-Deductible IRA Eligibility and Contributions

If your household AGI exceeds $160,000—or $160,000,000 for that matter—the only type of IRA you can use is a nondeductible IRA. Although not as tax advantageous, it does allow you to invest $2,000 annually (per working spouse) for retirement tax-deferred. It's the only tax-advantaged IRA game in town if you don't meet tax-deductible (traditional) IRA or Roth IRA eligibility requirements.

This IRA defers tax on all earnings until retirement. Your contributions are tax-free upon withdrawal after age 59$\frac{1}{2}$, because you've already paid taxes on them. That is, provided you've kept track of them. Keep a file of your year-end statements that show your annual contributions.

JUST A MINUTE

You don't necessarily have to do paid work to open an IRA. If your spouse has earned income of at least $4,000, but you have none, you can still contribute $2,000 each to any type of IRA for which your spouse qualifies—in a spousal IRA. If you don't take advantage, you're guilty of spousal (IRA) abuse.

Common Rules

How can you contribute to an IRA. Let's count the ways. You can do it all at once, starting January 1 of the tax year for which you're establishing it. In other words, you don't have to already have earned the amount you put in the IRA, just make sure you eventually do. Setting it up with the full amount as early as possible is preferable, because you're giving your money the longest opportunity to grow. However, you can also wait until your tax-filing deadline (plus extensions) the following year, or you can make your contributions in as many installments until then as you wish.

Regardless of what type of IRA you establish, be sure you carefully follow the eligibility and phaseout rules for contributions. If you contribute more than the eligible amount, you'll owe 6 percent excise tax on the amount by which you exceed the eligible amount. However, you can avoid the excess tax if you catch your mistake before the contribution deadline. You can "unwind" your contribution by withdrawing the money before your tax-filing date (plus extensions).

You can also unwind contributions by the deadline if you discover you don't want to contribute as much (but really, find a way to afford the full contribution!).

Whether you unwind due to a mistake or by choice, you also must withdraw any earnings on that money and pay taxes on those earnings. It's something you hope you will never have to do, but if you end up with an emergency or lose a job it gives you an escape valve. Your ability to unwind is why you should make the contribution as early as possible in the year and take advantage of the tax-free gains for a longer time.

IRA WITHDRAWAL RULES

Just like Marvin K. Mooney (Money?) of Dr. Seuss fame, the time will come when you have to go, go, go. Go, that is, to the financial institution housing your IRA and turn some of that loot loose—unless it's in a Roth IRA. IRS IRA rules say you can start making withdrawals at age $59^1/_2$, but must start making minimum withdrawals by April 1 of the year after reaching age $70^1/_2$—or pay a 50 percent excise tax on the amount not withdrawn as required.

GO TO ▶
These distributions are being simplified for future retirees, as discussed in the "Plan Trends" section later in this Hour. We'll take a closer look at retirement distribution management in Hour 23, "Managing Retirement Distributions."

Meanwhile, taxes on anything withdrawn from a traditional (tax-deductible) IRA are assessed at your ordinary-income rate (the rate on your last dollar of earnings at the time of withdrawal). Once you start withdrawing, you can take a lump sum, irregular chunks, or regular periodic distributions. However, because taxes will be due, it's best to minimize your tax hit by taking periodic distributions in order not to push part of a distribution up into higher tax brackets.

These distributions can be set on a formula based on your life expectancy, the joint life expectancies of you and your beneficiary, or a periodic distribution that you pick provided it does not exceed your life expectancy or life expectancy of you and your beneficiary. Don't withdraw too slowly; any money left in a traditional or nondeductible IRA after your death will be immediately taxable and reduce your heirs' inheritance.

For most people, though, the problem isn't taking too little money, too late, it's taking too much money, too soon. If you need your funds from any of the three IRA types before age 59½, they can be withdrawn, but (other than for a few exceptions covered below) you'll have to pay a 10 percent penalty plus taxes on a least part of the withdrawal. You will not have to pay a penalty or taxes on the contributions made into a Roth (as long as the money is deposited for five years or more) or nondeductible IRA, since you paid taxes on that money before it went into the IRA.

Taxation and penalties for premature, normal, and insufficient withdrawals from a nondeductible IRA are identical to tax-deductible IRAs, with one key exception: You don't pay taxes on the money you actually contributed. For example, if your contributions totaled $10,000 and your account is worth $20,000. You can take out the $10,000 in contributions and not owe tax. That money was taxed before it went into the IRA.

The Roth IRA has fewer restrictive rules on withdrawals, provided you leave the money in the Roth for at least five years. Once you've held the Roth for more than five years, you can take out any of the money you contributed without paying any taxes or penalties no matter what age you are.

You can also withdraw any earnings without penalty, but you will have to pay tax on the earnings if you begin withdrawing the money before age 59½. You can avoid the penalty if you meet one of these criteria:

1. You are disabled.
2. You are the beneficiary of a deceased IRA owner.
3. You are a first-time homebuyer and withdraw $10,000 or less. (No tax owed either!)
4. You need to pay significant unreimbursed medical expenses.
5. You are paying for medical insurance after a job loss.
6. You are using the money for qualified higher education expenses.
7. You are at least 55 and "separated from service" (retired or terminated from a job).

ROLLOVERS AND ROTH CONVERSIONS

The tax advantages of IRAs can be so valuable that you might be wondering if there's any way you can legally cheat and get more money into their tax-deferred and tax-free growth machines. Well, sort of.

Tax law allows your traditional IRA to be a tax-deferred (continuation) repository for funds received from a complete or partial (lump-sum) qualified retirement plan distribution. For example, upon termination, you can roll over your 401(k) account or defined-benefit lump sums from an ex-employer into an IRA—although you can't roll over normal monthly pension payments.

JUST A MINUTE

 Ideally, you should (and are allowed to) set up a new traditional (conduit) tax-deductible IRA for an ex-employer lump sum. That will allow you to roll them into a new employer's qualified retirement plan at any time if permitted and desirable. You'll be ineligible for the rollover, however, if you intermingle those funds with funds you contributed to an IRA.

Another type of "rollover" is actually a conversion of your traditional (tax-deductible) IRA into a Roth IRA. This is allowed at any time, providing you don't exceed the $100,000 AGI income ceiling in the year of the conversion. You're liable immediately for all taxes due on the conversion amount, as though it's an unpenalized distribution. You're far better off paying these taxes from funds outside your IRA, or the reduction in IRA assets will negate a considerable part of the advantage of converting.

GO TO ▶
Should you convert to a Roth? It involves a complicated analysis of the tax impacts of such a decision. We'll cover conversion strategies and decisions in Hour 18, "Retirement Plan Management."

Why do this? It could be a great move in a year when your tax rate is low, but you anticipate a higher tax rate when you'd be withdrawing those funds from the traditional (tax-deductible) IRA in retirement. You'd take care of the tax obligation now, and then not have to pay a dime ever on further earnings from the converted amount. For example, suppose you were laid off from your job, but got another one after a few months. If you have a good emergency fund, you could use it to pay the taxes on the conversion, which might only be 15 percent if your layoff-year income suffered enough.

COMPARE IRA ALTERNATIVES

Your head must be spinning right now with all the alternatives we've discussed. First, just to help you review the key points, here is a chart that summarizes the differences:

Comparison of IRA Alternatives

	Tax-Deductible	Roth	Nondeductible
Eligibility— must have earned income that at least totals the amount to be contributed (max $2,000 contribution per spouse) or be a spousal IRA.	Anyone who does not have an employer-sponsored retirement plan. Also, single— AGI $43,000,** married— AGI $63,000.**	Single—AGI $110,000** Married—AGI $160,000.**	No income limits even if you do have an employer-sponsored retirement plan.
Early withdrawals (before age 59^1/$_2$) for higher education, death, or disability.	Yes, tax must be paid on withdrawals.	Yes, tax must be paid on earnings withdrawn, but not on contributions.	Yes, tax must be paid on earnings withdrawn, but not on contributions.
Early withdrawal (before age 59^1/$_2$); first-time home purchase up to $10,000.	Yes, tax must be paid on withdrawals.	Yes, tax must be paid on earnings withdrawn, but not on contributions.	If held for more than five years, no taxes need to be paid. If held less than five years, taxes must not be paid on earnings, but on contributions.
Other early withdrawals.	10% penalties plus tax on withdrawals.	10% penalties on withdrawal of earnings plus tax on earnings with some exceptions.*	10% penalties on withdrawal of earnings plus tax on earnings with some exceptions.*
Taxability at age 59^1/$_2$.	Yes	No	Only on earnings, not on original contributions.

Exceptions include: medical expenses that exceed 7.5% of your AGI, or if you collect federal unemployment benefits for 12 consecutive weeks and use IRA withdrawals to pay for health insurance.

**All are subject to phaseout rules discussed above.*

If you qualify for both the tax-deductible IRA and the Roth IRA, your first question should be: Which is best? The key consideration is tax impact. If you expect your tax rate will be lower at the time of your retirement then you definitely are better off delaying taxes.

If you expect your tax rate will be the same or higher, the Roth makes more sense. All the money you invest using a Roth can be taken out tax-free. All the money withdrawn from the tax-deductible IRA will be taxed at your tax rate at retirement.

The following table compares a fully funded tax-deductible IRA and a partially funded Roth IRA. The Roth IRA figures are developed assuming that the amount you will need to pay in taxes will reduce the amount you can deposit into your Roth.

Contributions: Roth vs. Traditional (Tax-Deductible) IRA*

Type	Years	Amount	Tax Now	Tax Later	After-Tax Net**
Example 1					
Traditional	30	$2,560*	28%	28%	$25,048
Roth	30	$2,000	28%	28%	$26,535
Example 2					
Traditional	30	$2,560*	28%	15%	$28,497
Roth	30	$2,000	28%	15%	$26,535
Example 3					
Traditional	50	$2,300*	15%	28%	$124,919
Roth	50	$2,000	15%	28%	$148,715

*The amount over $2,000 comes from tax savings, and is invested in a mutual fund that will be taxed at the capital gains rate of 20% at the same time the traditional IRA is cashed in and taxes at the then ordinary income tax rate.

**Assume 9% annualized investment growth

The examples in this table show that the Roth is preferable unless you have the Example 2 situation of contributing when in a higher tax bracket than the one you'll be in when withdrawing. That might happen, but don't count on it. Example 1 uses the same starting and ending tax brackets, and the

Roth still comes out the winner by a slight bit. But that understates the Roth's advantage, because starting at age 70, you must take minimum annual distributions from your traditional IRA. However, you never have to take them from the Roth, so you continue tax-free growth that will never be taxed. Meanwhile, the traditional IRA has lost some of its power due to withdrawals and increasingly smaller amounts are growing tax-deferred.

Finally, Example 3 shows why the Roth is the clear-cut winner when you're young and in the lowest tax bracket and end up withdrawing in a higher tax bracket.

FYI This comparison is based on some very simple assumptions. If you would like to take a closer look at your specific set of circumstances, there is an excellent online calculator that compares the Roth to the traditional IRA at www.datachimp.com/articles/rothira/rothcalc.htm.

The only reason to choose a nondeductible traditional IRA is if you do not qualify for the Roth IRA. It does not make sense to put money that is already taxed into a tax-deferred vehicle rather than the tax-free Roth. Roth withdrawals at retirement are completely tax-free, while the earnings withdrawn from the non-tax-deductible traditional IRA will be taxed at your current income tax rate.

UNDERSTAND INVESTMENT ALTERNATIVES

Now that you know the various IRA alternatives, the next key decision is where to open your retirement account. IRAs can be opened through a bank, an insurance company, a mutual fund, or a brokerage company. Each alternative will have different investment possibilities.

In addition to the investment alternatives, you should also pay close attention to the administrative fees you will be charged. Also, remember that there will be investment fees depending on the type of investments you choose. If you choose to use mutual funds, then you will definitely have yearly operating costs that will be a drain on your investment. These can be as low as 0.18 percent if you choose an index fund, but as high as 3 percent in an aggressive fund. There could also be upfront sales loads that will reduce the amount put into your IRA, which usually range from 3 to 6 percent. If you choose to invest in stocks, then you will need to consider the costs of buying and selling those stocks.

GO TO ▶

In Hour 22, "Pre-Retirement Plan-ning," we will be exploring pre-retirement planning to review ways to structure your nest egg. We'll take a closer look at asset allocation and risk management.

How do people invest who currently have IRAs? According to an In-vestment Company Institute study, 49 percent of IRA funds are invested through mutual funds, 30 percent through brokerage companies, 10 percent through banks, and 9 percent through life insurance companies.

Once you decide where to open your account, you should next consider what types of investments to include in your IRA. You can buy stocks, bonds, equity mutual funds or bond mutual funds. You can also choose to deposit the money in certificates of deposits and money market funds.

Now that you have a good understanding of the IRA alternatives, we'll take a look at IRA changes and trends.

Plan Trends

We've already discussed the increased contributions under the new tax law. Another key change simplifies how you must take money out of your tradi-tional IRA. Since there are no distribution requirements for the Roth, it is not affected by this change. The new rules begin with distributions taken in January 2002.

Under the old regulations you had to make a final decision by age 70½ on how you wanted to take your IRA distributions and who would be your ben-eficiary. Once that choice was made there was no going back. The decision was irrevocable.

After January 2002, the beneficiary can be named at any time after distribu-tions start and in some cases can even be named after death. If you made these decisions prior to January 2001, you can change them after January 2002. They'll no longer be irrevocable.

GO TO ▶

We'll discuss the new minimum distri-bution rules in greater depth in Hour 23.

The big change, though, is the simplification of the minimum distribution rules. Earlier in this Hour we talked about the complicated process of IRA distributions. After January 2002, this requirement will end. Instead, the IRS has prepared a minimum distribution table that you can use to deter-mine your minimum IRA distribution for the year.

In most situations the minimum distribution amount will be less than was previously required. You are permitted to take out more than the minimum distribution amount you calculate. You just cannot take out less, or you risk excise taxes as mentioned earlier.

There is only one situation in which you might want to consider the old method of calculating distribution—if your spouse is your beneficiary and he or she is 10 years or more younger than you. In that situation it might make more sense for you to use the old "joint life and last survivor" rules.

No matter what your employer-sponsored retirement plan is, there's an IRA that meets your needs. Even if you are married but don't earn income, the spousal IRA enables you to save tax-deferred or tax-free for retirement.

HOUR'S UP!

It's time to find out whether you have learned the basics of IRAs:

1. You have no retirement plan at work, you are married, and you earn $50,000 a year. For which type of IRA or IRAs do you meet the eligibility requirements?

    a. Tax-deductible IRA

    b. Roth IRA

    c. Non-tax-deductible IRA

    d. All of the above

2. You are actively contributing to your retirement plan at work, you are married, and you earn $100,000 a year. For which type of IRA or IRAs do you meet the eligibility requirements?

    a. Tax-deductible IRA

    b. Roth IRA

    c. Non-tax-deductible IRA

    d. Only (b) and (c)

3. You are actively contributing to your retirement plan at work, you are not married, and you earn $115,000 a year. For which type of IRA or IRAs do you meet the eligibility requirements?

    a. Tax-deductible IRA

    b. Roth IRA

    c. Non-tax-deductible IRA

    d. Both (b) and (c)

4. You have been contributing for more than five years into a tax-deductible IRA and finally have gotten an opportunity to buy your first home. In order to do so you will need to take some money out of your IRA. Can you do it?

   a. Yes, but there will be a 10 percent penalty, but no other taxes.

   b. Yes, but taxes will need to be paid. There will be no penalty for early withdrawal.

   c. Yes, but there will be both a 10 percent penalty and taxes will be due.

   d. No, you cannot withdraw money from the IRA to buy a new home.

5. You have been contributing for more than five years into a Roth IRA and have decided to go back to college to earn a Master's degree. In order to do so, you will need to take some money out of your IRA to pay for tuition. Can you do it?

   a. Yes and you will be able to withdraw all the money tax-free.

   b. Yes, but you will have to pay taxes on everything you withdraw.

   c. Yes, but you will have to pay taxes on any earnings from contributions that you withdraw. You will not have to pay taxes on any contributions you withdraw.

   d. No, you cannot take money out for going back to college.

6. You have been contributing for more than five years into a non-tax-deductible IRA and you have just become disabled. You are still too young to begin withdrawing from the IRA for retirement, but need to take out some of the money anyway. Can you do it?

   a. Yes and you will be able to withdraw all the money tax-free.

   b. Yes, but you will have to pay taxes on everything you withdraw.

   c. Yes, but you will have to pay taxes on any earnings from contributions that you withdraw. You will not have to pay taxes on any contributions you withdraw.

   d. No, you cannot take money out for disability.

7. You are tired of working and decide to retire at age 55. You want to take a trip around the world and plan to use your Roth IRA to fund it. Can you do it?

    a. Yes, but you will have to pay a 10 percent penalty on everything you withdraw because you're quitting too early, plus you will have to pay taxes on all the money.

    b. Yes, but you will have to pay a 10 percent penalty on any earnings you withdraw, plus pay taxes on that money. You can withdraw your contributions without taxes or penalty as long as they have been in the IRA for more than five years.

    c. No, the government doesn't allow you to use your money before you reach their approved retirement age.

    d. Yes and you can withdraw the money completely tax- and penalty-free.

8. You are trying to decide whether to use a tax-deductible or Roth IRA. You do qualify for both. Which one would be preferable if you are certain that your tax rate will be lower at retirement?

    a. The Roth IRA would be best to avoid taxes at retirement time.

    b. The tax-deductible IRA would be best to avoid paying higher taxes on the money.

    c. Either is okay.

    d. An IRA does not make sense if you are going to have lower taxes.

9. You must begin taking your money out of your tax-deductible and non-tax-deductible traditional IRAs after you reach $70^1/_2$. There are new rules starting in January 2002, and these rules will …

    a. Make it simpler to calculate the minimum distribution requirement.

    b. Allow you to take out less each year, if you wish, than most of the older distribution rules.

    c. Allow you to change your beneficiary designation, which under the old rules was irrevocable.

    d. Allow all of the above.

QUIZ

10. If you have a retirement gap in your IRA, you will be allowed to increase the amount you make in contributions each year beginning with January 2002 under the tax law passed in May 2001. What are the new contribution limits?

a. $2,000 to $3,000 in 2002–2004, $4,000 in 2005–2007, and $5,000 in 2008.

b. If you are already over age 50, you will be able to make $5,000 contributions beginning in 2002, which will be indexed in $500 increments after 2004.

c. If you are over 50, you will be able to make catch-up contributions beginning in 2002.

d. Both (a) and (c) are correct.

Hour 14

Medicare and Private Supplementary Insurance

CHAPTER SUMMARY

LESSON PLAN:

In this Hour you will learn about ...

- Employer retiree health insurance cutbacks.
- Medicare enrollment, coverage, and reimbursement.
- Filling Medicare gaps with private Medigap policies.
- The crucial need for long-term care (LTC).

Everyone talks about the possibility of Social Security running out before they get to collect, but the program at even greater risk is Medicare. You might think that won't matter much because your employer provides good, free health insurance to retirees. Think again: Employers have no obligation to continue retiree coverage unless they've explicitly promised it. Consequently, and often in concert with conversion to cash-balance pensions, employers are starting to charge substantial amounts for retiree health coverage or dropping it altogether.

Therefore, it's critical you know how incomprehensive Medicare coverage is now, and the implications its weak financial condition has for future coverage cutbacks. You should also know how Medigap coverage shores up some of Medicare's sags, how much it costs, what it doesn't cover, and the likelihood its costs will increase along with medical inflation and the need to back up more of Medicare's deficiencies. And neither Medicare, Medigap, or employer retiree policies will cover most aspects of the kind of institutionalized, nonhospital care that almost half of current Boomers are likely to need—thus necessitating long-term-care insurance, which I'll discuss a little later in the Hour.

This all makes it urgent you plan much higher medical costs in your retirement budget than you now anticipate, as well as starting long-term-care coverage before retirement, while your health makes it affordable.

THE MEDICARE PROBLEM

While Medicare faces the same Baby Boom demographics as Social Security, its problems are compounded by the fact that, per enrollee, Medicare costs are expected to rise faster than income from wages. Medicare costs will place larger demands on the federal budget and beneficiaries than Social Security, according to the findings of the 2001 Annual Report by Trustees of the Social Security and Medicare trust funds. It's now projected that Medicare tax-revenue inflows will start falling short of outlays by 2016 and will be insolvent by 2029.

The trustees suggest two possible solutions for closing this gap to make Medicare solvent through 2075—raise the payroll tax immediately from 1.45 to 2.44 percent on both employers and employees, or immediately reduce outlays by 37 percent (in other words less coverage for beneficiaries now). It will most likely be solved by some combination of the two.

FYI Medicare has two trust funds: Hospital Insurance (HI), for inpatient hospital and related care, and Supplementary Medical Insurance (SMI), for physician and out-patient services. They can be used only for benefits and program administrative costs. The trust funds hold money not needed to pay current year costs. They must, by law, invest it in interest-bearing securities that are guaranteed by the U.S. Government.

At the end of 1999 there were over 39 million people on Medicare. In 2000, $222 billion were spent to cover the total expenses for Medicare. Eighty-seven percent of beneficiaries were over age 65 and the rest are people on disability. That is more than double the number of the recipients in its first year, 1966.

Closing the gap could get even more difficult as doctors bolt from providing care to new Medicare patients because these doctors object to the low levels of reimbursement. According to a 1999 study from the American Academy of Family Physicians, almost 30 percent of U.S. family physicians are not taking new Medicare patients. They blame excessive paperwork and low reimbursements. Medicare recipients in some areas of the country are reporting that it can take months to find a doctor who will accept Medicare. Even when they find one, some report that doctors are not giving them the full range of care and tests that is available to seniors who have supplemental coverage packages, such as Medigap.

UNDERSTAND MEDICARE BASICS

First, let's take a look at what Medicare covers. It has two parts. Part A is hospital insurance, covering care as an inpatient in a hospital or skilled nursing facility plus hospice care. In addition, it pays for some home care, including part-time skilled nursing care, physical therapy, occupational therapy, speech-language therapy, home health aide services, and durable medical equipment (such as wheelchairs, hospital beds, oxygen, and walkers). The home health costs are covered under Part A, provided they were part of hospital discharge orders. Otherwise these costs are paid under Part B.

Part B pays for medically necessary doctor services, outpatient hospital care, and some other medical services that Part A does not cover, such as physical and occupational therapists, and some home healthcare.

Most people don't pay for Part A. However, if both spouses have very limited work histories, they now pay either $165 or $300 each per month depending on how little they've worked. The premium for Medicare Part B is $50 per month. Each year there is a $100 deductible that must be met before receiving benefits.

FYI Each year Medicare puts out an all-inclusive handbook that spells out that year's benefits, entitled *Medicare and You*. You can get a copy for the current year by calling 1-800-MEDICARE (1-800-633-4227) or online at www.medicare.gov/Basics/Overview.asp.

When it comes time to enroll, you can select the original Medicare, which is administered by the Federal government through select private insurers, or pick one of two options in Medicare+Choice—a traditional fee-for-service plan or a Medicare managed-care plan, which is similar to an HMO. The Medicare+Choice programs are also answerable to the Federal government, but they, too, are based on laws governing state health insurance regulations. That's why you will find different benefits in different states. Congress made these new plans available to give Medicare recipients more choice and to allow more private insurers an opportunity to service the Medicare population. Currently, in most states only the HMO type of plan is available in Medicare+Choice.

The fee-for-service plan lets you pick the doctors you want to see. If your state does offer a fee-for-service plan, be sure to check out the doctors on the fee-for-service list to be certain there are ones that you would want to use. If you decide to use an HMO plan, you will have to see the doctors under the

HMO to get your medical costs paid. If you plan to travel during retirement, the fee-for-service plan is definitely your best choice. The HMO plans usually have doctors in only one community and you'll be restricted to emergency services only when you're away from home.

Why are people choosing to use Medicare+Choice plans? Money is the most common answer. It is usually cheaper to get full coverage with these types of plans than to use a traditional Medicare plan plus Medigap insurance. We'll look more closely at these cost issues when we discuss supplementary insurance later in this Hour.

UNDERSTAND THE ENROLLMENT WINDOW

If you are collecting Social Security, when you turn 65, Medicare Part A coverage is automatic. You will receive your Medicare card in the mail. If you are not yet collecting Social Security, enrollment rules vary and you must be careful not to make a mistake or you could end up delaying when you will be able to start coverage.

If you and your spouse are different ages and one of you retires before the age of 65, you will have to carry some kind of individual health insurance. Medicare is available only at age 65 and later. For example, if the husband is 65 and the wife is 60, the husband should apply for Medicare Part A and B. The wife should continue her current health insurance until she's 65.

If you are not collecting Social Security, you should go to your nearest Social Security office to sign up for Medicare three months before your 65th birthday. You have a total of seven months to apply for Medicare benefits starting with three months before you turn 65. If you fail to do so in time, you must wait until the next general enrollment period, January 1 to March 31.

You should apply for Medicare Part B coverage as soon as you get your Medicare Part A card. Otherwise, you'll be penalized 10 percent of the Part B premium for each year delayed.

As is always the case with government, there is an exception to these penalties. If at the age of 65 you are still working for a company with 20 or more employees (100 or more if you are disabled), you can remain on the company's health insurance policy. When you leave the company you must sign up for Medicare within eight months to avoid penalties.

JUST A MINUTE

Knowing your Medicare rights is very important. The Medicare Rights Center is a nonprofit organization that works to ensure that affordable healthcare is available for older adults and for people with disabilities. You can visit their Web site at www.medicarerights.org/Index.html.

If you work for a company with fewer than 20 employees, you must sign up for Medicare immediately when you turn 65, or risk penalties. In a small company plan, the private insurance usually will pay only what Medicare does not cover. This puts you at risk of not having full coverage, in addition to the possibility of having to pay penalties to get Part B.

If your employer provides health benefits as part of your retirement package, you should still sign up for Medicare. In these situations, the former employer's health insurance coverage will act as your Medigap coverage, which essentially fills the gap between what Medicare pays and what you must pay out of pocket. We'll be covering Medigap in greater detail later in this Hour.

If you are carrying private insurance, it cannot be used after the age of 65, so you must sign up for Medicare at age 65 if you're not starting Social Security until a later age. Insurers of small groups or individuals will become secondary insurers, covering only what Medicare will not. If you are happy with your private insurer, your best bet is to talk with them about their Medigap offerings. With continuous coverage using the same insurer, you should be able to avoid a problem with preexisting conditions.

UNDERSTAND MEDICARE REIMBURSEMENT

The amount paid by Medicare changes each year. In 2001, your first 60 days in the hospital costs the Medicare recipient a total of $792 per benefit period. Any hospital costs above that figure are paid by Medicare. A benefit period begins the first day you enter the hospital and ends when you have been out of the hospital for 60 consecutive days. There are no limits on the number of benefit periods you can have during any one year, but you must pay the deductible with each hospitalization.

After that there is a co-insurance paid by the Medicare recipient of $198.00 a day for the 61st to 90th day, which rises to $396 per day for the 91st to 150th day for each lifetime reserve day. A person has a total of 60 lifetime reserve days, which are nonrenewable. Once you use those up you've exceeded your lifetime benefit. In other words, if you are in the hospital for 120 days one year for a continuous period, you will have used 30 of your 60 lifetime reserve days.

For a skilled nursing facility, Part A covers 100 percent of the approved Medicare amount for the first 20 days. After that Medicare will pay all but $99 a day for each benefit period during day 21 to day 100. Once you have exhausted the 100 days, Medicare pays nothing.

You pay nothing for home healthcare services approved by Medicare, but you must pay 20 percent of any Medicare-approved durable medical equipment. Hospice care is paid for as long as the doctor has certified the need. Medicare Part A pays almost all of hospice costs. The only costs you may need to pay is for some outpatient drugs and inpatient respite care.

FYI At the time this book was written there was no coverage under Medicare for most outpatient prescription drugs. Legislation was under consideration in Congress to change this, so it's important to keep an eye on this critical issue. According to AARP, "On average, beneficiaries are expected to spend as much out-of-pocket for prescription drugs as for physician care, vision services, and medical supplies combined."

Medical expenses are paid under Part B. These include doctors' services, inpatient and outpatient medical and surgical services and supplies, physical and speech therapy, and diagnostic services as long as they are medically necessary. There are no limits on these services, but Medicare only pays 80 percent of the approved amount. You must pay a $100 deductible plus 20 percent of approved amounts in co-insurance, which is what the patient owes out of pocket or is covered under their Medigap plan.

Clinical laboratory services and home healthcare that is medically necessary, but not directly a result of a recent hospitalization, are covered at 100 percent by Part B. You are responsible for 20 percent of the costs of approved durable medical equipment.

Other medical items not covered by Medicare include: private duty nursing; custodial care, if skilled care is provided at the same time; most chiropractic services; cosmetic surgery; care outside the United States; acupuncture; eyeglasses after cataract surgery; and dental care.

You've probably realized by now that many significant medical costs aren't covered by Medicare. Since you might be on a fixed income in retirement, you definitely don't want substantial unanticipated medical expenses to shatter your carefully incubated retirement nest egg.

UNDERSTAND PRIVATE SUPPLEMENTARY INSURANCE (MEDIGAP)

To avoid financial catastrophe, your best bet is to have some type of Medigap coverage, but these plans can cost as much as $1,000 per month. As we mentioned earlier, there may also be some good Medicare+Choice options in your community. Although costing considerably less, they severely restrict from whom and where you can get care.

TIME SAVER

Medicare offers you an easy way to compare the Medicare+Choice plans on its Web site. You can compare costs and review quality ratings by state. You can search for options nearest your home by using zip code. To check out what is currently available, go to www.medicare.gov/MPHCompare/home.asp#NewSearch.

Medicare+Choice coverage options and costs vary widely by state, so it's important to not just consider both the amount and scope of coverage of the monthly fees. All plans require Medicare Parts A and B, and their fees are in addition to any fees for enrollment in Medicare.

In comparing several states, you will find that monthly costs and plans vary widely. In Georgia, for example, Medicare+Choice options were $40 to $50 a month at the time this book was written. Doctors visits were $10 to $15 per visit versus the uncertainly of a 20 percent cost with traditional Medicare. Hospital costs were capped at $200 or $250 per stay with no time limits versus Medicare's $792 for the first 60 days with considerable escalation after that to a point of no coverage at all for a longer stay. Prescription medications cost $10 to 21, but were capped at a maximum of $500 per year. Medicare right now provides no prescription coverage outside a hospital environment.

California plans were more costly per month. They varied from $50 to $75, but had per–doctor visits as low as $5. Hospital stay costs varied, but even the lowest coverage capped them at $500. Prescription drug costs ranged from $5 to $25 and were capped at a $1,000 limit for the year in many plan options.

Compared to Georgia and California, New Jersey had the greatest variation in price and coverage options. The monthly fees ranged from $0 additional dollars to $116 per month. The doctors' appointments ranged from $10 to $25. Many of New Jersey's plans had no cost for hospital stays, but also offered no prescription drug benefit.

As you plan your retirement budget, use the comparisons for your state to estimate what your medical insurance costs might be. When calculating your retirement gap (see Hours 6, "Retirement Gap Calculation," and 7, "Introduction to Retirement Gap Calculation"), consider separating out medical costs, and assuming double the normal inflation rate for them.

Unless there are changes made to the Medicare+Choice programs soon in Congress, they may not be an option when you retire. The Health Care Financing Administration (HFCA) was notified in July 2000 by some private insurers that they were pulling out of the program. This has been a trend for a number of years because insurers complain they're not receiving adequate reimbursements to cover their costs. Over 900,000 Medicare+Choice participants lost coverage in 2001. According to HCFA, that pattern is worsening each year.

HFCA believes that even if these plans do still exist they will probably offer fewer options or will raise their rates close to Medigap's. Let's take a closer look at Medigap as an option.

FYI You can compare Medigap options in your state on the Medicare Web site at www.medicare.gov/MGCompare/Home.asp. Telephone numbers for the private insurers are included, so you can call for additional information.

Medigap is private health insurance that supplements your healthcare costs not paid by Medicare, including deductibles and co-insurance. If you do not have Medigap, you will be liable for the medical costs out of pocket. Numerous plan types are available, all including these features at minimum:

- Hospital co-insurance
- Full coverage for 365 additional hospital days (after Medicare hospital reserve days are exhausted)
- Twenty percent co-payment for physician and other Part B services
- Three pints of blood

Optional Medigap coverage includes additional benefits depending on the plan you select. Obviously, the more benefits you want the higher the cost is likely to be. Additional benefits you can shop for include the following:

- Coverage of Medicare hospital deductible
- Skilled nursing facility daily co-insurance
- Coverage of Part B $100 deductible

- Eighty percent of emergency medical costs outside the U.S. for the first two months of a trip
- Coverage of doctors' fees that exceed the Medicare approved charge
- At-home custodial care in addition to Medicare-approved home care
- Prescription drug coverage
- Preventive care coverage

No single Medigap plan covers everything, and many things aren't covered by any plan: custodial care (such as feeding, bathing, and grooming) either at home or in a nursing home; long-term skilled care in a nursing home; unlimited prescription drugs; vision care; dental care; and private nurse. The following table, from the Health Care Financing Administration of the U.S. Department Health and Human Services, shows you what the various Medigap coverage options are:

Medigap Compare—Ten Standardized Medigap Plans

Optional Riders	A	B	C	D	E	F*	G	H	I	J*
Basic benefits	√	√	√	√	√	√	√	√	√	√
Part A: Inpatient hospital deductible		√	√	√	√	√	√	√	√	√
Part A: Skilled nursing facility co-insurance			√	√	√	√	√	√	√	√
Part B: Deductible			√		√					√
Foreign travel emergency			√	√	√	√	√	√	√	√
At-home recovery				√			√		√	√

continues

Medigap Compare—Ten Standardized Medigap Plans (continued)

Optional Riders	A	B	C	D	E	F*	G	H	I	J*
Part B: Excess charges						100%	80%		100%	100%
Preventive care					√					√
Prescription drugs								√ Basic Coverage	√ Basic Coverage	√ Extended Coverage

Plans F and J also have a high-deductible option with substantially lower premiums: You pay $1,580 out-of-pocket per year before they pay anything.

FYI The 10 Medigap options are standardized for all states except Massachusetts, Minnesota, and Wisconsin. They're covered in the following chart: www.medicare.gov/MGCompare/Search/StandardizedPlans/StandardPlans.asp.

Some employers provide medical coverage as part of their pension plans. If your company does, you will usually find the combination of Medicare and your retiree insurance is as complete if not better than what you will be able to find in a Medigap policy. When you are making decisions about whether to accept your company's health insurance benefits, be certain to carefully compare both options and costs.

Another reason to stick with you company plan, if offered, is if you have preexisting medical conditions. Medigap plans can exclude coverage of preexisting conditions for up to six months. If you are considering Medigap, be certain to sign up for it within six months of the time you enroll in Medicare Part B. As long as you sign up within six months, insurance companies must let you sign up for the plan of your choice without regard to your health or age. Switching from your employer plan to a Medigap plan after you have been on Medicare Part B for more than six months could also put you at risk of not having coverage for six months for any preexisting conditions. You may be able to switch to a Medigap plan offered by the same insurer and avoid the risk of no preexisting condition coverage for six months.

Once you sign a contract for a Medigap policy, you have 30 days to review the plan and cancel it without penalty. You can change or cancel your policy once a year. If you want to apply for more comprehensive coverage after your initial application, most states permit insurers to reject the more comprehensive coverage. Downgrading your coverage is a lot easier. So your best bet is to seek the most comprehensive plan you can afford and downgrade to lower cost options if money becomes a major stumbling block later.

TIME SAVER

Use the Internet to compare Medigap costs. Otherwise you will have to call insurance companies individually. For a quick comparison and ballpark estimate, check out www.einsure.com/health/.

UNDERSTAND SHOPPING FOR SUPPLEMENTARY INSURANCE

As you probably have realized by now shopping for supplementary insurance can be a formidable task. Your first step is to decide what you think you absolutely must have in the way of coverage and then make a list of your desired options. You may have to shorten your wish list as you start pricing policies in your state.

Pricing for Medicare+Choice and Medigap programs are both impacted by state law and vary greatly state by state. If you are thinking of retiring to a new state and are choosing from among several states, healthcare costs may help you narrow your final choices.

Once you choose your absolute necessities and your additional options, look at the 10 Medigap policies to see which ones meet your basic needs. Also, compare them against the Medicare+Choice options in your state.

You may have less physician choice, but more coverage in a Medicare+Choice HMO. When considering an HMO, talk with people you know who have had direct experience with the providers you're considering. You're stuck for a year once you sign a contract and you want to avoid making a major error. Also, if you decide to change coverage at a later time, but have developed a serious medical condition, it may be harder to find coverage at a cost you can afford when you want to make that change.

According to Medicare statistics, more than 80 percent of recipients stay in the same plan they initially selected—partly from inertia, but also because of the difficulties with changing. It can be crucial, however, to both your medical and financial retirement health, to think ahead about what you'll need and continually monitor whether your plan is meeting your needs.

UNDERSTAND LONG-TERM-CARE INSURANCE

You have seen how Medicare+Choice and Medigap can help you fill the gap in healthcare coverage. However, they still will not provide coverage if you are faced with a long-term illness that requires extensive 24-hour care just to fulfill the basic needs of daily living. They also will not cover extended care in nursing homes.

Nearly 50 percent of people over 65 will spend some time in a nursing home, which costs an average of $30,000 a year nationwide and as high as $100,000 a year in major metropolitan areas. The average nursing home stay is 19 months. Premiums for long-term-care insurance that is bought over the age of 65 can range from $2,000 to $10,000 per year. There are over 100 insurance companies offering long-term-care policies today.

The only way to get coverage for long-term care is through *long-term-care insurance*. As you grow older the possibility of needing long-term care is greater, but the premium costs rise steeply with increasing age.

STRICTLY DEFINED

As you get older, your chances of needing help with the basics of daily living increase. You may also need skilled nursing care longer than Medicare or a Medigap policy will provide. **Long-term-care insurance** fills this gap in your retirement planning.

Long-term-care policies are among the most difficult to select. Contracts are filled with unintelligible legal mumbo jumbo, and sales presentations often overstate what the policies will cover. Sales tactics usually are designed to scare seniors into making a quick decision. People buying policies usually do not understand what will be covered and only find out that their policy falls short when it is actually needed. Be sure to take your time researching and comparing insurance options.

It's money well spent to review a complicated LTC contract with an attorney before making a decision. It is better to pay legal fees up front than to find out you do not have the proper coverage when you need it.

Many long-term-care policies have strict restrictions and coverage limitations. They contain indecipherable definitions of when and where you can receive care. Some require you to be so severely ill before receiving benefits that you must need "continuous one-on-one assistance" (basically, intensive care!).

PROCEED WITH CAUTION

You want to be sure that the long-term-care company you choose will be around when you need the coverage. It is critical that you check the financial health of the company. Two of the key ratings allow you to research that online. They are A.M. Best (www3.ambest.com/ratings/Advanced.asp) and Standard and Poors (www.standardandpoors.com/RatingsActions/RatingsLists/Insurance/InsuranceStrengthRatings.html).

In addition to looking at where and when you will qualify for coverage, there are a number of key coverage considerations. First you must decide how long you want your benefits to last, usually from one to six years are given as options. Next you need to consider the elimination period, which is how soon your benefits will begin.

Another major question is how much coverage you want each month. Common variables are monthly amounts that range from $1,000 to $6,000 per month. There also are usually lifetime caps of total coverage available that can range from $36,000 to $450,000. Another option is the percentage of home care costs that will be paid, which usually range from 50 percent to 100 percent. Obviously the more coverage you select, the higher the monthly premium will be.

When picking a long-term-care policy be certain to check rates for renewing the policy each year. Sometimes you pay more in monthly costs, but can get a guaranteed rate that will not change as you get older. These guaranteed rates can become very important to your ability to continue the policy on a fixed retirement income.

Monthly coverage costs jump dramatically the closer you are to 65, and become unaffordable for most people by age 70. Many healthcare specialists believe you should shop for coverage between 55 and 60, when rates are still somewhat reasonable, but you won't be paying for coverage too long before possibly needing it. For this strategy to benefit you, it's critical to select a policy that offers guarantees regarding future premiums.

Some employers offer long-term-care group policies, and possible payment with pre-tax dollars. If yours does, examine the plan to determine whether it offers all the options you want. Normally, such plans are a bargain compared to what you'll pay for individual policies.

If you do decide on a group plan at work, be certain that you can continue the policy at an advantageous rate when you leave the company. If you have to renegotiate those rates when you leave, you're probably better off with an individual plan for which you can lock in a rate schedule permanently when purchased.

It used to be a common practice for financial advisors to recommend giving away assets so that you could qualify for Medicaid when you ran out of funds. That practice is not only unethical, but also illegal if you try to hide your assets. The Health Insurance Portability and Accountability Act of 1996 made it a crime penalized with jail time to deliberately spend down assets so you could go on Medicaid. That didn't go over well politically, so it was changed to penalize attorneys and estate planners instead. The current law makes it illegal for a lawyer to advise you to give away your assets, but only if you're later ruled ineligible for Medicaid.

HOUR'S UP!

It's time to find out whether you have learned the basics of healthcare benefits and costs you will face when you reach 65.

1. When you turn 65 and are collecting Social Security, Medicare Part A coverage is automatic. What does this coverage include?

   a. Inpatient care in a hospital or skilled nursing facilities

   b. Hospice care

   c. Part-time skilled nursing care

   d. Home health aide services

   e. All of the above

2. When you turn 65, Medicare Part B coverage is an option that costs $50 per month. If you choose this option, what does it cover?

   a. Medically necessary doctors' services

   b. Outpatient hospital care

   c. Some other medical services that Part A does not cover, such as the services of physical and occupational therapists

   d. Some home healthcare

   e. All of the above

QUIZ

3. Are there limitations on when you can decide to sign up for Medicare Part B?

    a. Yes, there is a seven month window of opportunity or you will have to wait until the next open enrollment period.

    b. Yes, if you delay applying for Medicare Part B, you may have to pay a penalty of 10 percent of the Part B premium for each year you waited.

    c. Yes, but you can delay signing up if you have healthcare coverage at work and you work for an company with more than 20 employees.

    d. Only (b) and (c) are correct.

    e. All the above are correct.

4. As a Medicare recipient, you must incur substantial medical costs for deductibles or co-insurance. How can you protect yourself against a cash crisis if you get sick?

    a. Get supplementary coverage through a Medigap policy.

    b. Chose at Medicare+Choice option rather than the traditional Medicare option.

    c. Skip taking Medicare completely and get private insurance.

    d. Pick either option (a) or (b).

    e. Pick either option (b) or (c).

5. Which of the following is a pro or a con relating to selecting Medicare+Choice?

    a. While choice is in the name, many of the Medicare+Choice options actually limit your choice of doctors.

    b. Medicare+Choice offers a way to cover healthcare costs not paid for by Medicare, at a cost that is much lower than a Medigap policy.

    c. Medicare+Choice options vary greatly by state and you must carefully research and compare all options.

    d. All are correct.

    e. Only (b) and (c) are correct.

6. Medigap polices must offer which of the following?

    a. Full coverage for 365 additional hospital days (to be used after Medicare hospital reserve days are exhausted)

    b. 20 percent co-payment for physician and other Part B services

    c. Three pints of blood

    d. Only (a) and (b)

    e. All of the above

7. Which are some key options available with Medigap policies:

    a. Coverage of Medicare hospital deductible

    b. Skilled nursing facility daily co-insurance

    c. Coverage of Part B $100 deductible

    d. Prescription drug coverage

    e. All of the above are possible options

8. If you already have a group of doctors you prefer to see and do not want to change your healthcare options, which plan(s) can you consider at age 65?

    a. Medicare Part A and Part B only.

    b. Medicare+Choice will give you the most choice.

    c. Medicare Part A and Part B plus Medigap.

    d. Only (a) or (c) will allow the range of choice you seek.

    e. Either (a), (b), or (c) is a reasonable option to guarantee your choice of medical providers.

9. While you have a 50 percent chance of needing long-term care in a nursing home in retirement once you reach the age of 65, Medicare and its supplemental insurance programs will not cover the costs. Which is your best option?

    a. You can buy a long-term-care policy that will cover you until you die.

    b. You can buy a long-term-care policy that will cover you for a period you determine at the time you buy the policy.

    c. You can hope your children will be able to care for you and do nothing.

    d. You can wait until you run out of money and let Medicaid kick in, leaving all care options to government approved programs.

    e. You can hope for a lot of luck and never need long-term care.

10. If you decide to purchase a long-term-care policy, what are some of the key feature options you will need to consider?

    a. You must decide how long you want your benefits to last, usually from one to six years are given as options.

    b. You can select the elimination period, which will determine how soon your long-term-care benefits will begin.

    c. You must decide upon how much coverage you want each month. Common variables are monthly amounts that range from $1,000 to $6,000 per month.

    d. You must select the percentage of home care costs that will be paid, which usually range from 50 to 100 percent.

    e. All the above are possible options.

QUIZ

PART IV
Assembling the Plan

HOUR 15   Integrating Retirement Sources

HOUR 16   Savings/Spending Priorities

HOUR 17   Retirement Road Detours

HOUR 18   Retirement Plan Management

HOUR 19   Completing the Plan

HOUR 20   Comprehensive Retirement Gap
Calculation Example

Hour 15

Integrating Retirement Sources

Chapter Summary

LESSON PLAN:

In this Hour you will learn about …

- Alternatives for building your long-term investment portfolio.
- Other investments to integrate into your retirement planning.
- Balancing business growth with other asset-building strategies.
- Inheritance and other windfalls.

At this point you might be asking, "Why all this detail? This author is just like my boss and work colleagues, spending so much time just trying to grow their assets."

Guilty as charged, but to properly address retirement planning, it's critical you understand the employer and government resources covered in Part III, "Employment/ Government Plans." Now it's time to find out how to integrate those resources with others you'll be building or receiving. As you put together your retirement plan, it's important to consider everything you own and how it will impact your ability to live the lifestyle you choose in retirement.

You may have a large stamp, coin, or baseball card collection. You have to decide whether to keep it or sell it. If you own a home, you will need to decide whether to keep it or use the assets from the sale of the home to buy a new home where you choose to retire. If you own a business, you will need to decide how to transfer those assets to your heirs or sell it. Or you might receive a substantial inheritance or other type of windfall. How you combine and handle all these assets greatly impacts the amount of money you'll have and how you'll be able to use it to generate retirement income.

Build a Long-Term Investment Portfolio

By the time you reach retirement, you and your spouse will probably have a variety of tax-advantaged retirement and other investment accounts from several different jobs, as well as several IRAs. You IRAs could have been ones that you contributed to religiously every year, or they may be made up of rollovers from previous employer-sponsored plans. Most likely they will come from both sources.

You may also have a variable life insurance policy or an annuity that you need to consider in the mix. Let's start with the retirement plan resources.

EMPLOYER/GOVERNMENT PLAN RESOURCES

As these accounts build, it is important to integrate them in your retirement planning and consider *asset allocation*. You may find yourself in a 401(k) that has great growth mutual funds, but is lacking good diversity for value or bond funds. In another 403(b), there may be excellent investments for safety but they lack the growth you think you'll need. By integrating the way you plan your allocations within each of these accounts, you can minimize risk and maximize growth potential.

STRICTLY DEFINED

Asset allocation is the method you use to proportionally allocate your assets among cash, bonds, or stocks. Numerous studies have shown that 90 percent or more of your portfolio's success may be attributed to overall asset allocation rather than the specific stocks, bonds, and mutual funds you choose.

To begin looking at integration, build a spreadsheet that shows all your investments regardless of their source. Include columns that indicate where the investment is held, the type of account, the total amount in the account, the percentage of total holdings, and the purpose for those holdings (for example, growth, safety, or income). Here is a sample worksheet.

Sample Worksheet for Integrating Retirement Assets

Investment	Account	Amount	% of Holdings	Purpose
Index mutual fund	403(b)—wife	$3,000	18%	Growth
Company stock	401(k)—husband	$5,000	29%	Growth
Bond mutual fund	403(b)—wife	$2,000	12%	Safety

Investment	Account	Amount	% of Holdings	Purpose
Value mutual fund	IRA—wife	$2,000	12%	Safety
Aggressive mutual fund	IRA—husband	$5,000	29%	Growth
Total assets	**$17,000**			

When you are finished you should have a roadmap to your actual retirement holdings. This will help you to quickly see your asset allocation and whether you may hold too much in one type of asset and not enough in another.

You can do an even more sophisticated approach by adding a column that gives more detail about the type of holding, such as small company funds, large company funds, bond funds, sector fund (such as technology or health). This more extensive view will be even more helpful if you want to review your balance by type of fund.

TIME SAVER

There are a number of sources on the Internet that let you track your portfolio for free and even monitor the change in value based on the number of shares held. One of the best is offered by Morningstar (http://portfolio.morningstar.com/portasp/allview.asp). This site even tracks the distributions and lets you decide whether to reinvest them or not. It helps you keep up to date on your total holdings.

You should do this type of review now and at least annually to ensure that the asset allocation in your portfolio continues to match your investment objectives and risk tolerance. To the degree it doesn't, you must do a reallocation to rebalance your portfolio. For example, not long before the tech stock plunge of the last year or two, this type of analysis and rebalancing would have revealed far too much risk in many portfolios. It might have saved tens of thousands of pre-retirees from the disastrous losses that have deferred their dreams.

In Hour 18, "Retirement Plan Management," we'll look at portfolio balancing and reallocation. In Hour 19, "Completing the Plan," we'll look at monitoring your portfolio and making adjustments.

OTHER SAVINGS SOURCES AT WORK

In addition to the traditional retirement plans, you may have other opportunities to sock away money for retirement. These options could include profit-sharing plans, employee stock ownership plans, employee stock purchase plans, thrift saving plans, and employee stock options. We'll cover these briefly here, but if they are available at your workplace, check out details and take advantage of them to build your nest egg.

PROFIT-SHARING PLANS

First, we'll look at the accurately named profit-sharing plan, a qualified defined-contribution retirement plan in which your company shares its profits with you. Contributions are made exclusively by your employer, and are completely discretionary. They can range from 0 to 25 percent of your compensation annually up to $200,000 under the new tax law passed in May 2001. For 2001 only, the old maximum was 15 percent of compensation up to $170,000. As qualified defined-contribution plans, profit-sharing plans are subject to the same kind of distribution rules upon termination as 401(k) and small-business retirement plans.

EMPLOYEE STOCK OWNERSHIP PLANS (ESOP)

Employee stock ownership plans are a sophisticated way for companies to provide employees with stock ownership while getting substantial tax deductions and additional working capital for the business. To employees, however, they're more straightforward. They receive a certain value in credited company shares each year, related to their level of compensation. Vesting rules are similar to those for the company contributions in a 401(k). However, the employee doesn't have any control of even vested shares until reaching age 55 with at least 10 years of service. And employees don't get actual possession until termination. Taxation and distribution of shares can be complicated and rollovers are possible.

JUST A MINUTE

If you have significant holdings in your ESOP, you'd be wise to consult a qualified financial advisor about your options.

EMPLOYEE STOCK PURCHASE PLANS

Employee stock purchase plans allow employees to purchase stock at a discount directly from the employer on a regular basis, for minimal commissions. The discount generally ranges from 5 to 15 percent and is treated as income, not capital gain, at the time you sell the shares. Unlike an ESOP, you have complete control of your shares from the moment you purchase them.

THRIFT PLANS

Thrift plans, not to be confused with federal-employee thrift savings plans, are private-sector 401(k)-type plans that allow employees tax-deferred savings with after-tax dollars, just like with a nondeductible IRA. Employers often provide partial matching and use these plans as an adjunct to the 401(k), allowing the employee to invest more than the 401(k) maximum, with the excess being tax-deferred rather than tax-deductible/-deferred. Only a small percentage of employers offer thrift plans, and they might soon become an historical footnote. That's because the just-enacted 2001 tax legislation allows employers to offer something better, starting in 2006. The Roth 401(k) will allow employees to make payroll after-tax contributions whose earnings will ultimately be tax-free.

EMPLOYEE STOCK OPTIONS

Employee stock options give employees the right to buy stock at any time over a designated time period (usually two to 10 years) at a price set at the time the option is granted. This can be a great advantage if hoped-for company growth results in stock that increases in value over time. The employee could then make a future purchase (called "exercising the option") at a potentially huge discount, allowing an immediate sale and instant profit.

If this sounds too good to be true, the tax laws governing options must be true, because they are too complex to just be the product of a cruel imagination. For example, these options come in two types, incentive stock options (ISO) and non-qualified stock options (NQSO), each with its own set of rules. Nevertheless, if you're in the enviable position of having options to buy many shares of stock at a substantial discount, it's well worth paying a good CPA for the tax advice that will maximize your transaction's contribution to your retirement nest egg. Like other employer-provided plans, stock options also have vesting periods, typically giving you full ownership of the options granted within four years. Your option exercise period begins when an option is vested.

VARIABLE UNIVERSAL LIFE INSURANCE AND VARIABLE ANNUITIES

Most people who own a *variable universal life (VUL)* insurance policy or a variable annuity in their portfolio probably are the victim of a smooth salesperson. That's because they're normally a drag on your retirement investing—with unnecessary fees and usually low-performing assets. Unfortunately, many retirement investors are stuck with annuities as part of their employer-sponsored plans, particularly 403(b) plans.

VUL and variable annuities might make sense if you have excess investment funds, are in a high tax bracket, and have invested the maximum allowed in your IRA and tax-advantaged employer or self-employment plans. They're also of interest to individuals who could be potential targets for lawsuits or providers of personal services who could be liable in a malpractice suit, because in most states assets in life insurance policies and annuities are credit protected. If you are considering an annuity for legal protection, be sure to seek the advice of an attorney who knows the law in the state in which you reside.

STRICTLY DEFINED

Variable universal life (VUL) is a combination life insurance/investment vehicle that is considered a hybrid between term and whole life insurance. You can have a level face value for the insurance or vary that amount. In addition to the life insurance portion of the policy, a tax-deferred investment portion can grow for eventual cashing out, or used to pay premiums.

VUL is the most flexible type of life insurance, term the cheapest, and (permanent) whole life the most expensive. Whole life contains a term-like protection piece and an investment (cash value) piece. Many planners will tell you it is best to buy term and invest whatever extra it would have required to buy the same amount of whole life. They say it's easy to outperform the insurance company's investment returns, particularly with their built-in fees and commissions. And they're right, despite the industry pushing variable whole life products that can offer better returns. However, you must be disciplined enough to save the money you don't use to buy whole life and then studiously invest it.

You can choose from a variety of investments, but if despite this lecture you're still VUL-vulnerable to an insurance pitch, be sure to check it out carefully. Chances are you were enticed by the VUL features allowing you to vary your annual or monthly premiums as long as you pay enough to keep the insurance part of the policy in force, and the borrowing option. But many VUL policies offer only conservative options that have low growth potential. And their biggest disadvantages are the fees you pay to the insurance company for maintaining the VUL, and the operating costs, deducted from your investment returns, of the mutual funds or other investments embedded in the policy.

Fees you need to research include the annual mortality and expense charge, the premium load (premium expense charge plus premium tax charge), sales load (if any), monthly administrative charge, monthly cost of insurance, and policy surrender charges for early withdrawal, if applicable. If you do decide to withdraw money prior to age 59½ you also will face the same kind of penalties and taxes that you do with IRAs.

The insurance fees can gobble up much of your investment and do not make sense unless you truly need the insurance. If you have maxed out your retirement investing alternatives, then one of the newer generation of lower-fee variable annuities might be a better option if your primary goal is an additional tax shelter.

Variable annuities are tax-deferred investment vehicles that have just enough of an insurance component (usually a death benefit equivalent to the premiums you've paid) to enable their IRS qualification for tax-deferred status. For tax purposes, think of them as nondeductible IRAs, because the amount you invest does not reduce your taxes. However, the annuity grows tax-deferred until you start annuitizing it and taking distributions.

PROCEED WITH CAUTION

Many financial advisors think you have to hold a variable annuity for 15 to 20 years before its tax-deferral advantages start to decidedly outweigh its fee and tax-rate disadvantages, and perform favorably in comparison to mutual funds. Whereas most mutual-fund gains are taxed at maximum capital-gains rates (currently 20 percent), variable annuity gains are taxed at ordinary-income rates, even though their underlying investments are often very similar to mutual funds.

As mentioned earlier with VULs, variable annuities are loaded with fees. Morningstar found that the average annual expenses on variable annuities total 2.08 percent versus an average of 1.34 percent for mutual funds. Other hidden costs you must watch out for in an annuity are sales loads (commissions) on the investment accounts and surrender charges if you decide to sell it early. Most will have a required holding period of about seven years to avoid highly punitive surrender charges. There are also contract charges of about $25 annually.

If after reading all this you still want to consider an annuity, shop carefully. Be leery of insurance companies, the traditional providers that have feasted on fat annuity fees—although a few are finally being forced by competition to offer more cost-effective products. Look first for lower-fee annuities now being offered by or through AnnuityNet.com, AnnuityScout.com, Vanguard, TIAA-CREF, and Fidelity. In addition to low fees, make sure the annuity provides a wide range of subaccount choices (each tantamount to a specific mutual fund).

Be clear that we're talking about variable annuities here, not the fixed annuities that new retirees (usually unwisely) buy to make their money last the rest of their lifetimes while exposing it to only minimal risk. These are absolutely the worst possible product you can consider if you're in active retirement investing mode because they grow only by virtue of puny fixed (annually adjusted) interest rates and lock up money you should be investing more aggressively.

 FYI TIAA-CREF provides retirement resources for local and state government and higher education. Their Web site (www.tiaa-cref.com) has an excellent section on individual annuities if you want to learn more.

OTHER INVESTMENTS

Now we'll take a look at other assets you are holding that can be part of your investment pie. Your largest share of other investments are probably in your personal residence. You may be lucky enough to have a vacation home as well. If you own a business, you have to consider what income or lump sum resources you may be able to capture from that business at retirement.

You also may be an avid collector. These collections give you lots of pleasure, but they could also turn into retirement resources, if necessary.

COLLECTIBLES

Are you a collector? Do you have an art collection that you have carefully built and use to decorate your home at the same time? Do you collect stamps, coins, or baseball cards?

All of these things have value and possibly more value than you even realize. As you begin thinking about integrating your retirement resources and figuring out ways to fill your retirement gap, don't forget to look at these items. They could be your saving grace if you fall short in retirement.

TIME SAVER

 If you don't know where to start, the Antiques and Collectibles Guide (www.acguide. com) by the American Directories Company can you help you find local resources. It can save you a lot of time finding a good appraiser in your area.

If you are collecting, be careful of the scam artists out there. For example, in May 2001, the attorney general of New York indicted six people for defrauding coin collectors and costing investors over $25 million during a seven year period from 1993 to 2000. Using a telemarketing scheme, coin collectors were sold used coins as though they were in mint condition. If investors questioned the validity of the coin's value, they were sent to one of five coin shops owned by the same company to verify the coin's value.

 Being on the alert for fraud is important, especially when you are investing your money, but also critical when spending and borrowing it. The National Fraud Information Center (www.fraud.org) is a great stop to make to find out more about the types of fraud and how you can avoid them.

If you do have a sizeable collection, you don't have to think about selling it up front. Enjoy it as long as you can and keep it for a safety net in case you do run short on funds in retirement. If you do plan to make your collection part of your retirement plan assets, be certain to have it appraised by a knowledgeable appraiser to be sure you are including the proper value.

HOME EQUITY AND OTHER REAL ESTATE

Your greatest personal asset is probably your home. By the time you reach retirement, you hopefully will have it paid off or be close to doing so. You may also own vacation property. In fact, you may have planned so well that vacation home may even be exactly where you want to live for retirement.

Your plan could be to sell your primary residence and live in your vacation home full-time.

You may also own rental properties. If you do, you will have to decide whether you want to continue managing those investments or just cash out and use the assets for retirement living.

All of the decisions, of course, come with tax consequences. As long as you have held the investment properties for more than a year, any capital gains will be taxed at a 20 percent capital gains rate.

Investment properties do have another catch if you decide to cash out. You most likely were renting them and offsetting the income with depreciation. All that depreciation is subtracted from your cost basis. You could end up owing taxes on the full sales price.

For example, you bought the rental property 20 years ago for $100,000. You depreciated it at $5,000 per year. Your cost basis would then be zero. You would have to pay a 20 percent capital gains tax on the sale of the property, which could be worth $500,000 if it gained an average of 8 percent per year during that 20-year period.

Luckily, your personal residence does not have the same rules. Tax law exempts the taxation of profits on the sale of a personal residence up to $500,000 for married couples and $250,00 for singles. For any gains over those limits you would have to pay 20 percent in taxes.

If you want to stay in your home, there are a number of ways to recapture the equity without moving. If your mortgage is paid off, you can consider taking a new mortgage to get cash if necessary. If you do make this choice, be sure the new monthly mortgage payments will not take too much of your monthly income and thereby negate the value of getting the cash.

PROCEED WITH CAUTION

Tread carefully if you decide to borrow on your home. Remember the risk you take with any of these mortgage options is that if you for some reason are not able to make payments on the loan, you could lose your property.

You can also access the money using a home-equity line of credit, which works like a credit card with a set limit, but does put your home at risk if you can't pay back your debt. One advantage this offers over a standard mortgage is that you can vary the amount you take. Pay it off and then use it again.

Capital-Based Business Opportunities

If you are a small business owner, your business could be your largest asset or your largest sink hole depending on its future worth. To get the business going you probably sunk a lot of time and money into the business. Obviously you did that with the expectation of future returns.

Is it living up to your expectations or do you find you are continuing to put money into the business with little idea of what will be there when it's time to retire? Is the money you are sinking into the business costing you dearly in what you could be saving for retirement?

These are questions you must ask yourself as you develop your retirement plan. How much has your business grown since you started? What are the prospects that it will continue to grow? Will it have a value at the time you want to retire? Do you have a lot of capital invested in the business? Will you be able to get that capital out or is it primarily made up of depreciating assets that won't have much value when you want to sell?

JUST A MINUTE

Did you know that almost 90 percent of all U.S. businesses are owned by families? These family businesses generate about half of the country's gross domestic product, half of the total wages, and are responsible for about 77 percent of all new job creation in the U.S. Only about 30 percent of family-owned businesses are successfully passed on from one generation to the next without being sold, closed, or liquidated for tax purposes.

As you think about retirement, it is important to balance your decision to continue to put money into the growth of your business or to diversify your assets further by investing them in other market opportunities. To answer this question, use the Sample Worksheet for Integrating Retirement Assets earlier in this Hour. Add a line item for what you think the business is now worth if you sold it.

What percentage of your total investments are represented by the amount tied to your business? Do you think you have enough diversification? If 50 percent or more is tied to your business, what would be the impact on your retirement if that business failed?

Now might be the time to look at diversifying your portfolio. You can set aside money for your retirement and avoid taxes as well if you make a concentrated effort to max out by fully funding one of the small business retirement plans mentioned in Hour 11, "Small Business/Self-Employed Plans."

In addition to making sure you put aside as much money as possible while you are working in the business, you also want to consider how to best maximize the assets you will get when you exit the business.

GO TO ▶
We'll cover the issues of selling a business in Hour 22, "Pre-Retirement Planning."

First, you need to realistically think about how much the business is worth if you tried to sell it. Does your business have saleable assets, such as land, buildings, or equipment that will be valuable even if the business failed? If so, separate your thinking into two possible scenarios. How much cash you could get out of the assets even if the business were not a going concern, and how much could you sell it for tomorrow as a going concern? This will give you a best-case and worst-case scenario for calculating what you might take into retirement when you exit the business.

Don't forget to consider the tax impact on the sale of the business. You probably have been depreciating any assets you could to minimize your tax hit through the years. You may have totally wiped out any cost basis and have to pay long-term capital gains taxes on everything you sell.

INHERITANCE AND OTHER WINDFALLS

Sometimes, just picking the right parents, lottery number, occupant of the other car in an accident, or answer on a television quiz show can blow a pile of cash into your life. Or you might own just the right tract of land that a developer needs for a major project.

These so-called windfalls are more common than you might expect. If you're a lucky recipient, indulge yourself just mildly with a fraction of your windfall, and then integrate the balance into your retirement assets. In fact, if you're a Baby Boomer, there's a strong chance you'll be receiving an inheritance windfall from the trillions your parents' generation is expected to leave behind.

Although it's an awkward subject, you should talk with your parents if they have assets that clearly exceed what they'll need, and have signaled their intent to give some to you. If they haven't engaged a high-quality financial advisor with estate-planning expertise, they should get advice now, especially in light of the inheritance tax phaseout included in the 2001 tax bill.

To give you an idea of some of the bill's provisions, and what's at stake in general regarding estate planning, see Hour 23, "Managing Retirement Distributions," which includes brief coverage of retirement estate planning.

FYI If you expect to be the recipient of a large estate or want to protect your own assets, there is an excellent Web site that collects links to the best estate planning information on the Internet. Check out www.estateplanninglinks.com.

Hour's Up!

It's time to find out how well you have learned the basics of integrating your retirement sources.

1. Which of the following resources should be considered when integrating your retirement plan?

    a. Employer-sponsored retirement plans

    b. Individual retirement arrangements (IRAs)

    c. Collectibles such as coins, artwork

    d. Your small business assets

    e. All of the above

2. When planning your asset allocation, what should you include?

    a. Stocks

    b. Bonds

    c. Cash

    d. Only (a) and (b)

    e. All of the above

3. You should consider buying an annuity if which of the following are true?

    a. You have maxed out on all your retirement investing options and still have money on which you want to defer taxes.

    b. You dislike your employer-sponsored retirement plan and are looking for another option.

    c. You may be facing a legal judgment and want to shelter your assets from that judgment.

    d. Only (a) and (c).

    e. All of the above.

QUIZ

4. If you are thinking about buying a variable universal life policy, what fees should you research?

    a. Annual mortality and expense charge

    b. Premium load (premium expense charge plus premium tax charge)

    c. Sales load (if any)

    d. Monthly administrative charges and cost of insurance

    e. All of the above and more

5. How long do many financial advisors believe you must hold an annuity before it becomes more tax efficient than a mutual fund?

    a. At least 5 years

    b. 5 to 10 years

    c. 10 to 15 years

    d. 15 to 20 years

    e. It is never better than a mutual fund

6. How are variable universal life and variable annuities taxed after you reach 59½?

    a. Taxation rules are similar to those of an IRA; all withdrawals are taxed at your current income tax rate.

    b. Taxation rules are similar to a Roth IRA; money is taken out tax-free.

    c. There are no tax incentives for an annuity.

    d. There are no tax incentives for variable universal life policies.

    e. There are no tax incentives for variable annuities.

7. Which are possible options to consider if you want to get some of your equity from your home at retirement without selling it?

    a. A new traditional mortgage

    b. A reverse mortgage

    c. An equity line

    d. Only (b) and (c) are correct

    e. (a), (b), and (c) are correct

8. If you decide to sell your home, how will it be taxed?

   a. If you are married, the first $500,000 of gain is exempt from taxation. The remainder will be taxed at the capital gains rate as long as you have held it for more than a year.

   b. If you are single, the first $250,000 of gain is exempt from taxation. The remainder will be taxed at the capital gains rate as long as you have held it for more than a year.

   c. All profits above the cost basis will be taxed at the capital gains rate.

   d. At retirement, you don't have to pay taxes on your home no matter how much gain you make.

   e. Both (a) and (b) are correct.

9. There are alternatives for saving offered by some companies. Which of these are possible?

   a. Employee stock purchase plan

   b. Thrift saving plan

   c. Employee stock options

   d. Profit-sharing plans

   e. All plans are possible, but it depends on what your company offers

10. If you are expecting an inheritance, what portion of the funds will you receive tax free?

   a. In 2001, the first $675,000 is exempt from estate or gift taxes.

   b. In 2002, $1 million will be exempt from estate taxes and that will gradually increase until it hits $3.5 million in 2009.

   c. In 2010, the estate tax will be repealed, but gift taxes will still be in place.

   d. Only (a) and (b) are correct.

   e. (a), (b), and (c) are correct.

HOUR 16

Savings/Spending Priorities

LESSON PLAN:

In this Hour you will learn about ...

- The never-ending struggle between saving and spending.
- The choices between saving, paying off debt, and protecting assets with insurance.
- The general choice between saving for immediate goals and retirement saving.
- Saving for a house down payment vs. saving for retirement.
- Investing in educating yourself vs. immediate retirement investing.

Regardless of which chorus you prefer in the current singsong debate over national energy policy debate, the lyrics offer a powerful and useful analogy to your retirement planning. Namely, what is the proper balance between production (making money) and conservation (budgeting)? Although it's true that our economy keeps growing, there are limits on how much of it we (collectively) and you (individually) can hope to harvest without exhausting its financial fossil fuel. That's where conservation and rationing come in—using limited financial resources wisely so that in retirement we don't end up as old financial-fossil fools.

Avoiding that fate will require a lot of renewable energy, of the creative kind. You'll have to figure out how to get what you want now while also getting what you want in retirement—at the same time singing to the truthful tune of the reality of rationing: "You can't always get what you want."

In other words, you must find the answer, my friend, to not blowing the powerful windfall of current and future economic opportunities from your work, your investments, and just plain luck. By hitting this Hour's high notes, you should warm up to the realization that carefully and intelligently rationing your limited financial resources is the only rational retirement strategy.

RATION OVERALL SPENDING VS. RETIREMENT SAVING

Ironically, many future retirees now feeling virtuous about heeding the clarion call to save more will nonetheless be singing the blues in their senior years. That's because they view retirement saving with tunnel vision—investing in their 401(k) and IRA accounts for the future, but making a thorough mishmash of their present finances. They're getting so deeply in debt that a substantial portion of it will accompany them home from their retirement parties.

One important reason is that today's mid-lifers married late and had kids even later. They will find themselves in their 50s, thinking seriously about retirement, at the same time that they're helping their kids think seriously about what college to attend. By necessity, kids are taking on more loan burden themselves, but parents still bear the brunt of it, either by the hazy legal obligation of "required parental support," or an instinctive sense of family obligation.

FYI Students graduating this year with baccalaureate degrees will carry an average of more than $15,000 of student-loan debt into their first jobs. That doesn't include loans their parents take to help pay for their education.

Given this pattern, many parents will find themselves already retired when it comes time to help children pay for weddings. Meanwhile, if they've also been sandwiched by helping support their own parents, they could very well be paying back high consumer debt, such as a considerable balance on a home-equity loan. On the one hand, they might have dutifully accumulated several hundred thousand in 401(k) and IRA accounts, yet—in addition to a mortgage—have tapped as much as a hundred thousand of the equity in their highly appreciated homes.

And let's not forget that mortgage. Buoyed by a strong employment market and soaring stock market, hundreds of thousands of Americans moved up to their dream homes in the '90s, confidently taking on mortgages in excess of $200,000, on $300,000 to $400,000 homes. They might have cashed in on the market boom to help with sizeable down payments, but were still left with very large monthly payments that leave little room in their budgets to save. In addition, with interest rates at their lowest in 30 years, millions of American refinanced their homes for a better rate, a good thing. But many turned that good thing into a dicey proposition by using the built-in equity to take a much larger mortgage with much higher payments, despite the lower interest rates.

Those same '90s saw the popularization of the car lease—allowing millions to drive a rich (wo)man's car without being rich. But unlike owning a good used family car after making several-hundred-dollar car-loan payments for a few years, they were left with nothing after the two years of even higher lease payments. Those who repeated that exercise several times missed out on the chance to invest several hundred more dollars a month once a car loan was paid off.

PROCEED WITH CAUTION

Of more than 15 million new cars forecast to be sold in the United States in 2001, more than four million will be leased. And with prices to buy cars becoming more attractive, many drivers who signed up for three-year leases in 1999 are regretting that they're stuck in them now.

If you recognize yourself in any of this, it's time to get a new lease on your retirement life. It's not enough to either live within your means or manage debt wisely during your working years. You must also recognize the retirement opportunity cost of unnecessary or excessive indulgences that keep you from investing more for the future. You might be making a trade that gives you a modicum of extra material comfort now in return for life-impairing financial discomfort later.

RATION HOUSE DOWN PAYMENT VS. RETIREMENT SAVING

One trade that does eventually make sense for young adults just starting to think about retirement is an apartment for a house. Conventional wisdom says you should do this as soon as possible, so that you're no longer "wasting" rent—instead getting tax benefits and equity build-up from home ownership. By some strange coincidence, these reasons are part of the oath that real estate agents take when they're sworn into service.

Because this book's sworn duty is to inform you objectively, here goes: Few real estate agents are trained financial advisors. The same goes for work peers, parents, and other well-meaning acquaintances who cheerfully heap the platitudes on the American Dream of home ownership. Listen and learn, but keep in mind that few of these folks will be part of your life when you're either comfortably settling into cushy retirement digs or cramming your stuff into a double-wide.

Instead, make your decision to buy a house based on your particular financial circumstances—taking into account your need to save for retirement. Call it practicing senior-safe saving, which gives you several reasons to retain your real-estate virginity until both you and your bank account are ready.

First, you're probably still in the 15 percent tax bracket and have very few deductions. For example, although interest on student loans is deductible, it's not an itemized deduction. Thus, even adding in mortgage interest and property tax, you might not be able to deduct much more than the generous standard deduction.

FYI These are the standard deductions for 2001: $3,800 filing married separately, $4,550 filing single, $6,650 filing head of household, and $7,600 filing married jointly.

Second, while you're in this low tax bracket, saving toward a down payment, you'll only be taxed at either 15 percent for earned interest, or as low as 10 percent for capital gains on stock held more than a year. Also, this is the time when fully funding a Roth IRA is clearly advantageous because you'd get minimal tax break from a deductible IRA and the Roth will grow tax-free forever. These facts work against the argument that delaying buying means you're badly missing out on tax-free appreciation of your home's value during this time.

True, you might miss out on some appreciation. And many real estate agents will tell you that you'll miss out on a house that appreciates rapidly because you won't be able to grow your down payment fast enough to still afford it. But that ignores the possibility that you might have to stop saving toward retirement if you've overextended yourself in buying the house.

The argument to buy early to catch the appreciation wave also ignores substantial amounts you could be saving monthly from the difference between rent and what you'd be paying monthly for mortgage and property taxes combined, plus upkeep. Most of that difference remains when you factor in the tiny little tax benefit you'd get from buying while in a low tax bracket, and how little equity you're building up from the miniscule principal payments in the early years of a mortgage loan.

And don't forget the closing costs involved in buying a house. Furthermore, like many young adults you might move within a few years of buying it for a job promotion or better opportunity. Keep in mind that it typically takes an average five years of first-home ownership before buying clearly becomes superior to continued renting. That number is even higher if you have a very good rental deal and the housing market is relatively cool.

FYI During 2000, United States homes appreciated an average of about 7 percent, and in several hot markets far more than 10 percent. It is expected to decrease substantially in the current cool economy, and historically averages up to 5 percent a year, but varies widely depending on the area.

All that said, a home is not purely an investment, so go ahead and buy one if it feels like the right time to do it. Just be sensible enough about it to at least continue saving something toward retirement both while you're accumulating the down payment and after you've become an owner.

TIME SAVER

Financenter.com has more than 100 useful financial calculators, including this neat one for doing a rent vs. buy analysis: www.calcbuilder.com/cgi-bin/HOM10.cgi/ FinanCenter.

Finally, you should definitely lean toward buying if the assumptions here don't apply to you. For example, if you're in the 28 percent (27 percent in 2002) or higher tax bracket, have many other deductions to itemize, and are paying high rent, you're a poster person for home ownership. After all, home ownership over the long term is a great retirement investment, given the $500,000 tax-free gain you can take away from its sale.

RATION DEBT PAYOFF VS. INVESTING

Once you've decided how to allocate limited investment funds between a Roth IRA and 401(k), the question is should you invest at all, if you're carrying high-interest debt?

Some financial experts take a totally analytical approach. They say to look at the total return you can get on your 401(k)—including the immediate tax benefit, the tax deferral, the employer match, and the actual return. Then compare that to the rate you're paying on your debt, adjusted down if it's tax-deductible debt such as a home equity loan. Whichever is higher, investing return or borrowing rate, act accordingly.

Talk to a good financial advisor, though, and you get a human, psychological perspective that can tilt a somewhat close decision either way. For some people, the knowledge that they're investing for retirement, even while still in considerable debt, is crucial to a positive mindset that they've gotten started and will get there. Unless debt is smothering, or rates on it astronomical, some advisors recommend that these individuals split available funds between debt payoff and retirement investment.

JUST A MINUTE

Financial advisors are applying knowledge of their clients' psychological types by using methods such as psychologist Dr. Kathleen Gurney's Moneymax profile. It identifies nine client types such as Safety Players, Perfectionists, and Money Masters. Similarly, financial advisor Ray Linder discusses how he uses the Meyers-Briggs personality types with clients in *What Will I Do with My Money: How Your Personality Affects Your Financial Behavior* (see Appendix B, "Resources").

In contrast, many advisors are emphatic about clients who've never met a budget they didn't bust—adopting a no-nonsense "this has got to change" stance with them. Even if the debt interest rate was reasonable, they'd put these clients on aggressive austerity programs until they wipe out their debt. Their reasoning: You must live on a budget during retirement, so it's more important to change habits while it's still possible, even if it means a harder road to reach retirement goals.

You probably don't need an advisor to know whether you are a "retirement or bust" type of saver, a budget-busting nonsaver, or fall in the heavily populated middle. If you have trouble managing money and sticking to a budget, the first step is to acknowledge the problem. Until you do, you'll undoubtedly always find rationalizations for financial strategies that keep you in debt.

Alternatively, you might already recognize your debt problem but aren't sure why you have it. If so, you might have difficulty distinguishing between good and bad debt. Good debt is for "living capital" such as houses, home improvements, functional furnishings, sensible cars, and emergencies that tap out a seemingly ample emergency fund. Bad debt is for frivolous fleeting-moment experiences and items associated with excessive travel, entertaining, and luxury.

Finally, you might be a solid, sensible, good-debt type. However, if you're so adamant about maximum saving that you refuse to run the numbers, you might be limiting how much you'll be able to invest ultimately because you've kept yourself in mathematically illogical debt. Your challenge is to channel your mild obsessive-compulsive instincts of paying down the debt into saving like a mad(wo)man again.

Don't worry, this Hour filled with psychobabble comes at no extra charge—except this: You're charged with responsibility to confront your debt situation, and determine the best way to deal with it to maximize your long-term retirement savings.

RATION EDUCATION VS. INVESTING

The other side of the debt coin plays a part in your decisions about allocating funds toward college savings vs. retirement. Namely, should you flip your priorities decidedly toward giving your kids the best possible education and worry about retirement later? Or, should you provide just enough to ensure their ability to attend a state school—possibly requiring they take modest loans and work throughout?

FYI A major recent study conducted over more than a 20-year period showed that ultimate career success was no better for graduates of private colleges than of public ones. Although the private-college graduates made more money in the first few years after graduation, over the long haul, things evened out in terms of both money and job satisfaction.

Because of the way college funding and financial aid work, this is actually far more than a philosophical question. In counting up family assets as part of determining a student's financial need, colleges don't include any funds you've invested in IRA and 401(k) accounts. Therefore, it normally makes sense to stuff the maximum you can into tax-advantaged retirement accounts while also maximizing financial aid. Of course, financial aid is not just free money. Normally it will be a package that includes at least 50 percent loans, so the less you've saved and the more expensive the college, the more you'll have to borrow. Worse, despite shielding that retirement money from the need analysis, you might not qualify for any aid and will have to borrow at a higher rate. During the years you spend paying back these loans, you might have to cut back on your retirement savings.

Usually, though, that's still the better option, because saving as early as possible toward retirement gives your money the maximum possible time to grow tax-deferred, or even tax-free. Given the choice of making maximum retirement investments when younger vs. when your children are college age, younger clearly wins. Besides, when you do pay back these loans, the interest on them is at least partially tax deductible, thus freeing up additional money to save toward retirement.

If that isn't enough reason to put your tax-advantaged savings first, consider the fact that you can withdraw money from an IRA prematurely to pay for college. You will owe the taxes, of course, but not the 10 percent premature withdrawal penalty. You can also tap your 401(k) in two ways that are less ideal: (1) You can take the early withdrawal, but you'll also owe the 10 percent penalty; or (2) you can take a loan against your 401(k) to avoid the penalty, but such loans have risks and disadvantages discussed in Hour 10, "401(k) and Related Plans." Before dismissing the 401(k) option, however, remember this: There's a good chance you'll be at least 59$^1/_2$ while you're still on the hook for either the direct college costs or paying back college loans. Then you'll be able to take withdrawals from the 401(k) without penalty.

So, are you now totally convinced that your retirement savings should come first? If so, Congress has just done its best to throw you for a loop with all the tax-favored education goodies included in the just-enacted 2001 tax bill. Some were mentioned in earlier Hours: expanded educational-loan interest deductibility and a $3,000 college expense annual deduction. However, even more importantly, Congress made important improvements to the previously feeble Education IRA and the attractive but flawed Section 529 plan.

The new, improved Education IRA allows you to sock away up to $2,000 annually in college investment, which is not tax-deductible. However, it works just like a Roth IRA, so you can withdraw investment plus earnings tax-free to apply toward education expenses.

Section 529 plans are even better—kind of a super Education IRA that you can use over and above the Education IRA. They enable you to invest essentially as much as you want after-tax toward educating your kids, although more than $10,000 per year per parent would trigger gift tax. At the time your child is ready for college, you can withdraw investment plus earnings tax-free to apply to college expenses.

However, Section 529 plans have some important limitations, the most important being that they must be used toward your child's (or another relative's) education, or you will pay taxes and substantial penalties to recover your money. Furthermore, unlike the IRA, you don't control your investments. Instead, you pick from among Section 529 plans offered by each state (you usually get a tax break investing in your own state's plan)—each one with its own administrator who controls your investments. You have to be careful about embedded investment fees and the fact that you have limited control over the strategy used to invest your money.

Once you're weighed the arguments, are you a bad parent if you put the feeding of your retirement kitty before the feeding of your kids' brains? Definitely not, especially if you simply save even more than the maximum you can contribute to retirement accounts; put the excess into moderate-growth mutual funds, in your name, with a long-term orientation. That gives you a flexible source of funds that you can tap at college time for your kids, or allow to keep growing for your own retirement. If you know you're going to use at least part of it for college, you can gift portions to your kids as needed before and during college. They can then cash them in at a lower capital-gains rate—using the proceeds to pay tuition and other expenses. How's that for a mutual (fund) admiration society?

JUST A MINUTE

The absolute guru of Section 529 plans is Joe Hurley, CPA, author of *The Best Way to Save for College* (see Appendix B). He maintains a Web site (www. savingforcollege.com) that contains the latest information on these plans, including a special section with updates for those who buy the book.

RATION BETWEEN OTHER CHOICES

Paying for college is important. But due to the many choices at different prices and availability of reasonable-rate loans, it's not as urgent as other needs—for example, making sure you can afford cancer surgery and chemotherapy. If you agree that's a more pressing need than both education and retirement saving, you've identified an important priority. Ultimately, you must look at all your categories of expenses and decide their relative priorities, allowing you to use a "what's leftover" approach to budgeting, including retirement savings.

JUST A MINUTE

For a different slant to a back-to-basics approach to budgeting, check out *Budget Yes!: 21st Century Solutions for Taking Control of Your Money Now*, by Jane E. Chidester and John L. Macko (see Appendix B).

SETTING PRIORITIES

Using the "what's leftover" approach, you'd start with food, housing, utilities, healthcare, transportation, and related budget "staples." You'd budget only for the essentials in each category, and they would all be included in the first and most important of three expense groups: non-discretionary life essentials. You'd rank these in order of importance for allocation purposes, but, hopefully, you'd always have enough income to cover all of them.

You'd then put all their "twin" discretionary categories into one of the two remaining expense groups, quality of life and would be nice. Those groups would also include categories not included in non-discretionary life essentials, such as vacation and travel, entertainment, and retirement saving.

Yes, retirement saving is discretionary, because you don't need it to stay alive today and tomorrow. But it should be at or near the top of the quality-of-life list—along with college saving, home maintenance, and other items you really shouldn't do without, but are still discretionary. Next to each item on this list, you'd put the amount you'd realistically like to spend on it annually.

If you were prudent in doing the first two lists, you should still have money left over for the would-be-nice list, which will include spillover twin (or triplet) categories from the first two lists, such as funds for expensive college, home remodeling projects, cushier retirement, and some new categories that are life enhancing but purely discretionary. Unless you accidentally picked up this book when you meant to get "Teach Yourself Outrageous Retirement Spending Sprees," you won't have enough money to cover all the items in this list. By prioritizing them, however, you'll know where to put the money when you get a raise or manage to cut your spending elsewhere.

INSURANCE VS. RETIREMENT SAVING

The priority approach is straightforward, but agonizing, nonetheless. For example, did you take pause when it came time to consider insurance? Sure, there are those who treat insurance as an investment. They're the ones who find ways to have a 1991 Hyundai still worth $10,000 stolen and be fully reimbursed. But most of us recognize that insurance is a cost of doing business: life business.

Like all business costs, therefore, we try to cut our insurance costs, but that can be riskier to your retirement than hang gliding. Just as we diversify an investment portfolio to reduce risk of unaffordable loss, insurance reduces that risk in a different way. If you're serious about retirement planning, you simply can't afford to be without good health insurance, although you can afford to cut costs with higher deductibles. Remember, insurance is meant to protect you from a financially fatal loss.

TIME SAVER

 Prominent financial planner and author Jonathan Pond provides a well-designed life-insurance needs calculation worksheet on his Web site at www.jonathanpond.com/lifeinsuranceneedsworksheet.html.

And sometimes it's to protect from a doubly fatal loss. If your spouse dies, how will you replace the income and pay for the extra services you need that your spouse might have provided through teamwork on childcare, home maintenance, and related matters. As you get older, you can cut back on life insurance, but at any time you need to have enough so that your retirement future won't die along with your spouse.

Hopefully, then, you put at least minimal insurance into non-discretionary life essentials—and added more into quality of life. For example, health insurance through an HMO might go into essentials, whereas the extra to have full choice health insurance would go into quality. We'll address these insurance choices more fully in Hour 17, "Retirement Road Detours." For now, recognize the cost of insurance as an important rationing decision you must make vs. retirement investing.

Finally, in making money-rationing decisions, consider the return on your investment. If you're already getting your full employer match from 401(k), it's easier to justify using funds for pressing nonretirement needs.

Similarly, if you're on a tight budget and don't have a 401(k), fully funding a Roth should be a high priority because its ultimate tax-free earnings are a big boost to its return.

If you're in the same situation and do have a 401(k), things get very interesting, because now it's a question of rationing limited funds between investment choices. Ideally, you'd want to get the full employer match and also fully fund the Roth IRA. But if that's not possible, don't automatically pick the 401(k). As we discussed in Hour 10, some 401(k) plans aren't okay—with minimal employer match, high fees, and an inadequate number of investment choices, often poor to boot. If you're in a 15 percent tax bracket, be sure to fully fund your Roth first before putting money into a substandard 401(k), even if it has a great employer match.

If you need any further convincing concerning the value of Roth investing, consider the fact that it makes one of your rationing decisions easier. Starting five years after opening a Roth, you can withdraw up to $10,000 totally tax- (and penalty-) free toward the purchase of a first home. Thus, young folks should stuff the Roth, and know they can tap it if they haven't raised enough down payment otherwise when they're ready to buy.

Hour's Up!

It's time to test what you've learned in this Hour about savings strategies. See how you do on the following quiz.

Answer True or False to the following statements:

1. Investing enough for retirement should always be your first priority, regardless of current life circumstances.

2. It sometimes makes sense to keep renting, providing more money to invest for retirement, instead of buying a house as soon as you can afford it.

3. It's not all bad to send your children to the school of hard knocks by not fully funding college for them.

4. It can be a financial burden to have children as a very young adult. But earlier awareness of financial responsibility means that young parents often end up ahead of those who wait until their 30s when it comes to playing the retirement-funding game.

5. As if paying for college isn't bad enough, it's an outrage that colleges expect you to deplete some or all of your retirement accounts to pay for it.

6. Insurance is important, but make sure you fully fund your 401(k) before you allocate funds for it.

7. One value of going to a good financial advisor is that you might get help making the difficult decision of how to split available funds between paying off debt and investing for retirement.

8. If you're obsessive-compulsive, you might have a hard time saving for retirement because you'll be constantly washing your hands of the whole business.

9. In some ways, buying a house is a lot like investing in a Roth IRA, because a married couple can sell it for up to $500,000 in tax-free gain.

10. It's important to take two years of algebra in order to make intelligent decisions about retirement-investing rationing, because you need to know when the numbers you come up with are based in reality, and whether they're rational or irrational.

QUIZ

Hour 17
Retirement Road Detours

Chapter Summary

LESSON PLAN:

In this Hour you will learn about …

- Unexpected problems such as medical crises, job difficulties, and divorce.
- Dealing with the "sandwich" of children and elderly parents.
- Expected problems for women such as career interruption for childbirth and widowhood.
- Insurance and liability-protection measures to guard your nest egg.

You might have heard the story about a couple visiting a city for the first time and renting a luxury car with a newly equipped computerized route-mapping system. It was late at night and they were relieved to be making it toward their destination smoothly, without trying to read an unfamiliar map with the interior car light. That is, until, they almost drove into a river.

Your road to retirement will sometimes cross such rivers. In some cases, you should know in advance that they'll be there, and in other cases, a flash flood will have created them. How they got there, though, is less important than you making sure not to wind up in them.

Let's take a little helicopter trip over your retirement road to map out these rivers so that you'll be able to better navigate them, and build a few bridges over them if necessary.

Expect the Unexpected

The challenge of planning retirement is that many things that probably won't happen to you nevertheless might. Don't wait for them to happen when it might be too late to do anything to financially compensate. Instead, build a cushion into your planning to allow for some unexpected adversity.

PREMATURE DEATH OR DISABILITY

If you're 30 years old, you have a one-in-six chance of dying before age 65. That's too big a possibility to ignore if others depend on you during your prime working years. Without life insurance, if you die, your spouse will fall helplessly behind in saving for retirement, not to mention possibly losing your future pension or Social Security. The nominal automatic life insurance (perhaps equal to salary) your employer might provide simply isn't enough. Through that same employer, you might be able to get good rates on supplemental term insurance, but you'll also lose that coverage when you terminate employment.

A better bet is to shop for your own term insurance, which is now priced very attractively due to the lower costs of offering it through toll-free numbers or via the Internet. You do need to be sure that the company is solid and solvent, which you can check out through Best's or other services that rate the financial health of insurance companies. It's not a crime to work with an agent, either, if that makes you more comfortable; but be prepared to be pitched permanent (whole life or variable life) insurance.

Such "permanent" insurance is a way to build up a tax-free or tax-deferred nest egg, but it's not a financial winner. Provided that you're disciplined, and you must be if you're reading this book, you can do better by using the old saw, "buy term and invest the difference." Buying whole life insurance when young is a mistake, if for no other reason, because it's likely to strip you of the funds you need to make full contributions to an IRA and 401(k). For more on choices, check out the *Life Insurance Buyer's Guide* at http://204.202.137.115/sections/business/Finance/insureprimer.html.

FYI A 30-year-old man is four times more likely to become disabled for at least three months than to die by age 65. A woman of 30 is 15 times more likely (although that statistic includes childbirth-related disability).

Life insurance is recognized as crucial, which is probably why almost twice as many working people carry it as carry disability insurance. Yet you're far more likely to suffer a disability keeping you out of work more than three months than to die during your working years. And most who do carry disability do so only because it's included in their employer benefit package. Many fail to realize that they don't have the coverage, and others who know they don't balk at the cost.

If you're among the reluctant, consider the impact of all those months or years without wages. Furthermore, your disability might keep you from performing even routine home upkeep. Therefore, you'll not only be unable to keep adding to your retirement investments, you also could end up having to tap them to pay for current needs. For less than $1,000 a year, you can get disability coverage that pays $2,000 tax-free dollars a month starting your 91st day of disability. That sounds expensive, but consider the alternative.

FAMILY MEDICAL CRISES

If the cause of a disability is a wage earner's serious illness, then retirement might be further jeopardized. The problem was less severe before medical technology made it far less likely that the victim would be "lucky enough" to die before depleting the family's resources. How much worse the tragedy to recover from a life-threatening illness only to face a life of poverty.

While there's no guaranteed solution, the best way to save your life and some of your savings is to get the best deal on good "choice" (vs. managed-care) medical insurance. You'll find costs much more palatable if you're willing to take on higher deductibles—say $2,000 annually—and maybe pay a portion of hospital costs instead of having them 100 percent covered.

JUST A MINUTE

As this book goes to press, a 2001 Congress altered by a party leadership change in the Senate started debating a national "Patient's Bill of Rights." It appears likely that this legislation will eventually pass and include provisions that loosen the control HMOs can exert over how doctors treat patients. Equally important, it will probably give patients substantial rights to sue an HMO for meaningful damages, heretofore virtually impossible.

True, when you're young and relatively healthy, you might find that all your medical expenses are essentially uninsured because you haven't hit the deductible. That will squeeze your current budget and require other sacrifices to keep up your retirement investing. But it will also mean that you're highly unlikely to take the devastating hit to your nest egg that occurs when you have conditions or require treatments that many managed-care policies won't cover.

Sudden Benefit Losses

As many dot-com workers discovered in this past year, you'll have a critical condition on your hands if you're abruptly laid off or your company goes bankrupt. On top of losing income, you could immediately lose benefits coverage and end up stuck with enormous uncovered bills—say for a coronary, upon discovering you're out of work.

The effects on your retirement planning are unspeakable.

FYI   During the year 2000, there were 20,335 Chapter-7 and 9,197 Chapter-11 business bankruptcy filings, and those numbers are expected to be sharply higher in 2001.

There's little chance of a bankruptcy occurring in a larger company without some forewarning—such as rounds of layoffs and media speculation. Seeing these signs, smart employees start polishing up their resumés, cutting back on spending, and looking for alternative sources of insurance. And even in a bankruptcy filing, larger companies often file Chapter 11, which means they keep operating, along with their benefit plans. You might even keep your job, and if you don't, you're eligible, under COBRA (Consolidated Omnibus Budget Reconciliation Act) provisions, to continue coverage for 18 months by paying 102 percent of the premium charged to the company per employee.

But the danger of the doors shutting without warning is much larger in a smaller company, if you're not alert to the signs. And when small employers shutter up, they usually choose Chapter 7, which means that creditors are paid first. Generally, that's the death knell for benefit plans, and recent news reports reveal that many smaller companies actually start siphoning off money from these plans before they close down. Meanwhile, you're uninsured and don't even know it.

Chances are that even your brilliant and heroic work efforts won't keep your sinking company afloat. But be prepared with your own life jacket. Your company's Summary Plan Document contains contact information for the insurance company. So, if you suspect hijinks, check with the insurer yourself to verify that you're covered. And start investigating alternatives while saving up to get new insurance. One good source to check immediately is your spouse's employer, which under some circumstances is required to enroll your spouse and you upon request within 30 days of you losing your coverage. Also, you might be eligible to convert your employer's plan to an individual policy, or as a "special individual" for other insurer's individual policies for which you might have otherwise been rejected due to health reasons.

Although you can lose these benefits abruptly, you shouldn't lose what you've earned in your pension plan, even if it is terminated. As discussed in Hour 12, "Defined-Benefit and Federal Pension Plans," the Pension Benefits Guaranty Corporation (PBGC) is a guarantor for a high percentage of (traditional) defined-benefit plans. If one of them should go under, PBGC will pay your pension directly, although it might take awhile to get everything sorted out, and coverage limitations will keep you from getting your entire pension if you're highly paid.

It's possibly a different story with 401(k) or other defined-contribution plans. Just as with health insurance, you should be concerned for the fate of your 401(k) if you work for a small company in trouble. Numerous instances of failing companies siphoning 401(k) contributions were reported and rumored during this past year's dot-com meltdown, and many companies have been caught with their hands in the employee contribution jar even before that.

DIVORCE

Fortunately, the majority of employers don't split with your 401(k) funds in tow, but 50 percent of spouses do split—sometimes with almost everything you've accumulated together for retirement. And that applies today whether you're a man or woman.

JUST A MINUTE

If you're heading for divorce and have reason to suspect that your spouse is hiding assets, hire a certified public accountant who specializes in forensic accounting, the art of finding hidden assets and other financial irregularities.

Due to increasing awareness of hidden assets and more protective laws, that kind of unfair split occurs less frequently. But when there's a battle, a fair split often goes three ways, the largest share sometimes to the attorneys involved. Each spouse is forced to live on less than half of the total pot, yet living apart costs each more than half of what it costs to live together.

For women especially, having more expenses on less money can virtually exterminate chances of a comfortable retirement if they never remarry. That's primarily because post-divorce statistics show that they usually have far less earning power than their husbands due to work disruptions or less education sacrificed for child rearing and homemaking. Furthermore, they live longer than men do so they end up accumulating far less and having to live on it longer—all on their own anemic Social Security, instead of their husband's.

It's small consolation that divorce settlements today often give spouses shares of each other's pensions. But those shares might be based only on current value, and not what the pension ultimately grows to become. Remembering the pension math from Hour 12, you can see that a woman divorced at age 45 might get her share of only 25 percent of her ex-husband's pension. That's despite her possibly having stayed home and raised the kids to make it possible for him to earn that pension.

JUST A MINUTE

You might want to look for a CPA or CERTIFIED FINANCIAL PLANNER with the relatively new Certified Divorce Planner (CDP) designation. A CDP has additional training that is geared toward looking down the road from the divorce instead of just "fairly splitting" current assets. Through knowledge of tax and retirement-plan intricacies and financial projections, the CDP attempts to suggest settlements that will keep both parties viable permanently.

This is not meant to be a gender-based polemic against divorce. But what's at stake for the parties, especially women (and always the children), makes it crucial to handle it in an equitable way, with minimum drain of assets. Counterintuitively, though, that might require hiring a financial advisor with specific, extensive divorce training. Although attorneys deal with money, they do so mostly in an adversarial fashion, rather than a big-picture fashion of helping guide the parties into financial life after the divorce. Here are some issues specifically related to retirement that any professionals you hire should know like the backs of their hands:

- How pension plans handle payments to a spouse under the separation and divorce agreements. Usually, this involves a qualified domestic relations order (QDRO). It must be consistent with the specific pension plan terms, and should always address the survivor benefits.

- How to evaluate a pension plan. What are the state laws on valuation? Is the pension indexed for inflation?

- Tax consequences of using pension benefits awarded to the ex-spouse before age 59$\frac{1}{2}$. Handled properly, there should be taxation, but no tax penalty.

EXPECT THE EXPECTED

You might very well reach retirement without hitting any of the "unexpected" detours, but you'll almost surely hit some expected ones. That's why financial advisors recommend a rainy-day or emergency fund of three to six months of take-home pay to get you through the kinds of unpredictably timed large expenses you're likely to encounter. And that's money over and above what you're saving for retirement, as it needs to be held in short-term safe savings instruments. About half should be accessible immediately (money-market fund), and the rest within months from short-term CDs or treasury bills.

JUST A MINUTE

Some financial advisors recommend you ladder your purchase of 91-day and 182-day treasury bills that you buy at a discount and cash in at for their full value upon maturity. The laddering refers to buying a combination of maturities each month for several months and then buying new ones when they come due. This way, a rung on the ladder comes due every month, and you average out interest rate fluctuations.

That stash is meant for major expenses not covered by insurance (hurricane-blown tree hitting your house) or not yet expected (a new furnace when the heat exchanger cracks), a sudden crunch of unusually high expenses, sudden opportunities to make a favorable-term major purchase that you hadn't budgeted (a heat pump to replace your antiquated heating/cooling system), and short periods of unemployment.

It's not enough, however, to cover larger expenses that can delay your arrival to full retirement financial preparedness. Here are "biggies" you must anticipate by more generous budgeting in your retirement savings plan.

FAMILY-NEED CRUNCHES

After years of two-income "yuppie-ism," with children mostly cared for institutionally, a recent retro-movement toward one parent at home has changed the financial outlook for many couples. Only one problem, things aren't what they were when single-income families were routinely able to succeed financially. Many of today's Boomers were raised in such '50s families, with mothers finally going to work outside the home when the nest emptied. Many of their fathers managed to retire with pensions and Social Security, that later-life mother's income helped pad an already comfortable retirement nest, and a large percentage of those couples retired together, still married.

By the time most of today's younger couples retire, they'll have been involved in a total of three or four marriages, combined, and few will be retiring to a comfortable company pension. Yet many are seduced by the warm memories of their family lives and by recently popular calculators that purport to show how you can often get along on one income because of overspending on two. Yes, well, those calculators don't include IRA and 401(k) contributions, which will be the bread and butter of most of today's younger generation's retirements.

They also don't take into account an important provision of the 2001 tax legislation—a partial remedy for the so-called marriage penalty in the taxation of two-income married couples.

JUST A MINUTE

The marriage penalty, a misnomer, resulted from mid-1900s tax code changes making rates more favorable to one-income families than to unmarried couples with one income. Unfortunately, those changes left approximately equal middle-income, two-income marrieds paying more tax combined than if they had remained single. The new tax law's wider 15 percent bracket erases most of that discrepancy.

So calculate this: Those who sit out of today's work force for any length of time, especially if they don't at least go to school to update or learn new skills, might be in line for a stale-bread retirement, with no butter. As it is, even two-income couples taking short family-leave breaks fall behind in retirement saving.

Consequently, in looking ahead to those breaks in income and retirement contributions, build up more savings in advance to make up for your shortfalls during those periods. And if you're taking longer breaks for traditional child rearing, add even more. Or, try to develop a home-based business that will enable you to contribute to one of the self-employed retirement plans discussed in Hour 11, "Small Business and Self-Employed Plans."

Of course, the burden on your budget only begins with the birth of a child and the possible break in one income. Although it varies widely by income, it's estimated to cost an average $200,000 in today's dollars to raise a child until age 18; college years are extra.

TIME SAVER

For a more exact idea of how much you might spend raising a child, try out the nifty calculators at www.calcbuilder.com/cgi-bin/calcs/BUD7.cgi/Kiplinger or www. bankrate.com/brm/calc/raiseChild.asp.

Although few couples specifically budget in advance for these younger-generation costs, parents are generally aware they're coming. What they don't see coming are costs for care of the older generation. These include the often-overlooked, difficult-to-quantify, adverse career effect on wage-earning women—on whom the burden of elder care normally falls.

Testimony in a recent Congressional hearing indicates that 22 million Americans provide informal care for seniors. About 14 million of them work, spending an average of one day's worth of time a week for eight years—often including several hours of work time when the cared-for person wasn't local. Although some caregivers are spouses, most are the cared-for person's adult children.

These numbers don't include millions that are receiving paid in-home, assisted living, or nursing-home care, often paid partly by the adult children. Chances are that you'll be involved in both ways at some point with care of your (or your spouse's) parents, starting with informal care and later with financial support. After all, somebody has to pay the $40,000 to $70,000 annually it costs for nursing homes, and that is increasingly less likely to be Medicaid.

If you doubt this sober reality, consider that only 10 percent of today's elderly have long-term care insurance—which etches the handwriting clearly on the wall. You must do something to avoid being overwhelmed by the time or money it will require to care for parents who haven't arranged it for themselves. That means talking to them about allocating resources to it, and not worrying about your inheritance—if that's even an issue—and working financially with them to arrange coverage, or setting aside more for your own retirement so the inevitable drain won't repeat the cycle across generations with you not having your own long-term-care arrangements.

EARLY RETIREMENT AND LAYOFFS

GO TO ▶
You'll recall that the Hour 12 coverage of pension plans included considerable discussion of early-retirement trends, their effects on pensions, and their implications for replacing income and insurance.

Of course, you'll have plenty of time to provide care for parents if you find yourself a victim of the kind of dramatic job cutbacks that began with the first hint of economic weakness during 2000. On top of actual layoffs, 2000 saw an acceleration of the early-retirement offer trend that has been part of the employment landscape since the mid-1980s downsizing.

So what's a future American retiree to do? If this seems like a philosophical question, maybe it is, because the answer comes from that American philosophical mecca, baseball. In Curt Flood's 1970 lawsuit that eventually led to the free-agency era of sports, one of the key arguments was that in the business world, employees are free agents, and baseball is just another business. Yet, ironically, it seems that modern sports stars are more proactive about free agency than business employees, who too often wait for the axe to fall, or stay with a losing "team" because they're afraid of losing accrued benefits.

Far too many workers still believe that loyalty is a virtue that their employers value and will reward. If it isn't clear by now that your only loyalty is to yourself, it's time for your own philosophical makeover.

As you approach retirement, be like a good baseball manager and think several batters (job-change possibilities) ahead. Otherwise, your retirement could be left stranded when you're given an intentional walk.

ANTICIPATE/HANDLE WIDOW(ER)HOOD

Widow(er)s have a similar early-retirement problem regarding spouses who involuntarily leave in a different way. Although only 6 percent of elderly couples are poor, almost two of every five widows have insufficient financial resources to live comfortably—half of this group is actually living in poverty.

The reasons are obvious, highlighted by this stunning statistic: 80 percent of widows now in poverty weren't poor before their spouses died. When a spouse dies, the widow's entitled to only half the spouse's pension, if there is one and they've elected joint and survivor benefits. Furthermore, if widow(er)s receives Social Security based on their own work (or as half of the spouse's benefit), they get half the spouse's benefit if it's larger, but lose their own benefit.

Furthermore, statistics show that excess medical costs associated with the spouse's death often eat up a substantial portion of the nest egg. Retirement poverty is a particularly serious problem for those widowed before age 60, because Social Security and pension benefits are also greatly reduced because of limited service.

Between widowhood and divorce, 80 to 90 percent of women eventually end up having to support themselves. The sobering reality of post-divorce and widowhood poverty is all the more reason why women should participate in the work force most of their lives to some degree. That's despite what families might perceive to be a wash in terms of the woman working and paying for childcare and homemaking expenses vs. staying at home.

Just the modest amounts that working mothers can put into employer retirement plans and IRAs can be crucial in retirement. And with the passage of the new tax bill, women over 50 should absolutely work full time in decently compensated employment. That's because of the catch-up provisions that allow everyone over 50 to contribute an extra $5,000 per year to their employer retirement plans. The language of that provision specifically cites the need for women to have adequate retirement resources.

PROCEED WITH CAUTION

Congress was wise enough to separate the catch-up provision from the amount you're allowed to contribute under the regular plan. You can make the catch-up contribution even if you're not allowed to contribute the maximum 401(k) amount due to overall plan participation rates in your company, or your own salary not being high enough. For example, if you're limited to making a $9,000 401(k) contribution in 2002 when the maximum will be $11,000, you can still make the allowed $1,000 catch-up contribution.

MINIMIZE THE DETOUR DAMAGE

Catch-up or not, neither men, women, or couples will have adequate retirement resources if they practice unsafe asset protection.

INSURANCE

Earlier in this and previous Hours, we discussed the importance of several types of insurance: life, disability, long-term care, and umbrella. Those are all types of insurance that people often consider discretionary, and if this book accomplishes nothing else, you're now convinced that they're mandatory.

We also covered health insurance, which most people know they need—and usually get through employment. But they fail to give enough thought to it until they end up without needed coverage or find out they're spending too much and could be taking larger deductibles. People also know they need homeowner's insurance, because a mortgage requires it, and auto insurance, because the law requires it. But people also tend to skimp on these in their haste to just get what's required.

Take homeowner's insurance. If your property has increased in value, or you're concerned about the effects of seemingly stronger and more frequent violent weather, it's time for a review. In order to get full replacement value for any damages to your structure, you must be insured for at least 80 percent of your home's replacement cost. Furthermore, it's a mistake to assume that your policy covers all sources of damage. You need separate flood insurance to be covered for that type of water damage, and must also have specific added coverage for sewer backups and other special situations.

And if you rent, make sure you have the renter's version of homeowner's insurance to cover your personal property and liability.

If necessary to make all this coverage affordable, set higher deductibles, which could save more than $100 on a typical annual premium. Doing so will reduce your temptation to make small claims that end up boosting rates or even prompt nonrenewal of your policy.

Regarding auto insurance, you're simply foolish to take anything less than the limits of liability that qualify you for umbrella insurance, and then get $2,000,000 of that. If you want to drop collision on an older car, fine, although it won't save you much. Here are the three main ways to save:

- Don't buy or lease luxury cars. You pay exorbitant rates because luxury cars are stolen at more than twice the (all-car) average rate and sustain 30 percent to 40 percent more than average accident damage. Contrast that to cars such as the four-door Taurus, stolen less than 50 percent as often and sustaining 20 percent less collision damage, on average.

- Don't try to fully cover yourself for loss. Increase your deductibles on liability and you could save 25 percent in total premium.

- Ease up on the foot so you don't foot the bill. Most states now mandate that insurers slap exorbitant surcharges for any traffic violation. If you get caught speeding a few times, your premium could increase 50 percent.

SHIELDING ASSETS

Insurance is certainly the key factor in protecting your assets. But if you either own a business or are self-employed, it's essential that you don't put your personal assets at risk of the consequences of your business activities. Usually, this means some form of incorporation, such as a C-corporation or limited liability company (LLC). These business structures (and S-corporations to a lesser degree) isolate your business assets so that creditors can't come after your personal assets.

In addition, though, you want to protect your business assets. If you work out of your home, be aware that your normal homeowner's policy doesn't cover losses associated with your business equipment. Thus, if the roof leaked into your home office and destroyed your equipment and records, you'd be out of luck without business insurance. And if your business desktop computer caught fire and it spread to the house, you might not even be covered for that damage if you don't have business insurance.

If you're performing a professional service, get errors and omissions insurance to cover any mistakes you might make, thus avoiding the need to liquidate your business to pay damages to a client. As you undoubtedly know, numerous and massive books have been written about business ownership, including extensive coverage of these topics. The key lesson is that while business income, capital gains, and tax-advantaged savings opportunities can help you create an enormous retirement nest egg, business carelessness can reduce your retirement savings to a goose egg.

HOUR'S UP!

If your road to retirement hits a detour, are you going to have to stop and ask for directions, or were you paying attention? Let's find out.

Answer True or False to the following statements:

1. Although it doesn't pay anything if you die, disability insurance can literally be a lifesaver in replacing income if you almost die.

2. Unemployment insurance is a bargain, and you can buy enough to get up to 80 percent of your income replaced if you're fired.

3. Fortunately, the law doesn't permit you to tap your IRA and 401(k) accounts if you lose your job, so at least you know they'll be there when you retire.

4. We could call it the sandwich generation because the financial strains of taking care of parents and kids can reduce you to eating peanut butter and jelly.

5. Umbrella insurance has a special provision that allows you to deposit extra money that grows tax deferred and provides you a rainy-day emergency fund.

6. If you're getting divorced, make sure to look under the place your spouse was sitting for any hidden assets.

7. A spouse's death is devastating, but an increasing number of companies are softening it by continuing the same pension payment to the surviving spouse.

8. When it comes to the chance that expensive new medical procedures will be covered, it might as well be called Managed-Dare Insurance.

9. The cost of setting up a protective corporate structure for your business can be a small price to pay to shield your personal assets.

10. To the relief of countless new mothers, recent studies have shown that it often doesn't pay to go back to work. Instead, by mothers caring for the kids, their husbands can concentrate on work and earn larger pensions to provide them both a comfortable retirement.

HOUR 18

Retirement Plan Management

CHAPTER SUMMARY

LESSON PLAN:

In this Hour you will learn about ...

- Key retirement-planning issues when changing jobs.
- How to take advantage of the new catch-up provisions in the 2001 tax bill.
- Portfolio balancing and investment reallocation.
- Rules for withdrawing your money without penalty, if you must.
- Roth conversion strategies.

You've explored retirement-plan management issues for each of the specific types of retirement plans. Now we'll take the time to orchestrate these options into one smooth symphony of retirement asset management.

Everyone is expected to change jobs, and possibly even careers, at least four times in their working lives and most will do it even more often. We no longer have a work-place environment that might have been true for your parents, who went to work for a company and stayed there until retirement. In fact, you may have watched your parents laid off from a job shortly before they got to take advantage of the full retirement package they expected.

Company loyalty used to be the norm. Now layoffs are so common people no longer can depend on a company keeping them around. Today's workers must plan their own retirement strategies and keep them in mind as they move from job to job. It gets more complex as you get older because you will also probably end up with numerous retirement accounts that need to be cross-managed in order to maintain a good portfolio balance.

CHANGING JOBS

Consider this: You've gotten exciting new job offers with higher salaries than you now earn and are ready to take one of them. Before you do, be sure to check out the fine print of the new retirement plans. You could be 100 percent vested in your current plan, but even under the new law you could end up waiting five years before any percentage is vested at the new company. A full discussion of how this works is in the following "Portability Options" section.

Another key point to check is how the employer's contributions are made and how much they match your contributions. The company could be offering the higher salary because their 401(k) contributions are very small or nonexistent. Also check to find out what the level of participation is of other employees in the 401(k) plan. It won't do you any good to have a great plan if you're a relatively high earner and can't contribute the max because there is poor employee participation.

Companies must pass what is called the average deferral percentage test. This means that a 401(k) plan generally must limit the average deferral percentage of highly compensated employees to no more than two percentage points above the average deferral percentage of the employees who are not highly compensated. If a company fails this test they can correct it in one of two ways:

- Make corrective contributions back to the highly compensated employees
- Make additional employer contributions to the employees who are not highly compensated

JUST A MINUTE

If you've received a great offer from a small company, be sure to ask about employee participation in the 401(k) plan and how this impacts your ability to contribute. Small companies have been successful raising their participation levels by shortening the time period for vesting. Be certain your new company does all it can to encourage participation.

Another related issue is the possibility of a company being found to have a "top heavy plan," which under the old law happened when 60 percent of the plan's assets are held by "key employees." If this is found to be true, the company could be required to make a contribution equal to 3 percent of each employee's salary.

The "top heavy plan" rules are somewhat simplified under the new tax law passed in May 2001. As long as an employer contributes at least a 3 percent match and offers 100 percent and 50 percent matching contributions at certain levels, the plan passes the "top heavy test." With these risks hanging over their heads, companies with low employee participation may end up limiting the contributions allowed by higher-paid employees.

PROCEED WITH CAUTION

Another key point to check out before taking that new job is what kind of plan the company is offering. The new company may offer a short vesting period and high percentage match, but the options may be so poor that your money wouldn't grow significantly.

Be sure to compare the investment options before you take the job. You could be stuck with them for the rest of your time at that company and it could be a real drag on your ability to build enough for retirement.

PORTABILITY OPTIONS

When you find a new job opportunity, and retirement plans are at least the same or better than the one you are currently part of, your next step will be to preserve your retirement planning by taking your already saved assets with you. Portability of the assets will be made much easier when the new tax bill provisions for retirement plans take effect December 31, 2001.

One big change that will help all workers is that they will become fully vested more quickly under the new law. There are two methods of vesting allowed employers who offer 401(k)s. One is called "cliff" vesting where the employee must wait a number of years before being 100 percent vested. Under the old law the waiting period allowed was five years. Under the new law that will switch to three years.

The second method is called "graded" vesting. Under the old law, a company could wait until the end of the third year before beginning to vest an employee's 401(k) contributions, and then begin vesting 20 percent per year for that and four more years. An employee would have to be with a company seven years before being fully vested. Under the new law, the company must start vesting at 20 percent per year starting at the end of the second year, and an employee must be fully vested by their sixth year on the job.

The new law also makes it easier for you to switch jobs because you have more rollover options. Under the old law a 401(k) could be rolled over only into another 401(k) or an IRA. A 403(b) could be rolled over only into another 403(b) or an IRA. A Section 457 could be rolled over only into another Section 457. Those savings plans could not even be rolled over into an IRA.

These restrictions made it much more complicated for people who wanted to switch jobs from the nonprofit to profit sector or even within the nonprofit sector. To simplify your life, the new law permits you to rollover qualified retirement plans into any of the other qualified retirement-plan options that accept rollovers. Distributions from a deceased employee's spouse's qualified retirement plan can also be rolled over into the surviving spouse's plan provided the employer permits rollovers.

Any after-tax contributions that you made into your employer-sponsored plan can be a bit more complicated to transfer. Under the old law they could not be rolled over into an IRA or another employer's 401(k). The new law allows these transfers to a new employer's plan, provided the new employer agrees to separately account for the after-tax dollars. They can also be rolled over into an IRA. You cannot do the reverse though, even under the new law.

PROCEED WITH CAUTION

 After-tax contributions to an IRA cannot be rolled over into a qualified plan, tax-sheltered annuity, or section 457 plan. This is one area of flexibility the new tax law does not allow.

USING THE CATCH-UP PROVISIONS

If you are over 50 and haven't saved enough for retirement, the new tax bill offers you a great opportunity to make up for it. This is particularly great for women who stayed out of the workplace for a while to raise a family.

In addition to the increase in IRA contributions that will be allowed for everyone, people over 50 will be able to contribute an additional $500 per year through 2005 and then an additional $1,000 per year beginning in 2006. Here is how the new contribution levels will work:

	Over 50	All Others
2002 to 2004	$3,500	$3,000
2005	$4,500	$4,000
2006 to 2007	$5,000	$4,000
2008	$6,000	$5,000

Catch-up provisions in the new law are also permitted for employer-sponsored plans. Here's how the new law impacts those plans:

	401K, 403(b), Section 457		Simple IRA	
	Over 50	*Others*	*Over 50*	*Others*
2002	$12,000	$11,000	$7,500	$7,000
2003	$14,000	$12,000	$9,000	$8,000
2004	$16,000	$13,000	$10,500	$9,000
2005	$18,000	$14,000	$12,000	$10,000
2006	$20,000	$15,000	Indexed plus additional $25,000	Indexed to inflation
Thereafter	Indexed to inflation		Indexed to inflation	

MAX OUT YOUR RETIREMENT SAVINGS OPTIONS

Your employer can also offer more generous benefits in plans beginning in 2002. The defined-contribution plan limit for a total of all your retirement plans will rise to $40,000.

Income limits rise under the new tax law as well. Under the old law the annual benefit limit was capped at $140,000 but now rises to $160,000. The $170,000 limit on compensation that could be taken into account under the old law now rises to $200,000. Also, contributions for profit-sharing and stock plans increase from 15 percent under the old law to 25 percent under the new law.

JUST A MINUTE

At the beginning of 2002, review all your contributions into employer-sponsored plans and be sure you are maxing out all your options under the more liberal new tax laws.

PORTFOLIO BALANCING AND INVESTMENT REALLOCATION

You are probably contributing to a number of plans, but are you looking at your portfolio balance across all of these plans? If you aren't doing that, stop reading and take a look at your most recent statements from all of your retirement plan options. It should not only show how your portfolio is performing, but also indicate how new deposits in each fund are being allocated. You should also get a statement of how all plan investment alternatives are performing. Compare the ones you selected with others available.

Do you still think you have made the best choices? If not, talk with your plan administrator about shifting your contribution allocation for your employer-sponsored plan. You can also talk with the trustee for any of your individual retirement plans, such as IRAs. You may want to shift funds already in the plan into other investment options, or decide to put new money into other investment opportunities to balance your asset allocation.

To get a handle on your overall asset allocation, review the retirement-plan holdings for you and your spouse. You may find you have great growth funds in your retirement-plan options and your spouse has better value or bond funds. By reviewing this together you can pick the best of both plans and reallocate accordingly.

FYI While allocations vary by age, Employee Benefit Research Institute/Investment Company Institute found on average, 53 percent of total plan balances are invested in equity funds, 19 percent in company stock, 10 percent in guaranteed investment contracts, 7 percent in balanced funds, 5 percent in bond funds, 4 percent in money funds, and 1 percent in other stable value funds for the year-end 1999.

What is the best asset allocation? That all depends on the number of years you have before retirement. If you are in your 20s or 30s, you have a long way to go before needing the funds. At this stage in life you can afford to take more risks because you have more time to recover from a drop in the stock market. If you are in your 50s and 60s, you are much closer to retirement and therefore should be careful about the risks you take.

It is generally believed that for younger employees an allocation of 70 to 80 percent in stock or stock funds and 20 to 30 percent in bonds or money-market funds is a good mix that will build a solid portfolio for the future. As you get closer to retirement, that allocation should be gradually shifted five to 10 years prior to retirement when the market conditions are right for re-allocating assets.

Remember the old adage "Buy low, sell high." As you look to reallocate your portfolio in your employer-sponsored retirement plan, be certain to sell assets at one of their highs and not when that type of asset is generally at a low. That is why it's wise to give yourself five to 10 years to reallocate your portfolio. By not forcing yourself into a time crunch so that you must sell an asset when it is in a down phase, you can wait for its recovery.

Most planners believe there should still be some significant percentage of growth stocks in your portfolio, given that people are routinely living 20 years or more in retirement and you don't want to run out of money. A good allocation in retirement actually reverses the allocation for folks in their 20s and 30s.

GO TO ▶

In Hour 21, "Retirement Gap Scenarios," we'll explore various cases that will review key investment and money management decisions at various ages and life stages.

Many mutual-fund companies are now offering life-cycle funds that repeatedly adjust and fine-tune your allocation according to your age and stage in life. Be careful, though, because many of these funds have embedded high fees that are difficult to clearly ascertain. You will usually be paying a fee for management of a life-cycle fund, as well as fees associated with each of the mutual funds that are part of the life-cycle fund. Sometimes these can be as much as double what you would have paid if you managed your own mutual fund alternatives.

EARLY WITHDRAWAL RULES WITHOUT PENALTY, IF YOU MUST

It's not wise to take your retirement money too early, but sometimes health issues or other emergencies make this necessary. There are ways to avoid the 10 percent penalty. If you have a traditional IRA you can "annuitize" the account using the IRS 72(t) method. Starting at any age, and continuing for five years or until the age of $59\frac{1}{2}$, whichever comes later, you can take annual cash withdrawals based on your life expectancy as mandated by the IRS. You'll pay taxes on your withdrawals as ordinary income, but no penalty. Once you've met the minimum duration requirements you can change to any other kind of withdrawal scheme you prefer.

FYI You can calculate your allowable annuity by using the IRS tables. You can download the necessary worksheets at www.irs.ustreas.gov/prod/forms_pubs/pubs/p93903.htm. What makes this method especially nice is that you can apply it to just one of your IRA accounts, and split up one big account to create a separate account with the amount you want to use for this treatment.

For example, if you are 55 and the IRS thinks that you will live until 80, you can take $\frac{1}{25}$ of the balance in your retirement accounts the first year. The next year you can take $\frac{1}{24}$. Using this method of withdrawal, you would need to pay taxes on the money withdrawn, but you would incur no penalties. During your payout period, your distributions schedule cannot change or you will be penalized. Check with a tax expert if you plan to take advantage of this early withdrawal option so you can be certain you understand the consequences of the choice and can avoid any risk of penalties.

If you have a short-term cash flow problem and are absolutely certain you can replace the money within 60 days, you can take a 60-day tax- and penalty-free loan from your IRA. This is viewed from the IRS perspective as a nontaxable rollover, but you can do this only once a year. If you miss the 60-day deadline you will have to pay taxes and penalties.

If you have a Roth IRA and the money has been in the account for at least five years you can withdraw your contributions both tax- and penalty-free. The disadvantage of doing this, though, is that if you treat the money as a loan to yourself and replace it, the amounts count against your annual contribution limits.

Roth Conversion Strategies

Now that we've talked about portability, rollover, and withdrawal options, there is one more cross-management issue to consider. Should you convert your qualified retirement-plan money into a Roth IRA? The Roth allows you tax-free withdrawals at retirement and doesn't require that you meet any minimum withdrawal rules at all. In fact, you never have to withdraw the money if you don't need it, instead leaving it to your heirs without incurring income tax.

Sound too good to be true? Well there are complications—remember it's still a government plan. In order to be eligible to even consider converting, your maximum income level is $100,000 whether single or married. A two-income family can easily top that in today's workplace environment. Another big drawback is that the money converted is taxed as current income. Worse, the more you convert, the more likely you'll throw yourself into a higher tax bracket that will make your conversion that much more costly. Also, if you do not have enough to pay the taxes with money held outside the retirement plans, any of the conversion money you use will be subject to the 10 percent penalty rules.

The good news is that you don't have to fully convert your holdings all in one year. You can do it over a number of years. If your money is held in accounts where some of it was after-tax money (such as a nondeductible

IRA) and some of it is taxable, you must add up all the accounts you plan to convert. Determine what percentage of the money is taxable and what percentage is tax-free.

PROCEED WITH CAUTION

Each year you convert the accounts, you must report the same percentage distribution of taxable vs. tax-free money. The rules do not allow you to pull out all the tax-free money one year and then the taxable money the next, or vice versa, for the purpose of Roth conversion.

Should you convert? It depends on your financial situation. Here are the benefits of conversion. Review your situation and see if your benefits would outweigh your costs. If you are certain your tax rates will be lower in retirement than at the time of conversion, conversion definitely would not make sense unless, for reasons of estate planning, you need to convert. Here's a brief look at the benefits after age 59$^{1}/_{2}$:

1. A Roth IRA of the same balance as a traditional IRA is worth more at the time of retirement. All the money in the Roth, both your contributions and the growth on those contributions are withdrawn tax-free.

2. You have more flexibility with the Roth, since you have no obligation to withdraw the money at any time or to meet any minimum distribution rules. All other qualified retirement plans require you to begin distributions by 70$^{1}/_{2}$ and you must meet the minimum distribution requirements set by the IRS.

3. Your heirs will love you, too, because they can avoid all but estate taxes. The Roth IRA does become part of your total assets at the time estate taxes are figured, but as long as you do not exceed estate tax limits, you heirs won't owe taxes on the Roth deposits held more than five years.

4. If you are certain that your taxes are lower now than they will be in retirement, it does make sense to convert. For example, if you are a two-income family and one of you has decided to go back to school, you know that you are now in the lowest tax bracket that you ever expect to be in. Take advantage of it and convert to a Roth.

QUIZ

HOUR'S UP!

It's time to find out whether you have learned the basics of retirement plan management.

Answer True or False to the following statements:

1. You are planning to change jobs. You have two options you like. One company has a slightly higher salary, but a poor retirement plan. The other offers a slightly lower salary, but matches a higher percentage of it in the 401(k) and has great investment options. Take the higher salary.

2. Under the tax law passed in 2001, you have greater flexibility in what you can do with your 401(k) at your current place of employment when you change jobs.

3. You are leaving a job in a nonprofit that has a 403(b) and moving to a for-profit with a 401(k). With the new tax law of 2001, you can now roll over the 403(b) into the 401(k) at your new employer if the company allows rollovers.

4. If you are a high-earning employee in a company with a lot of people earning low salaries, your contributions could be limited if there is poor employee participation.

5. There is no change in the 2001 tax bill that will result in your getting vested earlier after a job change.

6. You are 50 years old. You will be able to take advantage of catch-up provisions that let you sock away more for retirement beginning in 2002.

7. Between the age of 55 and 59$\frac{1}{2}$, you can "annuitize" you IRA and take money out earlier without penalty.

8. If you and your spouse are earning $125,000 combined, you can convert a Roth as long as each of you is earning less than $100,000.

9. Roth conversion is a good option if you know your taxes will be lower after retirement.

10. A Roth IRA is actually worth more than a traditional IRA if they both have the same balance at the start of retirement.

Hour 19

Completing the Plan

CHAPTER SUMMARY

LESSON PLAN:

In this Hour you will learn about ...

- Determining time frame, risk tolerance, and economic/return assumptions.
- Projecting contributions and allocating assets.
- Verifying the plan's suitability.
- Monitoring performance and making adjustments.

"Sounds like a plan." Wouldn't you just love to wipe that grin off the face of the next boss or work colleague who says that to you?

Sorry, can't help you with that, but this Hour will enable you to sincerely ask yourself, "sound like a plan?" And it will give you the tools to make sure you have a sound plan for your retirement. Those tools will put a face on your plan so that it looks like you: your station in life, stage in life, risk profile, and related parameters. But, scout's honor, no stupid grin!

DETERMINE PLANNING PARAMETERS

As long as we're into clichés, we can talk until we're blue in the face about a retirement plan. But it's not a plan until you've defined what retirement means to you. Regardless of how government or employers define it, your retirement age is when you plan to make that key adult transition. You'll have finished building your nest egg and will be ready to hatch and nurture it through the new phase of your life that it represents.

PLANNING TIME FRAME

By doing that, you've established what financial advisors call your planning time frame—the period over which investments are made to reach a goal. Actually, based on the unique approach in this book, you'll have as many as five planning time frames, unique to you, that will largely be determined by your choice of retirement date: your "until actual retirement" time frame, your "until-normal retirement age" time frame, and the three retirement phases. For now, let's focus on the immediate time frame from now until your personal retirement.

In Hour 7, "Introduction to Retirement Gap Calculation," we calculated, synchronized to retirement age, your post-retirement and preretirement cash flows. The calculation involved combining all inflows (income) with all outflows (expenses) over a period of time. Each inflow and outflow was converted to its value at the same point in time (usually the beginning or end of the time horizon), regardless of when it actually occurred. The synchronized flows were then combined to the present value or future value—which can be either positive or negative.

The combined net of all that represented your retirement gap (or surplus), stated in retirement-age dollars. We then determined how much more you'd have to add to positive preretirement cash flow to close the gap.

JUST A MINUTE

To put cash flow in perspective, a new business usually starts with a negative cash flow. That's because you create a large outflow with your startup costs and then have more outflows with heavy expenses in the first few years. Meanwhile, profits (inflows) start slowly, but if the business is successful they start becoming larger and more regular, making the overall cash flow positive after the first few years.

It's evident, then, that one way to close the gap is to change the time frames, with a longer preretirement time frame and, therefore, a shorter post-retirement one. That works on the assumption your cash flow is positive before retirement and negative afterwards, so that you'd be accentuating the positive, and (partially) eliminating the negative. That makes for a hit not only in Hollywood (for "Here Come the Waves" by Johnny Mercer), but also in your retirement—the calculation results being music to your ears.

Yet another way to accentuate the positive is to boost preretirement cash flow without changing the time frame. That relies on a possible combination of cutting expenses, increasing income, and higher investment return. It's important to realize that this flexibility with time frame gives you one set of gap-closing options, and rigidity gives you a different set. It's a question of identifying your priority—doing more total work by working harder in a shorter time frame or by continuing the same work pace for a longer time frame.

DETERMINE RISK TOLERANCE BY LIFE STAGE

While recognizing flexibility in time frames, there is a point at which you reach an important limitation. In general, the shorter your investment time frame, the less risk you can take. Conversely, the longer the time frame, the more you can expect the risk inherent in your chosen investments to be borne out by results.

To make this more clear, think about the exercise of tossing pennies and keeping track of how many heads and tails you get. The more times you toss, the closer the ratio of heads to tails will get to 50 percent. So think of a gambling game tossing coins in which you pick either heads or tails and you win if your choice occurs at least 45 percent of the time. Under which scenario would you bet the most money: 100 coin tosses or 1,000 coin tosses?

FYI What do pennies have to do with retirement saving anyway? Try this. Put one penny in a jar today. Tomorrow add two pennies, the next day four, the next day eight, and keep doubling the amount every day. After one month (31 days), take the jar (be careful of a hernia) to the bank and buy safe savings bonds with the more than $10,000,000 that just bought you a comfortable retirement.

The answer, of course, is 1,000, because short-term bad luck is less likely to cause you to lose. The odds are in your favor in the long run. Similarly, when investing in quality stocks, the odds are definitely in your favor in the long run. Thus, the longer the run, the more the chance you will achieve the historical annualized return on stocks of about 11 or 12 percent.

However, if you're now only 10 years from retirement, you'd be right to feel less confident of achieving that level of return. If you really need that level of return to reach your goals, it probably means you need to extend your time frame and go for a slightly lower return. From this line of reasoning comes the notion of risk tolerance according to age. The older you are, the less time you presumably have until retirement, and you can tolerate less risk in your investing. That said, it doesn't mean you should stop taking risks as you approach retirement age, but you might need to modify the risks by reducing your exposure to stocks and increasing your allocations to high-quality bonds and other safer (in protecting principal) investments.

Don't get the wrong impression. The risk level you assume as you near retirement is not the last word. Unless you accumulate a nest egg by retirement that would immediately cover 40 or more years of your retirement expenses, you'll need to continue investing during retirement. In fact, as you saw in the Hour 7 example calculation, assumptions about 8 percent growth until age 75 were made—a growth level that normally requires you be invested at least 50 percent in stocks.

PROCEED WITH CAUTION

To allow for investing a substantial portion of your retirement portfolio in equities, most financial advisors recommend that you have about three to five years' worth of it in highly liquid investments, so that you won't possibly be forced to sell equities when they're in a down cycle. This is covered more fully in Hour 23, "Managing Retirement Distributions."

ECONOMIC AND INVESTMENT ASSUMPTIONS

Even riskier than your actual percentage equity exposure, though, is your assumption about what rate of return that exposure will garner. Unlike the careful thought you put into the budget and asset forms providing the bulk of ingredients feeding the retirement-gap calculation, return assumptions are just a few numbers. But, just like a meticulously prepared dish can be totally ruined with a little over-spicing, overly optimistic return and inflation numbers can lead you down the primrose retirement-gap path.

For example, you might wonder how much small differences in growth and inflation could have in calculating a savings plan. Let's take an example of a couple who save all the take-home income from a part-time job that the wife has. Assume she now takes home $1,000 a month and will receive 4 percent annual inflation adjustments to her previous year's pay. We want to know how much she'll accumulate in 20 years, assuming a 9 percent rate of return. For simplicity sake, we'll assume she deposits $12,000 at the beginning of each year. The result: almost $1,150,000 accumulated in 20 years. Now let's change the example (seemingly) slightly. The employer uses only a 3 percent cost of living adjustment (COLA) for inflation and she earns only 8 percent on her investments. The result: about $300,000 less.

This comparison suggests that from here on you use the expression "a measly 1 percent" with considerable caution. More importantly, it tells you not to become too elated or deflated when you calculate your own retirement gap and the amount of extra savings you need to generate. Because these assumption make a huge difference, try this and any other financial calculations you do with several different (seemingly) close choices of rate of return and inflation rate. Then, when deciding a strategy, err on the side of being conservative in how favorable actual inflation and return will be to you.

Finally, don't forget that these numbers cut both ways. In the example we selected, a higher inflation rate was favorable because the employer was adjusting for it in giving salary increases. Yet, that higher inflation also means that annual expenses will increase. In calculating your retirement gap, then, inflation will be used for you and against you, so the overall effect of different choices won't be so dramatic. Nevertheless, you should still try those different choices.

TIME SAVER

If you want to go by the book, so to speak, then you might want the best historical data on inflation and rates of return for various asset classes. In 1999, for example, the highly respected Professor Roger Ibbotson made the following annualized forecasts through 2025: 11.6 percent return on large-cap stocks, 12.4 percent return on small-cap stocks, 5.4 percent on government bonds, 4.5 percent on Treasury bills, and 3.1 percent inflation.

INVESTMENT AMOUNTS AND ALLOCATIONS

By determining the planning parameters we've just discussed and incorporating them into the methodology in Hour 6, "Retirement Gap Calculation," and Hour 7, we've started to flesh out your specific retirement situation. The next step is to use your budget and asset information to estimate how much you'll be investing and how you'll be investing it.

PROJECT CONTRIBUTIONS TO PLANS/INVESTMENTS

What makes this approach to retirement planning different from most you'll see is that it's literally asset-backwards. In most models and calculators, you make assumptions about how much you'll need in retirement as a percentage of how much you're making now. Do any 35-year-olds have a clue of what that might be, with a salary and lifestyle so different than it will be as they approach retirement? Then, having made the assumption, they look at the difference between their current assets and the assets that will be needed in retirement to support that level of spending. They then complete the exercise by determining the savings and investment performance they'll need to get there.

That approach also ignores built-in spending habits you already have. Economists have long known that individuals can be at least partially characterized by their "propensity to consume." The theory around that says that you tend to spend in relation to what you have, no matter how much you have. Therefore, despite possibly dramatic changes in your income, you'll still tend to save at the same rate you're saving now. In other words, if you now make $80,000 a year and save $2,000, then you'll save about $4,000 if you make 160,000 a year.

This calculation uses that assumption in the way that it proportionately increases savings as your projected salary rises at the rate of inflation. In other words, it uses what you're likely to save based on current consumption tendencies, and then calculates the additional amount you'll need to save. Thus, the amount you discover you'll need to save will be either pretty sobering if you're now a lousy saver, or pretty comforting if you're a good one.

You might note that this reveals a possible limitation of this calculation, in that it assumes your salary will go up only by the rate of inflation. However, this limitation plays into the idea of the propensity to consume, in effect preventing you from assuming you're going to save tons more just because your salary might go up faster than your expenses. The propensity-to-consume theory says that your expenses will tend to go up with your salary, and that's as it should be.

You might then wonder why you can't assume both your salary and expenses will go up at a rate other than inflation. Well, they could and nothing stops you from using a different inflation rate here than the inflation rate you use in other parts of the calculation. However, be very wary of assuming a salary increase rate. You'll be on more solid ground by sticking with inflation, or perhaps an average of inflation and what you guess your salary increase rate will be.

DETERMINE ASSET ALLOCATION STRATEGY

Now let's jump back from salary and expense inflation (or rate of increase) to the rate at which your current and continuing investments will grow. To be realistic about that rate, you must take into account the earlier-mentioned considerations of time frame, your risk profile, and economic assumptions about growth and inflation. Together, these factors determine your asset allocation strategy—how you'll spread your investments (mainly) among stocks and bonds, and even what types.

In mid-life or before, the only other market investment assets you should normally be holding is your emergency fund split between money-market funds and short-term treasury notes. The return on this will be much less, but it should only (at least ultimately) be a very small percentage of your portfolio.

In general, the more you weight towards stocks, the higher return you can assume, but the greater risk you're taking. The more you weight toward bonds, the lower return you can assume, but the less risk you're taking. Although you don't need to actually decide on an asset allocation for the purpose of doing the calculations in this book, you do need to do it when you actually invest. Therefore some basics about stocks and bonds are in order.

BONDS

Money put into a savings account earns interest, usually on a monthly basis. If you leave the original amount on deposit and reinvest your interest in the account, interest helps to build your savings more quickly. You will not only earn interest on your initial deposit, but the interest will begin earning more interest.

Bonds are similar to savings accounts in that they do pay interest, but they differ by the fact that you are essentially loaning your money to someone else. Bonds are IOUs or loans that are bought and sold on the market. When you buy a bond, you are actually lending a specific sum of money to the company or institution that is issuing the bond.

Bonds can be issued by a corporation, a government entity, or some other borrowing institution. They are issued for a specific period of time, which is known as the term. In most cases the entity issuing the bond promises to make regular payments of interest to the investor at a rate set when the bond is issued. This is why bonds are often referred to as fixed-income investments. The term of a bond ends on the bond's maturity date at which time the bond issuer repays the investor the face amount listed on the bond.

If you hold the bond until its maturity date, you will receive the face value of the bond in full. Prior to reaching its maturity date, a bond price will fluctuate as economic conditions change. When interest rates go up, the price of a bond goes down because new bonds will be issued with higher interest rates, which make older bonds less attractive to investors. When interest rates go down, bond prices go up, because the older bonds are more attractive to investors since they are paying higher interest rates than the new bonds. Other factors that can impact bond prices are supply and demand, the financial health of a bond issuer, returns offered by other investments, and the maturity date of a bond.

You can see why it becomes more complex to figure out the rate of return from a bond. If you buy the bond when first issued, collect interest annually, and sell it when it matures, it is a simple interest calculation. Otherwise, to figure out your rate of return involves considering the price you paid for the bond, the interest earned for the number of years you held the bond, and the price at which you sold the bond. If the bond went up in value, you may have earned money in addition to your original cost, which would be a capital gain. If the bond went down in value and you had to sell it below the price originally paid, it would be a capital loss.

To find out how much your bond will earn annually, you must calculate the yield. To do that you divide:

Annual Interest ÷ Cost of Bond = Yield

STOCKS

Stocks and their returns get even more complex. Stocks are certificates that show you own a small fraction of a corporation. What you actually own is a small percentage of everything the company owns—buildings, computers, chairs, and so on. (No wonder you're squirming while you're reading this.)

Today, it's rare that paper certificates actually change hands. Most people leave their stocks on deposit with a broker to be handled electronically. Stock prices are set by the market and reflect what investors believe the company is worth. They can also be impacted by general economic conditions, news about the sector in which the individual stock falls, or news that affects the future earning potential of the individual company.

JUST A MINUTE

During the late '90s Internet mania, it seemed like what made stocks go up was what talking heads hyped on TV financial shows. In their view, traditional models of valuation failed to take into account net stocks' future potential from "monetizing eyeballs." As we've all seen, current earning power has now assumed at least equal weight in how the market values these companies.

The most critical factors that send a stock up or down in price are the perceived future growth rate of a company and its current earning power. When calculating the rate of return on a stock you include both dividends earned, if any, and capital gains. Dividends are paid in cash, usually quarterly, and are based on a company's profits.

Few growth companies pay dividends because they reinvest their profits toward growth of the company. Dividends are paid by older, more mature companies. Most investors count on an increase in stock price to earn the average 11 or 12 percent mentioned earlier. These earnings are primarily capital gains from selling the stock for more than it originally cost to buy.

For example, if you bought a share of stock for $10 and sold it for $20, your rate of return would be 100 percent. The other factor that must be calculated is the amount of time you held that stock in order to figure out your annual earnings on that money. To find your rate of return on a stock investment, you add dividends to the gain in value:

Gain in Value = Sales Price – Cost of Investment

Dividends + Gain in Value = Total Return

And then you can calculate the percentage return by dividing:

Total return ÷ Cost of Investment = Percent Return

Finally the percent return is divided by the number of years you held the investment to get the average annual return:

Percent Return ÷ Number of Years Held = Average Annual Return

Adjusting Calculations and Assessing Performance

With your certificate of completion for Portfolio Theory 101 now firmly in hand, you have all the requisite background for making sensible use of the calculation methods in this book. But no matter what you've learned here, nothing will be more important in using these tools than something uniquely yours—common sense. Assuming you have confidence in that, at every point in using these methods, ask yourself, "does this make sense." That, in fact, is the true power of eyeballs, your eyeball validation of your calculations, which could lead you to discover something important you left out, or a mistake in what you included.

Therefore, plan to do these calculations a few times just to gain a comfort level, and then to make adjustments based on what you discover. If you calculate a retirement gap the size of the Grand Canyon, and you've made no obvious mistakes, take an especially close look at your expenses—particularly those in retirement. Don't be surprised at such a large gap if you're planning an early retirement. It is simply darn hard to financially swing it.

On the other hand, if your calculations reveal you've got it made in the shade, then maybe you've been in the sun too long. Check and recheck to make sure your assumptions make sense, that you haven't accidentally added in salary twice, or that your expenses don't rely on eating macaroni and cheese for 50 years. Of course, if you cashed in on the Internet boom before it busted, your optimistic calculations are likely right on.

If, after all the careful checking, you find the extra amount you must save to be extraordinarily high, then it's time for remedial action. Perhaps you have credit-card problems and should pay a visit to a bona fide nonprofit credit counseling service. Maybe you need your kids to provide more for their college educations. Is it time for you to consider going back to school and upgrading your skills so that you can earn more? Revisit every area of the calculation to look for opportunities to reduce expenses and boost savings.

JUST A MINUTE

Although people tend to be overly optimistic about rate of return, some are too conservative. Financial advisors try hard to determine clients' true individual risk tolerances. In the end, you have to be able to sleep at night, but if you recognize that you're extremely conservative—say, believing that you can only achieve an average 8 percent return long term), then educate yourself more about investing and you might change your mindset.

Regardless, though, don't fret. At least you'll have learned that you have some serious work to do to accomplish your retirement goals. You can then use it positively to energize yourself. Then take a new look at things next year. You might be surprised to find that you'll discover more opportunities to cut the gap when you feel you've made a start and are in a more positive frame of mind.

HOUR'S UP!

A man, a plan, a canal, Panama. Okay, now it's time to show if you can complete your retirement plan forwards and backwards. If not, you know where you're going to retire!

Answer True or False to the following statements:

1. Your investment time frame is important in case you ever get investigated by the Securities and Exchange Commission (SEC). As the saying goes, if you do the crime, you must do the time—even if you were framed.

2. Risk tolerance is a highly individual trait that relates to your own personality, as well as the time frame.

3. Ibbotson is the child of the actor who made the frog ribbeting noise famous in the '60s comedy show *Laugh-In*.

4. The shorter your time frame until retirement, the more you're justified in taking greater investment risk to meet your objectives.

5. In projecting stock prices, most models give a weight of 15 percent to the average of the price projections given by TV networks CNBC and CNN.

6. The general rate of inflation is easier to predict than your likely rate of salary increases.

7. The calculations in this book are so straightforward, that there's very little chance of error. If you calculate a big gap, immediately start looking at drastic measures you can take to improve your situation.

8. Bonds go up in price in concert with interest rate increases, and down in price when interest rates fall.

9. Your propensity to consume affects your retirement gap because the less you consume, the more new clothes you have to buy to fill the gap caused by a shrinking stomach.

10. The dividends that stocks pay make them a little like a bond. In fact some stocks are very much like bonds in paying big dividends but not growing much.

Hour 20

Comprehensive Retirement Gap Calculation Example

Now that you have learned more about retirement issues and the complexities that can affect your retirement gap, we will revisit the retirement gap calculation and complete a more comprehensive problem. This will give you another chance to practice before using the blank retirement gap calculation in Appendix D, "Retirement Gap Data and Calculation Worksheets," for your own retirement planning.

Setting the Stage

First let's set the stage for this drama. We're going to revisit Mark and Mary Moneystrapped from Hour 7, "Introduction to Retirement Gap Calculation." This time we'll be stopping by 10 years into the future when Mark and Mary are 50 years old.

Their two teenagers have grown. One has only two years left in graduate school and will then be getting married. The second has five years left before finishing college and graduate school, but plans to get married the same year.

Fortunately, the grandparents set up a trust fund to cover college for their two children, but it only just became available. Up until now, they've been budgeting $10,000 per child annually to supplement the financial aid package and cover the cost of expensive private schools—leaving nothing in their budget for extra savings.

Unfortunately, their obligations to their kids aren't over, as they've promised them a combined $45,000 for the two weddings and gifts.

They have decided to retire early at age 60. Mary wants to write novels and Mark has worked out a consulting arrangement and expects to earn $70,000 a year until full retirement at 65. Their early-retirement phase will be ages 60 to 65.

At the age of 65, the Moneystrappeds plan to fully retire and take a major around-the-world vacation that will cost $90,000 in today's dollars. Upon return, they'll move into a rest-of-life retirement community arrangement that they project will cost them $750,000 at that time. They expect the proceeds of their current home to cover most of the costs.

Currently, their home is entering the sixth year of a 15-year mortgage they arranged upon refinancing at age 45. That enabled them to pay off their previous equity line and be free of housing debt upon early retirement at age 60. For planning purposes, the Moneystrappeds believe they'll reach Phase 2 of their retirement planning at age 75 and Phase 3 at age 80.

JUST A MINUTE

By age 80, will Mary and Mark Moneystrapped still be able to take care of themselves? They've thought about that and plan to buy into an active retirement community that is affiliated with a continuing-care retirement community. This will ensure them of total housing and care guaranteed and covered for the rest of their lives. They're also protecting themselves immediately against a financially devastating situation by taking long-term-care insurance in case something happens before then.

The Moneystrappeds have not saved as much as they hoped, but they're improving, and now plan to use their retirement plan catch-up options, authorized in the just-enacted 2001 tax legislation, to fill their retirement gap more quickly. They now have a joint gross income of $175,000. Their annual outlays total $155,000—including taxes and deposits in their 401(k)s—leaving a $20,000 surplus for net annual additional savings that is now available because they're no longer paying college costs. Their 401(k) savings will be increased to $15,000 annually, including $1,000 from employer match.

Again, we're going to calculate the Moneystrappeds' retirement gap assuming the inflation rate is 3 percent and their rate of return (growth rate) on investments until age 65 is 9 percent. From age 65 to 75, we'll assume they'll move investments into more conservative choices and earn an average of 8 percent. From age 75 to 80, they'll again shift to a more conservative investment allocation that earns 7 percent. Finally, after age 80 all investments are virtually safe, earning 6 percent.

Their retirement resources have grown. Currently they have $160,000 in their 401(k)s and $52,000 in their Roth IRAs. They are putting all extra cash into boosting their retirement assets. After having just cashed in a sizeable taxable capital gain (and already paying the tax), their taxable stock portfolio currently has a market value of $30,000 with a cost basis of $30,000. Their home is now valued at $450,000, and has a $300,000 mortgage balance (note the high $40,000 annual home ownership cost despite a very low interest rate) that will be paid off in 10 years, at early retirement. Their annual Social Security income at age 65 is now estimated to be $34,600.

JUST A MINUTE

Review your assumptions and calculations annually just to be sure you are on track. Now that their financial obligations for their children's college have ended, Mary and Mark Moneystrapped want to revisit their retirement gap and get more serious about filling it. The first step is to find out how large it is. They hope the cash that went toward college will be enough to fill that gap in time for early retirement.

Early retirement requires an additional budget with much higher costs for health insurance. The Moneystrappeds will begin to tap into their assets at age 60, but think they will be able to cover most of their costs with consulting fees Mark will earn totaling $70,000. Mary wants to write novels, but since the earnings are more uncertain, we will not include any possible income from her in these calculations.

The additional money needed will first be taken from their taxable savings, which are taxed at only the 20 percent capital gains rate. After that they will begin to draw from their tax-deferred retirement savings, leaving the tax-free Roth for use later.

They anticipate needing annual after-tax income, in today's dollars, of $100,000 at the beginning of Phase 0 (age 60), $90,000 at the beginning of Phase 1 (age 65), $50,000 at the beginning of Phase 2 (age 75), and $75,000 starting Phase 3 (age 80). Inflation will increase these amounts yearly during each phase.

PREPARING THE WORKSHEETS

As we did in Hour 7, we'll first complete the worksheets to be used in the retirement gap calculations.

Remember, Appendix D is where you will find a budget worksheet to set your own budget for now (your working years)—and Phases 0, 1, 2, and 3. We will again simplify this budget for Mark and Mary using the stated assumptions. When working up your own budget, use the more detailed one in Appendix D. The additional line-by-line detail will help you estimate each of these major line items.

Expense Item	Now	Phase 0	Phase 1	Phase 2	Phase 3
Home ownership	$40,000	$3,500	$3,500	$3,500	$15,000
Utilities	$4,000	$4,500	$5,000	$6,000	$3,000
Insurance	$5,000	$8,000	$8,500	$8,500	$9,000
Food/personal care	$7,000	$7,500	$8,000	$8,000	$10,000
Entertainment/ travel	$8,000	$10,000	$18,000	$3,000	$2,000
Transportation	$7,000	$9,000	$9,000	$3,000	$5,000
Clothing	$5,000	$8,000	$8,000	$4,000	$3,000
Religion/charity	$10,000	$10,000	$5,000	$0	$0
Savings/ investments	$14,000	$0	$0	$0	$0
FICA/taxes	$50,000	$30,500	$12,000	$2,000	$2,000
Health/child care	$3,000	$15,000	$10,000	$10,000	$23,000
Miscellaneous	$2,000	$4,000	$3,000	$2,000	$3,000
Total Outlays	**$155,000**	**$110,000**	**$90,000**	**$50,000**	**$75,000**
Income	$175,000	$70,000	Social Security	Social Security	Social Security
Additional savings	$20,000	$0	$0	$0	$0

JUST A MINUTE

Note that the Moneystrappeds' projected total outlays (expenses plus savings) for early retirement drop by $45,000. Is it realistic to think they can cut their budget by so much? Actually, when you take out the $20,000 for additional savings, the $14,000 added yearly to the 401(k), and lower taxes, it won't be hard to live with the cut in pay even though there are much higher health insurance costs outside a group plan.

We now need to develop the Retirement Ready Assets worksheet that you can find in Appendix D. This will include investments, luxury cars, valuables, personal property, real estate, and other miscellaneous assets. Here is a sample developed from Mark and Mary's assets in the "Setting the Stage" section at the beginning of this Hour:

Asset Category	Asset Name	Value	Cost to Sell	Basis
Investment	401(k)s	$160,000	-	-
Investment	Roth IRAs	$52,000	-	-
Investment	Stock	$30,000	$720	$30,000
Real estate	Home	$450,000	$10,000	$275,000

Now we are ready to put this more complicated case into practice. Hopefully, by the end of these calculations you will be even more confident that you can figure out your own retirement gap.

RETIREMENT NEED GAP CALCULATION PROCEDURE

When you started working through the Hour 7 calculation, you might have been overwhelmed; but by the time you finished Hour 7, you might have been saying "Hey, I finally get it!" The good news is that this procedure builds on Hour 7, so your success there will help here. The bad news is that this is longer and more complicated. Nevertheless, you will "get this" too if you stick with it, and it's well worth the effort. When you finish, you'll be confident of being able to calculate your own gap, so that you can use the advice throughout this book to start closing it!

To save space, this Hour doesn't repeat all the detail from the worksheet it uses in Appendix D. So refer to that worksheet (better yet, make a copy) and follow it closely as you work through this example. The answers are included, so you can check yourself for accuracy.

This procedure contains some simplifying assumptions, such as the way taxes are calculated, that will make the result different from a more detailed, exact procedure. But these simplifications are biased toward overstating your retirement gap. Thus, you won't get overconfident, and you'll still have a far better idea where you stand than you would with rule-of-thumb methods.

Step 1: Determine ages for each phase and determine expected annual budget amount in current dollars:

Ages for Phase 0 are __60–64__, Annual Budget _____$110K_____

Ages for Phase 1 are __65–74__, Annual Budget _____$90K_____

Ages for Phase 2 are __75–80__, Annual Budget _____$50K_____

Ages for Phase 3 are __80+__, Annual Budget _____$75K_____

Step 2: Determine the inflation-adjusted budget amounts for each year starting with normal retirement:

Phase 1: $90,000 \times 1.03^{15} = \$140,217$

Phase 2: $50,000 \times 1.03^{25} = \$104,181$

Phase 3: $75,000 \times 1.03^{30} = \$182,044$

Step 3: Determine inflation-adjusted income during each year of retirement from Social Security, pensions, and other already established annuities. In Mark and Mary's situation, we are including only Social Security and anticipated consulting fees during the early retirement phase.

Phase 1: $34,600 \times 1.03^{15} = \$53,905$

Phase 2: $34,600 \times 1.03^{25} = \$72,444$

Phase 3: $34,600 \times 1.03^{30} = \$83,983$

JUST A MINUTE

Step 3 is actually calculating the inflation-adjusted amounts for the first year of each normal retirement phase. The Step 5 calculation "invisibly" projects those amounts to the specific inflation-adjusted amounts for each year of retirement.

Step 4: Find the need gaps by subtracting amounts in Step 2 from amounts in Step 3. (The results of the subtraction are negative.)

Phase 1 GAP: –$86,300

Phase 2 GAP: –$32,400

Phase 3 GAP: –$98,100

Step 5: Combine the expected effects of inflation and rate of return on the Social-Security gap amounts from Step 4 to get total gaps at the beginning of each of the phases of retirement and then combine for total gap at the beginning of retirement.

Phase 1

$(^{1.08}/_{1.03}) - 1 = .0485$ (or 4.85%) is Inflation-Adjusted Interest Rate

Phase 1 Gap at Beginning of Phase 1 = –$703,800 (10-year phase)

So, Phase 1 Gap is –$703,800.

Phase 2

$([^{1.07}/_{1.03}]) - 1 = .0388$ (or 3.88%) is Inflation-Adjusted Interest Rate

Phase 2 Gap at Beginning of Phase 2 = –$150,300 (5-year phase)

Phase 2 Gap at Beginning of Phase 1 = –$69,480 (discounting 10 years with 8% growth rate)

So, Phase 2 Gap is –$69,480.

Phase 3

$^{1.06}/_{1.03} - 100 = .0291$ (or 2.91%) is Inflation-Adjusted Interest Rate

Phase 3 Gap at Beginning of Phase 3 = –$864,800 (10-year phase)

Phase 3 Gap at Beginning of Phase 2 = –$616,600 (discounting 5 years with 7% growth rate)

Phase 3 Gap at Beginning of Phase 1 = –$285,160 (discounting 10 years with 8% growth rate)

So, Phase 3 Gap is –$285,160.

Total Gap

Add final Gaps from Phases 1, 2, and 3 above:

–$703,800 + (–$69,480) + (–$285,160) = –$1,058,440

Step 6: Calculate the amount available to save annually.

401(k): $15,000

Roth: $10,000

Taxable: $20,000

Step 7: (Using alternative Step 7 for Early Retirement that you'll find after Step 10 on the Retirement Gap Calculation worksheet in Appendix D): Project the amount that your invested ongoing savings will grow to by the time you retire. Don't include money already saved. That is used in Step 8.

Please note that these calculations all use the inflation-enhanced interest rate to project your annual investments forward to early retirement. They then use the normal growth rate to project the amounts accumulated by early-retirement to normal retirement.

401(k):

Annual savings until early retirement:

$15,000 for 10 years @ 12.3% = $299,900 ($1,000 of the $15,000 is employer match)

Lump sum saved from early retirement to full retirement:

$299,900 @ 9% projected forward 5 years = $461,430

After-Tax Lump Sum:

$461,430 @ .75 = $346,070

This assumes the new law's eventual ordinary-tax rate of 25% (down from current 28%).

After-Tax Invested Taxable Savings:

Annual savings until early retirement:

$20,000 for 10 years @ 12.3% = $399,910

Lump sum saved from early retirement to full retirement:

$399,900 projected forward five years @ 9% = $615,310

After-Tax Lump Sum:

615,310 – [.2 × (615,000 – 200,000)] = $532,250 (after-tax)

Applying capital gains rate of 20 percent to the difference between the before-tax lump sum and the basis of $200,000 (20,000 for 10 years) invested.

Roth:

Annual savings until early retirement:

$10,000 @ 12.3% for 10 years = $199,950 tax-free

Lump sum saved from early retirement to full retirement:

$199,950 projected five years at @ 9% = $307,650

PROCEED WITH CAUTION

Although their income seems too high, note that it is Adjusted Gross Income (AGI) that determines Roth qualification, and they just barely make it. Also, if the $10,000 contribution seems too high, note that they are taking advantage of the catch-up provisions in the just-enacted tax act to contribute this much.

Total After-Tax Savings:

Sum the Type 1, 3, and 4 savings. They have no Type 2 (nondeductible IRA) amounts.

$346,070 + $532,250 + $307,650 = $1,186,000

Early Retirement Negative Cash Flow:

Continuing in Alternative Step 7b, there are no additional savings to be calculated during early retirement, but there are "anti-savings." Their budget is $110,000 with only $70,000 in income from consulting. Therefore, there is a $40,000 shortfall. This must be carried forward as a negative number in the calculations to the full retirement period. The $40,000 annual shortfall (income minus outlays) for the first year of early retirement must be adjusted for inflation from current dollars to dollars as of 10 years from now.

–$40,000 @ 3% = –$53,757

Calculate lump-sum shortfall through early retirement:

$53,800 for 5 years @ 12.3% = $386,100 shortfall at normal retirement.

Then subtract that from the total lump-sum savings at normal retirement, calculated earlier in this Step:

$1,186,000 – $386,100 = $799,900

Thus, total ongoing invested savings grows to approximately $800,000 at normal retirement.

Step 8: Calculate Mary and Mark's current and anticipated retirement-ready assets and then apply 9 percent growth (or other rates, as appropriate) to those assets to determine their value at age 65, completing the calculation by subtracting taxes. Note that some of these "assets" are actually liabilities, which must be expressed in dollars as of their normal-retirement year.

Cash on Hand:

$45,000 for weddings: –$145,699

Project $45,000 forward 2 years at rate of inflation to the time of the weddings, and then project that amount 13 years forward at the growth rate to determine liability as of retirement.

$90K for trip: –$187,000

Assuming a 5 percent rate of inflation for travel expenses projecting this amount forward 15 years.

Then, offset this $187,000 in age 65 dollars for the trip with a $5,000 tax-free gift for travel from the company at retirement.

Thus, –$182,000 is the net liability for the trip at retirement.

Roth IRA is $52,000 @ 9% for 15 years = $123,103

401(k) is $160K at 9% for 15 years = $378,779

After-tax = $284,084 (applying 25% ordinary-income tax rate)

Taxable Investments are $30,000 at 9% for 15 years = $71,021

71,021 – [.2 × (71,021 – 30,000)]

After-tax = $62,817 (Basis is $30,000)

Their home is now worth $450,000. It is anticipated to appreciate to approximately $700,000 (3 percent annually for 15 years) by the time of full retirement at age 65. The Moneystrappeds will then combine that $700,000 with an additional $50,000 to buy into the retirement community.

Now, combine everything in this step, with home value cancelled out and subtracting the additional $50,000 outlay for the retirement community:

Total retirement-ready assets at age 65: approximately $90,000

Step 9: Calculate the Retirement Gap.

Total Gap from Step 5: approximately –$1,050,000

Total Savings from Step 7: approximately $800,000

Total Assets from Step 8: approximately $90,000

Total Retirement Gap (summing these) = –$160,000

Step 10: Determine additional annual savings needed to close the Step 9 gap.

(i) 5 × Total Retirement Gap (Step 9) = $800,000 (call this result the Full Numerator)

(ii) 1 + Growth Rate = (suggest 1 + .09 = 1.09) = 1.09 (call this result the Growth Factor)

(iii) [(Growth Factor)$^{\text{Years to Retirement}}$] – 1 = 2.64

Raising Growth Factor of 1.09 to the power of the number of years (15) from now to retirement. Then subtract 1 from that result.

Multiply results of Steps (ii) and (iii) = 2.88

Multiply Step (iv) result by 4 = 11.56 (call this the Partial Denominator)

(vi) (Partial Denominator) ÷ Growth Rate = 128.4

Use .09 Growth Rate from Step (ii).

(vii) (Years to Retirement) + (Step (vi) Result) = –143.4 (call this result the Full Denominator)

(viii) Full Numerator ÷ Full Denominator = $5,578

Step (i) result (800,000) divided by Step (vii) result (143.4)

You can now confirm that this is the correct amount as follows:

Determine the Future Value of 15 years of $5,578 payments at a 9 percent growth rate, which is about $179,000.

Determine the Basis: 15 × $5,578 = $83,670

Find taxes: .2 × (179,000 – 83,670) = approximately $19,000

$179,000 – $19,000 = $160,000 (your retirement gap)

Remember, this is the Moneystrappeds' retirement *gap*, not the total amount needed for retirement. Thus, the $5,578 is an *additional* amount they must save and invest yearly, over what they are now budgeting, if they are to meet their rather extravagant retirement goals.

USE OF ESTIMATIONS AND ASSUMPTIONS

We have visited a fictitious family, but in reality you will need to make up your own future in order to plan for retirement and figure out your gap. As we discussed in Hour 5, "Retirement Finance Basics," sometimes the hardest thing to do is figure out your ages you should pick for the various phases and think about when you will die.

You can start by looking at family history. How long did your parents live or are they still alive? If they are still alive, how long did their parents and grandparents live? Are there health problems that seem to hit each generation? Looking back at family history helps you to make your own assumptions about your future.

Budgeting is another place where a lot of unknown estimates become a big part of finding the retirement gap answer. You can take some of the guesswork out of these estimations by finding out what today's costs are for the various things you may want to do in retirement. Remember, you will be adjusting all these numbers by inflation.

FYI If after working through the retirement gap calculation you are still finding this too difficult, you can at least get a very rough ballpark estimate of your savings need using a simpler worksheet developed by the American Savings Education Council. It can be used as an online interactive calculator, or you can download a worksheet at www.asec.org/ballpark.

HOUR'S UP!

You can't put it off any longer. It's time to do your own calculations. Let's review some key points and see how much you have learned.

Answer True or False to the following statements:

1. When considering early retirement, you must do an additional budget.
2. One of the key costs unique to early retirement is related to health insurance.

QUIZ

3. Once you complete the retirement gap calculation, you never have to do it again.

4. Long-term care insurance adds significantly to your monthly insurance bill, but reduces the risk of devastating your retirement savings.

5. The sale of your residence can be used to buy a retirement home and allow you to live mortgage- or rent-free in retirement.

6. You don't need to do any special adjustments to calculate lump sums as long as they are paid before the start of retirement.

7. When considering early retirement, be certain to add its impact to all the retirement gap steps as appropriate. It's not just a budget calculation.

8. It's impossible to make reasonable assumptions about the ages for your various retirement phases.

9. You can put together reasonable budget estimates by checking on current costs for the things you plan to do.

10. It is important to revisit your retirement gap calculations yearly, just to be sure you are on track and to make any adjustments as you know more about your estimates and assumptions.

QUIZ

PART V

Road to Retirement

Hour 21 Retirement Gap Scenarios

Hour 22 Pre-Retirement Planning

Hour 23 Managing Retirement Distributions

Hour 24 Retirement Pitfalls, Shortfalls, and Surpluses

HOUR 21
Retirement Gap Scenarios

CHAPTER SUMMARY

LESSON PLAN:

In this Hour you will learn about ...

- Retirement planning strategies for typical young singles.
- Retirement planning strategies for typical young married couples.
- Retirement planning strategies for typical permanent singles.
- Retirement planning strategies for typical mid-life couples.
- Retirement planning strategies for typical mid-life divorced couples.
- Retirement planning strategies for typical preretirees.
- Choosing the right financial advisor.

Now that there's a (retirement) gap in your education, and 20 Hours behind you on how to fill it, the question is, what's the next step? What we're going to do in this Hour is look at retirement planning strategies for six typical life situations. Hopefully, one of them will be at a place that's close to fitting you.

This lesson won't include any specific numerical information about salary, savings, and the like. However, it will talk about typical financial situations for each of the six cases, and the typical retirement-planning strategies that best serve those situations.

You've probably seen so-called "money makeovers" in newspapers and magazines, in which specific people and couples get professional financial planning help. Think of these six scenarios, then, as generic retirement-planning makeovers for six types of financial-planning clients.

TYPICAL YOUNG SINGLE SITUATION

If, as an unmarried young person in your 20s who is now out of school, you fall into this first generic retirement makeover, consider yourself lucky. You know very well that you can't afford a financial planner, yet your situation is enough like millions of others that this advice will probably sound like it fits you personally. And if you're older but admit to a case of arrested financial development, follow along, because this case touches on all the basics.

PLANNING ADVICE

As a young single you probably have at least one student loan. Furthermore, you've likely piled up credit-card debt on top of student loans, so focus on that higher-interest debt first. Don't neglect your obligation to Sallie Mae, but because her rates are so favorable, you might want to consider her "interest only" deferral plan for repayment. It has the added advantage of making your payments fully tax-deductible, even though you probably don't have enough deductions to itemize.

FYI The Sallie Mae Web site (www.salliemae.com/) provides extremely helpful information on refinancing student loans. And, for those reading this who are parents of future college students, the Sallie Mae and companion Web site, Wired Scholar (www.wiredscholar.com/paying/content/index.jsp), are rich sources of information on college funding.

Be anxious to pay off your debt, but don't go overboard by taking risky steps. Don't think you can make a quick killing in the stock market, even though it's now showing some signs of recovery from a very bad year.

Instead, invest your immediate efforts in budgeting and paying off your debts, and start saving and investing for longer term. Every dollar you invest now for the long term is so much more valuable than what you invest 20 years from now. It has all those years of compound growth, and time to ride the bumps toward the ultimate upward trend of the stock market.

Speaking of long term, what about Social Security for you? Yeah, right! Don't count on a traditional pension or retiree medical coverage, either—or help from Mom and Pop. Your Baby-Boomer parents, who lived through an era of corporate downsizing, raised you and put you through school, have increasing care responsibilities for aging parents, are short on their own retirement needs, and will live longer than any previous generation. Consequently, any help you get from parents or once-paternalistic companies will be an unexpected bonus.

However, the government, sometimes with your company as agent and collaborator, does help a lot—with 401(k) or similar plans, Roth and other IRAs, and the new cash-balance pensions. Here's how to take advantage:

- When considering job offers or changes, take the quality of the 401(k) (or similar) plan into account. A good 401(k) will have a generous company match of 50 percent or more on your contributions of 6 percent of your salary, short (maximum two years) vesting periods, and low administrative fees of preferably less than 1 percent annually. (Read the summary plan document and fund prospectuses to determine this.) It will also offer several different investment choices, including a good index fund.

- Definitely make the maximum, nondeductible (pay tax now) $2,000 contribution to a Roth IRA and then reap all the gains it rings up over the years, totally tax-free. Furthermore, after you've had the Roth for five years, you can make up to a $10,000 tax-free first-time home-buyer's withdrawal. Even better, starting in 2002, you can put $3,000 annually in your Roth, going up to $5,000 by 2008. Furthermore, in 2006, the Roth 401(k) kicks in, allowing you to make nondeductible payroll reductions that you direct into an employer retirement plan that combines the features of a Roth and 401(k)—such as matching contributions.

GO TO ▶
Hour 12, "Defined-Benefit and Federal Pension Plans," reveals why conversions to cash-balance plans are the nadir of mid-life employee existence.

- Although it's often bad news for Baby Boomers, it's good news for you if your company offers a cash-balance pension plan. Each month, the company puts up to 5 percent (over and above) of your gross monthly salary into an account that grows at a specified interest rate (usually prime rate related). If you've stayed long enough for it to be vested, when you leave the company, you take the current balance with you, and defer tax by rolling the lump sum into your own tax-deferred IRA, or your new company's 401(k).

SAVINGS ADVICE

To make every possible dollar available for saving, don't spend money unnecessarily:

- Run, don't walk, away from salespeople pushing whole-life insurance or tax-deferred annuities. You don't really need life insurance, with nobody depending on you now.

- You'll probably share health-insurance costs with your employer, and you can limit or eliminate your contribution by taking a good HMO, or the highest deductible, highest out-of-pocket "choice" plan. Chances are that you're healthy enough that you'll owe a smaller balance of your medical bills than what you'll save by reducing your employee contribution. But if you can't get company health insurance, you must get your own (although you might still be covered by a parent's plan). Also, it's wise to get renter's insurance.

- Finally, don't pay someone else and forfeit the "pleasure" of doing your taxes, which is a good way to stay in touch with your financial situation. Simplify it with software such as Tax Cut or Turbo Tax—especially used in conjunction with data you can regularly record in Quicken and Microsoft Money.

- If marriage is in your future, think hard about alternative uses for a $25,000, or even more expensive, wedding. If you spend $5,000 instead, that extra $20,000 invested in an index mutual fund should grow to more than $500,000, after taxes, at age 65.

TYPICAL YOUNG MARRIED SITUATION

Now that you're married, don't you wish you'd had that last piece of advice before you first met with a wedding planner? Well, all is not lost; you're still young.

Of course, you're probably planning to buy a house, and then maybe have kids—not necessarily in that order. Perhaps you already have both, which means that you might view as crazy any thoughts that you can now save even a dime toward retirement.

DEBT AND HOUSES

GO TO ▶
Hour 15, "Integrating Retirement Sources," talks about your various assets and their utility for retirement.

But as a young married, you're hopefully at least out of debt, or well on your way out. You're in the asset-building stage, whether those assets are going to go toward a house or retirement. Remember, a house is a retirement asset although it doesn't grow in value over the long term nearly as much as a stock-market investment.

Therefore, you don't want to put all your eggs in the house-buying basket. At the very least, make sure that you're fully funding IRAs and contributing at least as much as your employer matches in a 401(k) or similar plan.

When you do buy a house, make sure you don't allow the real-estate agent to become your financial planner. Too many agents want to tell you what you can afford, but your income isn't nearly the whole story. Research the true cost of home ownership, including ongoing maintenance. Then go into the hunt knowing what you can truly afford, and don't budge from it.

KIDS

If you have kids, make sure to take advantage of any pre-tax employer dependent-care account you might have available. If you're in at least the 28 percent tax bracket (27 percent starting in 2002), you might be able to pay up to $5,000 a year in child-care expenses this way and save $1,350 or more on taxes.

And, although you should have done it when you married, now it's especially important to get life insurance. If either of you died, you'd be leaving the other in an awful financial bind without it. Forget about whole life. Just buy what you need in term insurance.

When your kids get older, give them the same experience they've undoubtedly given you: Put them on a budget. Much like a relationship with a dog, your family's relationship to a budget needs to be one of dominance and submission. In other words, don't let the expenses control your family, your family must control the expenses.

JUST A MINUTE

Want to book some time with experts on teaching your kids about money? Try the following: *Piggy Bank to Credit Card: Teach Your Kids the Financial Facts of Life* by Linda Barbanel, and *Money Doesn't Grow on Trees: A Parent's Guide to Raising Financially Responsible Children* by Neale S. Godfrey and Carolina Edwards. (See Appendix B, "Resources," for details.)

The only way that will happen is if you set the example. If children observe you using credit cards to pay for everything, and then hear arguments about money when the bills come due, what are they to think? Much better that they learn the immediate disappointment but ultimate satisfaction of dealing with deprivation.

Fortunately, if you allow it, you can also easily deprive yourself of much of the life you led before you had kids. And you need to, once you've been in a house a few years and your kids are starting to grow. Then it's time to start seriously building up your retirement assets. At this point make sure that you are contributing the maximum you are allowed to your 401(k) and IRA. You should also be starting to contribute monthly to one or more mutual funds outside of your tax-advantaged savings.

You'll be glad that you boosted these savings because you'll soon be entering the difficult mid-life phase where saving can get tougher. Besides, the more you save when you're farther from retirement, the better.

TYPICAL MID-LIFE COUPLE SITUATION

If you've reached mid-life, retirement has probably become a serious proposition, because you've spent about as long as an adult as you'll continue spending until retirement. So you can actually start visualizing what that life might be like.

At mid-life, you should have accumulated some reasonably substantial assets in your 401(k) and IRA accounts, perhaps as much as $100,000 and $50,000 respectively, including investment growth. Because of potentially difficult sandwich generation years ahead, you should also have fully funded a short-term emergency account of approximately three to six months of take-home pay.

FYI If you've saved more than $100,000 toward retirement by mid-life, you're way ahead of your peers, according to the most recent Retirement Confidence Survey jointly conducted by the Employee Benefit Research Institute along with the American Savings Education Council. Only 25 percent of respondents had saved that much by age 45.

If you don't have assets like this, it's time to take some drastic measures if your earning power is limiting you. You should seriously consider further education that will enable you to get a better job. If you're not worried about your savings because your company offers a good pension plan, think again—because it might not be here 10 or 20 years from now. And what you've accumulated at the time your plan might be terminated could fall far short of what you're now expecting in the future.

Even if you do have healthy assets, be careful not to compromise them too much in helping fund your children's education. Keep in mind that statistics show that more expensive isn't necessarily better in terms of the payoff from a college education. Depending on your age when your children start college, you might actually be retired by the time they finish. At that point you'll be able to tap your tax-deferred retirement accounts without penalty to help repay college loans.

There are two pieces of good news concerning payment of college expenses. The new tax bill provides for a deduction of up to $4,000 (by 2006) for payment of college expenses. That's a wonderful new alternative when the following credits aren't available or wouldn't be as beneficial: the existing Hope credit of up to $1,500 per student annually for the first two years of college, or the lifetime learning credit of up to $1,000 per family annually.

In addition, now when paying back student loans, interest is deductible until the loan is paid back, just as it would be if you took a home-equity loan. But this way you needn't put your home at risk in order to borrow for college.

Whatever your situation, mid-life is an excellent time to consider hiring a financial advisor. Proper use of your assets from this point on is critical to your achieving a successful retirement. An advisor's unbiased view can help you see your situation more clearly and get you back on right track. The last section in this Hour includes guidelines for finding the right advisor to meet your needs.

TYPICAL DIVORCED COUPLE SITUATION

When you find you're no longer well-advised to stay with your spouse, it's time to take financial action to protect your interests, preferably long before the actual divorce. Hour 17, "Retirement Road Detours," raised several financial issues related to divorce—particularly regarding its impact on women. Here are suggestions for best dealing with both financial and emotional gaps from this difficult life transition:

- Consider hiring a financial advisor versed in divorce issues, such as one with the additional credential of certified divorce planner.

- Make sure you're not hoodwinked by an asset-hiding spouse. As soon as you know you might be getting divorced, make meticulous records of all the financial documents relating to accounts that you and your spouse have. If necessary, consider hiring a forensic accountant to trace possible missing assets.

- Make sure you get your fair share of the retirement assets, and that means future assets, not just what the retirement is worth now. Remember, you had a stake in building that retirement fund, so you deserve your full proportional share of the part you helped build.

- Structuring your divorce to optimize taxes is critical. To the extent possible, you want to receive child support instead of alimony because child support is not taxable. Also, make sure no mistakes are made in the assignment of any retirement-fund monies to you, or you could end up with a whopping tax bill.

- Consider using mediation instead of adversarial attorneys in order to come to a fair resolution. Keep in mind that the ideal resolution has probably been reached when each party thinks the other has gotten the better deal. You'll still want to have an attorney representing you, but the fee should be much lower because you'll be doing most of the work. You can always make an agreement that the mediation is non-binding so that either party can resort to the traditional adversarial approach if necessary. Under no circumstances should you share an attorney.

- For women especially, don't try to save a bad marriage by not working outside the home. Take the opportunity to go to school when you sense trouble is on the horizon so you can upgrade your skills as quickly as possible to maximize your earning power after the divorce.

- In determining a fair settlement, if you've taken a leave from your career to raise children, make sure to factor in the losses to your pension.

- To preserve funds, it is becoming more common for a separated husband and wife to continue living in the same house until the divorce is final.

- If your settlement includes a requirement that your spouse maintain you as a beneficiary to life insurance in order to guarantee support for children, make sure that the payments continue to be made after the divorce.

- If you have kids who will later be going to college, make sure that the divorce agreement specifies that your spouse is 50 percent responsible. Many people mistakenly assume that the spouse must pay because it's a child support issue. Wrong!

- Don't use visitation in custody as a financial lever for a better agreement. Remember that the terms must still be enforced, and that's less likely if you haven't acted in good faith.

- Financial burdens presented by the divorce may put you behind in contributing to retirement accounts for a few years. Once you can, save like crazy to build up the assets necessary to make catch-up contributions to your tax-deferred retirement accounts after you're 50.

- For those unmarrieds reading this, two words: prenuptial agreement. To ensure that it's enforceable, both parties must be properly represented at the time it's drafted, and no coercion must be involved.

PROCEED WITH CAUTION

One of the biggest mistakes women make regarding divorce settlements is putting undue importance on getting the house. Unfortunately, emotional attachment gets in the way of seeing the house for what it might be—a money-sucking asset that sometimes ends up getting foreclosed. Even women who can afford ownership often find themselves in a low tax bracket where home ownership tax deductions don't help much.

TYPICAL PERMANENT SINGLE SITUATION

If you've always been single, it's obvious nobody has coerced you into marriage, or perhaps you're not married due to sexual preference. In either event, if you're likely to be single all your life, your strategies are obviously somewhat different. For one thing, your single tax bracket is a disadvantage compared to what it would be if you were married to someone who isn't working. You should look long and hard at legitimate tax shelters, of course starting with the absolute maximum contribution to employer tax-deferred plans.

Although you might not think you need the space of a house, the tax advantages of home ownership are too good to overlook. The other big thing, of course, is less a retirement issue than an estate-planning issue. Although the tax bill passed in May 2001 will liberalize the estate tax starting in 2002, increasing the tax-free estate that you can pass on to your designated heir each year from now until 2010, experts cast considerable doubt on whether these provisions will remain. Because you don't have the unlimited marital deduction available to you, you would be wise to get good estate planning advice, anyway, if you're not elderly and already have an estate plan.

Otherwise, your strategy should be based upon the appropriate parts of the advice given earlier to young singles and marrieds.

PRE-RETIREES

If you're in late mid-life, you're in a totally different situation than those in the previous categories. We devote Hour 22, "Pre-Retirement Planning," to your situation.

THE RIGHT FINANCIAL ADVISOR

With the possible exception of young singles, due to the cost, virtually anyone planning for retirement can benefit from consultation with a quality financial advisor. Here are some suggestions for hiring good advisors.

MAKE SURE THEY HAVE GOOD QUALIFICATIONS

CERTIFIED FINANCIAL PLANNERS (CFP), certified public accountants (CPA), and personal finance specialists (PFS) have passed tests on a broad spectrum of personal-finance topics. If the advisors you're considering don't have these credentials, ask how they've become knowledgeable in economics and finance, taxes, budgeting and debt management, insurance, investing, em-ployee benefits, self-employment and small-business issues, retirement and estate planning, and related topics. Also, credentials or not, try to determine if your planner is prepared to deal with all these topics.

JUST A MINUTE

To find a CFP, call the Financial Planning Association (FPA) at 1-800-282-PLAN. To find a CPA or PFS, call the American Institute of Certified Public Accountants toll-free at 1-888-999-9256, and ask for the AICPA-PFP Division.

FIND AN ADVISOR WITH A COMPATIBLE STYLE

Is your prospective advisor a paternalistic, take-charge person, or someone who'll treat you as a "partner"? Does he or she talk about money only, or ask about what part money plays in your life dreams, goals, and aspirations? Does the advisor seem likely to make sure you understand what he or she is having you do with your money and why, or is he or she more a "sign here" type? Is the advisor willing to go the next step and help you increase your wealth of financial knowledge along with your monetary wealth?

None of these questions suggests the "right way" for your advisor and you to relate to each other, but you should think about them to be sure you're comfortable with your advisor's relationship style. Most important, your advisor's style should engender your trust.

FIND A COMPATIBLE ADVISOR

It might not seem politically correct, but it's often a plus to pick an advisor in your demographic sphere. For example, if you're a woman who feels inexperienced in financial matters, you might do better with a female advisor who's "been there." Or, because you're nearing retirement and possibly feeling your mortality, you might prefer an older advisor. For many people, these differences don't matter, but it's not necessarily discrimination if they matter for you.

TIME SAVER

 If you know right off the bat that you want to find a fee-only advisor, start by contacting the National Association of Personal Financial Advisors (NAPFA) toll-free at 1-888-FEE-ONLY.

UNDERSTAND HOW YOUR ADVISOR GETS PAID

It's crucial to understand the implications of how your advisor charges for services. If your advisor is compensated for "assets under management," you're charged anywhere from 0.5 percent to 2 percent of your assets annually (typically lower the higher your asset base) for comprehensive planning that includes complete investment management and extensive yearly reviews of your entire financial picture.

During the recent raging-bull market, 2 percent might have seemed like a bargain, but you might have felt badly overcharged if your million-dollar portfolio lost 5 percent last year, even though that would have been above-average performance. Furthermore, there's a potential conflict of interest if you need a lot more insurance protection or should lower your debt. That's because any money removed from your investable assets to cover those needs would lower your advisor's compensation.

Another form of percentage-based charging is the old-fashioned commission on the investments and insurance you purchase through your advisor—a method often used for people with limited assets. An advisor charging this way might "throw in" or minimally charge for some basic written financial plan that provides the framework for the investment strategy and other asset deployment.

If you have good reason to trust your advisor, this arrangement would be entirely legitimate if it were fully disclosed. Watch out, though, because the potential for conflict of interest is evident. If you had a lot invested in a corporate 401(k) plan, your advisor wouldn't earn any commissions from that, so be leery when an advisor suggests you might reduce your contribution percentage to such plans.

JUST A MINUTE

However compensated, check that your advisor is registered as an investment advisor with the SEC, and operates under a code of ethics. Check with the Securities and Exchange Commission, National Association of Securities Dealers (NASD) Regulation Public Disclosure Program, and state securities agencies.

Still another compensation arrangement avoids those potential conflicts, but comes at a pretty steep price, usually $150-plus an hour for any services your advisor provides. Sometimes, though, advisors set fixed charges for certain types of services, such as portfolio reviews, basic plans, or comprehensive plans.

HAVE CONFIDENCE IN THE METHODS YOUR ADVISOR USES

Did your advisor talk about his or her overall philosophy and approach, and show you what the plans look like and how they'll be communicated to you? Do the questions the advisor is asking you and information he or she is requesting suggest that the advisor is taking into account everything he or she should be? In other words, make sure you're not getting some generic plan, but a high-quality comprehensive one that is really customized to you.

HOUR'S UP!

This book is no substitute for your parents. Nevertheless, it has now told you how to financially act your age. Let's see if you're able by answering these questions correctly.

Answer True or False to the following statements:

1. Roth IRAs are a bad investment for young singles because they provide no immediate tax break.

2. It's important for young singles to have life insurance because it's one way of helping parents who might not have adequately prepared for retirement.

3. If you're young married, it's tempting to spend a lot on leisure activities before you have parental commitments. But you'd be wise to think twice, because this is a crucial saving time for you.

4. If you have kids, it's possible to save $1,350 or more a year if your employer has a special program for you to make pre-tax contributions for child care.

5. Young marrieds should definitely be contributing the absolute maximum to their 401(k) account. There's no excuse not to.

6. Mid-life is the time to finally start accumulating assets. It's very hard to have much put away for retirement before you're 50.

7. It's critical that mid-lifers put their children's needs for college ahead of their own retirement.

8. Divorce presents an incredible number of challenges in trying to plan a prosperous retirement.

9. Fortunately, there's a special provision now in the tax code that lets people over 50 make catch-up contributions to tax-deferred retirement accounts. This can be very helpful to those divorced in their 50s.

10. If you're gay or otherwise permanently single, you have a distinct advantage over marrieds in financial and estate planning.

HOUR 22

Pre-Retirement Planning

CHAPTER SUMMARY

LESSON PLAN:

In this Hour you will learn about …

- Assessing retirement readiness.
- Decisions about current job and possible new retirement jobs.
- Decisions to explore, start, or terminate a business.
- Restructuring your nest egg for retirement.
- Decisions about life insurance, long-term care, medical insurance, and Medicare.

Even the greatest of traditional Hollywood filmmakers might be severely challenged to develop and produce a movie capturing the drama underlying a decision to retire. But let's imagine they're up to the task.

At about 11:58 A.M. on a sunny day, a big crowd of people gathers on the patio outside a popular downtown restaurant. Among them is a cluster of dressed-down 20-somethings chattering about how they left in the wee hours from their latest romantic conquests and drove straight to work. On the far side is a section crowded with strollers, baby chairs, and bedraggled young parents chasing their kids around, and in the middle, some sober-looking silver-haired types dressed as though they just walked out of the corporate boardroom.

In front of the crowd, a tall, rugged-looking man with a mild resemblance to an older Gary Cooper waits patiently for the crowd noise to die down and begins, precisely as the clock strikes high noon: "You probably know why we're here. Over the past several years, I've tried to bring you young folks on board to the way we like to do things and I've run out of ideas. To my neighbors with all your kids running amok, I say, spare the rod and spoil my rose bushes. And to my faithful company peers, I acknowledge that no man can stand alone. Now my work is done here; it's time for someone else to chase our bad-guy competitors out of the marketplace."

Just like that, no shots fired, the weary man unbuttons and removes his suit coat, unclips suspenders on each side, and plunks them on the table, the metallic sound startling the chortling office and neighborhood gossips. Removing a 20-gallon hat, he slowly, silently walks away.

Chances are that your retirement high noon won't be nearly as dramatic, or framed in such a clear-cut manner. Maybe you'll keep working at your company after you formally retire, and be tempted to share what's happening in your bedroom due to the giddy freedom of no longer having to go to work every day. Perhaps you'll live in the same neighborhood and teach its younger kids how to plant rose bushes, or their parents how to pull off million-dollar deals. Or perhaps those suspenders and the other clothes you're wearing will be so worn that you won't take them off, because you don't have new ones into which you can change. So, before you're ready to shoot your personal climactic retirement scene, here are some script suggestions.

REVISIT RETIREMENT SCENARIO

To plan your appearance in the retirement scene, you have to know how close it is to your personal high noon. Certainly, you've been assuming when that will be, but now it's time for a reality check.

DETERMINE THE ATTAINABILITY OF YOUR ORIGINAL GOAL

Start with your most recently stated goals of when you're going to retire and what kind of financial shape you're going to be in when you do. Except for possible changes in tax, growth, and inflation rates, even years from now you should be able to use this book's retirement gap methodology to see where you are.

Remember this methodology projects where you'll stand at retirement, based on where you are at the time you make the calculation, and the future cash flows and expenses you expect. So, if you're not comfortably in the plus zone when you make the calculation, your retirement plan is hanging by a few weak threads.

On the other hand, what if you do the calculation within five years of your planned retirement and it shows a gap, but not an overwhelming one? The good news is that the closer you are to retirement, the more reliable the calculation. Thus, the data you've assembled to make the calculation should serve as an excellent blueprint for remodeling your plan and retiring on or close to when you'd originally intended. If the gap is large, though, it's time to rebuild your plan from scratch.

JUST A MINUTE

Financial advisors can help determine your readiness for retirement, but many financial advisors aren't trained to look at the bigger psychological/emotional picture. You might want to consider a session with one of the new breed of retirement counselors who aren't financial advisors, including gerontologists and professionals holding the Certified Retirement Counselor credential from the International Foundation for Retirement Education.

DETERMINE WHETHER YOUR OBJECTIVES HAVE CHANGED

As a reader of this book, though, it's highly unlikely that you're going to approach retirement financially unprepared (insert authors' smiling faces). But this book is powerless to deal with the psychological and emotional changes you'll go through as you approach retirement, and that's as it should be.

For example, you might discover that you want a more materially comfortable retirement than you'd originally planned—that you're not really cut out for the Spartan, away-from-civilization life that perhaps had originally appealed to you. Conversely, you might just get sick and tired of stuff and a highly programmed life of events, and want a much more modest, much less structured lifestyle. Or situations involving children and grandchildren might have caused you to establish totally new objectives.

Obviously, changed objectives often translate into different financial needs, so whatever gap you thought you had is now virtually meaningless. Although you'll be able to keep all the income and asset numbers you previously used in your plan, you're going to have to totally redo the expense side, and run through a fresh gap calculation from start to finish.

REVISE RETIREMENT SCENARIO

If you do change your plan, however, don't limit yourself to just the obvious changes. Use the opportunity to rethink every aspect of your plan.

CONSIDER YOUR CURRENT LIFE CIRCUMSTANCES AND HEALTH

While changing lifestyle and financial objectives are important reasons for revising retirement plans, health is probably the number-one trigger for revising them. Declining health can lower energy levels of mid-life workers and stop their advancement to higher-paid positions. Frequently, it causes early retirement, either by the worker's own choice or by the employer easing out the worker when he or she is seen as "not cutting it" any more.

A spouse's declining health is also often the cause of retirement-plan changes. When couples see progressive, debilitating disease as closing the window on opportunities to fulfill life dreams, they sometimes try to beat the calendar. The suffering party might fully retire, while the other spouse finds a more flexible work arrangement. Because many women marry men several years older, their careers can often be cut short when the husband takes ill. And women also are often the ones who sacrifice their careers early when ill elderly parents need caretaking.

GO TO ▶
Hour 17, "Retirement Road Detours," includes detailed coverage of the retirement challenges faced by divorced women.

And then there's ill will, resulting in divorce and total rethinking of retirement plans. The '80s saw the beginning of a marked trend for men in their 50s to remarry late-30s women racing their biological clocks. They were grabbing for both a rejuvenating relationship and a chance to be a better father the second time around. But that meant that instead of winding down their careers, they needed to gear up to continue earning aggressively to meet growing family needs and retirement preparation—often after paying out substantial settlements to scorned, discarded partners.

Meanwhile, those newest members of the first wives' club might not have been left empty-handed, but they suddenly faced a totally new life and new needs on which to base their retirement preparation. In many cases, that meant going back to school after the kids were gone, to prepare for new (or first) decent-compensation careers offering them their own retirement-saving opportunities.

CONSIDER YOUR DESIRE/ABILITY TO CONTINUE WORKING

Sometimes, though, it's the woman in a healthy long-term marriage who feels the urgency to work, not only toward, but beyond retirement—their husbands' retirement that is. Many of these women are just hitting their stride professionally at a time when their husbands want to gear down. Even though the couple might not "need the money," the wife needs the psychological rewards that the job provides just as much. Furthermore, she might have a different opinion about need for the money, seeing the extra income from work and later retirement benefits as a form of emancipation from an earlier life of comparative economic drudgery.

Warding off unplanned economic drudgery is one reason that up to two thirds of men and women plan to do paid work during retirement. But as many as half of retirees plan to work just because they're not ready to give it up. They might also volunteer, but paid, part-time work, where they have considerable total hours and scheduling flexibility, meets different non-economic needs they have. In reality, companies would find large numbers of workers who would continue working to normal retirement age and beyond if they allowed them to cut back hours and choose work schedules. Because these options might be more available in the near future, keep them in mind for your own retirement planning.

ENVISION RETIREMENT LIFE MORE REALISTICALLY

In the end, the financial, family, and work-related complexities of planning your retirement are a relative piece of cake next to the stark reality of anticipating a life with virtually no responsibility. As a child, you probably were able to play as much as you'll be able to in retirement, but you were also still controlled, and had responsibilities. Then came work and family life, with nothing but responsibilities. But in retirement, given that you're financially solid, chances are that you'll have nobody to answer to except a spouse, and those demands will be much lighter.

If anything, the problem with retirement is just that—more about compensating for what you don't have to do than of what you do have to do. For most people, all the expeditions, cruises, and other leisure pursuits they waited so long to pursue don't fill the need to be needed. In making your plan, you must find the proper balance between "decadent" leisure and connectedness.

JUST A MINUTE

 One way to avoid boredom is by becoming a volunteer. Use your business experience as a volunteer Service Corps of Retired Executives (1-800-634-0245). Or light up the lives of those less fortunate by contacting The Points of Light Foundation (1-800-879-5400). Many experts recommend starting to get involved in such activities a few years before actual retirement.

PRE-RETIREMENT LIFESTYLE AND WORK ACTIONS

Once you're on solid financial and life-planning ground about your retirement, the next step is to start the transition into your retirement agenda.

CONTINUING WORK OR STARTING A BUSINESS

Do you feel confident about your relationship with your employer, and would like to effect a "phased retirement"? If so, come to your employer with the same type of business case you might use in an actual work project. What would your schedule be? How would your reduced compensation be handled? How would it affect your benefits? Why would doing this pay off for your employer? Because these arrangements often involve breaking new human resources ground, these answers might require that you research how other employees with other employers are making such arrangements.

If, instead, you have every intention of making your employer history and working elsewhere during retirement, start searching out those opportunities a few years beforehand. Those who do volunteer work before retirement have a better track record of doing it once retired. And by looking in advance at what's really available to you in both volunteer and part-time paid work, you might discover that neither are really what you want. Instead, you might be better suited for self-employment or starting a business.

But that's something you must get started with in advance as well. For one thing, if you need funding for your business, you're more likely to get it, or a better deal on it, while you're still fully and gainfully employed before retirement. Too, making it part of your life before retirement will make it that much more likely you'll actually do it. And because you'll still be busy with your main job, you're more apt to get your business started as a smaller side business before retirement, getting your feet wet before risking too much. If you wait until retirement, feeling you can put all your energy into it, you might start too big and lose big before you discover it's not right for you.

PHASING DOWN OR OUT OF A BUSINESS

Your problem, though, might be just the opposite—starting to separate yourself from a business that is right for you, the one you've been running most of your working life. If you want this business to survive, don't make the mistake of keeping it too much to yourself. By putting the next generation or people outside your family in meatier roles before you retire, you'll develop confidence that your business is in good hands. That will enable you to disengage more comfortably and gradually before and during retirement. It will also mitigate against any potential power struggle with those who might feel you're meddling too much when you're now only a retirement part-timer.

If you have a partner in your business, another major consideration is how you part ways when one of you wants to retire. Do you have a *buy/sell agreement* in place?

STRICTLY DEFINED

A **buy/sell agreement** is a contract developed between you and your partner(s) that defines how one of the owners will sell his or her part of the business and how the other owner(s) will buy that interest based on a set of given circumstances.

There are a number of common ways to structure these agreements. These include:

1. An **entity purchase agreement** specifies that the corporation or partnership will buy back the interest of the departing owner. This type of agreement is used most often when there are a number of partners.

2. A **cross-purchase agreement** sets the terms of sale between owners based on some prearranged basis value. The partners agree that if one partner wants to exit the business they will automatically sell to the other partner.

3. A **wait-and-see agreement** gives owners more flexibility on how they want to dispose of the business.

The decision about whether to use an entity purchase or cross-purchase agreement will be determined based on the most tax-wise strategy at the time of sale.

To be sure your business will survive the death of your partner and that you will still have a business from which to retire, it's important to protect these agreements with life and disability insurance. You want to be certain that enough money will be available to purchase the business and pay whatever taxes may be necessary. Many businesses end up closing their doors because they are forced to liquidate after the death or disability of one of their owners.

Using life insurance guarantees the proceeds will be available at an owner's death to purchase his or her interest, and allows for the buildup of tax-deferred cash value for a future buyout for something such as retirement. If an entity purchase agreement is used, the partnership or corporation is the owner and beneficiary of the life insurance on the shareholders or partners. In the case of a cross-purchase agreement, policies are owned by the individual shareholders or partners on the lives of each other.

If you are at the point where you are ready to sell your business, the first question you need to ask is, do you want a lump-sum cash payment or do you want to consider an installment sale? The primary advantage of financing at least part of the sale is that you can spread out the tax hit using IRS installment sales rules.

FYI Seller financing of at least part of a business sale is common in 30 percent of all business sales. In tough economic times when there is a bank-credit crunch, such as the early '90s, 90 percent of business sales will likely be financed at least partially by seller financing.

If you can wait for some of the cash and finance the business sale, this can serve two purposes. It may be easier to find a buyer if he or she doesn't need to fully finance the purchase through a lending institution, and it may allow you to defer some of the tax you will have to pay until you actually receive the cash in future installments.

You can use the installment method as long as you will receive at least one of your payments after the year of the actual sale. Unfortunately many, if not most, of your assets may not be eligible for installment sale treatment. The general rule of thumb is that gains which would normally be treated as ordinary income will not be eligible for installment sale treatment. This includes payments for inventory, accounts payable, and any property you have held for less than a year.

The installment sale method works best if you have considerable gain on assets that have appreciated in value beyond their original purchase price. For example, if you have been in business for a long time, one big item for which the installment sale method works is the intangible asset, goodwill.

Another way to sell a business and continue getting a cash flow from it is an *earnout* arrangement. Typically, you receive additional money if the business reaches certain preset goals determined at the time of sale. This is a particularly good arrangement if you sell your business, but plan to stay as an employee or consultant to the buyer. If you do choose to use an earnout option, be certain to specify who will be reviewing the books and verifying performance of the business.

STRICTLY DEFINED

An **earnout** is an arrangement in which you will receive additional money if the business reaches certain preset goals determined at the time of sale. The earnout is a way to negotiate a lower initial price of the business with the promise of later, contingent payments. This can be risky because it depends on the new business owner's abilities for keeping the business going.

PRE-RETIREMENT FINANCIAL ACTIONS

Phasing out of that business, though, requires no longer financially being dependent on it. Assuming that within a few years of retirement you're close to your target critical mass of money and capital, here are some things you must do to get it working for you as you need it.

RESTRUCTURE INVESTMENTS FOR RETIREMENT

By now, hopefully, you no longer buy into the once-sacred maxim that you must put all your money into safe investments upon retirement. That's because your money might need to grow for a many years after retirement as it did before.

But there's one crucial difference that does dictate a subtle conservative shift in how you invest once retired. In general, you're no longer adding to your investments, other than reinvesting the growth and possibly dividends. That means a change from once relying on dollar-cost averaging of investments to buy more shares in bad times. Eventually, all those shares were likely to be lifted in the rising tide of individual company or overall market performance.

And, if that didn't always work because of a few bad choices, you were able to supplement it with "performance averaging." That meant that you dug down deep into your savings bag of tricks to put more money into new, hopefully better, investments to make up for your losers. Unfortunately, retirement strips you of that option. Although you still hope to ride a rising tide that keeps your portfolio growing, you must also slow down the rate that your ship (portfolio) eventually slips below the surface as you exhaust it.

Your primary strategy to forestall your ultimate sinking should be to make sure you have the ballast of three to five years worth of liquid, safe investments in reserve—your retirement emergency fund. Now, if your systematic liquidation of your portfolio by the 4 percent or some similar rule is thrown off by an underperforming market, you won't be forced to dip further into your invested capital. Instead, just make up the difference by drawing from your liquid investments. And you needn't replenish this fund because that much in liquid form should be enough to meet those excess needs on a cumulative basis throughout retirement.

SOCIAL SECURITY, MEDICARE, LONG-TERM CARE

That liquid-asset safety-net strategy, however, works only if you have your other safety nets in order—starting with Social Security. In only rare instances should retirees plan on taking Social Security earlier than normal age. In fact, if you're planning on doing significant part-time work, don't plan on tapping it until the latest possible age, 70. That's true even if you're not in great health, as long as you've accumulated an ample nest egg.

Why? Well it's all in Social Security's equivalent of the scientific name for a popular prescription drug, "Old Age Survivor's Insurance" (OASI). Just as too many people file shady car and other insurance claims to recoup their insurance investment, too many people view recouping what they paid into Social Security as a moral imperative. Hence the thinking, "the earlier I start getting it out, the more likely that I'll ultimately break even on all that payroll tax." Instead, though, they should be thinking, how neat an insurance policy Social Security is. "By simply paying the extra premium of delayed gratification until as late as age 70, more will be there for me if I really need it to meet monthly expenses down the line."

Of course, if you don't need the Social Security early, but do plan to treat it as investable savings to further build your nest egg (or at least offset its shrinkage), then that's at least a meritorious argument for taking it early. In effect, then, you're setting up your own form of Social Security privatization—hoping for a better ultimate return than simply the inflation rate—and you don't have to rely on Congress to approve it.

The other piece of OASI is Medicare, and there's little reason to ever delay starting to use it. In fact, the big problem is that you can't use it until age 65, even though you might be retiring earlier and no longer have employer health insurance. Therefore, be prepared to fill that gap with a spouse's plan, good private individual or group insurance, a spouse's employer plan, or your own employer's continued insurance under an early-retirement arrangement.

Once you're eligible for Medicare, you'll want to pay for both Parts A and B, plus a Medigap policy—collectively giving you merely adequate health insurance. You might be lucky enough to also have employer retiree health insurance, but treat it as gravy, because such insurance is a case of, "there but for the grace of Wall Street go I." As soon as companies judge that they can afford the public-relations hit in return for a better financial return, they'll ditch retiree health insurance, unless they've explicitly promised it— and there's been a lot of recent momentum among companies doing just that.

FYI Some sobering statistics on the decline in retiree health coverage: Since the 1980s, the percentage of early retirees with ex-employer health benefits has plummeted from 70 percent to 37 percent. Since the early 1990s, the percentage of normal-age (Medicare-eligible) retirees with ex-employer coverage has dropped from 40 percent to 24 percent.

Therefore, you must "self-insure" for the gap between what your Medicare-centered coverage will pay, and possibly considerable out-of-pocket expenses for prescription drugs and overall medical care. In other words, make sure that such out-of-pocket expense is estimated realistically in your budget. Furthermore, recognize that long-term care almost certainly won't be covered by any of this insurance. You must purchase a quality long-term-care (LTC) insurance plan that will guarantee you a level premium for the rest of your life (subject to universal rate adjustments for rising medical costs).

The earlier in life you buy such a policy, the less you'll pay monthly. Although, obviously, the LTC carrier will be collecting years worth of premiums during a time you're not that likely to need the coverage. But don't forget, early-onset Alzheimer's and other conditions are occurring more frequently, so it can be critical to have LTC as early as age 50.

Your coverage is subject to a medical exam, so the earlier you apply, the less likely you'll be rejected. Before you panic, realize that LTC doesn't cover normal hospital care—only nursing homes, assisted living, and the like. Thus, you're normally not rejected for routine heart conditions and other things that could hospitalize or kill you, but don't currently suggest you'll need long-term care. Taking all this into account, most people are safe waiting until age 60, at which time a premium of about $100 monthly buys them a few thousand dollars per month for life of LTC coverage.

VIATICAL SETTLEMENTS

It's hard to say whether you'll need a nursing home, but at some point you might need to nurse a sickly portfolio. As a last resort, some retirees resort to three sources of regular cash payments that all have the dubious distinction of being tilted heavily in the favor of the institutions offering you the cash.

Let's start with the worst offender, barely viable *viatical settlements* of your life insurance policy.

STRICTLY DEFINED

Viatical settlements provide early access (in other words, while the insured is still alive!) to a substantial portion of the death benefit provided by a life insurance policy. They're usually used to ease financial burdens connected with a terminal illness. They are offered either by the insuror that issued the policy or a third party who buys the policy from the insured for a discount from its death benefit.

On the surface, viatical settlements seem to meet a need that went wanting until the mid-'90s—how to help terminally ill patients benefit from life insurance.

Viaticals were perhaps triggered by the AIDS epidemic, in which thousands of men were dying broke and in great suffering because they had no insurance to cover expensive drugs and care. What if they had life insurance, which in most cases wasn't really needed by their beneficiaries, and could somehow use it to help themselves while still alive? Viaticals were the answer, with newly established financial companies swooping in like vultures circling the near dead. "Oh, you have a term insurance policy that pays $200,000 upon your death. Sign it over to us and we'll pay you $100,000 right now."

Wouldn't you like an investment that paid a 100 percent return (minus the minor ongoing premiums) within a few months or a few years? Those companies sure did. Although their offers did meet a real need, they clearly smacked of exploitation.

For a while, that's as far as viaticals went, but companies saw that to grow they'd have to expand. Why not buy policies from nonterminal folks in ill health, giving them a way to enjoy the rest of their shortened lives by, in effect, winning the lottery? And why not buy from healthy folks with cash-value insurance—offering them more than their cash value, but less than what the policy would pay them upon death? Thus, a 70-year-old man with diabetes who has $200,000 whole life and a cash value of $75,000 might be offered $125,000 for the policy—that company hoping for a good chance to cash out the $200,000 within the man's remaining five-year life expectancy.

PROCEED WITH CAUTION

The viatical industry has spawned many fraudulent schemes. One common one involves selling fraudulent viaticals as an investment to gullible retirees. It starts by getting an uninsurable terminally ill patient to get insured by trickery or criminal collusion with a shady agent. The policy is then sold to a willing sucker, who finds out that it's worth nothing upon the insured's death because it was obtained by fraudulent means.

So, should you deny yourself a viatical just because the company who makes a deal with you is going to make a killing upon your "killing"? Consider these points: Your heirs might need the insurance; you might get a better offer elsewhere; or your financial advisor might be in line to make a fat commission if the offer came through him, which is typically the way these companies now work. Bottom line: It's vital that you get good unbiased advice from a financial adviser who doesn't stand to benefit, except from your fee. This obviously takes away from what you could be getting.

REVERSE MORTGAGES

The equivalent of a commission—a fat lender's fee—also takes away from another questionable source of retirement funds, the reverse mortgage. Think of this arrangement as selling your house back to the bank in a way that lets you stay in it until you die. In actuality, it's a loan you take against your house that doesn't require you to make payments. Instead, you're the one receiving payments—monthly—each adding to what you'll owe the bank, with interest accruing on that balance. Thus, it's a way of using your paid-off house to add to your Social Security and other monthly income.

The neat feature is that although you could end up owing more than the house is worth, your liability is limited to the house's value. If this happens, when you and your spouse die, the bank forecloses on the house and sells it to get back as much of their loan as possible. But don't feel sorry for the bank, for the following reasons:

- Your loan amount is immediately cut by up to $5,000 in closing costs to set up such an arrangement.

- Your house usually increases in value, even though you get a loan based only on the value when it was originated. The bank would then clear far more than it paid out, and it's meanwhile benefited from a handsome interest-rate return on its money—which has the effect of limiting your monthly payment on what's sometimes called a reverse amortization schedule. In fairness, some loans include an equity-sharing arrangement that lets you benefit from part of the appreciation.

- Most contracts include provisions that allow the loan to be terminated and paid back immediately if you fail to keep up the property or certain other events occur that could put the bank's investment at risk.

Reverse mortgages are probably best left to those who've suffered financial reverses. They're simply not the best use of the capital in your home, for a number of other reasons that aren't worth stating here. Instead, rely on good planning to put you in a position that would never have you even thinking about this option.

ANNUITIES

To reinforce the point that bad things come in threes, let's add annuities to the mix. On the surface, it seems like a great idea, a guaranteed lifetime income. Although there are many kinds of annuities, let's focus on the type that makes the most sense for some retirees, the single-payment immediate annuity.

PROCEED WITH CAUTION

Annuities can be immediate (start now) or deferred (start at specified later date); be purchased with one payment or a series of payments; be fixed (payment known in advance) or variable (payment based on investment performance); have a number of survivorship and guaranteed payment options; bind you with severe premature surrender penalties; and drive you to drink with tax complexity.

The principle here (pun intended) is giving an amount to an insurance company in exchange for the promise to pay you back a fixed amount monthly until you die, or until you and a survivor die. You might do this if you're sure that the amount you're being paid—in combination with Social Security, pensions, and other income—will definitely cover your monthly expenses the rest of your life. The calculation of the payment you have coming to you uses the time value of money methods we discussed in Part II, "Your Retirement Gap," and is based on your life expectancy. Thus, if you live longer than expected, you won't run out of money.

The flip side is that if you live shorter than expected, you'll have nothing left to pass on to heirs. Okay, that's not great, but it is a minor strike against annuities compared to several more major ones. Start with the lack of inflation adjustment. If you do live a long time, those monthly payments you thought would do you suddenly look anemic. In addition, those payments are usually based on a fairly stingy interest rate, meaning that you're giving the insurance company cheap use of your money, on which they can earn lots more. Finally, there's the commission earned by the friendly salesperson who signed you up, further cutting into your payment.

Despite these negatives, annuities aren't inherently bad if you address all these potential shortcomings and feel that despite them, you're getting a pretty good deal that will meet your needs. But most folks would be far better off lopping a few thousand off a big chunk of money and paying a reputable financial advisor to help them figure out how to get that money to do more for them than an annuity would. Of course, that means finding such an advisor who won't try selling you one him- or herself, and being willing to put some effort into keeping up with the investing approach recommended.

HOUR'S UP!

Find out if you're ready for your golden years with these questions on pre-retirement.

Answer True or False to the following statements:

1. For most people, a carefully constructed plan put together years before retirement usually can be relied on to execute as is once retirement is reached.

2. Two of the biggest reasons that people change their retirement plans are that they're either sick and tired of work, or just plain sick and tired.

QUIZ

3. Women generally plan and think about retirement almost exactly the same way men do.

4. Their second wives' biological clocks are often the reason that men still get up to an early alarm clock every morning well beyond the years they originally thought they'd retire.

5. Most workers approaching retirement wish their companies would be more flexible regarding hours and schedule for long-time employees.

6. The greatest thing about retirement is that most people hunger for the time when it no longer matters to anyone what they choose to do each day.

7. It's best to put off volunteer work until after retirement instead using the years before to earn as much as possible to eliminate the need for paid work during retirement.

8. A lot of thought and planning should go into either starting a business for retirement or phasing out of one.

9. Investing and portfolio structure during retirement is really no different than before, except for being a little more conservative.

10. You're far better off thinking of Social Security as the "insurance" embedded in it's other name, old-age and survivor's insurance.

Hour 23

Managing Retirement Distributions

Chapter Summary

LESSON PLAN:

In this Hour you will learn about ...

- Traditional pension distribution options.
- Various distribution options to consider with all your non-pension retirement assets.
- Evaluating your withdrawal options.
- Widow and widower benefits.
- Why you should revisit your withdrawal options annually.

What makes retirement unique is the fact that at some time during your golden years, you're going to start being dependent on dipping into savings for month-to-month living expenses. It might not be the first year, or the first few years, during which you might be able to live on income from your nest egg. But it will probably be sooner rather than later, and then for the rest of your life.

Sounds easy enough to just start taking out money sparingly and carefully. But it turns out that taking out money is scarier than the first time you were either taken out on a date or took someone out. And unlike dating, where you finally grew comfortable with taking out someone, it might never feel comfortable to keep taking money out of your nest egg. In fact, by the time you see how complex the decision is, the only taking out you might want to do is your frustration on your helpless authors—who are simply messengers bearing wealth-preservation warnings.

And these complexities come just when you thought you'd finished the most complex undertaking of all—saving for retirement. As you now know, it took a lot of planning, time, and a bit of luck for the economic forces that determine the success of your retirement investments to work in your favor. While economic factors worked in your favor some of the time during your savings years, you undoubtedly experienced some years of high stress as the markets took a dive. This stress doesn't end at retirement, but careful management of your withdrawals from retirement funds can certainly take away some of the fear that you won't have enough to last through your lifetime.

In this Hour, we will explore all the rules regarding withdrawals and then start looking at the question of how to determine what is safe for you. The good news is that, for many of the plans available to you, you don't have to make a decision at retirement that you will have to live with for the rest of your life. Pensions and Social Security (see Hour 9, "Social Security") are the big exceptions to this flexibility. We will briefly visit the issue of widow or widower benefits, because that is something that could change your distributions during retirement.

PENSIONS

As we pointed out in Hour 12, "Defined-Benefit and Federal Pension Plans," traditional pensions are a rapidly disappearing part of the retirement environment. When you get to retirement you may be among the privileged minority left with this option. Pensions have the potential to guarantee you income for the rest of your life—and, with the proper choices, through the life of your spouse as well, whoever lives longer.

PROCEED WITH CAUTION

 The way you choose to take your pension is set in stone. Do not make this decision lightly, and be certain you understand all the consequences of the option you choose before signing away the rest of your pension-producing life.

LUMP SUMS VS. ANNUITIES

Your first choice will be whether to take the pension as a lump sum or an annuity. Once you make that choice there are a number of ways to then withdraw the funds. It is basically a choice about whether you want to manage the funds in retirement or let your old company do so.

The annuity option offers you the security of knowing that preset payments will come on a regular basis without regard to how your investments are doing. It gives you the ability to more easily plan your retirement income, and also gives you the peace of mind that you won't outlive your money.

One big disadvantage of most pension annuities is that they are not indexed for inflation, which means your constant regular payments will buy far less as time goes on. Another danger is that your plan could be unsafe or under-funded and fold during your retirement. It's important that you know the financial status of the company from which you are retiring.

FYI If the pension is guaranteed by the Pension Benefit Guarantee Corporation (PBGC), you can feel much more secure the money will be there when you need it. The PBGC guarantees nearly 38,000 defined-benefit pension plans, which currently protects the retirement income of 43 million American workers. It was created in 1974 under Title IV of the Employee Retirement Income Security Act (ERISA). To learn more about these protections, go to www.pbgc.gov/about_pbgc/faqs/faq.htm.

If you choose to manage the funds yourself, then there are two ways to take out the money—as a lump sum in cash or as an IRA rollover. First we will take a closer look at the annuity withdrawal options. Then we'll discuss the lump-sum options.

Annuity Withdrawal Options

You may remember that we discussed annuities in Hour 15, "Integrating Retirement Sources." A simple annuity is a series of equal payments over a set period of time. For pension plans there are several annuity options. One is based on a single life, which is also known as straight life. In this type of annuity, your life span is estimated based on actuarial calculations. The payments are averaged over this anticipated life span. The greatest danger of this choice is that if you are the first to die and you are the pension recipient, your spouse will get nothing after your death.

PROCEED WITH CAUTION

 Be sure you understand the full impact of the decision to take the single life annuity option. The Employee Benefit Research Institute reports that women's average pensions are $535 per month compared to $955 for men. This gap is primarily caused by the years a woman is absent from work to raise a family or take care of other family members.

A second type of annuity is the joint and survivor annuity. For this type of annuity you can usually choose a 100 percent or 50 percent option. If you choose a 100 percent joint and survivor annuity, it means that whichever spouse dies first, the surviving spouse will continue to get the same regular pension payments. The 50 percent option guarantees the spouse only 50 percent of the pension payments received when both spouses were alive. Obviously, the payments when both spouses are alive will be larger for the 50 percent-to-survivor option than for 100 percent-to-survivor.

The joint and survivor annuity is the most common option and is the one the law requires as an automatic default for married employees. In fact, the spouse must sign a waiver to allow you the employee to take a single life annuity. The disadvantage of the joint and survivor election is that the payments will be lower than the single life annuity. If your spouse dies first and you are the retiree, then you may be sorry you took the lower payment.

If your spouse is significantly younger than you, or you want to provide for a child, you may also select a period-certain single life annuity, with payments generally higher than joint and survivor, but lower than regular single life. That's because period-certain guarantees payments for the designated period, usually 5 to 10 years, even if the employee dies. The payments for the rest of the period then go to the surviving spouse or another beneficiary. Think of the period-certain choice as being a lottery winner and having what's left of the annual payments go to a survivor if you should die during the payoff period. (Unfortunately, payments are much smaller!)

LUMP-SUM WITHDRAWAL OPTIONS

The lump-sum withdrawal options give you much greater flexibility in deciding how you want to receive your money each year of retirement, but it also comes with greater risks because you are responsible for making sure that money lasts. The advantages are that you can invest those funds to beat inflation rather than accept an annuity payment that is not indexed for inflation. You also don't have the worry that your former employer could change its pension policy or that a pension plan could go bust.

You can take the money as a cash distribution or as an IRA rollover. The amount is a present-value equivalent of what the employer determines would have been the stream of payments had you chosen the annuity option. Errors in these calculations are common, which will be covered in the next section.

If you take it as a one-time cash distribution, the tax hit is tremendous (unless you were born before 1936 and can use something called 10-year averaging). You must pay taxes on that money as though it were current income, and you might be pushed up into a much higher tax bracket on part of it. Furthermore, if you take the distribution before age 55, you'll owe a 10 percent additional penalty for a premature distribution unless you deposit it in a traditional IRA.

The primary advantage of the cash distribution is that you can use the money immediately. There are no limits on the amount you can withdraw or when and how you withdraw it. In addition to the tax consequences another major disadvantage is that you have a greater risk of spending the money too fast.

The IRA rollover allows you to delay taxes until you withdraw the funds and you can continue to benefit from tax-deferred growth. In the long term you may end up paying more taxes and you will have to start withdrawals by age $70^{1}/_{2}$.

Once you decide how you want to take your funds, then you have to decide what you want to do with this large chunk of money. Will you get it by check? Will the funds be wire-transferred to an account at your bank or a broker? How will you transfer the funds into an investment account? If you are selecting an IRA rollover, it's best to have the money directly transferred from your ex-employer to the broker, bank, or mutual fund company that will handle the funds. Otherwise, you could wind up having 20 percent of it withheld for taxes, even though you'll get that money back in the next year's filing if you did your own rollover.

There is one asset that may be in your employer-sponsored retirement account that you may be better off holding in a taxable account rather than rolling it over to your IRA—the company stock. By holding on to the stock you do not have to liquidate it.

Rather than paying tax on the current market value, the tax would be based on the amount actually paid for it. This likely would be considerably lower than the current market value. The difference is net unrealized appreciation and it would not be taxable until you sell the shares. When you do actually sell, as long as you hold the stocks for more than a year after receiving the distribution from your employer, this capital gains would be taxed at the 20 percent capital gains tax rate rather than your current income tax rate.

However, there is one important disadvantage. If the company stock represents a big chunk of money, you have an undiversified investment, and if the stock goes way down, you lose much more than you'll save in taxes.

GO TO ▶
Once the funds are in place, you must decide how to invest them. Asset allocation issues were discussed in Hours 15, 19, "Completing the Plan," and 21, "Retirement Gap Scenarios." The rules for withdrawal of funds rolled over into an IRA are discussed in detail later in this Hour.

PENSION PLAN ERRORS

Once you decide how you want to get your pension benefits, you still must carefully review whether you are getting your fair share. Hour 12 detailed many types of errors that companies routinely make when calculating your proper pension amount, so you shouldn't just accept the figures given you. Be particularly wary if you're taking a lump sum, because a number of employers have been found to base their present-value calculations on higher-than-appropriate rates of return. This "overdiscounts" your future payments, giving you a lower lump sum than you deserve.

Your pension is a big part of your retirement income. This is not the time to rush into a quick decision. Carefully weigh your options, attend any retirement planning sessions offered by your company, and don't make a decision until you are comfortable that you understand the decision you are making. If you still are not sure after researching this yourself, work with a qualified financial advisor to be certain you are making the right decision given your circumstances.

ALL OTHER RETIREMENT PLANS

Now that you've read all about the complications of pension withdrawals, you may be thinking I'm really glad I don't have to worry about all those issues. Unfortunately, you're not immune to problems when your retirement assets are only in 401(k)s, 403(b)s, IRAs, Keoghs, and any other employer retirement-savings plans. They all also require that you carefully consider your options to comply with IRS rules and best suit your circumstances. Some companies do offer annuity options for the money in your defined-contribution plans, but a majority of companies will require you to select a lump sum option. Again, the best option is to roll the money over into an IRA.

UNDERSTAND DIFFERING IRS WITHDRAWAL RULES

You are in control of your money, but the IRS certainly has its say in how and when it is withdrawn. The rules were simplified in a new proposed set of regulations released by the IRS on January 11, 2001. These changes were optional for folks retiring in 2001 and become mandatory in 2002. It's not a bad thing. The rules actually make the mathematics of calculating withdrawals more straightforward, and give you more flexibility with how you withdraw your funds than was possible under the previous regulations.

PROCEED WITH CAUTION

You can begin to take out your funds at age $59^1/_2$ but are not required to do so until age $70^1/_2$. Once you are older than $70^1/_2$, if you do not comply with the minimum distribution requirements, you may have to pay a 50 percent excise tax on the amount not distributed as required.

You should be asking, "What are those required amounts?" Luckily, you no longer have to deal with a maze of calculations that were required until this year. Now there is a simple IRS chart based on life expectancy figures:

Age	Life Expectancy Divisor	Age	Life Expectancy Divisor
70	26.2	85	13.8
71	25.3	86	13.1
72	24.4	87	12.4
73	23.5	88	11.8
74	22.7	89	11.1
75	21.8	90	10.5
76	20.9	91	9.9
77	20.1	92	9.4
78	19.2	93	8.8
79	18.4	94	8.3
80	17.6	95	7.8
81	16.8	96	7.3
82	16.0	97	6.9
83	15.3	98	6.5
84	14.5	99	6.1

Calculating the minimum required is simple:

$$\frac{\text{Total Assets in Retirement Account}}{\text{Life Expectancy Divisor}} = \text{Required Minimum Distribution}$$

For example, if you are 78 years old and have $500,000 in your IRA, you would be required to take out $5,208.33 ($500,000 ÷ 19.2) that year. This is considerably less than the planner's rule of thumb of 4 percent, which would be $20,000. You can see that you would need a very sizeable portfolio before you would have any worry about minimum distribution requirements unless you weren't planning to take money from the IRA that year.

There are certain circumstances where you may want to use the old rules. These are primarily useful in situations where your beneficiary is considerably younger than you and you want to be sure that there are assets left for your beneficiary. The old rules will still be available for these special planning situations.

Under the old rules you had to name a beneficiary before beginning to withdraw the funds and this beneficiary could not be changed. Under the new rules you are not even required to name your beneficiary before you start taking out the money and you can change your beneficiary even after naming one. But, for inheritance purposes don't put off naming a beneficiary for long.

 FYI   According to census data, 9 percent of the population (about 25 million Americans) is 70 years old or older. The Investment Company Institute estimates there are 16 million households with a head of household who is 70 years or older and approximately 5.2 million of these households own an IRA subject to these required minimum distribution rules. As the Baby Boomer population ages, these numbers will only increase.

UNDERSTAND TAX RAMIFICATIONS OF WITHDRAWALS

Unless your funds are sitting in a Roth IRA or the new Roth-style 401(k), you will owe taxes on your retirement-plan distributions. If all the money went into the retirement fund tax-deferred, which is the case in all but the nondeductible IRA, everything you take out will be taxed at your then current ordinary-income tax rate.

Funds that you contributed to a traditional nondeductible IRA can be withdrawn tax-free, but all the gains will be taxed at your current tax rate. The only way to avoid taxes on withdrawals is to withdraw the money from a Roth IRA. Most planners believe it is best to leave Roth IRA withdrawals for the last, since they also give you the most flexibility in how and when they can be withdrawn.

Although every case must be analyzed individually, most people do best with a counterintuitive approach to withdrawing funds from their mix of accounts. Setting a clear "taxability-first" priority usually has the least long-term tax impact. In general, you'll do best liquidating and withdrawing your (capital gains) taxable investments first. Then draw from your tax-deferred investments—both originally tax-deductible (such as 401(k) and non-deductible (IRA, thrift plan, and variable annuity). Finally, if needed, draw from your tax-free Roth (which can otherwise pass to your heirs income-tax free). One immediate complication in applying these rules is an additional form of income taxation at the state level. In fact, you might have heard horror stories about how various states were levying income tax on retirement distributions made by former residents, because some of those assets were earned while domiciled in the state. Fortunately, a 1996 federal law put a stop to this "source taxation" nightmare, which had some retirees filling out forms from five or more states at tax time.

Nevertheless, most states do tax their residents to some extent on the pensions and Social Security they receive, and their withdrawals from 401(k), IRA, and other qualified retirement-plan accounts. Differences between states can be substantial, so it's worth taking a look at the income tax policies of the "short list" of retirement-candidate states. That comparison could prove an effective tiebreaker if you're clearly undecided. However, most state taxes are a nuisance rather than impossible burden, and policies can change, so they usually shouldn't drive your decision.

JUST A MINUTE

States also vary markedly in property tax, sales tax, and taxes on the value of your overall assets (for example, intangibles tax). So don't look at income tax in isolation. A useful resource for making overall comparisons of state tax policies is Kiplinger's Bankrate.com State Tax Roundup (www.bankrate.com/kip/story_home.asp?web= kip&story=itax/edit/state/profiles/state_tax_Cal&prodtype=itax).

Another area of concern about how you withdraw your funds is possible estate taxation of remaining balances. Here are the rules as they stand under current tax law. The first question is whether the beneficiary is a spouse or a nonspouse. The spouse can roll over the IRA, consider the inherited IRA as part of his or her assets, and continue calculating distributions as before but with a larger base of assets.

The next question to be answered is whether the IRA holder died before or after his or her required beginning date, which is April 1 of the year following reaching of age 70$^1/_2$. If death is before that time the entire IRA balance must be withdrawn within five years and will be taxed at the recipient's current tax rate. How the funds are withdrawn during this five-year period is optional. They can be withdrawn all at once or in a series of equal or unequal payments.

If the owner dies after the required beginning date, more options are available. Most IRA or qualified plans allow the recipient to opt out of the five-year rule and select instead a life expectancy rule, which will provide for a much longer payout period. To take advantage of this longer period, you must take the first distribution by December 31 of the IRA owner's year of death. Missing that deadline can be costly because then the recipient must use the five-year rule.

Another common misconception about inheriting IRAs relates to the Roth. Many people believe that the Roth IRA is completely free of taxes even for beneficiaries. This is not the case. The Roth becomes part of the base for estate tax calculation. If the Roth IRA owner's estate exceeds the tax-free threshold, then the Roth will be taxed under estate tax rules.

If you are sure you are going to die in 2010, when according to the new tax bill there will be no estate taxes, then this need not concern you, but it's not a certainty you can count on. You also have to believe that the tax bill passed in 2001 will go unchanged in the next 10 years. If you follow U.S. tax politics, you know the chances of that are slim and none.

Another area where a mistake can be made on an inherited Roth IRA is if contributions were made to the Roth less than five years before the IRA owner's death. An inherited Roth that is made up of contributions that were added less than five years earlier, should not be withdrawn until the funds are in the Roth for at least five years, or taxes will need to be paid on the gains.

EVALUATE RETIREMENT WITHDRAWAL OPTIONS

Now that you know all the rules, let's look at how you can evaluate your options to be certain you won't outlive your assets. You can plan the withdrawals based on your lifetime, the joint lifetime of you and your spouse, or the joint lifetime of you and your beneficiary. Basically, what you are trying to do when looking at these choices is to decide how long you want your money to last.

FYI How much should you withdraw each year? For years, the rule of thumb for planners was 4 percent, with few arguing that you should risk anything more. Recently, there have been some mathematical findings challenging this absolute rule, depending on the aggressiveness of the portfolio and the retiree's expected longevity.

Once you have figured that out, you need to consider how conservative or aggressive your portfolio will be and the level of confidence you want to have that you won't outlive your money. Earlier in this Hour it was mentioned that 4 percent is the rule of thumb as a safe withdrawal percentage. There has been much controversy recently questioning that percentage. Here is a chart that you can use to help decide the issue for yourself. It shows the percentage of confidence you can have of your money lasting you the rest of your life with a particular withdrawal rate. It shows this for three different levels of confidence, five different investment allocations, and four different life expectancies.

Distribution Withdrawal Rate Chart

Asset Allocation	Level of Confidence	Years Expected in Retirement			
		10 Years	20 Years	30 Years	40 Years
Conservative					
25% Stocks	95%	9.7%	5.3%	3.9%	3.3%
40% Bonds	85%	10.5%	5.9%	4.4%	3.8%
35% Cash	50%	11.9%	6.9%	5.3%	4.5%
Conservative Growth					
40% Stocks	95%	9.4%	5.3%	4.0%	3.3%
40% Bonds	85%	10.4%	6.1%	4.6%	4.0%
20% Cash	50%	12.2%	7.3%	5.8%	5.0%
Balanced					
50% Stocks	95%	9.2%	5.2%	4.0%	3.3%
35% Bonds	85%	10.3%	6.1%	4.7%	4.0%
15% Cash	50%	12.4%	7.6%	6.0%	5.3%
Moderate Aggressive					
60% Stocks	95%	9.0%	5.2%	4.0%	3.3%
35% Bonds	85%	10.3%	6.2%	4.8%	4.1%
5% Cash	50%	12.7%	7.9%	6.3%	5.6%

continues

Distribution Withdrawal Rate Chart   (continued)

Asset Allocation	Level of Confidence	Years Expected in Retirement			
		10 Years	20 Years	30 Years	40 Years
Aggressive					
75% Stocks	95%	8.7%	5.0%	3.9%	3.3%
25% Bonds	85%	10.2%	6.1%	4.9%	4.3%
0% Cash	50%	12.9%	8.1%	6.6%	5.8%

This excellent chart was developed using calculations of Morningstar's director of financial planning, Sue Stevens, from her Income Worksheet for Retirees. You can download the full worksheet at http://news.morningstar.com/pdfs/Income_Worksheet_Retire.pdf. In developing these withdrawal percentages, Sue Stevens assumed the following growth rates: large-cap stocks, 5.5 percent; mid- or small-cap stocks, 6.5 percent; international stocks, 6 percent; bonds, 3 percent; and cash, 1.5 percent. Withdrawals increase annually by rate of inflation. She also assumes a $0 dollar portfolio balance at death.

As you can see from the variables in this chart, it is not a simple answer. For example, if your retirement planning is for a 10-year period and you want to be 95 percent certain that you will have enough money throughout that period, you can get your highest percentage withdrawal rate in the most conservative portfolio allocation—9.7 percent. If you want that same 95 percent certainty but over a 30 year retirement period, your highest withdrawal rate is 4 percent—the general rule of thumb recommended by financial advisors. You'll find that in three portfolio options: conservative growth, balanced, and moderate aggressive.

FYI Determining your withdrawal options can be very complex and is so critical to your ultimate success in managing your money, you may want to read further about it. One of the experts in this, Barry R. Picker, CFP and CFP/PFS, wrote an excellent *Guide to Retirement Distribution Planning.* You can order it by calling 1-800-809-0015 or directly from his Web site at www.bpickercpa.com/Guide2.htm.

SOCIAL SECURITY RULES FOR WIDOWS AND WIDOWERS

The Social Security Administration reports that there are five million widows or widowers receiving benefits based on their deceased spouse's earnings records. It is more common for widows to choose to use their spouse's records than their own, since women tend to have lower earnings through their lifetime because of breaks in work for raising a family and for other reasons.

Even if a widow has worked, she may want to collect under her deceased husband's Social Security benefits. If she began collecting under her benefits at retirement but her deceased spouse had a higher benefit, she may switch to his pension after his death.

A widow or widower can collect on a spouse's Social Security benefits as early as age 60 at reduced benefit rates, but must wait until full retirement age to get full benefits. Disabled widows or widowers can begin receiving spouse's benefits as early as age 50, provided they qualify under disability rules.

If he or she has a child under the age of 16, a widow or widower can collect survivors's benefits for taking care of that child at any age. Divorced spouses also have the right to collect on their ex-spouse's benefits provided they did not remarry and were married at least 10 years. Details are provided at www.ssa.gov/survivorplan/onyourown4.htm.

REVISITING YOUR WITHDRAWAL OPTIONS ANNUALLY

This is not the first time you are hearing this refrain, but you do need to revisit this issue annually and be certain you are staying on track. You may find that health problems have destroyed all your budget planning and you need to rethink your withdrawal options or find a way to live more cheaply by moving to a less costly housing arrangement. Or more positively, you may find you're health is better than expected and you now want to plan for a longer retirement period.

Your portfolio might have taken a larger drop than you expected and you may need to reallocate that portfolio more conservatively to be sure you will have enough through retirement. In making this kind of adjustment, you want to be certain you are not reacting too quickly to a short-term market correction.

Any portfolio allocation change should be made slowly and with the least amount of loss. Remember it is only a paper loss until you actually sell the asset. If you still think it is a good investment, you may want to be patient and allow it to recover. This is easier to do if you have a good portfolio allocation with investment alternatives that are not in a loss position and liquid, such as cash or money market funds. In fact, many financial advisors recommend that you avoid the pressure to sell during a market down cycle by starting retirement with three to five years worth of living expenses invested in liquid assets.

HOUR'S UP!

It's time to find out whether you have learned the basics of retirement distribution.

Answer True or False to the following statements:

1. If you will be collecting a traditional pension you must allow the company to continue to control the money and select an annuity payout option.

2. If you select a lump-sum payout, you can take that as a cash distribution or roll the money over into an IRA.

3. Annuities can be based on a single life or the lives of both you and your spouse.

4. If you are married, the law requires the company to offer a joint and survivor annuity. To select a single life annuity, your spouse must sign a waiver.

5. The biggest advantage of taking a lump-sum payment as a cash distribution is that the tax bite is low.

6. The rule of thumb for calculating how much to take out each year of retirement is 4 percent, but other individual circumstances may justify a different option.

7. If you will be collecting a traditional defined-benefit pension, your choice of withdrawal option is set in stone and cannot be changed.

8. Once you decide on a withdrawal method for your IRAs, your choice cannot be changed.

9. If you are a widow or widower collecting Social Security based on your own benefits, when your spouse dies you do have the option to change to his or her benefits if they are higher.

10. You should revisit your retirement withdrawal plans yearly to be certain you're on track and don't need to change the withdrawal options you have selected.

HOUR 24

Retirement Pitfalls, Shortfalls, and Surpluses

CHAPTER SUMMARY

LESSON PLAN:
In this Hour you will learn about …

- Monitoring your money situation.
- Keeping the financial wolves from your nest egg's hen-house.
- Absorbing late-life changes without changing your financial fortunes.
- Protecting yourself against fraud.
- Allocating your abundance of wealth.

After all the planning, fretting, and expended emotions, the actual beginning of retirement will likely seem either anticlimactic or unreal, depending on how you start it. Many experts suggest you choose the mundane route, living in your first year of retirement at the same standard you lived in your last year of work—or perhaps the other way around.

In other words, while you still have the security of a paycheck, live the way your retirement plan dictates you live once you do retire. That way, you'll either know you can, or might change your retirement plans if you discover within a few months that it's not working. You'll then have to determine if you need to be older and more mature to pull it off, or if you need more years of work to accumulate the amount that will enable you to live at the level of comfort you really need.

It's not easy to make it through that last work year lived like your first retirement year, and your first retirement year lived like your last work year. But after you do, you'll be ready for the relatively unrestrained celebration with a temporary feel-good budget, knowing that you've already proven your retirement fiscal restraint and will then come back to it. In other words, in your first year, live together with retirement but don't share a bed, to make sure you'll still be able to respect your fiscal restraint the mornings after you do splurge.

With those preliminaries out of the way, you'll be ready to do the other financial things that keep your retirement on track: monitoring the performance of your plan, avoiding the sharks who want to feed on seniors' financial flesh, remarrying or making other life changes without getting off track, dealing with living below the standard you'd wanted if you made major retirement-preparation mistakes, and making arrangements for handling your financial affairs or leftovers if you should become incapacitated or die.

MONITOR YOUR RETIREMENT PLAN'S PERFORMANCE

Does your heart quicken when you look at a list, table, or bar chart showing how your money is doing? No plug intended (although the pun was), in retirement you no longer have an excuse not to put your financial life on Quicken, Microsoft Money, or any good competitive product that might emerge (we're all still waiting).

Why? Because you have much less margin for error when the money coming in is less than the money going out. So, in a sense, you're going to invest sweat equity into being a smart consumer. That doesn't mean you have to use coupons every time you go shopping (save that for your slower Phase 2 if you'd like), but it does mean developing a much better daily understanding of what's happening to your money. Be assured, awareness will tighten the clasp on your pocketbook.

More importantly, having your data on these neat programs makes it a cinch to size up your big-picture financial situation virtually any time you want.

Pictures indeed, those vivid color graphs really emphasize the important aspects of your finances. And speaking of virtual, these programs allow you to easily download up-to-the minute (on the Internet) balance information from your IRA, 401(k), mutual-fund, and other financial accounts. In fact, these programs can even be set to do automatic download updating.

Of course, all the monitoring in the world won't help unless you act on the information. If you're off track, it's time to adjust your budgets by changing spending patterns, bringing in more income, modifying your portfolio, or some combination. The really good news is that at this point, you have permission to burn the retirement-gap worksheets (or at least burn some copies for symbolic purposes). That's because both Quicken and Microsoft Money (deluxe versions) have the capability to do all the financial projections you need during retirement.

JUST A MINUTE

We think of the retirement gap calculation in this book as sort of an unofficially patented approach to doing an essential financial evaluation before retirement that no other book or software now does.

AVOID RIPOFF RETIREMENT "OPPORTUNITIES"

If your brand-new, pride-and-joy, tuned-to-perfection car is involved in a violent collision, you know enough to expect performance problems, even after the body is repaired. Similarly, your well-tuned retirement plan will sputter and stall out if you collide with one of thousands of high-speed, high-stakes fraud perpetrators who prey on seniors.

The most tempting and dangerous of these might be prime bank "certificates"—especially in these low-inflation times when money-market accounts and Treasury bonds are paying such low rates of interest. Seniors "reaching for yield" have been suckered by legitimate-looking advertisements in *USA Today*, the *Wall Street Journal*, and other highly respected publications whose managements had no way of knowing they were placed by incredibly brazen fraud perpetrators. Gathered from the U.S. Government SEC and Commerce Department Web sites, here are verbatim excerpts describing how these schemes are operated:

> Prime bank programs often claim investors' funds will be used to purchase and trade "prime bank" financial instruments on clandestine overseas markets in order to generate huge returns in which the investor will share. However, neither these instruments, nor the markets on which they allegedly trade, exist. To give the scheme an air of legitimacy, the promoters distribute documents that appear complex, sophisticated, and official. The sellers frequently tell potential investors that they have special access to programs that otherwise would be reserved for top financiers on Wall Street, or in London, Geneva, or other world financial centers. Investors are also told that profits of 100 percent or more are possible with little risk.

> Despite having credible-sounding names, the supposed "financial instruments" at the heart of prime bank schemes simply don't exist. Exercise

caution if you've been asked to invest in debt obligations of the top 100 world banks, medium-term bank notes or debentures, standby letters of credit, bank guarantees, offshore trading programs, a roll program, bank-issued debentures, high-yield investment programs, or some variation on these descriptions. Promoters frequently claim that the offered financial instrument is issued, traded, endorsed, or guaranteed by the World Bank, International Monetary Fund, International Chamber of Commerce, Federal Reserve, Department of Treasury, or an international central bank.

Another prime fraud perpetrated by those who have an affinity for taking other people's money is the "affinity fraud." From the same U.S. government sources, here's the scoop:

Affinity fraud refers to investment scams that prey upon members of identifiable groups, including religious, elderly, ethnic, and professional groups. The fraudsters who promote affinity scams are group members, claim to be members of the group, or enlist respected leaders within a group to spread the word about an investment deal. In addition, fraud-sters are increasingly using the Internet to target groups with e-mail spams. These scams exploit the trust and friendship that exist in groups of people who have something in common. Because of the tight-knit structure of many groups, it is usually more difficult for regulators or law enforcement officials to detect an affinity scam. Victims of such scams often fail to notify authorities or pursue their legal remedies, but are more likely to try to work things out within the group.

Many affinity scams involve "Ponzi" or pyramid schemes where new investor money is used to make payments to earlier investors to give the false illusion that the investment is successful. This ploy is used to induce or "trick" new investors to invest in the scheme and to lull existing investors into believing their investments are safe and secure. In reality, the fraudster almost always steals investor money for personal use. Both types of schemes depend on an unending supply of new investors; when the inevitable occurs, and the supply of investors dries up, the whole scheme collapses and investors lose most, if not all, of their money.

As pervasive and harmful as they are, prime bank and affinity frauds are only the top layer of a seamy underworld of financial frauds targeted at seniors and others. Here are brief annotated descriptions of the worst of the rest:

- **Credit and charge-card fraud.** These aren't offers to invest, but rather schemes to get at your credit information so that it can be used to make large purchases for which you'll be left holding the bag. In the majority of cases, these criminals obtain the information both surreptitiously (the Internet and other places you use your charge card), or after you carelessly discard credit information. In other cases, they pose as authorities trying to entrap someone who is trying to steal your information, and they're asking for "verification" of your information so the perpetrators can be stopped and arrested.

- **Identity theft.** Taking credit theft many steps further, these scamsters infiltrate your entire "financial infrastructure" and take over control of your credit and assets. Many identity-theft victims have spent months or years undoing damage, including proving to authorities that they're the innocent parties who've been victimized.

- **Fraudulent charities.** Using names that sound like legitimate organizations, such as American Cancer Syndicate, they illicitly solicit billions in donations from kind-hearted folks.

- **Boiler-room schemes.** They work just like in the hit movie *Boiler Room*—high-pressure telephone sales of totally phony investments. Sometimes a first modest investment in a nonexistent security is sold to a "mark" and it proves a "winner"—so the "profits" are sent to the investor. Then a much larger second phony investment is sold and proves a loser, setting up a third even bigger one to be sold to recover the loss on the second one. To add insult to injury, the scheme also includes people posing as authorities who want to involve the victims in an entrapment scheme to catch the operators, and only require that they put up the money to lure them, assuring them they'll soon get it back, plus, hopefully, the money taken from them previously. Not only don't they get it back, they never seem to "get it"—period!

- **Other schemes.** These include living trusts that will supposedly save you tens of thousands in taxes, but end up netting the trust designers your fat fees, with you left holding a meaningless document. Next are foreign lotteries that supposedly are inaccessible to Americans, but lucky you are being given the opportunity—at much better odds than U.S. lotteries! Usually, there is no lottery.

Many multilevel marketing enterprises are legitimate, but few have any real potential to net their participants any more than what amount to moderate discounts on highly marked-up products that they purchase for themselves. It's the ones that aggressively convince you otherwise, and require that you front significant funds, that are potentially criminal.

Then there are flawed franchises and multilevel marketing enterprises that elicit substantial front money from you, but have little potential to ever make you any money. Finally, there are travel and vacation frauds that offer you huge savings for upfront cash payments, and various bargain financing offers that give you cheap rates to borrow money, but surreptitiously tie the loan to your house. These loans have hidden rollover provisions that make them very difficult to ever pay back, and you can end up losing your house altogether.

So, how do you avoid getting ensnared in these schemes? Here's more directly quoted SEC (U.S. government) advice:

> With any investment, whether recommended in person, by mail, telephone, or on the Internet, you should always slow down, ask questions, and get written information. Take notes so you have a record of what you were told in case you have a dispute later. Here are some questions to ask:

- Is the investment registered with the SEC and the state where I live?

- Is the person recommending this investment licensed with my state securities agency? Is there a record of any complaints about this person or the firm (for which) he or she works?

- How does this investment match my investment objectives?

- Will the sales representative send me the latest reports that have been filed on this company?

- What are the costs to buy, hold, and sell this investment? How easily can I sell?

- Who is managing the investment? What experience do they have? Have they made money for investors before?

- What is the risk that I could lose the money I invest?

- What return can I expect on my money? When?

- How long has the company been in business? Is it making money, and if so, how? What is their product or service? What other companies are in this business?

- How can I get more information about this investment, such as audited financial statements, annual and quarterly reports, a prospectus?

To learn more about questions you should ask before you invest, visit the SEC's Web site at www.sec.gov, or call 1-800-SEC-0330. Order the SEC publications *Get the Facts on Saving and Investing* or *Ask Questions*.

REMARRIAGE AND OTHER COMPLICATIONS

Although many retirees are victims of fraud perpetrated by strangers, a large percentage are also victimized by mishandling unexpected, yet common, life changes such as widowhood, divorce, and remarriage. Combine the 250,000 annual marriages involving people over 50 with the 40 percent of people over 65 who are widowed or divorced, and it's obvious that a lot of financial and legal footwork is needed to protect retiree assets. This includes asset retitling, beneficiary redesignations, prenuptial agreements, rearranging insurance coverage, minimizing taxes when giving up one of two homes, dealing with the effects of Social Security and pension changes, and a slew of other estate-planning issues.

All this especially affects 8.6 million widows and almost 1 million divorced female seniors. Despite major strides in educational and professional equity in the last 30 years, many of these women were traditional homemakers who had little involvement in the "big-picture" aspects of family finance. That makes them ill-prepared to deal with finances now—thus vulnerable to both intentional manipulation, and errors of ignorance when dealing with life changes during retirement.

GO TO ▶
Some estate planning basics are covered in the last section of this Hour.

These issues are far too complex for adequate coverage in this book. Therefore, any readers confronting them, or helping someone who is, should seek competent legal and financial-planning advice. These matters have the potential to blow an otherwise well-planned retirement right out of the water, so they shouldn't be ignored.

RETIREMENT DREAMS DEFERRED

Although you can, at later peril, ignore potential financial consequences of retirement life changes, you can't ignore the stark reality of an investment portfolio pulverized by the recent stock market plunge.

Are you among the not-long-ago market virgins who quickly graduated from Crisco shortening in your pantry to shorting Cisco in your portfolio? Or from Jane Russell's full-figured 18-hour bra to fully figuring on the Russell 5000 to shape up your investment results?

If so, you might be feeling used right now by all those sexy market seers who seduced you into believing you'd keep doubling your money every few years. If, instead, you're suffering from mourning-after (bull market) sickness and have lost 50 percent of your wealth weight, you've plenty of company among chastened (pre)retirees.

Given the legitimacy that the media conferred on the '90s market hysteria, you or anyone else burned by it are justified in being angry. But all the victims were consenting adults, so it's time to move on. In many cases, there's no escaping the obvious consequences—a delayed or more modest retirement, and a return to, or increase in, part-time work.

But just as it's necessary for the victims to own up to their mistakes, it's equally important that they not overreact by getting even more insanely aggressive or overconservative in their investment philosophies.

The '90s market was a once-in-a-lifetime event, so there's no hope of catching lightning in a bottle again and then being smart enough to keep it there. But you do need to keep the bottle open and at least catch a few rays of market sunshine.

If it seems this advice is too heavy on metaphor and too light on method, that's intentional. If your retirement plans have been markedly altered by market reversals, you're literally suffering something like post-traumatic disorder. You must first make the needed emotional and attitudinal adjustments before you make the mental and mechanical ones. Think of yourself as getting to a place where you can slap on a bumper sticker reading "I survived the bull-you-know-what market" on your Toyota Echo (sorry, no Infiniti now for you, pal!).

RETIREMENT SWEET DREAMS, FOR GOOD

You don't have to own an Infiniti, however, or have anything like infinite wealth, in order to have the opposite problem. If, despite your bumper sticker about spending the grandkids' inheritance, your money will survive you, now's the time to keep it from being consumed by either the phasing-out inheritance tax, or the just-enacted future capital gains tax on inherited wealth.

One common practice to minimize these taxes is to give money to your heirs over a number of years before your die. You and your spouse can each give up to $10,000 per year per recipient without incurring any federal gift tax.

If your gifts have built-in capital gains, your recipients will eventually owe tax on them, but that's as little as 10 percent of the gain if you're giving capital gains property to kids. In contrast, under the current law scheduled to end in 2010, any of your capital gains property that your heirs receive will be inherited on a stepped-up basis. For example, if your heirs get your stock that was purchased for $50 and it is now worth $1,000 on the market, it's as though they purchased it for $1,000 in determining gain for income tax purposes when they eventually sell it. If your heirs were to sell that stock five years down the road for $1,500, their capital gains tax would be based on the $500 gained since they received the stock as an inheritance. Meanwhile, your estate paid estate taxes on the $1,000 property value.

But starting in 2010, things flip-flop. Your estate will not be taxed for what you bequeath to your heirs. But your heirs will be taxed on the difference between what you paid for what you're giving them, and its value when they sell it. Thus, if they inherit that same stock and then sell it for $1,300, they'll pay income tax on the difference between the $1,300 sale price and your original $50 acquisition price.

Another big factor for most estates is the *unified credit*. This applies to any gifts over the $10,000 allowed per year as well as up to $675,000 of whatever is left. For example, if a gift of $50,000 were given in one year to a person, then $10,000 would qualify toward the annual gift tax exclusion, but $40,000 would be used to reduce the lifetime unified credit to $635,000.

STRICTLY DEFINED

Almost everyone is entitled to take advantage of the **unified credit** when doing their estate planning. This lifetime credit exempts the first $675,000 of your estate from gift and estate taxes, and that amount will increase several times between now and the inheritance-tax phaseout in 2010.

The unified credit is phased out for estates over $10 million. The unified credit is important in estate planning because there is no estate tax on estates of $675,000 or less. Once the estate tops $675,000, then taxes start at 37 percent on amounts in excess of $675,000 and escalate to 41 percent on amounts over $1 million and 55 percent on anything over $3 million.

The current unlimited marital deduction allows you to give, upon your death, any amount to your spouse without estate tax. However, your spouse's estate will be taxed on any amount over $675,000 when he or she dies. To reduce that tax burden, the current law allows spouses to each set up something called a credit-shelter trust. Upon the first spouse's death, everything above $675,000 goes to the surviving spouse in a marital trust. The $675,000 goes to another heir, but only after the spouse has used income from it until he or she dies. In essence, this technique doubles the amount that spouses can bequeath free of inheritance tax.

Under the just-passed bill, the unified credit keeps increasing and the estate tax rates drop between now and estate tax repeal in 2010. The unified credit, now on the first $675,000 of assets, will rise to $1 million in 2002. After that, it will gradually increase until it eventually hits $3.5 million in 2009.

The top estate tax rate will drop from the current 55 percent to 45 percent by 2007. The estate tax will be repealed in 2010, though gift taxes will remain in effect. However, it will also be reinstated in 2011 unless Congress takes further action. Many financial planners will tell you that considering all the quirks and flaws in this legislation, and the government's likely increased need for revenue, you shouldn't hang your hat on any aspect of this legislation just yet. Many believe the bill will be substantially modified in a more permanent future treatment of inheritance taxation.

The lesson here is that if your heirs are lucky enough to be getting inheritance from you, you can maximize their good fortune by keeping a close eye on developments concerning the supposed phaseout of the estate tax.

Whatever you do, however, don't include this book in your estate. As you've undoubtedly discovered, it's so valuable that it will blow sky-high either inheritance tax or your heirs' ultimate capital gains tax.

HOUR'S UP!

Retirement is the pits if you don't have enough money, and even if you do, there are pitfalls to keeping it. Try pitting your knowledge of these challenges against these questions.

Answer True or False to the following statements:

1. Most successful retirements begin with an ultra-frugal first year.

2. During retirement, you'd do well to find a soft place in your heart for financial-planning software.

3. After you've spent most of your life trying to look and act young, you can be excused for not trotting out the grocery coupons during the first phase of retirement.

4. Scam artists are a serious problem in this country, but most at least have the compassion to avoid exploiting helpless seniors.

5. Prime bank certificates pay an average of major bank prime rates—a great way for retirees to boost their fixed-income yields.

6. Both "Affinity" and "Infiniti" seem to fit this Hour to a "Ti."

7. It's wise to watch out for identity theft scams involving cosmetic surgeons. When seniors get face lifts, their head impressions are sold to criminals who get their own surgery done to enable them to physically assume the identity of their victims.

8. The movie *Boiler Room* might have been chilled by all the cold-hearted cold-calling concerning hot investments, but male and female movie fans (respectively) definitely couldn't cool down after watching hot Nia Long and Ben Affleck.

9. The best thing to do when offered an unsolicited living trust is anything but (trusting it).

10. The unified credit was a special tax break in the just-passed tax cut to encourage immigrant marriages between former residents of East Germany and West Germany, North Korea and South Korea, and any two former Balkan states.

APPENDIX A
20-Minute Recap

Hour 1

You know why you think you should be reading this book, but in this Hour you'll learn the real reasons why it's nothing less than a manifesto for a survival strategy in retirement. You'll find out a new way to think about your retirement in three very different segments, and why you can't rely on anybody but yourself to get you through those segments.

Hour 2

Hour 1 wasn't a lie—you must meet a major challenge to be financially prepared for retirement. But there is hope, and it starts with taking the time to envision your own specific retirement, instead of the generic brand painted in almost every panic article about retirement saving. You'll feel like wearing a painter's smock when you admire your own artistry in picturing your retirement future.

Hour 3

Going from the abstract to the concrete, this Hour covers details about what kinds of costs you can expect in retirement, and how to determine how much they'll be for you. Referring to one of the book's appendixes, you're asked to complete current and future budgets that will be needed in later retirement calculations.

Hour 4

Continuing the data preparation started in Hour 3 for the calculations you'll be doing in later Hours, you'll turn your attention to your assets. You'll learn how to inventory and value them, and determine their applicability toward your retirement nest egg. You'll then refer to the same appendix you started completing in Hour 3, and fill in the details of your inventory.

Hour 5

Now that you've tabulated most of the data you'll need, you're ready to learn about how you'll be using it. Before getting into the actual calculation methods covered in Hours 6 and 7, you'll learn here about the concepts underlying them. If you ever find yourself having cocktails with Alan Greenspan, you'll be ready to pontificate on inflation, interest rates, investment returns, and taxes.

Hour 6

With data in your left hand and concepts in your right, now you'll get a detailed overview of how they go hand in hand in computing what this book calls your personal *retirement gap*. That's the amount of additional money you'll need to accumulate by your retirement year, through investment of additional savings generated by either higher income or lower expenses. Steps are explained in two syllables (okay, maybe three or four occasionally) to avoid scaring you from plunging into the detailed calculation in Hour 7.

Hour 7

Using a somewhat simplified but realistic example of a married couple doing retirement planning, in this Hour you'll follow the complete detail of the calculation of their retirement gap.

Hour 8

With an actual retirement gap calculation fresh in your mind, you'll certainly want to know what can be done to close such a gap. Here you'll learn principles for improved budgeting, appropriate investment strategies, ways to reap tax advantages, and how to exploit benefits—all in order to squeeze out more savings and get better investment results from them in closing your personal retirement gap.

Hour 9

Okay, be honest, other than having "lockbox" and "privatization" playing in your head like an annoying old song, did you really learn anything about Social Security from the 2000 Presidential debates? After this Hour, you will have.

Hour 10

So you thought your employer was being such a good guy offering you that 401(k) plan? Well, maybe, but after everything you'll learn here, you'll really know, and not just accept your employer's propaganda.

Hour 11

And if your "good guy" employer isn't a big guy, he might be offering only a Keogh, SEP-IRA, or SIMPLE-IRA for small businesses. Learn more about what you are getting, or why you might want to be suggesting these plans to your employer if you don't have one. Or, if you're self-employed or a business owner, you'll learn why you should be setting one up for yourself.

Hour 12

Your employer probably is a good guy if he still offers an old-time pension plan. But if he did offer one and converted it to a cash-balance plan, he might now be on your personal America's Most Wanted Scoundrels list. When you've finished this Hour, you'll know what all the pension passion is about.

Hour 13

Do you have a 401(k) and pension, but no IRA? In that case you deserve some good old-fashioned rear-end corporal punishment for not using any common sense. Avoid coming up short for your retirement needs by learning why you can and should invest in one of the three IRA types—even if you didn't think you qualified.

HOUR 14

Just spend a few hours with some seniors and you'll get an unhealthy dose of reality about their frequent and expensive adventures with the medical community. Medicare is your after-65 health lifeline, and you'll need some supplementary coverage to comfortably swim above water financially. Dive in by learning all about it here.

HOUR 15

Now you know all about your gap, and the retirement-saving and expense-paying resources covered in Part III to deal with it. Now it's time to figure out how it all goes together as a foundation for building a plan to close your gap. In this Hour you'll learn about how your current assets will play a part in your ultimate retirement nest egg.

HOUR 16

How's this for a big *duh*: The crux of your retirement gap-closing plan will be the priorities it establishes for spending vs. savings. But you might not have thought through all those priorities, such as house down payment vs. retirement investing—or even be aware that you are, by default, acting on them. Now you'll know, and you'll decide.

HOUR 17

Potholes aren't just problems in New York City and Los Angeles. They lie ahead on your road to retirement, and some are sure to cause detours: disability, divorce, unplanned job changes, family crises from third generation to first. You'll find out here how to keep moving toward your retirement destination.

HOUR 18

It's not enough to invest as much as possible in the plans described in Part III. You'll learn how to manage those investments properly, taking into account each plan's rules, rules for moving money between plans, tax consequences, your investment objectives, and the structure of your overall portfolio.

Hour 19

At this point, you've assembled and stirred all your retirement plan ingredients, but you're not yet cooking with gas. Learn how to adjust the temperature for your planning time frame, risk tolerance, and speculations on how the overall economy and your investments will perform. Then learn to check to see if you're really done when the retirement timer rings.

Hour 20

You thought Hour 7 was fun? Get real—really—with this full-blown example of calculating a retirement gap. Then really do your own calculations.

Hour 21

Sometimes stereotyping can be good. Here you can pick the category in which you best fit, and learn more about the specific retirement challenges your group faces. But don't skip the other ones, you'll learn something from their challenges, too.

Hour 22

No matter how carefully constructed your retirement plan is, it's crucial to revisit it when you anticipate retirement within five years. Your objectives and life circumstances might have changed, and your "modern maturity" might have given you a totally different perspective on retirement from the one you had when you put together your plan. You'll learn what to review, and revise if necessary.

Hour 23

It's not that financial advisors (among those who are Christian) don't believe in the holy trinity. It's just that they're devout followers of the fraternity of four—the 4-percent rule for the amount you're supposed to be able to withdraw from your nest egg each year during retirement so your money will last. But new theories have come to the fore, and it's important that you learn all this Hour has to say about the variables, regulations, and tax rules involved in deciding on the how to and how much of annual distributions of your retirement accounts.

HOUR 24

We're warning you—start with us! Start your retirement, that is, with the approaches outlined in this Hour: Don't go hog wild; learn to deal with life reversals or recent market crashes; and dodge repeated attempts by fraudsters and swindlers to part you from your money. And also kill some time finding out what you have to do so that your heirs get the most when you die.

APPENDIX B
Resources

BOOKS

Anthony, Mitch. *The New Retirementality*. Dearborn Trade, 2001.

Barbanel, Linda. *Teach Your Kids the Financial Facts of Life*. Crown Trade Paperbacks, 1994.

Better Homes and Gardens Second Home. Better Homes and Gardens Books, 2000.

Carter, Jimmy. *The Virtues of Aging*. Ballantine Books, 1998.

Chidester, Jane E., and John L. Macko. *Budget Yes!* TulipTreePress, 1997.

Chilton, David. *The Wealthy Barber*. Prima Publishing, 1998.

Cunningham, Timothy W., and Clay B. Mansfield. *Pay Yourself First: A Commonsense Guide to Life-Cycle Retirement Investing*. John Wiley & Sons, 1996.

Dacyczyn, Amy. *The Complete Tightwad Gazette*. Random House, 1999.

Dempsey, Mark. *Robbing You Blind*. William Morrow and Company, 2000.

Dominguez, Joe, and Vicki Robin. *Your Money or Your Life*. Penguin USA, 1999.

Edwards, Carolina, and Neale S. Godfrey. *Money Doesn't Grow on Trees*. Fireside–Simon and Schuster, 1994.

Eldred, Gary W. *The Complete Guide to Second Homes for Vacation, Retirement, and Investment*. John Wiley & Sons, 1999.

Fox, Richard L. *America's 100 Best Places to Retire*. Vacation Publications, 2000.

Freedman, Marc. *Prime Time: How Baby-Boomers Will Revolutionize Retirement and Transform America*. Public Affairs, 2000.

Greenwald, Robert. *50 Fabulous Planned Retirement Communities for Active Adults*. Career Press, 1998.

Hinden, Stan. *How to Retire Happy*. McGraw-Hill Professional Publishing, 2001.

Hoffman, Ellen. *The Retirement Catch-Up Guide*. New Market Press, 2000.

Howells, John. *Retirement on a Shoestring*. Globe Pequot Press, 2000.

———. *Where to Retire: America's Best and Most Affordable Places*. Globe Pequot Press, 2000.

Hurley, Joe. *The Best Way to Save for College: A Complete Guide to 529 Plans*. BonaCom Publications, 2001.

Jaffe, Charles A. *The Right Way to Hire Financial Help*. MIT Press, 2001.

Kaplan, Lawrence J. *Retiring Right: Planning for a Successful Retirement*. Square One Publishers, 2001.

Linder, Ray. *What Will I Do with My Money?* Northfield Publishing, 2000.

Lubow, Joseph M. *Choose a College Town for Retirement*. Globe Pequot Press, 1999.

O'Shaughnessy, Lynn. *Retirement Bible*. Hungry Minds, Inc., 2001.

Otterbourg, Robert K. *Retire and Thrive*. Kiplinger Books, 1999.

Rosenberg, Steven M., and Steven Rosenberg. *Last Minute Retirement Planning*. Career Press, 1998.

Sander, Peter J., and Jennifer Basye Sander. *The Pocket Idiot's Guide to Living on a Budget*. Alpha Books, 1999.

Savageau, David. *Retirement Places Rated*. Hungry Minds, Inc., 1999.

Schwab, Charles R. *You're Fifty—Now What?* Crown Publishers, 2000.

Smith, Mary Helen, and Shuford Smith. *101 Secrets for a Great Retirement.* Lowell House, 2000.

——. *The Retirement Sourcebook.* Roxbury Park, 1999.

Stanley, Thomas J., and William D. Danko. *The Millionaire Next Door.* Pocket Books, 2000.

Tuller, Lawrence W. *The Small Business Valuation Book.* Adams Media Corporation, 1998.

Vacation and Second Homes: 465 Designs for Recreation, Retirement and Leisure Living. Home Planners, LLC, 1999.

Wasik, John F. *Retire Early—and Live the Life You Want Now.* Henry Holt, 1999.

GENERAL WEB SITES

ABC News MONEYScope (www.abcnews.go.com/sections/business)

Don't expect the ABCs of money here, but it's a sure bet you'll find articles with sophisticated financial information and strategies. Look for the weekly financial makeover, which takes on some ugly money messes.

Age Venture News Service (www.demko.com)

A fantastic archive of encouraging, helpful articles about virtually every aspect of retirement and aging.

Bankrate (www.bankrate.com)

Great articles and competitive financing information to help you deal with financial institutions in the most cost-effective way.

CBS MarketWatch (www.cbsmarketwatch.com)

Shout a big "Aye!" to its well-organized, broad coverage of business, the markets, and your money.

CNNfn (www.cnnfn.com)

To the best of its "cablebilities," this site offers a wealth of in-depth business news, sector analysis, and personal-finance articles.

Errold Moody (www.erroldmoody.com)

Frequently awarded site on all aspects of financial planning, including retirement. Be prepared to read at the college level, but it's worth the effort.

Insure.com (www.insure.com)

Everything you ever wanted to know about insurance can be found here. Many excellent articles on virtually every type of insurance. For example, if you're an animal lover, you'll probably do anything for your pets. But health care for them can be almost as expensive as for yourself. Go to www.insure.com/personal/pets.html for a great article on getting pet insurance to avoid catastrophic costs that can bury your retirement faster than your dog buries bones.

Investing in Bonds (www.investinginbonds.com)

A wealth of material to help you better understand these financial instruments that should be part of your wealth-building and maintenance strategy.

Kiplinger's (www.kiplinger.com)

Once publisher of *Changing Times*, Kiplinger's has changed with the times and offers this snappy and savvy collection of articles and online financial tools covering virtually every personal finance subject and need.

Money Magazine (www.money.com)

Not as glossy as the print version that targets the comfortably affluent, but contains everything you can find there, plus more. Middle-income folks grudgingly allowed.

MSN MoneyCentral (www.moneycentral.com)

That pain in the (Windows) glass, Bill Gates, undoubtedly wants to make sure you can pay for more software. This great site helps, offering financial advice in the context of real life, rather than the sterile fashion in which you often find it.

New York Times (www.nytimes.com)

Its Sunday edition has the best single-day business section in the world, with thoughtful (yet useful) commentary, analysis, and advice. But read it before it disappears into the paid archives.

Suze Orman (www.suzeorman.com)

Best-selling personal finance author Suze Orman's Web site is well worth the visit. It includes a specific directory with links to pages of terrific resources on retirement and related topics, such as long-term care (www.suzeorman.com/resources/index.html).

Tim Younkin's 401(k) Advocate Site (www.timyounkin.com)

A lot of good information on 401(k) investing is available at other sites tied to the financial industry, but Tim has no such connections. He amasses a great collection of reprinted (with permission) articles and links to many other articles and useful Web sites.

USA Retirement (www.usa-retirement.com)

This senior-oriented Web site has a great list of links on lifestyle, research information, and activities for retirees at www.usa-retirement.com/links.html.

Washington Post (www.washingtonpost.com/wp-srv/business/yrmoney.htm)

Overall, it's the best daily newspaper business section, with particular emphasis on personal finance. Michelle Singletary's "Color of Money" column aims first to keep African-American readers in the financial know—and is useful to virtually everyone.

Washington Post Seniors Guide Post (http://washingtonpost.com/wp-srv/health/seniors/main.htm)

Although it's classified under "health," this section of the Washington Post's Web site has a number of excellent features on all aspects of senior life—including very useful resources on Medicare, long-term care, and estate planning. Also, check out Stan Hinden's Retirement Journal, an occasional feature by the now-retired, long-time personal-finance columnist, at http://washingtonpost.com/wp-dyn/business/columns/personalfinance/retirementjournal.

Women.com Money (www.womenswire.com/money)

The financial features help you shape up a sagging portfolio with thoughtful, well-written pieces by a stable of fine financial journalists.

Specific Resources

AARP (www.aarp.org)

Once called the American Association of Retired Persons, it's become such a strong and powerful lobby that it's no longer an acronym. You're eligible to join at age 50, and it's well worth the modest membership fee to qualify for group insurance and other discounts. But even without membership, take advantage of the articles and resources provided on the Web site, such as the following:

- **Information on your specific pension plan.** If you work for a middle-sized or large company, there's an excellent chance that it had to file a Form 5500 with Department of Labor concerning its pension and benefit programs. At one time (and still) you could only get this information by writing to the Department of Labor, or showing up in person. Now it's accessible through www.freeerisa.com, which also contains a valuable page of links to other financial information at www.freeerisa.com/info/fit14.asp.

- **Smart consumerism and fraud protection.** Uncle Sam tells you how to avoid money molestation in the *Consumer Action Handbook*, available free by writing Handbook, Federal Consumer Information Center, Pueblo CO 81009; or by calling 1-888-878-3256. The handbook is also available online, along with an immense collection of additional useful consumer and fraud avoidance information, at www.pueblo.gsa.gov/crh/respref.htm.

Administration on Aging (www.aoa.gov)

Yet another example of how your tax dollars really are used for good purposes can be found at this U.S. government Web site. You'll find information on almost anything related to aging, and there's a specific section of excellent resources on retirement and financial planning at www.aoa.gov/retirement/default.htm.

Benefits Checkup for Seniors (www.benefitscheckup.org)

Go to this Web site to find out what federal and state assistance programs are available to seniors, or call the U.S. Department of Health and Human Services at 1-800-677-1116. The service runs weekdays from 9 A.M. to 8 P.M. EST.

Bureau of the Public Debt
(www.publicdebt.treas.gov/bpd/bpdhome.htm)

Information of all kinds of treasury debt, including savings bonds. Enables you to buy treasury securities directly and avoid commission and financial sales pitches.

Moneymax Profile System
(www.kathleengurney.com/money_mastering_tools/moneymax.html)

For a better understanding of your psychological orientation to money—why you handle it the way you do and how you can handle it better—complete Dr. Kathleen Gurney's online Moneymax profile. For a reasonable fee, you'll get a detailed report identifying your money type and what it means.

Retirement, Aging, and the Law

A successful retirement takes being in good form—wills, trusts, powers of attorney, healthcare directives, employment-related and financial paperwork, and so on. Nolo Press, which specializes in making legal complexities comprehensible to the average person, has a wide array of software, publications, and online articles on legal matters and forms related to retirement and aging at www.nolo.com/category/ret_home.html.

Retirement Distributions

Barry Picker, CERTIFIED FINANCIAL PLANNER and CPA (nationally recognized retirement plan expert), offers this *Guide to Retirement Distribution Planning* and *The New Minimum Required Distribution Rules* by calling 1-800-809-0015 or by ordering directly from his Web site: www.bpickercpa.com/Guide2.htm.

Retirement Publications Provided by the U.S. Government

They provide 46 hardcopy publications on topics such as pension rights, 401(k) plan fees, health insurance rights when terminating from a job (COBRA), and changing health insurers (HIPAA). Find out what's available by calling 1-800-998-7542. The Web site (www.dol.gov/dol/pwba/public/whatsnew/ftsht800.htm) contains some items not available in hard copy.

Social Security Earnings and Benefits Estimate Statement
(www.ssa.gov/online/ssa-7004.html)
(www.ssa.gov/planners/calculators.htm)

Use the first link to request, complete, and submit the EBES online; or download it and mail it in. Or you can call Social Security at 1-800-772-1213. Use the second link to generate your own benefits estimate.

Student Financial Aid and Loans for College

The Sallie Mae main site (www.salliemae.com) provides extensive information on all the various financing, refinancing, and repayment options for college loans. The Wired Scholar companion site (www.wiredscholar.com/paying/content/index.jsp) has more of that, and a lot of useful information on the overall financial-aid process and scholarship searching.

Women's Social Security Site (www.ssa.gov/women)

Women really are different, in a way that has nothing to do with *Maxim* magazine—but does have to do with the difficulty of maximizing retirement prosperity. This Social Security Administration site highlights why, and provides guidance to overcoming built-in obstacles that women face in amassing retirement nest eggs.

CALCULATORS AND SOFTWARE

Online Subscription Software

The following Web sites offer services that provide a detailed portfolio asset-allocation recommendation, personalized to your personal demographic variables, risk tolerance, and objectives:

Bankrate.com Calculator
(www.bankrate.com/brm/calc/retire_smm.asp)

ClearFuture
(https://cf.morningstar.com/login/login.asp)

Financial Engines
(www.financialengines.com)

Links to several other retirement calculators
(www.ifigure.com/money/retire/retire.htm)

Mpower
(www.mpower.com)

MSNBC Retirement Planner
(www.msnbc.com/news/358710.asp)

Quicken's Online Tax Estimator
(www.quicken.com/taxes/estimator)

Retirement Expense Data and Projections
(www.uslaw.com/vsimplify/forms/F_RPexpense.htm)
(www.usnews.com/usnews/nycu/money/retspend.htm)
(www.calcbuilder.com/cgi-bin/calcs/ret1.cgi/usnews)
(www.extension.umn.edu/distribution/businessmanagement/DF3791.html)
(www.scils.rutgers.edu/rfa/rfaretlist.html)

Retirement Plan Required Minimum Distribution Calculator
(www.calctools.com/newrmd.htm)

Social Security Calculator
(www.ssa.gov/retire2/calculator.htm)

EXCELLENT ARTICLES ON SPECIFIC RETIREMENT ISSUES

Early Retirement
(www.findarticles.com/cf_0/m1318/1_54/58342789/p1/article.jhtml?term=
early+retirement)

Decisions at Retirement
(http://money.philly.com/retirement/guide99a/choice08.asp)

Don't Get Rich, Get a Life (Scott Burns)
(www.scottburns.com/001224SU.htm)

Finding Paradise Right Down the Road
(http://inq.philly.com/content/inquirer/2000/05/08/business/NEARBY08.
htm?template=/retirement/index.htm)

House Rich Elders Can Get Help ("House Rich" refers to owning a high-
value house with a paid-off mortgage; the article is about ways to tap that
home equity) (http://news.excite.com/news/ap/010222/07/on-the-money)

Living Until You're Very Old
(http://inq.philly.com/content/inquirer/2000/11/30/business/PERS30.htm)

Long-Term Care
(http://washingtonpost.com/wp-srv/health/seniors/resources072099.htm)
(www.ahca.org/brief/nr990407.htm)

Options in Retirement Living
(www.washingtonpost.com/wp-srv/health/seniors/stories/retliving/
retirement.htm)

Retirees' Difficulties Obtaining Credit
(www.msnbc.com/news/527795.asp)
(http://stage.bankrate.com/real/news/pf/20010328a.asp)

Retirees Need to Figure Out How Not to Outlive Their Money
(http://inq.philly.com/content/inquirer/2000/05/08/business/OUTLIVE08.
htm?template=/retirement/index.htm)

Retirement Personality Types
(www.findarticles.com/m0EIN/1999_June_15/54892779/p1/article.jhtml)

Retirement Plans During Divorce
(www.findarticles.com/cf_0/m1318/3_55/70770252/p1/article.jhtml?term=
early+retirement)
(www.washingtonpost.com/wp-dyn/articles/A21914-2001Apr1.html)
(www.businessweek.com/bwdaily/dnflash/may2000/nf00518d.htm)

Spouses with Different Retirement Dates
(www.findarticles.com/cf_0/m1318/11_54/66278799/p1/article.jhtml?term=
early+retirement)

The Middle-Aging of the Boomer Population
(www.washingtonpost.com/wp-dyn/health/seniors/news/A62315-
2001Mar26.html)

What to Look for in a CCRC Facility
(http://washingtonpost.com/wp-srv/health/seniors/stories/look042099.htm)

Studies and Surveys

1999 AARP Survey of Baby-Boomer Retirement Attitudes
(http://research.aarp.org/econ/boomer_seg_toc.html)

2001 ASEC Retirement Confidence Survey Summary
(www.asec.org/2001rcs/01rcses.pdf)

Baby Boomer Inheritance
(www.clev.frb.org/Research/Com2000/1001.htm)

EBRI Small Employer Retirement Survey
(www.ebri.org/sers/2001/index.htm)

Retirement Savings of American Households: Asset Levels and Adequacy (Ohio State University Study) (www.consumerfed.org/econ.pdf)

Survey of Cash Balance Plans
(www.pwcglobal.com/extweb/ncsurvres.nsf/DocID/7C89EE478C4CD479852 568FB00721096)

APPENDIX C

Answers to Quiz Questions

Hour 1

1.	a	6.	b
2.	d	7.	c
3.	b	8.	b
4.	c	9.	c
5.	b	10.	a

Hour 2

1.	b	6.	b
2.	c	7.	a
3.	a	8.	c
4.	b	9.	b
5.	c	10.	a

Hour 3

1.	F	6.	T
2.	F	7.	T
3.	T	8.	F
4.	F	9.	T
5.	T	10.	T

Hour 4

1.	F	6.	F
2.	T	7.	T
3.	F	8.	F
4.	F	9.	F
5.	F	10.	T

Hour 5

1.	d	6.	d
2.	d	7.	c
3.	b	8.	d
4.	c	9.	d
5.	d	10.	c

Hour 6

1.	F	6.	F
2.	F	7.	F
3.	T	8.	F
4.	T	9.	F
5.	T	10.	T

Hour 7

1. T		**6.** T	
2. T		**7.** T	
3. F		**8.** T	
4. T		**9.** F	
5. T		**10.** T	

Hour 8

1. F		**6.** F	
2. T		**7.** T	
3. T		**8.** T	
4. F		**9.** T	
5. F		**10.** F	

Hour 9

1. c		**6.** d	
2. c		**7.** a	
3. a		**8.** d	
4. d		**9.** b	
5. d		**10.** d	

Hour 10

1. c		**6.** a	
2. a		**7.** d	
3. d		**8.** a	
4. b		**9.** d	
5. d		**10.** a	

Hour 11

1. b		**6.** c	
2. c		**7.** c	
3. a		**8.** d	
4. d		**9.** d	
5. d		**10.** d	

Hour 12

1. F		**6.** T	
2. F		**7.** F	
3. T		**8.** T	
4. F		**9.** F	
5. T		**10.** T	

Hour 13

1. d		**6.** c	
2. d		**7.** b	
3. c		**8.** b	
4. b		**9.** d	
5. c		**10.** d	

Hour 14

1. e		**6.** e	
2. e		**7.** e	
3. d		**8.** d	
4. b		**9.** b	
5. d		**10.** e	

Hour 15

1.	e	6.	a
2.	e	7.	e
3.	d	8.	e
4.	e	9.	e
5.	d	10.	e

Hour 16

1.	F	6.	F
2.	T	7.	T
3.	T	8.	T or F (check 10 more times to be sure.)
4.	T	9.	T
5.	F	10.	T

Hour 17

1.	T	6.	T
2.	F	7.	F
3.	F	8.	T
4.	T	9.	T
5.	F	10.	F

Hour 18

1.	F	6.	T
2.	T	7.	T
3.	T	8.	F
4.	T	9.	F
5.	F	10.	T

Hour 19

1.	F	6.	T
2.	T	7.	F
3.	F	8.	F
4.	F	9.	T
5.	F	10.	T

Hour 20

1.	T	6.	F
2.	T	7.	T
3.	F	8.	F
4.	T	9.	T
5.	T	10.	T

Hour 21

1.	F	6.	F
2.	F	7.	F
3.	T	8.	T
4.	T	9.	T
5.	F	10.	F

Hour 22

1.	F	6.	F
2.	T	7.	F
3.	F	8.	T
4.	T	9.	F
5.	T	10.	T

HOUR 23

1.	F	6.	T
2.	T	7.	T
3.	T	8.	F
4.	T	9.	T
5.	F	10.	T

HOUR 24

1.	F	6.	T
2.	T	7.	F
3.	T	8.	T
4.	F	9.	T
5.	F	10.	F

APPENDIX D

Retirement Gap Data and Calculation Worksheets

EXPENSES, PLANNED EXPENDITURES, AND LIABILITIES

Fill in the following table by referring to Hour 3, "Quantifying Retirement Costs." You should note several things:

- Each entry allows you to fill in values for your current budget, a Phase 0 early-retirement budget, and Phases 1 through 3 of your retirement budget.

- Each entry also allows you to indicate any expenses that are not annual, but instead are one-time (lump sum) anticipated expenses, and to indicate what year (lump-sum year) you're planning to make that purchase. Do not make any assumptions about whether you'll be making a future purchase with either a loan or with cash. Simply indicate the dollar amount and year of the purchase, stated in today's dollars.

- The Expense Item column of the table includes some blank lines so that you can add categories that haven't been covered. You might want to use some of these lines for separate entries if you have both current expenses and anticipated one-time expenses for a particular type of expense.

- All debts are shown in a subsection at the end of the table. Note several things: The "credit card carryover" category should include only debt you've been carrying, not ongoing debt due to using your credit cards frequently for convenience or bonuses, and then paying them off right away. For each type of debt, fill in how much you now owe, the original number of years for which you took the loan (if it is a mortgage, car, or other amortized loan), when the debt is due, and the interest rate on the debt (indicating whether it's variable or fixed). Finally, note that the debt subsection groups together all debts instead of associating them with other seemingly logical subcategories (such as mortgage with home ownership).

- All insurance costs are in one subsection, instead of being associated with otherwise logical categories (health insurance with medical expenses, for example).

Expenses, Planned Expenditures, and Liabilities Worksheet

Expense Item	Now	Phase 0	Phase 1	Phase 2	Phase 3	Lump Sum	Lump Sum	Lump Sum Year
Home Ownership								
Current rent								
Homeowner' association								
Condominium association								
Retirement home buy								
Retirement community membership								
Retirement rent								
Landscaping/lawn care								
snow removal								
Heat/air conditioning service								
Plumber/electrician								
Other maintenance								
Other repairs								
Furnishings/furniture								
Household supplies								
Home Utilities								
Cable/satellite TV								
Internet service								
Phone (regular, cell)								
Electricity								
Gas or oil								

Expenses, Planned Expenditures, and Liabilities Worksheet (continued)

Expense Item	Now	Phase 0	Phase 1	Phase 2	Phase 3	Lump Sum	Lump Sum	Lump Sum Year
Home Utilities								
Sewer/septic								
Water/well								
_____								
_____								
Insurance								
Life								
Auto								
Health								
Dental								
Vision								
Long-term care								
Disability								
Homeowner's/renter's								
Umbrella								
Pet								
Legal								
Flood								
Medicare								
Medigap								
_____								
_____								

Expense Item	Now	Phase 0	Phase 1	Phase 2	Phase 3	Lump Sum	Lump Sum	Lump Sum Year
Food/Personal Care								
Groceries								
Alcohol/tobacco								
Dining out (at work)								
Dining out (personal)								
Snacks and sundries								
Toiletries, cosmetics, etc.								
Hair care, massages, etc.								
_____								
_____								
Entertainment/Recreation								
Vacations/travel								
Equipment								
Activities (golf, etc.)								
Sporting events								
Movies/theater/concerts								
Parties hosted at home								
Fitness club								
Country club								
Concerts, CDs, etc.								
Other hobbies								
Buy boat, RV, etc.								
Pet ownership/vet								

Expenses, Planned Expenditures, and Liabilities Worksheet (continued)

Expense Item	Now	Phase 0	Phase 1	Phase 2	Phase 3	Lump Sum	Lump Sum	Lump Sum Year
Entertainment/Recreation								
Nonbusiness computers								
Kids' recreation								
Books, magazines, videos								
_____								
_____								
Transportation								
Car payments								
Auto maintenance								
Parking, car pools, tolls								
Public transportation								
Gas								
Registration, taxes, fees								
_____								
_____								
Clothing								
Purchases, rentals								
Dry cleaning, laundry								
Mending, repair								
_____								
_____								

Expense Item	Now	Phase 0	Phase 1	Phase 2	Phase 3	Lump Sum	Lump Sum	Lump Sum Year
Religion/Charity								
Church/temple dues								
Religious school								
Religious activities								
Charitable donations								
Weddings, bar mitzvahs								
_____								
_____								
Savings/Investments/Taxes								
FICA								
Federal income tax								
State/local income tax								
Property tax								
401(k), 403(b), SEP, etc.								
Nonemployer funds, etc.								
Employee stock purchase								
College fund								
Business seed money								
_____								
_____								

Expenses, Planned Expenditures, and Liabilities Worksheet (continued)

Expense Item	Now	Phase 0	Phase 1	Phase 2	Phase 3	Lump Sum	Lump Sum	Lump Sum Year
Health								
Out-of-pocket doctors	___	___	___	___	___	___	___	___
Out-of-pocket hospital	___	___	___	___	___	___	___	___
Nonprescription meds	___	___	___	___	___	___	___	___
Out-of-pocket prescriptions	___	___	___	___	___	___	___	___
Vitamins and supplements	___	___	___	___	___	___	___	___
Parents' healthcare	___	___	___	___	___	___	___	___
_____	___	___	___	___	___	___	___	___
_____	___	___	___	___	___	___	___	___
_____	___	___	___	___	___	___	___	___
Child/Parent Care								
Private school	___	___	___	___	___	___	___	___
Tuition	___	___	___	___	___	___	___	___
College tuition	___	___	___	___	___	___	___	___
Child care/babysitting	___	___	___	___	___	___	___	___
Nonmedical parents' support	___	___	___	___	___	___	___	___
_____	___	___	___	___	___	___	___	___
_____	___	___	___	___	___	___	___	___
Professional								
Attorney	___	___	___	___	___	___	___	___
Accountant	___	___	___	___	___	___	___	___

Expense Item	Now	Phase 0	Phase 1	Phase 2	Phase 3	Lump Sum	Lump Sum	Lump Sum Year
Mortgage/Debts/Obligations								
Financial planner								
Nonbusiness professional dues, etc.								
_____								
_____								
Primary mortgage								
Vacation home mortgage								
Home equity loan								
Credit card carryover								
Auto loan								
College loan								
401(k) loan								
Stock-secured loan								
Unsecured loan								
Investment real estate								
Attorney/child support								
_____								
_____								
_____								

RETIREMENT-READY ASSETS

Complete the following table with all of your significant assets by referring to Hour 4, "Quantifying Retirement Assets." It explains how to calculate their current value, when to include a cost to sell, and how to determine basis (the amount invested in the asset).

Give each asset its full value, even if you took a loan to purchase it. Such loans are accounted for in the Expenses, Planned Expenditures, and Liabilities Worksheet shown earlier in this appendix.

Retirement-Ready Assets Worksheet

Asset Category	Asset Name	Value	Cost to Sell	Basis
Employer Retirement 401(k)	403(b)			
	Section 457			
	SEP-IRA			
	SIMPLE IRA			
	Keogh			
	Profit Sharing			
	Thrift Plan			
	Cash-Balance Pension			
	Pension Lump Sum			
	Other			
Other Employer Plans	ESOP			
	Stock Purchase			
	ISO Stock Options			
	NQSO Stock Options			
	Other			
Personal Retirement Plans	Traditional IRA			
	Roth IRA			
	Nondeductible IRA			
Non-Retirement Market Investments	Mutual Funds			
	Individual Stocks			
	Treasury Bills			

Retirement-Ready Assets Worksheet (continued)

Asset Category	Asset Name	Value	Cost to Sell	Basis
Non-Retirement Market Investments	Treasury Bonds	____	____	____
	Treasury Notes	____	____	____
	U.S. Savings Bonds	____	____	____
	Corporate Bonds	____	____	____
	Municipal Bonds	____	____	____
	REITs	____	____	____
	Options, Warrants, etc.	____	____	____
	Other	____	____	____
Cash Accounts	Checking	____	____	____
	Savings	____	____	____
	CDs	____	____	____
	Money Market	____	____	____
	Other	____	____	____
Real Estate	Home	____	____	____
	Vacation Property	____	____	____
	Rental Property	____	____	____
Special Education Savings	Education IRA	____	____	____
	Crummey Trust	____	____	____
	Section 529/QSTP	____	____	____

Asset Category	Asset Name	Value	Cost to Sell	Basis
Special Education Savings	UGMA/UTMA			
	Other			
Insurance	Life Insurance Cash Value			
	Annuity Surrender Value			
	Other			
Other Investment Assets	Value of Business			
	Precious Metals			
	Antiques and Collectibles			
	Other			
Future Assets	Trust Fund Value			
	Structured Settlement			
	Expected Inheritance			
	Other			
Valuable Personal Property	Luxury Cars			
	Jewelry			
	Furs			
	Other			
Miscellaneous				

RETIREMENT GAP CALCULATION

This calculation will determine the amount of additional savings you must generate and invest, starting now, in order to achieve the retirement needs expressed in the budgets you prepared earlier in this appendix. It is a lengthy calculation, but don't let the length overwhelm you before you even start. For one thing, about half of the pages of this worksheet, which comprise Preliminary Step 5 and Alternative Step 7 at the end, are only relevant to a small percentage of readers. Preliminary Step 5 is for those readers who are confident that they will be receiving pension payments during retirement, and Alternative Step 7 is for those readers seriously planning retirement before the usual age of 65.

Even if you are planning early retirement, it's best to first do this worksheet as though you are planning normal-age retirement, and see how prepared you are for that. If you have doubts about receiving a substantial pension, you can assume you won't and see where that leaves you.

The message here is that this lengthy worksheet is not necessarily as bad as it looks, and is definitely a useful and doable exercise if you've bought into the general theme of this book—that you will have a retirement gap, and you must take steps to close it. To make it clearer, Hour 20, "Comprehensive Retirement Gap Calculation Example," contains a full-blown example to follow details on how this worksheet is used.

So, let's get started.

Step 1:

Determine your ages for each phase and determine your expected annual budget amount in current dollars. Your figures will come from the budget worksheet earlier in this appendix. (Calculate Phase 0 only if you are considering early retirement; otherwise, start calculations with Phase 1.)

Ages for Phase 0 are _____ to __64__; Annual Budget _____

Ages for Phase 1 are __65__ to _____; Annual Budget _____

Ages for Phase 2 are _____ to _____; Annual Budget _____

Ages for Phase 3 are _____ to _____; Annual Budget _____

Step 2:

Determine the inflation-adjusted budget amount for Phases 1, 2, and 3 (P1, P2, and P3). Use the inflation factor, which is 1 plus the fractional inflation rate. (For example, for an inflation rate of 4 percent, the inflation factor is 1 plus .04 equals 1.04.) The formula raises that inflation factor to the power of the number of years from now until the beginning of each phase:

Budget Amount × (Inflation Factor)$^{\text{Years to Phase}}$

For Phase 1:

_____	×	(1._____)$^{-----}$	=	_____
Budget Amount		Inflation Factor	Years to Phase 1	P1 Inflation-Adjusted Budget Amount

For Phase 2:

_____	×	(1._____)$^{-----}$	=	_____
Budget Amount		Inflation Factor	Years to Phase 2	P2 Inflation-Adjusted Budget Amount

For Phase 3:

_____	×	(1._____)$^{-----}$	=	_____
Budget Amount		Inflation Factor	Years to Phase 3	P3 Inflation-Adjusted Budget Amount

Step 3:

Determine your Inflation Adjusted Social Security Income. Note: Your full retirement age for Social Security could be 66 or 67, but for simplicity, we'll assume it's 65 (start of Phase 1) and you'll get whatever benefit is coming to you starting then.

For Phase 1:

_____	×	(1._____)$^{-----}$	=	_____
Social Security Income Amount		Inflation Factor	Years to Phase 1	P1 Inflation-Adjusted Social Security Income

For Phase 2:

_____	×	(1._____)$^{-----}$	=	_____
Social Security Income Amount		Inflation Factor	Years to Phase 2	P2 Inflation-Adjusted Social Security Income

For Phase 3:

$$\underline{\hspace{3cm}} \times (1.\underline{\hspace{1.5cm}})^{-----} = \underline{\hspace{3cm}}$$

| Social Security Income Amount | Inflation Factor | Years to Phase 3 | P3 Inflation-Adjusted Social Security Income |

Step 4:

Find the Social Security Need Gap using the Inflation-Adjusted Budget amounts from Step 2.

For Phase 1:

$$\underline{\hspace{3cm}} - \underline{\hspace{3cm}} = \underline{\hspace{3cm}}$$

| Inflation-Adjusted Budget Amount | Inflation-Adjusted Social Security Income | Phase 1 Gap |

For Phase 2:

$$\underline{\hspace{3cm}} - \underline{\hspace{3cm}} = \underline{\hspace{3cm}}$$

| Inflation-Adjusted Budget Amount | Inflation-Adjusted Social Security Income | Phase 2 Gap |

For Phase 3:

$$\underline{\hspace{3cm}} - \underline{\hspace{3cm}} = \underline{\hspace{3cm}}$$

| Inflation-Adjusted Budget Amount | Inflation-Adjusted Social Security Income | Phase 3 Gap |

Step 5:

This step calculates the total gap between retirement income and retirement expenses as of the beginning of retirement. It does this by combining the expected effects of inflation and rate of return on the gap amounts from Step 4 to get your total gaps at the beginning of each of the phases of retirement.

Note: Social Security income is inflation-adjusted, and pension/annuity income normally isn't, so if you are one of the lucky few with a pension, you should first do Preliminary Step 5, later on in this worksheet, and then come back to complete this step.

First find the inflation-adjusted interest rate. This is different for each phase, with a suggested inflation rate of 3 percent (or inflation factor of 1.03), and the following suggested growth rates/factors: Phase 3 = 6 percent or 1.06, Phase 2 = 7 percent or 1.07, Phase 1 = 8 percent or 1.08. Do not feel bound to these choices; feel free to use what you think makes sense.

(_____ ÷ _____) − 1 = _____

    P1 Growth Factor   Inflation Factor   P1 Inflation-
                                                                  Adjusted
                                                               Interest Rate

(_____ ÷ _____) − 1 = _____

    P2 Growth Factor   Inflation Factor   P2 Inflation-
                                                                   Adjusted
                                                               Interest Rate

(_____ ÷ _____) − 1 = _____

    P3 Growth Factor   Inflation Factor   P3 Inflation-
                                                                   Adjusted
                                                               Interest Rate

For Phase 1:

Using your financial calculator (remember to set it in begin mode and one payment per year), enter ...

    N (number) = Number of years in the Phase
    I (interest) = P1 Inflation Adjusted Interest Rate
    PMT (payment) = Phase 1 Gap from Step 4
    FV (future value) = N/A
    Solve for PV (present value) = _____

                                 P1 Gap at Start of P1

For Phase 2:

Using your financial calculator (remember to set it in begin mode and one payment per year), enter ...

    N (number) = Number of years in the Phase
    I (interest) = P2 Inflation Adjusted Interest Rate
    PMT (payment) = Phase 2 Gap from Step 4
    FV (future value) = N/A
    Solve for PV (present value) = _____

                                 P2 Gap at Start of P2

Then discount back to the beginning of retirement (Phase 1) using the Phase 1 growth rate (suggested 8 percent or .08) by entering ...

FV = PV just found (P2 gap at start of P2)
PMT = N/A
N = Number of years back from Phase 2 to Phase 1
I = Growth rate for Phase 1 (not inflation adjusted)
Solve for PV (present value) = _____

P2 Gap at Start of P1

For Phase 3:

Using your financial calculator (remember to set it in begin mode and one payment per year), enter ...

N (number) = Number of years in the Phase
I (interest) = P3 Inflation-Adjusted Interest Rate
PMT (payment) = Phase 3 Gap from Step 4
FV (future value) = N/A
Solve for PV (present value) = _____

P3 Gap at Start of P3

Then discount back to the beginning of Phase 2 using the Phase 2 growth rate (suggested 7 percent or .07) by entering ...

FV = PV just found (P3 gap at start of P3)
PMT = N/A
N = Number of years back from Phase 3 to Phase 2
I = Growth rate for Phase 2 (not inflation adjusted)
Solve for PV (present value) = _____

P3 Gap at Start of P2

Then discount back to the beginning of retirement (Phase 1) using the Phase 1 growth rate (suggested 8 percent or .08) by entering ...

FV = PV just found (P3 gap at start of P2)
PMT = N/A
N = Number of years back from Phase 2 to Phase 1
I = Growth rate for Phase 1 (not inflation adjusted)
Solve for PV (present value) = _____

P3 Gap at Start of P1

Add the just-calculated gaps (as of the beginning of Phase 1) for Phases 1, 2, and 3 to find the total Social-Security gap at the beginning of retirement:

_____	+	_____	+	_____	=	_____
P1 Gap at Beginning of P1		P2 Gap at Beginning of P1		P3 Gap at Beginning of P1		Total Social Security Gap

If you did complete Preliminary Step 5 for Pensions, add the Total Pension Income to Total Social-Security Retirement Gap Income. This is your total retirement gap. In most cases, you'll be adding a negative number (Total Social Security Gap) to a positive number (pension/annuity total income) to get what will still be a negative number (Total Income-Expense Post-Retirement Gap):

_____	+	_____	=	_____
Social Security Retirement Gap		Pension/Annuity Total Income		Total Income-Expense Post-Retirement Gap

Step 6:

Calculate the amount you have available to save annually. This calculation will have two steps. The first step determines the current amounts you have available to save, and the second step calculates amounts you'll later have available to save when your current mortgage and any other major regular monthly-payment loans are paid off. (This does not include car loans, for example, because you'll later buy another car. It also doesn't include home equity borrowing or credit-card balances because they're not regular monthly-payment loans.) You'll find all these figures from the current budget you filled out earlier in this appendix.

Step 6a: Using the information from your current budget (refer to the Expenses, Planned Expenditures, and Liabilities Worksheet earlier in this appendix), calculate the amounts you save annually:

Your retirement contribution at work _____

Employer's added contribution to it _____

If married and your spouse works, his or her
retirement contribution at work _____

Employer's contribution to it _____

Your IRA contributions (indicate type of IRA) _____

Your spouse's IRA contributions (and type)   _____

Total Plan Investments (Add all above lines)   _____

Total Other Investments (from Budget)
(such as payroll deductions to mutual funds,
contributions to college savings, etc.)   _____

Total Expenses (Budget)   _____

Total Outlays (add three previous lines)   _____

Total Income (Budget)   _____

Then, using the previous two lines:

Total Income – Total Outlays =   _____
(Additional Savings)

Finally, using previous line and a few lines up:

Additional Savings + Total Other Investments =   _____

This amount is Type 3 Savings (to be used in Step 7).

Step 6b: Determine the amounts you'll have available upon paying off your current mortgage. If you have another major nonbusiness amortized loan you expect to pay off before retirement (for example, college loans for your kids) and then have more money for savings, also include that here:

_____   _____

Annual Mortgage Payment   Years Until 65 After
Paying Off

_____   _____

Other Major Loan Payment   Years Until 65 After
Paying Off

Step 7:

Do this step unless you're planning to retire significantly earlier than normal retirement age (65). If you are planning such early retirement then, instead, do Alternative Step 7 for Early Retirement (later in this appendix).

This step uses the results of Step 6 to project the value of your ongoing savings to retirement age. It does not include money you've already saved, which is dealt with in Step 8.

First, find the enhanced rate of return resulting from combining the growth rate from now until retirement (suggested 9 percent) with the yearly increase in savings from salary inflation. To do that, calculate:

$$(1 + \underline{\hspace{2cm}}) \quad \times \quad (1 + \underline{\hspace{2cm}}) \quad - \quad 1 = \underline{\hspace{2cm}}$$

  Growth Rate   Inflation   Enhanced Growth
             Rate   Rate

Then, using the results of Step 6a, you'll do the four calculations below—each for a particular type of savings and investing—according to its tax treatment:

1. Deductible tax-deferred accounts, such as 401(k)
2. Tax-deferred nondeductible IRAs and thrift plans
3. Taxable accounts (other savings and investments)
4. Nontaxable accounts such as Roth

You might be wondering how we can assume the amounts you can invest in Types 1, 3, and 4 can go up with inflation, given they're limited by tax laws. The just-enacted 2001 tax legislation finally phases in higher maximums over the next several years. Because that's finally been done, it's reasonable to assume the maximums will be increased for inflation in the future.

Each of these calculations will result in the lump-sum future value (FV) for your regular contributions to one of the four accounts:

Payment = Total Type 1 savings in Step 6a
N = Number of years until retirement
I = Enhanced growth rate
PV = N/A
Solve for Type 1 FV _____

Payment = Total Type 2 savings in Step 6a
N = Number of years until retirement
I = Enhanced growth rate
PV = N/A
Solve for Type 2 FV _____

Payment = Total Type 3 savings in Step 6a
N = Number of years until retirement
I = Enhanced growth rate
PV = N/A

Solve for Type 3 FV _____

Payment = Total Type 4 savings in Step 6a
N = Number of years until retirement.
I = Enhanced growth rate
PV = N/A
Solve for Type 4 FV _____

For future savings (Step 6b) after debt is paid off, do the following calculation to find the future value (FV) of the stream of cash created when the mortgage loan ends. For N, the number of years until retirement, use "Years Until 65 after loan payoff" that you indicated in each Step 6b. Assume that you'll invest this cash stream in taxable accounts:

Payment = Amount of mortgage payment no longer made.
N = Number of years from loan end until retirement.
I = Enhanced growth rate
PV = N/A
Solve for FV _____

After-Mortgage Lump Sum from Extra Savings

If you have other (nonmortgage) major regular-payment (amortized) loans (for one-time major expenditures, such as a boat) that will be paid off before retirement, do the following calculation once for each of them:

Payment = Amount of mortgage payment no longer made.
N = Number of years from loan end until retirement.
I = Enhanced growth rate
PV = N/A
Solve for FV _____

After-Mortgage Lump Sum from Extra Savings

Now calculate your Total Lump Sum from Debt Payoff:

_____   +   _____   =   _____

| After-Mortgage Lump Sum from Extra Savings | After-Loan Lump Sum from Extra Savings | Total Lump Sum from Debt Payoff |

Then do the following calculation to add this total lump sum to the total lump sum from (Type 3) taxable investing that you calculated above:

_____   +   _____   =   _____

| Total Lump Sum from Debt Payoff | Type 3 FV Above | Enhanced Type 3 Lump Sum |

Now it's time to calculate the after-tax amounts for each of the account types. (Note: Your Type 4 Roth after-tax amount will not change from what you calculated above.)

First, calculate your after-tax lump sum on Type 1 tax-deferred retirement accounts. Use your ordinary-income tax rate, which is the rate you expect to be paying on the last dollar of retirement income (probably = .25):

1 – _____ = _____

  Current Tax Rate   After-Tax Remainder Rate

_____ × _____ = _____

| After-Tax Remainder Rate | Tax-Deferred Lump Sum (Type 1) | Tax-Deferred Account After-Tax Lump Sum (Type 1) |

Then calculate your after-tax lump sum on Type 2 tax-deferred earnings (for example, nondeductible IRA) retirement accounts. Use the same tax rate as in the previous (Type 1) calculation:

(_____ – _____) × _____ = _____

| Tax-Deferred Earnings Lump Sum (Type 2) | After-Tax Contributions | Current Tax Rate | Tax Owed |

_____ – _____ = _____

| Tax-Deferred Earnings Lump Sum (Type 2) | Tax Owed | Tax-Deferred Earnings After-Tax Lump Sum (Type 2) |

Then calculate your after-tax lump sum on taxable accounts. Your Capital Gains Tax Rate probably equals .20:

_____ – _____ = _____

| Enhanced Lump Sum (Type 3) | Investment Cost Basis | Adjusted Lump Sum |

_____ × _____ = _____

| Adjusted Lump Sum | Capital Gains Tax Rate | Capital Gains Tax Paid |

_____ – _____ = _____

| Enhanced Lump Sum (Type 3) | Capital Gains Tax Paid | Net Capital Gains Lump Sum (Type 3) |

Now, add all your after-tax savings:

_____	+	_____	+	_____	+	_____	=	_____
Tax-Deferred After-Tax Lump Sum (Type 1)		Net Capital Gains Lump Sum (Type 3)		Roth Lump Sum (Type 4)		Tax-Deferred Earnings After-Tax Lump Sum (Type 2)		Total Savings Lump Sum

Step 8:

Use Hour 4 and the retirement-ready assets from the worksheet in this appendix to calculate your current and anticipated (inheritances and gifts, for example) net retirement-ready assets (taking liabilities from your expense worksheet into account). You'll then apply the appropriate rates of return to the different types of assets to determine their value at your full retirement age, completing the calculation by subtracting taxes.

For all investment assets, you should apply an appropriate investment return (suggested 9 percent), and then apply tax at the appropriate rates for Type 4 nontaxable retirement accounts (0 percent tax); Type 1 tax-deferred retirement accounts such as the 401(k); Type 2 tax-deferred earnings retirement accounts such as the nondeductible IRA (ordinary-income rate, suggested 25 percent); and Type 3 other investments (capital gains rate, suggested 20 percent).

For all cash assets that exceed current liabilities, you should apply an appropriate "safe investment return" (suggested 4 percent after tax). If your current liabilities that aren't being paid off with regular monthly payments exceed your cash assets, you'll apply an investment return growth factor to the excess of those liabilities over available cash to determine how much you would owe on them at retirement.

You'll separately apply a real-estate appreciation (suggested inflation) rate to your home(s) (primary and vacation) to determine their values at full retirement age. For other complex assets, such as investment real estate and collectibles, you'll be on your own to establish an after-tax retirement value that you'll plug in at the end of this step. These assets are simply far too varied, complex, and unique to your circumstances to provide any meaningful calculation methods here.

To start all these calculations, set your calculator in the end mode and for one payment per year. For each calculation (except number 2), enter ...

N (number) = Number of years until retirement _____
I (interest) = Growth Rate _____
PV (present value) = Current Asset Value _____
Solve for FV (future value) _____

1. Determine the retirement value of current net cash or net debt (credit card, home equity line, etc.). Don't include the balances of mortgages, car loans, or other regular payment (amortized) loans already in your annual expense budget:

_____ – _____ = _____

Current Cash   Current Total   Current Net
                    Debt   Cash or Debt

Now choose the applicable one of these two calculations, depending on the Current Net Cash or Debt result:

(a) If the result is positive, do this calculation ...

FV at a suggested 4 percent growth rate = _____

Cash at Retirement

(b) If the result is negative, do this calculation ...

FV at a suggested 9 percent growth rate = _____

Debt at Retirement

Note: If this result is positive, we'll ignore income taxes on the low-rate growth of the assets.

2. Determine the retirement value of future major debts (weddings, college expenses, etc.) or unusual expected cash inflows (inheritances, gifts, etc.). Each must be calculated separately and then the results must be added together to get a lump sum of future debts and inflows as of retirement. Use these two steps for each item:

N: Number of years from now received/incurred _____
I (interest) = Inflation Rate _____
PV: Asset/Liability Value when Received/Incurred _____
(in today's dollars)
FV in dollars when received (calculate) _____

Now project the FV you just found forward to normal-retirement age, and compute after-tax value:

N: Number of years from receipt until retirement _____
I (interest) = Growth Rate _____
PV (present value) = Current Asset Value _____
FV at retirement _____

If this value is an asset (positive), compute its after-tax value as follows:

Taxes = .2 × (FV Retirement − FV Received) = _____

FV Received − Taxes = After-Tax Asset Value _____

Sum of all Liability and After-Tax Asset Values _____

(Note that you might be adding positives and negatives.)

3. Determine the retirement value of Type 1 401(k) and other employer or self-employed tax-deferred accounts:

Current combined 401(k), other tax-deferreds _____

FV at a suggested 9% growth rate _____

Net after taxes: .75 × FV = _____

4. Determine the retirement value of Type 2 nondeductible IRA accounts and other tax-deferred earnings vehicles such as variable annuities:

Current combined value _____

FV at a suggested 9% growth rate _____

Taxes: .25 × (FV − After-Tax Contributions) = _____

Net FV after taxes: FV − Taxes = _____

5. Find retirement value of Type 3 taxable investments:

Current Taxable Investments _____

FV at a suggested 9% growth rate _____

Net after taxes:

FV − (.2 × (FV − Basis)) = _____

6. Determine the retirement value of Type 4 (nontaxable) Roth IRA accounts:

Current Roth IRA Value _____

FV at (suggested) 9% growth rate = _____

7. Determine the retirement value of primary residence:

Current Home Value _____

FV at (suggested) 3% (inflation-estimated) growth rate =

_____

8. Other assets: These include collectibles, investment real estate, or other assets beyond these categories. For such investments to make sense, you should be either sophisticated enough to do these types of calculations to determine their after-tax retirement value, or at least reasonably estimate it. Or, you should be relying on a good advisor from whom you'll get this information. Enter the result of those calculations here:

After-tax retirement age value of other assets _____

9. Add the final lines of each of the eight previous items to yield total net retirement assets/liabilities:

Total net retirement assets/liabilities _____

Step 9:

Calculate the retirement gap:

_____ + _____ + _____ = _____

Total Income-Expense Retirement Gap (Step 5)	Total Net Retirement Assets or Liabilities (Step 8)	Net Ongoing Invested Savings at Retirement (Step 7)	Total Retirement Gap

Note: For the third blank in the previous formula, if you're retiring early, use the amount from Alternative Step 7c (shown later in this appendix) instead of the regular Step 7 result (skipped because of early retirement).

Step 10:

Determine additional annual savings needed to close the Step 9 Total Retirement Gap. There's no direct way to do this with financial-calculator functions, so instead, this calculation is based on adapting the formulas behind those calculator functions. Thus, you'll use only normal calculator arithmetic.

(i) 5 × Total Retirement Gap (Step 9) = _____

  (Call this result the Full Numerator)

(ii) 1 + Growth Rate = (suggest 1 + .09 = 1.09) _____

  (Call this result the Growth Factor)

(iii) [Growth Factor]$^{\text{Years to Retirement}}$ − 1 = _____

  (Raising Growth Factor to the power of the number of years from now to retirement and subtracting 1 from that result)

(iv) Multiply results of Steps (ii) and (iii) = _____

(v) Multiply Step (iv) result by 4 = _____

  (Call this the Partial Denominator)

(vi) (Partial Denominator) ÷ Growth Rate = _____

  (Use Growth Rate from Step (ii), suggest .09)

(vii) (Years to Retirement) + [Step (vi) Result] = _____

  (Call this result the Full Denominator)

(viii) Full Numerator ÷ Full Denominator = _____

  (Step (i) result divided by Step (viii) Result)

The Step (viii) result is the annual additional amount you must generate and invest annually between now and retirement so that you will close your retirement gap.

Preliminary Step 5 for Pensions

Do this step only if you are reasonably certain you will receive an annual pension from your employer, or annual payments from an annuity you already own, on top of your Social Security and any additional earnings you'll have in retirement. After completing this step, return to the beginning of the regular Step 5 and complete it. You'll use the final result of this Preliminary Step 5 in the final calculation of regular Step 5.

Now, let's start.

Find the present value, at beginning of Phase 1, of Pension and annuity payments received during retirement. Note: If you are retiring early and receiving a pension before normal retirement, those years won't be included in this step. Instead, that pension amount is one of the sources of income reflected in your Phase 0 budget, used in the Step 6 calculation that determines amounts you're regularly investing during working years.

Normally, pensions are not inflation adjusted. If yours will be, instead of the growth rate, you'll be using the inflation-adjusted interest rate with some of the calculations that follow (per Notes that are included). The rates you'll use are different for each phase, with a suggested inflation rate of 3 percent or factor of 1.03, and the following suggested growth rates/factors: Phase 3 = 6 percent or 1.06; Phase 2 = 7 percent or 1.07; Phase 1 = 8 percent or 1.08; Phase 0 = 9 percent or 1.09.

For Phase 1:

Using your financial calculator (remember to set it in begin mode and one payment per year), enter …

> N (number) = Number of years in the Phase
> I (interest) = Growth rate (suggested 8%); see Note below
> if pension is inflation adjusted
> PMT (payment) = Annual pension/annuity payments
> FV (future value) = N/A
> Solve for PV (present value) = _____

Phase 1 Total at
Beginning of Phase 1

Note: Normally, pensions are not inflation adjusted. If your pension will be, then instead of using the growth rate above, use the inflation-adjusted interest rate resulting from this calculation:

(_____ ÷ _____) − 1 = _____

Growth Factor	Inflation Factor	Inflation-Adjusted Interest Rate

For Phase 2:

Using your financial calculator (remember to set it in begin mode and one payment per year), enter …

> N (number) = Number of years in the Phase
> I (interest) = Growth Rate (suggested 8%); see Note below
> if pension is inflation adjusted
> PMT (payment) = Annual Pension/Annuity Payments

FV (future value) = N/A

Solve for PV (present value) = _____

Phase 2 Total at
Beginning of Phase 2

Note: Normally, pensions are not inflation adjusted. If your pension will be, then instead of using the growth rate above, use the inflation-adjusted interest rate resulting from this calculation:

(_____ ÷ _____) – 1 = _____

Growth Factor   Inflation Factor   Inflation-Adjusted Interest Rate

Then discount Phase 2 total back to the beginning of retirement (Phase 1) using suggested 8 percent growth rate by entering …

FV = Beginning of Phase 2 present value
PMT = N/A
N = Number of years back from Phase 2 to Phase 1
I = Growth rate for Phase 1 (not inflation adjusted)
Solve for Present Value = _____

Phase 2 Total at
Beginning of Phase 1

For Phase 3:

Using your financial calculator (remember to set it in begin mode and one payment per year), enter …

N (number) = Number of years in the Phase
I (interest) = Growth rate (suggested 7%); see Note below
if pension is inflation adjusted
PMT (payment) = Annual pension/annuity payments
FV (future value) = N/A
Solve for PV (present value) = _____

Phase 3 Total at
Beginning of Phase 3

Note: Normally, pensions are not inflation adjusted. If your pension will be, then instead of using the growth rate above, use the inflation-adjusted interest rate resulting from this calculation:

(_____ ÷ _____) – 1 = _____

Growth Factor   Inflation Factor   Inflation-Adjusted Interest Rate

Then discount Phase 3 total back to the beginning of Phase 2 using a suggested 7 percent growth rate by entering ...

FV = Beginning of Phase 3 present value
PMT = N/A
N = Number of years back from Phase 3 to Phase 2
I = Growth rate for Phase 2 (not inflation adjusted)
Solve for Present Value = _____

Phase 3 Total at
Beginning of Phase 2

Then discount Phase 3 total as of beginning of Phase 2 back to the beginning of Phase 1 using suggested 6 percent growth rate by entering ...

FV = Beginning of Phase 3 present value
PMT = N/A
N = Number of years back from Phase 2 to Phase 1
I = Growth Rate for Phase 1 (not inflation adjusted)
Solve for Present Value = _____

Phase 3 Total at
Beginning of Phase 1

Add solutions for Phases 1, 2, and 3 to find total pension/annuity income at beginning of retirement:

_____	+	_____	+	_____	=	_____
P1 Total at Start of P1		P2 Total at Start of P1		P3 Total at Start of P1		Total Pension Income

Now return to the beginning of regular Step 5. You'll use the Total Pension Income you calculated in this Preliminary Step 5 in the last calculation of regular Step 5.

Alternative Step 7 for Early Retirement

You should be doing this step (instead of the regular Step 7) only if you're planning to retire significantly earlier than age 65. This step projects your preretirement and early-retirement ongoing savings forward to normal retirement age (65). It doesn't include money you've already saved, which is dealt with in Step 8.

Because you have a different budget for early retirement than you do until early retirement, this step has two parts, one you do with your preretirement budget, and the other with your early retirement budget.

Alternative Step 7a: Lump Sum Value at Normal Retirement Age of Ongoing Savings from Now Until Early Retirement

First, find the enhanced rate of return resulting from combining the growth rate with the yearly increase in savings from salary inflation. To do that, calculate:

$$(1 + \underline{\hspace{1.5cm}}) \times (1 + \underline{\hspace{1.5cm}}) - 1 = \underline{\hspace{2.5cm}}$$

      Growth   Inflation   Enhanced Growth
        Rate   Rate   Rate

Then, using the results of Step 6a, you'll do the four calculations below—each for a particular type of savings and investing—according to its tax treatment:

1. Deductible tax-deferred accounts, such as 401(k)
2. Tax-deferred nondeductible IRAs and thrift plans
3. Taxable accounts (other savings and investments)
4. Nontaxable accounts such as Roth

Note: You might be wondering how we can assume the amounts you can invest in Types 1, 3, and 4 can go up with inflation, given they're limited by tax laws. The just-enacted 2001 tax legislation finally phases in higher maximums over the next several years. Because that's finally been done, it's reasonable to assume the maximums will be increased for inflation in the future.

Each of these calculations will result in the lump-sum future value (FV) for your regular contributions to one of the four accounts:

    Payment = Total Type 1 savings in Step 6a
    N = Number of years until *early* retirement
    I = Enhanced growth rate
    PV = N/A
    Solve for Type 1 FV _____

    Payment = Total Type 2 savings in Step 6a
    N = Number of years until *early* retirement

I = Enhanced growth rate
PV = N/A
Solve for Type 2 FV _____

Payment = Total Type 3 savings in Step 6a
N = Number of years until *early* retirement
I = Enhanced growth rate
PV = N/A
Solve for Type 3 FV _____

Payment = Total Type 4 savings in Step 6a
N = Number of years until *early* retirement
I = Enhanced growth rate
PV = N/A
Solve for Type 4 FV _____

Do you have a mortgage loan that will be paid off before your early retirement date? If not, skip to the nonmortgage loan step below. Otherwise, calculate future savings (Step 6b) after debt is paid off with the following calculation to find the future value (FV) of the stream of cash created when the mortgage loan ends. Assume that you'll invest this cash stream in taxable accounts …

Payment = Amount of mortgage payment no longer made
N = Number of years from loan end until *early* retirement starts
I = Enhanced growth rate
PV = N/A
Solve for FV_____

After-Mortgage Lump Sum
from Extra Savings

Do you have other (nonmortgage) major regular-payment (amortized) loans (for one-time major expenditures, such as a boat) that will be paid off before your early retirement date? If not, skip to the paragraph after this calculation. Otherwise, do this calculation once for each of this type of loan that will be paid off before early retirement …

Payment = Amount of mortgage payment no longer made
N = Number of years from loan end until *early* retirement
I = Enhanced growth rate
PV = N/A

Solve for FV_____

After-Loan Lump Sum
from Extra Savings

Now calculate your Total Lump Sum from Debt Payoff:

_____ + _____ = _____

After-Mortgage Lump	After-Loan Lump	Total Lump Sum
Sum from Extra	Sum from Extra	from Debt Payoff
Savings	Savings	

Then do the following calculation to add this total lump sum to the total lump sum from (Type 3) taxable investing that you calculated above:

_____ + _____ = _____

| Total Lump Sum | Type 3 FV Above | Enhanced Type 3 |
| from Debt Payoff | | Lump Sum |

Now it's time to calculate the after-tax amounts for each of the account types. (Note: Your Type 4 Roth after-tax amount will not change from what you calculated above.) In each case this will require two steps. First, each of the above lump sums (Type 1 through Type 4) must grow from its early-retirement amount to its normal retirement amount. Second, the after-tax amount of that must be calculated.

To start all these calculations, set your calculator in the end mode and for one payment per year …

N (number) = Number of years from early to normal retirement

_____

I (interest) = Rate of return _____
PV (present value) = Type 1 Lump Sum (above) _____
Solve for FV (future value) _____

The calculated FV is the Type 1 tax-deferred lump sum.

Now, calculate your after-tax lump sum on Type 1 tax-deferred retirement accounts. Use your ordinary-income tax rate, which is the rate you expect to be paying on the last dollar of retirement income (probably = .25):

1 − _____ = _____

Tax Rate   After-Tax Remainder Rate

_____ × _____ = _____
　　After-Tax　　　　　　　Tax-Deferred　　　　Tax-Deferred Account
　Remainder Rate　　　　　　Lump Sum　　　　　After-Tax Lump Sum
　　　　　　　　　　　　　　(Type 1)　　　　　　　(Type 1)

N (number) = Number of years from early until normal retirement _____
I (interest) = Growth Rate _____
PV (present value) = Type 2 Lump Sum (above) _____
Solve for FV (future value) _____

The FV is the Type 2 tax-deferred earnings lump sum.

Now, calculate your after-tax lump sum on Type 2 tax-deferred earnings (e.g., nondeductible IRA) retirement accounts. Use the same tax rate (suggested .25) as in the previous (Type 1) calculation:

(_____ − _____) × _____ = _____
　Tax-Deferred　　　　After-Tax　　　　Current　　　Tax Owed
　　Earnings　　　　Contributions　　　Tax Rate
Lump Sum (Type 2)

_____ − _____ = _____
　Tax-Deferred　　　　Tax Owed　　　Tax-Deferred Earnings
　　Earnings　　　　　　　　　　　After-Tax Lump Sum
　Lump Sum　　　　　　　　　　　　　(Type 2)
　(Type 2)

N (number) = Number of years from early until normal retirement _____
I (interest) = Growth Rate _____
PV (present value) = Type 3 Lump Sum (above) _____
Solve for FV (future value) _____

The FV is the Type 3 taxable lump sum.

Then calculate your after-tax lump sum on taxable accounts. Your Capital Gains Tax Rate is probably = .20:

_____ − _____ = _____
　　Enhanced　　　　Investment Cost　　　　Adjusted Lump Sum
Lump Sum (Type 3)　　　　Basis

_____ × _____ = _____
　　Adjusted　　　　Capital Gains　　　　Capital Gains
　Lump Sum　　　　　Tax Rate　　　　　　Tax Paid

_____ − _____ = _____

| Enhanced
Lump Sum (Type 3) | Capital Gains
Tax Paid | Net Capital Gains
Lump Sum
(Type 3) |

N (number) = Number of years from early until normal retirement

_____

I (interest) = Growth Rate _____

PV (present value) = Type 4 Lump Sum (above) _____

Solve for FV (future value) _____

The FV is the Type 4 Roth lump sum.

Now, add all your after-tax savings:

_____ + _____ + _____ + _____ = _____

| Tax-Deferred
After-Tax
Lump Sum
(Type 1) | Net Capital
Gains
Lump Sum
(Type 2) | Roth
Lump
Sum
(Type 4) | Tax-Deferred
Earnings
After-Tax Lump Sum
(Type 2) | Total
Savings
Lump Sum
(Working
Years) |

You'll combine this last result—Total Savings Lump Sum (working years)—with the results of Alternative Step 7b in Alternative Step 7c.

Alternative Step 7b: Lump Sum Value at Normal Retirement Age of Ongoing Savings from Early Retirement Until Normal Retirement at Age 65

For the remainder of this step, think of yourself as now being at the beginning of your early retirement. Using your Early Retirement budget from earlier in this appendix, calculate the amounts available to save annually. This calculation will involve two steps. The first step determines the current amounts you have available to save, and the second step calculates amounts you'll later have available to save when your current mortgage and any other major regular monthly-payment loans are paid off. (This does not include car loans, for example, because you'll later buy another car. It also doesn't include home equity borrowing or credit-card balances because they're not regular monthly-payment loans.)

Note: Many of these might not apply if you will have a true leisure early retirement. However, the majority of early retirees work.

Your retirement contribution at work _____

Employer contribution _____

Spouse's retirement contribution at work _____

Employer contribution _____

Your IRA contributions _____

Spouse's IRA contributions _____

Total Plan Investments (add all preceding lines) _____

Total Other Investments (Early Retirement Budget) _____
(such as payroll deductions to mutual funds,
contributions to college savings, etc.)

Total Expenses (Early Retirement Budget) _____

Total Outlays (add three previous lines) _____

Total Income (Early Retirement Budget) _____

Then, using the previous two lines:

Total Income – Total Outlays = _____
(Additional Savings)

Finally, using previous line and a few lines up:

Additional Savings + Total Other Investments = _____

This amount is Early Retirement Type 3 Savings.

Note: If your expenses are going to exceed your income in early retirement, your Early Retirement Type 3 Savings could be a negative number.

Because Early Retirement Type 3 Savings is expressed in current dollars, it must be projected to the beginning of early retirement using the inflation factor …

N = Number of years from early to normal retirement _____
I = Inflation Rate _____
PV = Early Retirement Type 3 Savings (Current) _____
Solve for FV_____

Projected Early Retirement Type 3 Savings

Next, find the enhanced rate of return resulting from combining the growth rate with the yearly increase in savings from salary inflation. To do that, calculate:

$$(1 + \underline{\hspace{2cm}}) \quad \times \quad (1 + \underline{\hspace{2cm}}) \quad - \quad 1 \quad = \quad \underline{\hspace{3cm}}$$

$$\text{Growth} \qquad\qquad \text{Inflation} \qquad\qquad\qquad \text{Enhanced Growth}$$
$$\text{Rate} \qquad\qquad\quad \text{Rate} \qquad\qquad\qquad\qquad \text{Rate}$$

Then, using the information you just completed concerning your ongoing savings, you'll do the following four calculations—each for a particular type of savings and investing—according to its tax treatment:

1. Deductible tax-deferred accounts, such as 401(k)
2. Tax-deferred nondeductible IRAs and thrift plans
3. Projected Early Retirement Type 3 Savings (this could be a negative number)
4. Nontaxable accounts such as Roth

Each of these calculations will result in the lump-sum future value (FV) for your regular contributions to one of the four accounts:

Payment = Total Type 1 savings
N = Number of years from *early* to *normal* retirement
I = Enhanced growth rate
PV = N/A
Solve for Type 1 FV _____

Payment = Total Type 2 savings
N = Number of years from *early* to *normal* retirement
I = Enhanced growth rate
PV = N/A
Solve for Type 2 FV _____

Payment = Total Type 3 savings
N = Number of years from *early* to *normal* retirement
I = Enhanced growth rate
PV = N/A
Solve for Type 3 FV _____

Payment = Total Type 4 savings in Step 6a
N = Number of years from *early* to *normal* retirement
I = Enhanced growth rate
PV = N/A
Solve for Type 4 FV _____

Do you have a mortgage loan that will be paid off during early retirement? If not, skip to the nonmortgage loan step below. Otherwise, calculate future savings after debt is paid off with the following calculation to find the future value (FV) of the stream of cash created when the mortgage loan ends. Assume that you'll invest this cash stream in taxable accounts ...

Payment = Amount of mortgage payment no longer made
N = Number of years from loan end until *normal* retirement
I = Enhanced growth rate
PV = N/A
Solve for FV _____

After-Mortgage Lump Sum from Extra Savings

Do you have other (nonmortgage) major regular-payment (amortized) loans (for one-time major expenditures, such as a boat) that will be paid off during early retirement? If not, skip to the paragraph after this calculation. Otherwise, do this calculation once for each of this type of loan that will be paid off before early retirement:

Payment = Amount of mortgage payment no longer made
N = Number of years from loan end until *early* retirement
I = Enhanced growth rate
PV = N/A
Solve for FV _____

After-Loan Lump Sum from Extra Savings

_____	+	_____	=	_____
After-Mortgage Lump Sum (Extra Savings)		After-Loan Lump Sum (Extra Savings)		Total Lump Sum from Debt Payoff

Then do the following calculation to add this total lump sum to the total lump sum from (Type 3) taxable investing that you calculated above:

_____	+	_____	=	_____
Total Lump Sum from Debt Payoff		Type 3 FV Above		Enhanced Type 3 Lump Sum

Now it's time to calculate the after-tax amounts for each of the account types. (Note: Your Type 4 Roth after-tax amount will not change from what you calculated above.)

Calculate your early-retirement after-tax lump sum on Type 1 tax-deferred retirement accounts. Use your ordinary-income tax rate, which is the rate you expect to be paying on the last dollar of retirement income (probably = .25):

1   −   _____   =   _____

              Tax Rate   After-Tax Remainder Rate

_____   ×   _____   =   _____

After-Tax   Tax-Deferred   Tax-Deferred Account
Remainder Rate   Lump Sum   After-Tax Lump Sum
                (Type 1 FV)   (Type 1)

Calculate your after-tax lump sum on Type 2 tax-deferred earnings (e.g., nondeductible IRA) retirement accounts. Use the same tax rate as in the previous (Type 1) calculation:

(_____   −   _____)   ×   _____   =   _____

Tax-Deferred   After-Tax   Current   Tax Owed
Earnings   Contributions   Tax Rate
Lump Sum
(Type 2 FV)

_____   −   _____   =   _____

Tax-Deferred   Tax Owed   Tax-Deferred
Earnings   After-Tax   Earnings
Lump Sum   Lump Sum
(Type 2 FV)   (Type 2)

Calculate your after-tax lump sum on taxable accounts. Your Capital Gains Tax Rate is probably = .20:

_____   −   _____   =   _____

Enhanced   Investment Cost   Adjusted Lump Sum
Lump Sum   Basis
(Type 3)

_____   ×   _____   =   _____

Adjusted   Capital Gains   Capital Gains
Lump Sum   Tax Rate   Tax Paid

_____   −   _____   =   _____

Enhanced   Capital Gains   Net Capital Gains
Lump Sum   Tax Paid   Lump Sum
(Type 3)   (Type 3)

Now, add all your after-tax savings:

_____	+ _____	+ _____	+ _____	= _____
Tax-Deferred After-Tax Lump Sum (Type 1)	Net Capital Gains Lump Sum (Type 3)	Roth Lump Sum (Type 4)	Tax-Deferred Earnings After-Tax Lump Sum (Type 2)	Total Savings Lump Sum (Early Retire)

This last result, Total Savings Lump Sum from Early Retirement, will now be used in Alternative Step 7c.

Alternative Step 7c: Total Normal Retirement Lump Sum when Retiring Early

To determine the total amount to be used from Alternative Step 7 in Step 9, simply add the results of Alternative Steps 7a and 7b:

Total Normal Retirement Lump Sum when Retiring Early =
Total Savings Lump Sum (Working Years) + Total Savings
Lump Sum (Early Retire)

Index

Symbols

401(k) plans, 132-136
    allocation alternatives,
        140
        rules, 141
    borrowing rules, 142-143
    contributions, 138-139
    income-tax impacts, 141
    rights, 144
    trends, 143-144
    vesting rules, 142
403(b) plans, 132-138
50 Fabulous Places to Retire in
    America, 26

A

AARCs (Active Adult
    Retirement Communities),
    35-36
AARP (American Asso-
    ciation of Retired Persons),
    survey of Baby-boomer
    retirement attitudes, 21
Active Adult Retirement
    Communities. See AARCs
active phase of retirement, 5

actuaries, 157
ADEA (Age Discrimination
    in Employment Act), 169
adjusted gross income. See
    AGI
administrative fees, IRA
    investment alternatives,
    191
advisors, financial. See finan-
    cial advisors
affinity fraud, "Ponzi," 346
after-tax cash flow, calculat-
    ing, 64-65
Age Discrimination in
    Employment Act. See
    ADEA
Age Venture News Service,
    20
AGI (adjusted gross income),
    phaseouts, 183
AICPA-PFP Division
    (American Institute of
    Certified Public
    Accountants), 308
allocations
    401(k) plans, 140
        rules, 141

investments, retirement-plan management, 275-277

America's 100 Best Places to Retire: The Only Guide You Need to Today's Top Retirement Towns, 26

America's Best Places to Retire, 26

American Association of Retired Persons. *See* AARP

American Institute of Certified Public Accountants. *See* AICPA-PFP Division

annuities
joint and survivor, 331
pension distributions, 330-331
withdrawal options, 331-332
period-certain single life, 332
surrender value, 50
variable, 49

answers to quiz questions, 373-376

articles, resources, 369-370

Ask Questions publication, 349

assets, 47
allocation, retirement-plan management, 276-277
cash-equivalent savings, 48-49
compiling inventory, 55
disposable, 55-56
employer retirement benefits, 50-51
FV (future value), 78
gifts and inheritance, 53
government (aided) retirement benefits, 51
home equity and real estate, 52
market and insurance investments, 49-50
personal retirement assets, 50
property, collectibles, business value, 52-53
retirement-ready net worth, 54-55
retitling, 349
shielding, minimizing the damage of unexpected problems, 259

assumptions, 67-69
calculating retirement gap, 294
economic and investment, retirement-plan management parameters, 274-275

averages
inflation, 60
rate of return, 62

B

Baby Boomers, 3
AARP survey of retirement attitudes, 21
Medicare problem, 198

beneficiary redesignations, 349

benefit multiplier factor. *See* BMF

benefits
cutbacks, 10
employer cutbacks, 10-11
government cutbacks, 11-12
Social Security
anticipated revisions, 125-128
anticipated trends, 125-128
delayed retirement options, 122
early retirement options, 121-122
estimating benefit, 120-121
supplementary income effects, 122-123
taxation of benefits, 124-125
sudden losses, 250-251
utilization as retirement gap solution, 107-109

Best Way to Save for College, The, 241

BMF (benefit multiplier factor), 166

boiler-room schemes, 347

bonds
retirement-plan management, 277-278
savings, current value, 48

book resources, 361-363

borrowing from 401(k) plans, 142-143

Budget Yes!: 21st Century Solutions for Taking Control of Your Money Now, 241

budgets
assembling an expense budget, 43-44
retirement gap solution, 102-104
spending time to save money, 103

Burk, Martha (NCWO Chair), 127

business value, inventory of benefits, 52-53

buy/sell agreement, 319

C

CA (Current Amount), 77
calculations
    adjusting and assessing
        performance, 279-280
    after-tax flow, 64-65
    retirement gap, 87-88,
        283-287, 390-416
        comprehensive exam-
            ple, 283-287
        estimations and
            assumptions, 294
        financial formulas,
            74-79
        need gap, 79-85,
            287-294
        procedure, 90-99
        worksheets, 88-90
    time value of money, vari-
        ables, 66-67
calculators
    Hewlett Packard HP12C,
        65
    MSN MoneyCentral, 69
    resources, 368-369
    Texas Instrument BA II,
        65
capital value. See CV
capital-based business oppor-
    tunities, integrating retire-
    ment resources, 227-228
cash distribution (lump-sum
    withdrawal), 332
cash-balance defined-benefit
    pensions. See CBPs
cash-equivalent savings,
    48-49
catch-up provisions, persons
    who have not saved
    enough, 264-265

CBPs (cash-balanced defined-
    benefit plans), 169-171
    formula, 170-171
CCRCs (Continuing Care
    Retirement Communities),
    36-37
CDPs (Certified Divorce
    Planners), 252
Certified Divorce Planners.
    See CDPs
Certified Financial Planners.
    See CPAs
changing jobs, retirement-
    plan management, 261-263
    catch-up provisions,
        264-265
    portability options,
        263-264
charge-card fraud, 347
charities fraud, 347
Civil Service Retirement
    System. See CSRS
clothing, estimating retire-
    ment costs, 41
COBRA (Consolidated
    Omnibus Budget
    Reconciliation Act), 250
COLA (cost of living adjust-
    ment), 81
collectibles
    integrating retirement
        resources, 225
    inventory of benefits,
        52-53
Comparison of IRA
    Alternatives chart, 188-190
Comparison of SEP-IRAs,
    SIMPLE IRAs, and Keogh
    Plans chart, 159-160
compatibility, financial advi-
    sors, 308-309

comprehensive retirement
    gap calculation, 283-287
Concentrated Retirement
    Care Living Options, 37-38
    homeowner's insurance,
        38
Consolidated Omnibus
    Budget Reconciliation Act.
    See COBRA
Consumer Price Index. See
    CPI
Continuing Care Retirement
    Communities. See CCRCs
contributions
    401(k) plans, 138-139
    IRAs, 181-186
        Contributions: Roth
            vs. Traditional (Tax-
            Deductible) IRA
            chart, 190-191
        non-tax-deductible IRAs,
            185
    projecting to plans and
        investments, retirement-
        plan management,
        275-276
    Roth IRAs, 185
    Social Security, 117-120
Contributions: Roth vs.
    Traditional (Tax-
    Deductible) IRA chart,
    190-191
controversial conversions,
    pensions, 171-173
conversions
    pensions, 171-173
    Roth IRAs, retirement-
        plan management,
        268-269
cost of living adjustment. See
    COLA

costs of retirement, 33-34
  assembling an expense budget, 43-44
  estimations
    clothing costs, 41
    food and shelter costs, 34
    healthcare costs, 38-39
    insurance costs, 42
    leisure and travel costs, 39-40
    local transportation costs, 41
    personal care costs, 40-41
    professional service costs, 42
    taxes and lump-sum expenses, 43
CPAs (Certified Financial Planners), 252
CPI (Consumer Price Index), 60
credit card fraud, 347
CRS Retirement Planning Guide, 178
CSRS (Civil Service Retirement System), 178
Current Amount. *See* CA
current value
  rule, defined-benefit pensions, 168
  savings bonds, 48
cutbacks, benefits, 10
  employer cutbacks, 10-11
  government cutbacks, 11-12
CV (capital value), 61

D

declining health and dependence phase of retirement, 5-6
deduction phaseout, 183
defined contribution plans, 11
defined-benefit Keogh plans, 156
defined-benefit pensions, 165-169
  cash-balance. *See* CBPs
  current value rule, 168
  formula, 166-167
  late-loading, 167
  normal and early retirement options, 173
    miscalculations, 175
    payout, 173-175
  OWBPA, 169
defined-contribution salary-reduction plans
  401(k) plans, 132-136
    allocation alternatives, 140-141
    borrowing rules, 142-143
    contributions, 138-139
    income-tax impacts, 141
    rights, 144
    trends, 143-144
    vesting rules, 142
  403(b) plans, 132-138
delayed retirement, Social Security options, 122
Demko, David, "neo-years," 20
demographic trends, 6
  disability, 9
  divorce, 7-8
  retirement gender gap, 8-9
  sandwich generation, 6-7

Department of Labor Pension and Welfare Benefits Administration. *See* DOL PWBA
Department of Labor. *See* DOL
disability, 248-249
  demographic trend, 9
disposable assets, 55-56
Distribution Withdrawal Rate Chart, 339-340
distributions, managing retirement distributions, 329-330
  compliance with IRS rules, 334-338
  evaluating withdrawal options, 338-342
  pensions, 330-334
  Social Security rules for widow(er)s, 340-341
divorce, 251-253
  demographic trend, 7-8
  remarriage financial consequences, 349
  typical divorced couple retirement gap, 305-307
DOL (Department of Labor), 133
DOL PWBA (Department of Labor Pension and Welfare Benefits Administration), 133
  warning signs, company abuses of 401(k) plans, 135
  Web site, 133
dual-purpose resources, utilization as retirement gap solution, 109
  earning potential investments, 111-112

home, 109-110
tax-deferred retirement savings, 110-111

E

early retirement
defined-benefit pensions, 173
miscalculations, 175
payout, 173-175
emergency funds, 256
Social Security options, 121-122
early retirement fraction. *See* ERF
earning potential, investments, utilization as retirement gap solution, 111-112
Earnings and Benefits Estimate Statement. *See* EBES
earnout arrangements, 320-321
EBES (Earnings and Benefits Estimate Statement), requesting with Form SSA-7004, 51
EBRI (Employee Benefits Research Institute), 149
Small Employer Retirement Survey, 150
economic trends, 12-13
eligibility
non-tax-deductible IRAs, 185
Roth IRAs, 184-185
SEP-IRAs, 152
SIMPLE IRAs, 154
Social Security, 117-119
Social Security Full Retirement and Reductions by Age chart, 119-120

traditional IRAs, 183-184
emergency funds, 253
early retirement and lay-offs, 256
family-need crunches, 253-255
widow(er)s, 256-257
employees
401(k) plan contributions, 138-139
benefit plans, cutbacks, 10
employer cutbacks, 10-11
government cutbacks, 11-12
stock options, 221-222
stock purchase plans, 49, 221
Employee Benefit Research Institute/Investment Company Institute, 266
Employee Benefits Research Institute. *See* EBRI
Employee Retirement Income Security Act. *See* ERISA
Employee Stock Ownership Plans. *See* ESOPs
employer
401(k) plan contributions, 138-139
benefit plans, inventory of benefits, 50-51
employment, part-time, 26-27
enrollment window, Medicare, 200-201
equality, SEP-IRAs, 151
ERF (early retirement fraction), 166
ERISA (Employee Retirement Income Security Act), 134, 331

errors, pension plan distributions, 334
ESOPs (Employee Stock Ownership Plans), 220
estate planning, maximizing your fortune, 350-352
estate taxes, phaseout, 351-352
Estimated Taxes. *See* ET
estimating retirement costs
assembling an expense budget, 43-44
calculating retirement gap, 294
clothing, 41
food and shelter, 34
AARCs, 35-36
CCRCs, 36-37
Concentrated Retirement Care Living Options, 37-38
healthcare, 38-39
insurance, 42
leisure and travel, 39-40
local transportation, 41
personal care, 40-41
professional services, 42
taxes and lump-sum expenses, 43
ET (Estimated Taxes), 64
expense gap, 78
expenses
assembling an expense budget, 43-44
inflation-adjusted annual retirement expenses, 78
Expenses, Planned Expenditures, and Liabilities Worksheet, 377-378, 385

F

family medical crises, 249
Fed (Federal Reserve), 60
Federal employee pensions, 177
  CSRS/FERS, 178
  Thrift Savings Plan, 178-179
Federal Employees Retirement System. *See* FERS
Federal Insurance Contributions Act. *See* FICA
Federal Reserve. *See* Fed
fee-for-service plan, Medicare, 199
fees, financial advisors, 309-310
FERS (Federal Employees Retirement System), *Retirement Planning Guide*, 178
FICA (Federal Insurance Contributions Act), 118
finance, 59
  assumptions, 67-69
  inflation, 59-61
    averages, 60
  interest rates, 59-61
  return on investment, 61
    formula, 61
    rate of return, 61-62
  taxes, 63
    after-tax cash flow, 64-65
  time value of money, 65
    calculating variables, 66-67
  understanding estimation, 67-69

financial advisors, 308
  compatible style, 308-309
  fees, 309-310
  qualifications, 308
financial assets, 47
  cash-equivalent savings, 48-49
  compiling inventory, 55
  employer retirement benefits, 50-51
  gifts and inheritance, 53
  government (aided) retirement benefits, 51
  home equity and real estate, 52
  market and insurance investments, 49-50
  personal retirement assets, 50
  property, collectibles, business value, 52-53
  retirement-ready net worth, 54-55
Financial Planning Association. *See* FPA
food costs, estimating retirement costs, 34
Form 5500-C, 157
Form 5500-R, 157
Form 5500EZ, 157
Form SSA-7004, requesting EBES, 51
formulas
  calculating retirement gap, 74
    inflation, 75-76
    return on investment, 76-77
    synchronizing for growth with inflation, 78-79

CBPs, 170-171
  defined-benefit pensions, 166-167
FPA (Financial Planning Association), 308
fraud
  affinity fraud, "Ponzi," 346
  charge-card, 347
  charities, 347
  credit card, 347
Future Value. *See* FV
FV (Future Value), 66
  assets, 78

G

gap (retirement), 73-74
  calculations, 74, 87-88, 283-287
    comprehensive example, 283-287
    estimations and assumptions, 294
    inflation, 75-76
    need gap, 79-85, 287-294
    procedure, 90-99
    return on investment, 76-77
    synchronizing for growth with inflation, 78-79
    worksheets, 88-90
  scenarios, 299
    pre-retirees, 308
    typical divorced couple situation, 305-307
    typical mid-life couple situation, 304-305
    typical permanent single situation, 307
    typical young married situation, 302-304
    young singles, 299-302

solutions, 101
  benefit utilization, 107-109
  budgeting, 102-104
  dual-purpose resources, 109-112
  exercises, 112
  investments, 104-105
  utilization of tax reduction/deferral, 105-107
gender gap (demographic trend), 8-9
Get the Facts on Saving and Investing publication, 349
gifts, inventory of benefits, 53
goals, leisure and travel, 27-28
government (aided) retirement benefits, inventory of benefits, 51
Greenspan, Alan, 60

H

HCFA, table of Medigap coverage options, 205
Health Care Financing Administration. *See* HFCA
Health Insurance Portability and Accountability Act of 1996, 210
healthcare benefits
  long-term-care insurance, 208-210
  Medicare, 198-202
  PSI (Medigap), 203-207
healthcare costs, estimating retirement costs, 38-39
Hewlett Packard HP12C calculator, 65
HFCA (Health Care Financing Administration), 204

HI (Hospital Insurance), 198
historical yardsticks, rate of return, 62
home, utilization as retirement gap solution, 109-110
home equity
  integrating retirement resources, 225-226
  inventory of benefits, 52
homeowner's insurance, 38
Hope Credit or Lifetime Learning Credit, 111
Hospital Insurance. *See* HI

I

Ibbotson Associates, 69
identity theft, 347
incentive stock options. *See* ISOs
income
  inflation-adjusted annual retirement income, 78-81
  retirement-year, 78
income-tax
  impact on small business and self-employed plans, 158
  impacts on 401(k) plans, 141
increasing life spans, effect on retirement planning, 4-5
index mutual funds, 105
individual retirement arrangement accounts. *See* IRAs
inflation, 59-61
  adjusted annual retirement expenses, 78
  adjusted annual retirement income, 78, 81

averages, 60
financial formulas for calculating retirement gap, 75-76
inheritances
  integrating retirement resources, 228-229
  inventory of benefits, 53
insurance
  estimating retirement costs, 42
  homeowner's, 38
  investments, 49-50
  long-term-care, 208-210
    monthly coverage costs, 209
    restrictions and coverage limitations, 208
  Medicare, 197
    Baby Boom demographics, 198
    enrollment window, 200-201
    fee-for-service plan, 199
    Medicare+Choice programs, 199
    Medigap coverage, 201-207
    Part A, 199
    Part B, 199
    reimbursement, 201-202
    Rights Center, 201
  minimizing the damage of unexpected problems, 257-258
Integrating Retirement Assets worksheet, 218
integrating retirement resources, building a long-term investment portfolio, 217

capital-based business opportunities, 227-228
employer/government plan resources, 218-219
inheritances, 228-229
investments, 224-226
savings sources at work, 220-224
interest rates, 59-61
Internal Revenue Code, 118
Internal Revenue Service. See IRS
Investment Company Institute, 151
investments
alternatives for IRAs, 191-192
administrative fees, 191
determining amounts and allocations, retirement-plan management, 275-279
earning potential, utilization as retirement gap solution, 111-112
integrating retirement resources, 224
collectibles, 225
home equity/real estate, 225-226
reallocation, retirement-plan management, 265-267
as retirement gap solution, 104-105
IRAs (individual retirement arrangement accounts), 181
Comparison of IRA Alternatives chart, 188-190
contributions, 181-186

Contributions: Roth vs. Traditional (Tax-Deductible) IRA chart, 190-191
investment alternatives, 191-192
administrative fees, 191
non-tax-deductible contributions, 185
eligibility, 185
nondeductible, 183
rollovers, 187-188
lump-sum withdrawal, 332
Roth conversions, 188
Roth, 183
contributions, 185
eligibility, 184-185
traditional, 182
eligibility, 183-184
trends, 192-193
withdrawals, 186-187
avoiding penalties, 187
IRS (Internal Revenue Service), 151
compliance with rules, managing retirement distributions, 334-338
Publication 590, 182
"Retirement Plans for Small Business" publication, 151
Web site, 151
ISOs (incentive stock options), 221

J

job changes, retirement-plan management, 261-263
catch-up provisions, 264-265
portability options, 263-264

joint and survivor annuity, 331

K

Keogh plans (tax-deferred retirement plans), 51, 150-157
complexity, 155
defined-benefit, 156
income-tax impacts, 158
money-purchased defined-contribution, 156
paired plans, 157
profit-sharing defined-contribution, 156
vesting, 158-159
Kiplinger's, 133

L

laddering treasury bills, 253
late-loading, defined-benefit pensions, 167
layoffs, emergency funds, 256
leisure goals, 27-28
estimating retirement costs, 39-40
overall living standard, 28
liabilities, 53-54
Life Insurance Buyer's Guide, 248
limitations, long-term-care insurance, 208
limited liability company. See LLC
LLC (limited liability company), 155
local transportation, estimating retirement costs, 41
locations for retirement, 23
choices, 25-26
considerations, 24-25

long-term-care insurance, 208-210
  monthly coverage costs, 209
  restrictions and coverage limitations, 208
long-term investment portfolio, 217
  capital-based business opportunities, 227-228
  employer/government plan resources, 218-219
  inheritances, 228-229
  investments, 224
    collectibles, 225
    home equity/real estate, 225-226
  savings sources at work, 220
    employee stock options, 221-222
    employee stock purchase plans, 221
    ESOPs, 220
    profit-sharing plans, 220
    thrift plans, 221
    VUL insurance and variable annuities, 222-224
lump-sum distributions (pensions), 330-331
  withdrawal, 332-333
    cash distribution, 332
    IRA rollovers, 332
lump-sum expenses, estimating retirement costs, 43

M

management
  retirement distributions, 329-330
  compliance with IRS rules, 334-338
  evaluating withdrawal options, 338-342
  pensions, 330-334
  Social Security rules for widow(er)s, 340-341
  retirement-plan, 261-280
    adjusting calculations and assessing performance, 279-280
    changing jobs, 261-265
    determining investment amounts and allocations, 275-279
    early withdrawal rules without penalty, 267-268
    economic and investment assumptions, 274-275
    maxing out retirement savings option, 265
    portfolio balancing and investment reallocation, 265-267
    risk tolerance by life stage, 273-274
    Roth conversion strategies, 268-269
    time frames, 271-272
market investments, 49-50
market plunges, 349-350
married persons, retirement gap, 302-305
  children, 303-304
  debt and houses, 302-303
maxing out retirement savings option, 265
medical crises, 249
Medicare, 197
  Baby Boom demographics, 198
  enrollment window, 200-201
  fee-for-service plan, 199
  Medicare+Choice programs, 199
  Medigap coverage, 201-207
    comparison of ten standardized Medigap plans, 205-206
    coverage options, 205
  Part A, 199
  Part B, 199
  reimbursement, 201-202
  Rights Center, 201
Medicare+Choice programs, 199
Medigap coverage, 201-207
  comparison of ten standardized Medigap plans, 205-206
  options, 205
mid-life couples, retirement gap, 304-305
Millionaire Next Door, The, 7
millionaire-next-door types, 7
minimizing the damage of unexpected problems, 257
  insurance, 257-258
  shielding assets, 259
miscalculations, defined-benefit pensions, normal and early retirement, 175
Money, 133
Money Doesn't Grow on Trees, 104
money-purchased defined-contribution Keogh plans, 156
monitoring plan performance, 344-345

monthly coverage costs, long-term-care insurance, 209
Morningstar Web site, 219
MSN MoneyCentral
calculator, 69
Web site, 69

N

NAPFA (National Association of Personal Financial Advisors), 309
NASD (National Association of Securities Dealers), Regulation Public Disclosure Program, 310
National Association of Personal Financial Advisors. See NAPFA
National Association of Securities Dealers. See NASD
National Council of Women's Organizations. See NCWO
National Fraud Information Center Web site, 225
NAV (net asset value), 49
NCB (new cash balance), 170
NCWO (National Council of Women's Organizations), opposition to privatization, 127
need gap calculation, 79-85
comprehensive example, 287-294
"neo-years," as defined by David Demko, 20
net asset value. See NAV
net worth, retirement-ready, 54-55
new cash balance. See NCB

non-qualified stock options. See NQSOs
non-tax-deductible IRA
contributions, 185
eligibility, 185
nondeductible IRAs, 183
normal retirement, defined-benefit pensions, 173
miscalculations, 175
payout, 173-175
NQSOs (non-qualified stock options), 221

O

obstacles (unexpected retirement issues), 247
divorce, 251-253
emergency funds, 253
early retirement and layoffs, 256
family-need crunches, 253-255
widow(er)s, 256-257
family medical crises, 249
minimizing the damage, 257
insurance, 257-258
shielding assets, 259
premature death or disability, 248-249
sudden benefit losses, 250-251
OCB (old cash balance), 170
old cash balance. See OCB
Older Workers Benefit Protection Act. See OWBPA
overall living standard, deciding on travel and leisure goals, 28
OWBPA (Older Workers Benefit Protection Act), defined-benefit pensions, 169

P

paired Keogh plans, 157
parameters, retirement-plan management, 271
economic and investment assumptions, 274-275
risk tolerance by life stage, 273-274
time frames, 271-272
Part A Medicare coverage, 199
Part B Medicare coverage, 199
part-time employment, 26-27
passive phase of retirement, 5
pay inequity, 8
Payment. See PMT
payout, defined-benefit pensions, normal and early retirement, 173-175
PBGC (Pension Benefits Guaranty Corporation), 175, 251, 331
PC AGI (phaseout ceiling AGI), 183
PCT (percent factor), 170
penalties, IRA withdrawal rules, 186-187
Pension Benefits Guaranty Corporation. See PBGC
pensions
cash-balanced defined-benefit plans. See CBPs
defined-benefit pensions. See defined-benefit pensions
employee rights, 175-176
managing retirement distributions, 330
annuity withdrawal options, 331-332
errors, 334

lump sums versus annuities, 330-331
lump-sum withdrawal options, 332-333
politics/controversial conversions, 171-173
trends, 176-177
U.S. Federal employee pensions, 177
CSRS/FERS, 178
Thrift Savings Plan, 178-179
percent factor. *See* PCT
performance
investments, retirement-plan management, 279-280
monitoring, 344-345
period-certain single life annuity, 332
personal care, estimating retirement costs, 40-41
personal finance specialists. *See* PFS
personal responsibility, 13-14
personal retirement assets, 50
PF AGI (phaseout-floor AGI), 183
PFS (personal finance specialists), 308
phaseout ceiling AGI. *See* PC AGI
phaseout of the estate tax, 351-352
phaseout-floor AGI. *See* PF AGI
phaseouts, 183
Piggy Bank to Credit Card, 104
plan performance, monitoring, 344-345
planning advice, young singles, 300-301
PMT (Payment), 66

Pocket Idiot's Guide to Living on a Budget, The, 102
politics, pensions, 171-173
Pond, Jonathan (financial planner), Web site, 243
"Ponzi" (pyramid schemes), 346
portability of assets, changing jobs, 263-264
portfolios, balancing, retirement-plan management, 265-267
post-conversion account-growth adjustment. *See* wearaway
PPI (Producer Price Index), 60
premature death, 248-249
prenuptial agreements, 349
Present Value. *See* PV
pre-retirement financial actions, 321-327
pre-retirement work actions, 318-321
phasing out a business, 318-319
starting a business, 318
privatization, NCWO opposition, 127
problems (unexpected retirement issues), 247
divorce, 251-253
emergency funds, 253
early retirement and layoffs, 256
family-need crunches, 253-255
widow(er)s, 256-257
family medical crises, 249
minimizing the damage, 257
insurance, 257-258
shielding assets, 259

premature death or disability, 248-249
sudden benefit losses, 250-251
Producer Price Index. *See* PPI
professional services, estimating retirement costs, 42
profit-sharing defined-contribution Keogh plans, 156
profit-sharing plans, 220
property, inventory of benefits, 52-53
Prosperous Retirement, The, 68
Protect Your Pension pamphlet (DOL), 134-135
PSI
Medigap, 203-207
comparison of ten standardized Medigap plans, 205-206
coverage options, 205
shopping for insurance, 207
Publication 505 ("Tax Withholding and Estimated Tax"), 124
Publication 590 (IRS), 182
Publication 915 ("Social Security and Equivalent Railroad Retirement Benefits"), 124
publications
Ask Questions, 349
Get the Facts on Saving and Investing, 349
"When to Retire" (Social Security Administration), 21
PV (Present Value), 66
pyramid schemes. *See* "Ponzi," 346

Q

qualifications, financial advisors, 308

quantifying retirement assets, 47

cash-equivalent savings, 48-49

compiling inventory, 55

employer retirement benefits, 50-51

gifts and inheritance, 53

government (aided) retirement benefits, 51

home equity and real estate, 52

market and insurance investments, 49-50

personal retirement assets, 50

property, collectibles, business value, 52-53

retirement-ready net worth, 54-55

quantifying retirement costs, 33-34

assembling an expense budget, 43-44

estimations

clothing costs, 41

food and shelter costs, 34

healthcare costs, 38-39

insurance costs, 42

leisure and travel costs, 39-40

local transportation costs, 41

personal care costs, 40-41

professional service costs, 42

taxes and lump-sum expenses, 43

quizzes

401(k) plans, 145-146

403(b) plans, 145-146

assets, 56

estimating retirement costs, 44-45

finance, 70-72

fraudulent schemes, 353

healthcare benefits, 210-213

integrating retirement resources, 229-231

IRAs, 193-195

managing retirement distributions, 342

pensions, 179

retirement gap, 85-86, 100

calculation, 294-295

scenarios, 311

solutions, 112

retirement hopes and dreams, 29-32

retirement realities, 14-16

retirement-plan management, 270, 281

savings strategies, 244-245

self-employed plans, 160-161

small business plans, 160-161

Social Security, 128-130

troubleshooting unexpected problems, 259-260

R

RAABP (recent average annual base pay), 166

rate of return, return on investment, 61-62

averages, 62

historical yardsticks, 62

rationing, saving versus spending

debt payoff versus investing, 237-239

education versus investing, 239-241

house down payment versus retirement saving, 235-237

overall spending versus retirement saving, 234-235

prioritizing, 241-244

real estate

integrating retirement resources, 225-226

inventory of benefits, 52

realities of retirement, increasing life spans, 4-5

reallocation of investments, retirement-plan management, 265-267

recent average annual base pay. See RAABP

Regulation Public Disclosure Program (NASD), 310

reimbursement, Medicare, 201-202

remarriage, 349

resources, 361

articles, 369-370

books, 361-363

calculators, 368-369

software, 368-369

studies, 370

surveys, 370

Web sites, 363-368

restrictions
  long-term-care insurance,
    208
  SEP-IRAs, 153
Retire & Thrive, 25
retirement gap, 73-74
  calculations, 74, 87-88,
    283-287, 390-416
    comprehensive exam-
      ple, 283-287
    estimations and
      assumptions, 294
    inflation, 75-76
    need gap, 79-85,
      287-294
    procedure, 90-99
    return on investment,
      76-77
    synchronizing for
      growth with infla-
      tion, 78-79
    worksheets, 88-90
  scenarios, 299
    pre-retirees, 308
    typical divorced couple
      situation, 305-307
    typical mid-life couple
      situation, 304-305
    typical permanent sin-
      gle situation, 307
    typical young married
      situation, 302-304
    young singles, 299-302
  solutions, 101
    benefit utilization,
      107-109
    budgeting, 102-104
    dual-purpose resources,
      109-112
    exercises, 112
    investments, 104-105
    utilization of tax
      reduction/deferral,
      105-107

retirement gender gap (demographic trend), 8-9
Retirement Places Rated, 26
"Retirement Plans for Small
  Business" publication (IRS),
  151
Retirement Ready Assets
  worksheet, 287, 386-389
retirement scenarios
  revising, 315-317
  revisiting, 314-315
retirement-plan management,
  261
  adjusting calculations and
    assessing performance,
    279-280
  changing jobs, 261-263
    catch-up provisions,
      264-265
    portability options,
      263-264
  determining investment
    amounts and allocations,
    275
    asset allocation strat-
      egy, 276-277
    bonds, 277-278
    projecting contribu-
      tions to plans,
      275-276
    stocks, 278-279
  early withdrawal rules
    without penalty, 267-268
  maxing out retirement
    savings option, 265
  parameters, 271
    economic and invest-
      ment assumptions,
      274-275
    risk tolerance by life
      stage, 273-274
    time frames, 271-272

  portfolio balancing and
    investment reallocation,
    265-267
  Roth conversion strate-
    gies, 268-269
retirement-ready net worth,
  54-55
retitling assets, 349
return on investment, 61
  financial formulas for cal-
    culating retirement gap,
    76-77
  formula, 61
  rate of return, 61-62
    averages, 62
    historical yardsticks, 62
reverse mortgages, 325-326
revisions, Social Security
  benefits, 125-128
revising retirement scenarios,
  315-317
revisiting retirement scenarios, 314-315
rights
  401(k) plans, 144
  pensions, 175-176
Rights Center, Medicare, 201
ripoff retirement "opportunities," 345-349
risk tolerance, retirement-
  plan management parame-
  ter, 273-274
Robbing You Blind, 133
rollovers
  IRAs, 187-188
    Roth conversions, 188
  lump-sum withdrawal, 332
Roth IRAs, 183
  contributions, 185
  conversions, 188
    retirement-plan man-
      agement, 268-269
  eligibility, 184-185
rules, allocations, 141

S

S&P 500 index fund, 105
SAL (salary base), 170
salary base. *See* SAL
salary reduction provision,
SEP-IRAs, 152
Salary Reduction SEP. *See*
SARSEP-IRAs
Sallie Mae Web site, 300
sandwich generation (demographic trend), 6-7
SARSEP-IRAs (Salary
Reduction SEP), 152
savings
advice for young singles,
301-302
bonds, current value, 48
cash-equivalent, 48-49
sources at work, 220
employee stock
options, 221-222
employee stock pur-
chase plans, 221
ESOPs, 220
profit-sharing plans,
220
thrift plans, 221
VUL insurance and
variable annuities,
222-224
spending time to save
money, 103
versus spending
debt payoff versus
investing, 237-239
education versus
investing, 239-241
house down payment
versus retirement
saving, 235-237

overall spending versus
retirement saving,
234-235
prioritizing, 241-244
Savings Incentive Match
Plan for Employees. *See*
SIMPLE
scams
avoiding ripoff retirement
"opportunities," 345-349
operation, 345
scenarios (retirement gap),
299
pre-retirees, 308
typical divorced couple
situation, 305-307
typical mid-life couple situation, 304-305
typical permanent single
situation, 307
typical young married situation, 302
children, 303-304
debt and houses,
302-303
young singles, 299
planning advice,
300-301
savings advice,
301-302
schemes
avoiding ripoff retirement
"opportunities," 345-349
boiler-room, 347
operation, 345
SECA (Self-Employment
Contributions Act), 118
Section 457 plans, 132
self-employed plans, 149-150
*Comparison of SEP-IRAs,
SIMPLE IRAS, and
Keogh Plans* chart,
159-160

income-tax impacts, 158
Keogh plans, 155-157
complexity, 155
defined-benefit, 156
money-purchased
defined-contribution,
156
paired plans, 157
profit-sharing defined-
contribution, 156
SEP-IRAs, 151-153
eligibility, 152
equality, 151
restrictions, 153
salary reduction provi-
sion, 152
SIMPLE IRAs, 153-155
eligibility, 154
vesting, 158
withdrawals, 158-159
Self-Employment
Contributions Act. *See*
SECA
SEP (Simplified Employee
Pension), 50
SEP-IRAs, 150-153
eligibility, 152
equality, 151
income-tax impacts, 158
restrictions, 153
salary reduction provision,
152
vesting, 158
withdrawals, 158-159
SERVFACT (service factor),
170
service factor. *See* SERV-
FACT
shelter costs, estimating
retirement costs, 34
AARCs, 35-36
CCRCs, 36-37

Concentrated Retirement Care Living Options, 37-38

shielding assets, minimizing the damage of unexpected problems, 259

shift to personal responsibility, 13-14

simple (interest) return, 61

SIMPLE (Savings Incentive Match Plan for Employees), 50

SIMPLE IRAs, 150-155
  eligibility, 154
  income-tax impacts, 158
  vesting, 158
  withdrawals, 158-159

Simplified Employee Pension. See SEP

single persons
  permanent singles, retirement gap, 307
  young persons, retirement gap, 299-302

small business plans, 149-150
  Comparison of SEP-IRAs, SIMPLE IRAs, and Keogh Plans chart, 159-160
  income-tax impacts, 158
  Keogh plans, 155-157
    complexity, 155
    defined-benefit, 156
    money-purchased defined-contribution, 156
    paired plans, 157
    profit-sharing defined-contribution, 156
  SEP-IRAs, 151-153
    eligibility, 152
    equality, 151

restrictions, 153
salary reduction provision, 152
SIMPLE IRAs, 153-155
  eligibility, 154
  vesting, 158
  withdrawals, 158-159

Small Business Valuation Book, The, 53

Small Employer Retirement Survey (EBRI), 150

Smart Money, 133

SMI (Supplementary Medical Insurance), 198

Social Security, 51
  anticipated revisions, 125-128
  anticipated trends, 125-128
  calculating expected benefit, 51
  contributions, 117-120
  delayed retirement options, 122
  distribution rules for widow(er)s, 340-341
  early retirement options, 121-122
  eligibility, 117-119
    Social Security Full Retirement and Reductions by Age chart, 119-120
  estimating standard benefit, 120-121
  exempt persons paying, 118
  supplementary income effects, 122-123
  taxation of benefits, 124-125
  Trust Fund, 117
    dates of concern, 126

Social Security Administration. See SSA

Social Security Full Retirement and Reductions by Age chart, 119-120

software, resources, 368-369

solutions, retirement gap, 101
  benefit utilization, 107-109
  budgeting, 102-104
  dual-purpose resources, 109-112
  exercises, 112
  investments, 104-105
  utilization of tax reduction/deferral, 105-107

SPD (summary plan document), 176

spending versus saving
  debt payoff versus investing, 237, 239
  education versus investing, 239-241
  house down payment versus retirement saving, 235-237
  overall spending versus retirement saving, 234-235
  prioritizing, 241-244

SSA (Social Security Administration), 51
  calculating expected Social Security benefit, 51
  Web site, 51

stages of retirement, 5
  active phase, 5
  declining health and dependence phase, 5-6
  passive phase, 5

standard benefit, Social
Security, estimating,
120-121
state employees, Section 457
plans, 132
stock market plunges,
349-350
stock purchase plans, 221
stocks, retirement-plan management, 278-279
studies, resources, 370
summary plan document. See
SPD
supplementary income,
effects on Social Security,
122-123
supplementary insurance
Medigap, 203-207
comparison of ten
standardized Medigap
plans, 205-206
coverage options, 205
shopping for insurance,
207
Supplementary Medical
Insurance. See SMI
surrender value, annuities, 50
surveys
AARP, Baby-boomer
retirement attitudes, 21
resources, 370
Small Employer
Retirement Survey
(EBRI), 150
synchronizing for growth with
inflation, financial formulas
for calculating retirement
gap, 78-79

T

Tax Sheltered Annuities. See
TSAs
tax-deductible IRAs. See traditional IRAs
tax-deferred retirement savings, utilization as retirement gap solution, 110-111
taxes, 63
after-tax cash flow, 64-65
calculating, 64-65
deferral, as retirement gap
solution, 105-107
estate, phaseout, 351-352
estimating retirement
costs, 43
reduction, as retirement
gap solution, 105-107
Social Security benefits,
124-125
tax-saving tips, 106-107
withdrawal of retirement
distributions, 336-338
Teachers Insurance and
Annuity Association-
College Retirement Equities
Fund. See TIAA-CREF
Texas Instrument BA II calculator, 65
thrift plans, 221
Thrift Savings Plan, 178-179
TIAA-CREF (Teachers
Insurance and Annuity
Association-College
Retirement Equities Fund),
140
Web site, 224
time frames, retirement-plan
management parameter,
271-272
time value of money, calculating variables, 65-67

timing your retirement, 19-20
cost of when, 21-22
when to say when, 22-23
total years of service. See TYS
traditional IRAs, 182
eligibility, 183-184
transportation, estimating
retirement costs, 41
travel goals, 27-28
estimating retirement
costs, 39-40
overall living standard, 28
treasury bills, laddering, 253
"Treasury Direct" Web site,
48
trends
401(k) plans, 143-144
demographic, 6
disability, 9
divorce, 7-8
retirement gender gap,
8-9
sandwich generation,
6-7
economic, 12-13
IRAs, 192-193
pensions, 176-177
Social Security benefits,
125-128
Trust Fund, Social Security,
117
dates of concern, 126
TSAs (Tax Sheltered
Annuities), 132
TYS (total years of service),
166

U

U.S. Federal employee pensions, 177
CSRS/FERS, 178
Thrift Savings Plan,
178-179

understanding estimation, 67-69

unexpected problems, 247
divorce, 251-253
emergency funds, 253
early retirement and layoffs, 256
family-need crunches, 253-255
widow(er)s, 256-257
family medical crises, 249
minimizing the damage, 257
insurance, 257-258
shielding assets, 259
premature death or disability, 248-249
sudden benefit losses, 250-251

unified credit, 351-352

V

variable annuities, 49, 222-224

variable universal life insurance. *See* VUL insurance

vesting
401(k) plans, 142
small business and self-employed plans, 158

viatical settlements, 324-325

VUL insurance (variable universal life insurance), 222-224

W

wearaway (post-conversion account-growth adjustment), 172

Web sites
DOL PWBA (Department of Labor Pension and Welfare Benefits Administration), 133
IRS (Internal Revenue Service), 151
Jonathan Pond's life-insurance needs calculation worksheet, 243
listing of resources, 363-368
Morningstar, 219
MSN MoneyCentral, 69
National Fraud Information Center, 225
Sallie Mae, 300
SSA (Social Security Administration), 51
TIAA-CREF, 224
Tim Younkin, 137
Treasury Direct, 48
Wired Scholar, 300

"When To Retire" (Social Security Administration's publication), 21

where to retire, 23
choices, 25-26
location considerations, 24-25

Where to Retire: America's Best and Most Affordable Places, 26

widow(er)s, emergency funds, 256-257

Wired Scholar Web site, 300

withdrawals
annuities, 331-332
early withdrawal rules without penalty, 267-268
IRAs, 186-187
avoiding penalties, 187

lump-sum, 332-333
cash distribution, 332
IRA rollover, 332
retirement distributions
evaluating options, 338-342
IRS rules, 334-336
tax ramifications, 336-338
small business and self-employed plans, 158-159

worksheets
Expenses, Planned Expenditures, and Liabilities Worksheet, 377-385
Integrating Retirement Assets, 218
retirement gap calculation, 283-287, 390-416
Retirement Gap Calculation Worksheet, 99
Retirement Ready Assets, 287, 386-389

World's Top Retirement Havens, The, 26

X-Y-Z

young married persons, retirement gap, 302
children, 303-304
debt and houses, 302-303

young singles, retirement gap, 299
planning advice, 300-301
savings advice, 301-302

Younkin, Tim ("401 Krusader") Web site, 137

Your Money or Your Life, 28